MALAYSIA

A World Bank Country Economic Report

PENINSULAR MALAYSIA

THAILAND

PERLIS

KEDAH

PENANG

PERAK

KELANTAN

TRENGGANU

SELANGOR

Kuala
Lumpur

P A H A N G

NEGRI
SEMBILAN

MALACCA

JOHORE

Strait of Malacca

South China Sea

KILOMETERS
0 20 40 60 80 100

0 20 40 60
MILES

MALAYSIA

⊛ National Capital

----- State Boundaries

-·-·- International Boundaries

SINGAPORE

MALAYSIA

THAILAND

PHILIPPINES

PENINSULAR
MALAYSIA

BRUNEI

SABAH

SARAWAK

Celebes Sea

SUMATERA

SINGAPORE

KALIMANTAN

SULAWESI

I N D O N E S I A

KILOMETERS
0 200 400

0 100 200 300
MILES

Malaysia

Growth and Equity
in a
Multiracial Society

Kevin Young
Willem C. F. Bussink
Parvez Hasan

Coordinating Authors

PUBLISHED FOR THE WORLD BANK

The Johns Hopkins University Press

BALTIMORE AND LONDON

HC
445.5
.Y68

Library of Congress Cataloging in Publication Data

Young, Kevin, 1945–
    Malaysia, growth and equity in a multiracial society.

    (A World Bank country economic report)
    Includes bibliographical references and index.
    1. Malaysia—Economic conditions.
    2. Malaysia—Economic policy. I. Bussink, Willem C. F., 1929–   joint author. II. Hasan, Parvez, joint author. III. Title. IV. Series: World Bank country economic reports.
    HC445.5. Y68   330.9595'053   79-3677
    ISBN 0-8018-2384-6
    ISBN 0-8018-2385-4 (pbk.)

Foreword

THIS IS THE NINETEENTH in the current series of World Bank country economic reports, all of which are listed on the following page. They are published, in response to a desire expressed by scholars and practitioners in the field of economic and social development, to facilitate research and the interchange of knowledge.

The Bank regularly prepares economic reports on borrowing countries in support of its own operations. These surveys provide a basis for discussion with governments and for decisions on Bank policy and operations. Many governments use the reports as an aid to their economic planning, as do consortia and consultative groups of governments and institutions providing assistance in development. All Bank country reports are published subject to the agreement of—and several have been published by—the governments concerned.

HOLLIS B. CHENERY
Vice President for Development Policy
The World Bank

Contents

ꙎꙎꙎ

Figures and Tables

Figures

Tables

Acronyms and Initials

ANRPC	Association of Natural Rubber Producing Countries
c.i.f.	Cost, insurance, and freight
FELCRA	Federal Land Consolidation and Rehabilitation Authority
FELDA	Federal Land Development Authority
FIDA	Federal Industrial Development Authority
f.o.b.	Free on board
GDP	Gross domestic product
GNP	Gross national product
ICOR	Incremental capital-output ratio
IMF	International Monetary Fund
LNG	Liquefied natural gas
MARA	Majlis Amanah Rakyat, Council of Trust for Indigenous Peoples
MARDI	Malaysian Agricultural Research and Development Institute
MCA	Malayan [now Malaysian] Chinese Association
MCP	Malayan Communist Party
MIC	Malayan [now Malaysian] Indian Congress
OECD	Organization for Economic Cooperation and Development
PERNAS	Perbadanan Nasional Berhad, National Trading Corporation
PETRONAS	Petroliam Nasional Berhad, National Petroleum Corporation
RISDA	Rubber Industry Smallholders Development Authority
SEALPA	South-east Asian Lumber Producers Association
SITC	Standard international trade classification
UMNO	United Malays National Organization
UNCTAD	United Nations Conference on Trade and Development

Currency Equivalents

THE RINGGIT (M$) is pegged to an undisclosed basket of currencies of Malaysia's principal trading partners. The weights are based on trade shares and the importance of currencies used in settlement. Since 1975 the composition of the basket has not changed. The exchange rates listed below are period averages.

Through 1970   US$1.00 = M$3.06
        1971   US$1.00 = M$3.05
        1972   US$1.00 = M$2.82
        1973   US$1.00 = M$2.44
        1974   US$1.00 = M$2.41
        1975   US$1.00 = M$2.40
        1976   US$1.00 = M$2.54
        1977   US$1.00 = M$2.46
        1978   US$1.00 = M$2.32

Preface

THIS BOOK IS A PRODUCT of the World Bank's economic work on Malaysia during the last several years. It reviews the performance of the Malaysian economy since 1960, discusses current issues, and assesses future prospects. There have been a number of notable achievements since 1960. A marked increase in the level of investment led to a high and sustained level of economic growth. The allocation of resources among sectors was generally good. The public sector expanded considerably at the same time that the private sector grew vigorously. Financial stability and a strong external position were continuously maintained. There also was progress in social areas, especially in expanding opportunities for education and improving health conditions.

Nonetheless, the gains from growth were not equally shared, and widespread poverty and income inequality persisted. The continued socioeconomic imbalances threatened national unity and in the early 1970s prompted government to introduce a new policy designed to reduce poverty and racial imbalances. This policy—the new Economic Policy—is the focus of this book. A principal theme is that continued rapid growth of the population and labor force make rapid economic growth the keystone for achieving these objectives. Sustained industrial growth, and the employment opportunities it would engender, are of particular importance in reducing poverty and increasing the participation of Malays in the modern sectors of the economy. In this light the report emphasizes the importance of providing a policy framework conducive to a high rate of investment in the manufacturing sector. It also recognizes that poverty will continue to be concentrated in rural areas. Thus a concerted effort to accelerate the pace of rural development is needed. The strong resource position of the public sector makes such an acceleration financially possible. The main constraint is the capacity of the public sector to design projects that can affect large numbers of rural poor.

Despite the difficulties inherent in reducing poverty and redressing racial imbalances, the outlook is brighter now than it was in 1955, when the World Bank's first report on Malaya was published.[1] That report, prepared under the direction of Sir Louis Chick, highlighted three main constraints on the country's impressive economic potential: a low rate of investment; inadequate public sector resources; and a high rate of population growth. As indicated above, the first two of these constraints were overcome. But the continued rapid population growth and a secular decline in the terms of trade for agricultural exports severely limited the increase in per capita incomes in the 1960s—and widespread poverty and inequality persisted. Since then, however, the rate of population growth has started to come down; exports, including petroleum, have boomed; the government has become much more active; and the demand for labor has accelerated. All this has contributed to an accelerated growth of real incomes and has started to reduce the incidence of poverty.

The historical analysis of this book generally covers the period from 1960 to 1976; the discussion of future prospects covers events through 1990. The report was drafted in 1978. Although the coverage is not fully up to date, recent developments do not significantly change the report's findings, and the discussion of future issues and prospects of Malaysia's development remains valid.

Except for chapter five, which is the partial result of a separate research project, the book draws to a varying degree on the findings of two economic missions. The first, in 1975, was led by Orville McDiarmid (consultant) and consisted of the following members: Montek Ahluwalia, Rutilas Allen (consultant), Alice Galenson, Michael Lav, George Parazich (consultant), Christopher Perry, Peter Pollak, Geoffrey Shepherd, Townsend Swayze, Suresh Tendulkar, John Tillman, and Virginia Konionoff (secretary). The report of this mission focused on the issues for the Third Malaysia Plan, for 1976–80, and offered suggestions while the plan was being developed. The second mission visited Malaysia in 1977 and consisted of Kevin Young (mission leader) and Alice Galenson. The report of this mission reviewed the final version of the plan and reassessed long-term prospects in the light of events during 1975 and 1976.

Chapters two and three benefited from an analysis of population trends and issues by Nwanganga Shields. The analysis in chapter four reflects work by Sudhir Anand on income distribution, Dipak Mazumdar on labor markets, and Graham Pyatt and Geoffrey Round on social

1. World Bank, *The Economic Development of Malaya* (Baltimore: Johns Hopkins Press, 1955).

accounting. Chapter eight draws on the report of a 1974 mission on rural poverty led by John DeWilde under the auspices of a cooperative program of the World Bank and the Food and Agriculture Organization of the United Nations. The national accounts data presented in appendix C are based on estimates prepared by Raquel Fok.

Bruce Ross-Larson and David Howell Jones edited the final manuscript for publication. Charlotte Jones assisted in coordinating the various contributions and in the technical editing. Christine Graunas and Winifred Gaughan read and corrected proofs through the Word Guild, Pensri Kimpitak prepared the charts, Florence Robinson indexed the text, and Christine Houle coordinated production of the book. The map was compiled by Yung D. Koo and drawn by Larry A. Bowring under the supervision of the World Bank's Cartography Division.

We are especially grateful for the assistance of the Malaysian government, particularly the Ministry of Finance, the Economic Planning Unit, and the Department of Statistics. Without their collaboration and assistance, this book would not have been possible.

KEVIN YOUNG
WILLEM BUSSINK
PARVEZ HASAN

⌐⌐

MALAYSIA

⌐⌐

Kevin Young

Overview

MALAYSIA IS ONE OF THE MOST PROSPEROUS COUNTRIES in Southeast Asia. It is the world's leading exporter of tin, rubber, and palm oil; it also is a principal exporter of tropical hardwoods and has significant reserves of oil and natural gas. By exploiting its rich natural resources, the country achieved a gross national product (GNP) of about US$1100 per capita in 1978. Moreover the manufacturing sector, although still small in relation to the rest of the economy, has registered substantial growth in recent years. The rapid growth of this sector and the increased investment by the public sector have been the main reasons underlying the acceleration of the growth rate from 6 percent a year during the 1960s to about 8 percent in the mid-1970s. The expansion of production has been achieved in the context of economic freedom and stability; the expansion of the public sector has neither competed with nor constrained the private sector. Given this pattern of development, the Malaysian economy has been very open to external influences: exports and imports are both equivalent to almost half of GNP.

A look beyond macroeconomic aggregates nevertheless reveals that a substantial part of the population is poor. The Malaysian government has estimated that about 40 percent of the population in 1976 had incomes that were insufficient to provide minimum requirements of food, shelter, clothing, and other basic needs. Although Malaysia's poverty line, when compared with international standards, appears to overestimate the extent of absolute poverty, the problems of poverty and an uneven distribution of income remain serious. Furthermore the incidence of poverty among Malays is disproportionately high. Their per capita income is only half that of Chinese and two-thirds of the national average.

How can such poverty be reconciled with rapid growth and a relatively high per capita GNP? First, the development of the agricultural sector, the main source of employment in the economy, has been highly dualistic. Despite the presence of an estate sector that is relatively

3

high in productivity, most agricultural households have been engaged in low-income, traditional activities on rice and rubber smallholdings. This dualism has significant racial connotations. Malays have generally stayed in traditional agriculture; the immigrant groups of Chinese and Indians have entered the sectors that proved to be more dynamic: tin mining, agricultural estates, commerce, and manufacturing. As a result, most of the poor are Malay, and many Malays are poor.

A second reason for Malaysia's high level of poverty is rapid population growth, which averaged almost 3 percent a year during the 1960s. Consequently the growth rate of output per capita was only about half the rate of total growth during that decade. In addition, the country experienced a serious and sustained terms-of-trade loss in the 1960s, a loss which further reduced average growth of real incomes. Of particular significance was the decline in the price of rubber: in one decade the unit value of this main export product was halved in real terms. Because rubber tapping has been one of the principal occupations of poor Malaysians, this decline had a serious negative effect on the efforts of government to alleviate poverty. As a result of these conditions, the position of many of Malaysia's poor improved slowly during the 1960s.

This generally disappointing outcome occurred despite the effectiveness of programs undertaken by government and the private sector to increase agricultural productivity. These programs resulted in a growth of smallholder output which was almost as high as the 6 percent annual growth in agricultural output. Rubber and rice smallholders made substantial gains, which after 1970 were no longer offset by a decline in the real price of rubber.

Because of a vigorous replanting program, the output of rubber smallholders grew more than twice as fast as that of estates during 1960–75. As a result, the share of smallholders in production increased from 40 percent to almost 60 percent during the period. Large irrigation projects, the Muda scheme in particular, substantially increased the output of rice smallholders. Government also instituted a large program of land development, which opened up virgin territory to poor and landless farmers. This program provided incomes above the poverty line to many poor households; it also relieved pressure on land already being farmed. The private sector, as well as government in some of its land development schemes, moved from rubber into oil palm and contributed to the long-term diversification of the economy. Government also expanded the provision of social services, and there were substantial increases in the education and medical care provided to the poor. These programs have significantly increased the welfare of many of the poor, as is evidenced by the substantial decline in mortality rates and the increase in life expectancy for all segments of Malaysian society. Primary education now is almost universal.

The foregoing discussion illustrates that it would be inappropriate to judge government policies only on the basis of incomes of the poor, incomes which generally did not show much improvement until 1970. Instead the improvements made in raising production levels, diversifying output, and improving social services deserve emphasis. If there had not been a poor external environment, the effect on rural incomes would have been greater. If there had not been significant government intervention, Malaysia's poor would have been much worse off.

Because the problem of poverty is large and persistent, government has given top priority to eradicating poverty. This is one of the twin objectives of the New Economic Policy introduced by government in 1971. The second objective of that policy is to reduce the racial imbalances in income, employment, and the ownership of assets. It is targeted that the incidence of poverty will be reduced by two-thirds by 1990, that the pattern of employment will reflect the racial composition of the population, and that the share of bumiputras in the ownership of the corporate sector will increase from 2 percent in 1970 to at least 30 percent by 1990.[1] Although government intervention will continue to be an important means of achieving these targets, the New Economic Policy gives new emphasis to the need for rapid growth in the modern sector as the only context in which the objectives will be attainable. The government's long-term plan is based on the requirement that 2.1 million, or almost 90 percent, of the new jobs to be created during 1975–90 would be in industry and services. This requirement implies a substantial reduction in the share of agricultural employment. It also implies a net shift out of agriculture of more than a million jobs from the number that would be employed if present employment patterns were to persist.

If the targets of the New Economy Policy are to be reached, the economy must maintain a long-term GNP growth rate of at least 8 percent a year. The growth of the manufacturing sector will have to be even more rapid. Without this expansion, employment growth of more

---

1. Bumiputra literally means "son of the soil." The word is used to refer to Malays and other indigenous groups.

than 3 percent a year will not materialize if rural incomes are to be significantly increased. A more moderate growth rate would substantially reduce the creation of new employment in the modern sector and make it more difficult to achieve the targets for restructuring employment and reducing poverty. Government policy is completely in line with this general argument. It stresses that the goals of the New Economic Policy have to be achieved in a context of rapid economic growth.

Given the need for rapid growth, what are the prospects for achieving it? Since the drafting of Malaysia's third plan, for 1976–80, there have been significant changes in factors affecting growth. Resource prospects are much better as a result of larger exports now being projected for oil and natural gas and general improvements in the price outlook for Malaysia's other export commodities. During the period of the third plan, for example, exports could be as much as 15 to 20 percent higher than initially projected and increase the foreign exchange resources available for growth. These improved prospects for exports, especially for oil, will also increase government revenue. Public revenue could rise from the equivalent of 26 percent of GNP during 1971–75, the period of Malaysia's second plan, to more than 30 percent during the 1980s. Thus the availability of resources, which has not been a serious problem in the past, is expected to be even less of a constraint in the future. Compared with most other developing countries, Malaysia is fortunate in this respect.

Although Malaysia appears to have the financial capacity to achieve rapid growth, the economy will no longer be able to rely so heavily on rapid growth of primary production. Although Malaysia still is rich in natural resources, which will provide a reliable base for the expansion of the economy, the growth rates of the production of such commodities as rubber, palm oil, petroleum, and forest products are all likely to be lower than in the past. With growth decelerating in the resource sectors, rapid industrial growth will increasingly become essential to successful economic performance. This imperative arises not only from the viewpoint of production and the creation of real incomes, but also from the viewpoint of employment and its restructuring. Because of the decline in manufacturing investment during 1975 and 1976, however, the economy was not well poised for sustained rapid industrial growth at the beginning of the third plan period. A substantial increase in manufacturing investment was needed to keep the manufacturing growth rate from faltering.

In addition to rapid industrial growth, successful achievement of the targets of the New Economic Policy will require a concerted effort to accelerate the pace of rural development. Most of the poor live in rural areas. Although rapid growth of industrial employment can ease the problem of rural poverty by absorbing migrants from rural areas, poverty will continue to be a largely rural phenomenon. Thus, even if there is rapid sustained growth of employment in industry and services, the projections of the third plan indicate that more than three-quarters of Malaysia's poor will be in rural areas in 1990. An expansion of income and employment opportunities for rural Malaysians is of high priority. Furthermore the expected decline in growth rates of the production of rubber and palm oil make an expansion of government programs even more necessary: for example, accelerating land development programs, increasing the settler participation in those programs, expanding programs of replanting for rubber smallholders, expanding extension and credit for rice farmers, intensifying efforts to promote intercropping by coconut smallholders, and improving the access of poor families to such basic services as education, electricity, housing, and water supply—all of which deserve priority because of the substantial impact they can have on reducing poverty.

The greater availability of public resources will enable government to undertake that expansion. But the main constraint on mounting a more effective attack on rural poverty appears to be the capacity of the public sector to identify and prepare projects that can affect large numbers of rural poor. In this regard a plan to improve the identification, preparation, and implementation of public programs deserves high priority. In addition, because the scarcity of qualified manpower in the public sector appears to be a serious constraint on expanding the development program, government might consider making greater use of the skills available in the private sector until the public sector can be expanded.

Government does not have the direct control over private investment that it has over public investment, but it can play a strong role in providing a policy framework conducive to vigorous growth in the private sector. Because the more obvious areas of import substitution have been exhausted, sustained rapid growth in manufacturing will have to rely increasingly on export expansion. Policies will therefore have to ensure a favorable export environment. In its management of exchange rates, government will have to give careful consideration to the effect on manufactured exports. An attempt to offset high rates of world inflation by substantially appreciating the Malaysian dollar could undermine Malaysia's competitive position; it could also exacerbate the maldistribution of income. With regard to institutional factors, government has already acted to alleviate fears in the private community about the Industrial Coordination Act and the Petroleum Development Act. Government has also stressed that it will implement the Industrial Coordination Act in a flexible and pragmatic manner so as to encourage investment and growth. Because much of the concern in the private sector has been over how that act will be implemented, flexible implementation by government should help to ease the concern in the business community.

The restructuring targets of the New Economic Policy present a challenge. Not only does the economy have to provide productive employment for a rapidly growing labor force, it also has to provide for a considerable change in the racial composition of employment by sector and occupation. Achieving the targets for restructuring employment will require modification of the patterns into which new employment is channeled. The most sweeping changes are to be in agriculture, which would be required to absorb only 5 percent of the Malay net addition to the labor force. This absorption implies that about 75 percent of the new places in agriculture would be taken up by non-Malays. Many observers have raised questions about the realism of these targets.

It may not be easy to meet the targets of the New Economic Policy for restructuring employment, targets that are embedded in rather high targets for the growth of employment, at least for the modern sectors. It is stated in the third plan that not much improvement in productivity has been assumed in the services and that some underemployment in that sector may persist. Because policy instruments have not yet been devised to induce workers to leave agriculture under these conditions, the estimates may overemphasize the relative shift in employment from agriculture to services. If employment in the modern sectors expands less rapidly than foreseen, more workers will remain in agriculture, and the restructuring targets, especially those for agriculture, will be even more difficult to reach. This is not to say that the targets for restructuring employment should be put aside as unrealistic or impractical. It appears, however, that it would not be desirable to enforce the restructuring targets regardless of the cost. Such enforcement conceivably could endanger the economic growth that is crucial to any reasonable effort at restructuring.

Under these circumstances it seems appropriate to conclude that the objective and the process of restructuring are more important than the specific numerical targets. The main goal is to foster national unity, which would be jeopardized if the enforcement of targets were to cause a slowdown in economic growth. Thus the efforts to reduce the identification of race with economic function should be continued. But as government has stipulated, those efforts should be continued in a way that enables the main groups in society to feel that they are participating significantly and continuously in the country's growth and development. If engendering this feeling were to involve softening some of the numerical targets—for example, by counting the Malays benefiting from land development schemes among those whose jobs have been restructured—the cost would be relatively small, particularly if it were to make possible the retention of the objective and process of restructuring. In addition, given the relatively comfortable resource position Malaysia will enjoy in the coming years, more use can be made of incentives to attain the restructuring objectives than of regulations, which could dampen business activity and the growth context in which restructuring must take place.

The general process of restructuring, especially the restructuring of occupations, will also require a considerable expansion in the number of technically trained Malays. Given the progress in increasing Malay enrollments during the period of the second plan, 1971–75, while at the same time allowing for significant growth in non-Malay enrollments, government obviously attaches a high priority to this issue. Nevertheless the projections of the third plan have raised the spectre of substantial shortages of technical manpower by the early 1980s. A reassessment of long-term educational requirements may therefore be warranted.

In summary, the prospects appear to be good for achieving rapid growth and for ameliorating the twin problems of poverty and racial imbalances. Certainly there should be no serious constraint imposed by the availability of resources. To achieve the targets of the New Economic Policy will nevertheless require vigorous action by government along a number of fronts. The policy framework will have to be readjusted to promote the rapid recovery and sustained growth of the industrial sector. A pragmatic attitude will be needed in interpreting and implementing the quantitative restructuring targets to ensure that sight is not lost of the overall goal of improving the racial balance. Growth in the supply of technically trained manpower will require close scrutiny to ensure that it does not constrain the restructuring potential made possible by rapid economic growth. Finally, larger and more effective programs to reduce poverty by direct action will require a concerted effort to expand the capacity of the public sector to prepare and implement such programs.

𐂃𐂃𐂃𐂃𐂃𐂃𐂃𐂃𐂃𐂃𐂃𐂃𐂃𐂃𐂃𐂃𐂃𐂃𐂃𐂃𐂃𐂃𐂃𐂃𐂃𐂃𐂃𐂃𐂃𐂃𐂃𐂃𐂃𐂃

Social and Political Setting

MALAYSIA IS A FEDERATION of thirteen states: eleven in the Malay Peninsula and two in the northern part of the island of Borneo. The peninsular states account for 40 percent of the land area; the Borneo states of Sabah and Sarawak, more than 400 miles to the east across the South China Sea, account for 60 percent. A mountain range covered with tropical rain forest divides the long, narrow Peninsula into two distinct regions. West of the range, rolling foothills have been converted to rubber and oil palm plantations. Alluvial plains, formed by short rivers flowing from the mountains, are suitable for the cultivation of rice and in places are rich in tin deposits. Because of this natural wealth, most of the urban and manufacturing concentrations have sprung up in the western part of the Peninsula, and the road system there is exceptional. East of the range, rain forest still covers most of the foothills, which are increasingly being converted to rubber and oil palm schemes for smallholders, and rice cultivation near the coast is the main economic activity. In Sabah and Sarawak, mountains, rain forest, long rivers, and a coastal fringe of alluvial plains and mangrove swamps dominate the landscape. The rugged terrain makes overland travel difficult, and most of the economic activity is along rivers and the coastal fringe.

With about 12 million inhabitants in 1975, Malaysia has a population density of about 100 persons a square mile. Of the 10.2 million dwellers in the Peninsula, roughly half are Malay, a third are Chinese, and a tenth are Indian. This tripartite division nevertheless oversimplifies strong ethnic alignments that are based on origins from different islands in the archipelago, different provinces in China, and different regions in the subcontinent—alignments that often are as rigid as those among the main groups. The residential and occupational stereotypes of the three groups are as follows. Most Malays live in rural areas and engage in smallholder agriculture and fishing; urban Malays generally work in the government bureaucracy, the armed forces and police, and the lower rungs of the manufacturing and services sectors. Most Chinese live in urban areas, where they dominate commerce; rural Chinese engage in tin mining and in agriculture as smallholders. Most Indians live in the rubber and oil palm estates; urban Indians are in the professions and services. Recent changes have made these stereotypes increasingly inapplicable, but they continue to be indicative of residential and occupational patterns.

The population is even more diverse in Sabah and Sarawak, where migrations throughout the past two or three millenia have successively displaced dwellers along the coast and beside the rivers, pushing early arrivals farther and farther inland. Having little contact with one another, the various ethnic groups developed independently and today retain much of their tribal individuality. As in the Peninsula, indigenous groups are for the most part engaged in agriculture and live in rural areas. Chinese generally live in the towns and dominate commerce, but a substantial number of them are smallholders in agriculture.

Until recently Malaysia's diverse territories and peoples were essentially separate, a condition that has complicated the creation of a sense of loyalty to the Malaysian state and a sense of belonging to the Malaysian nation. The common heritage of the thirteen states is the history of British colonial administration, but it takes more than this shared heritage to transcend the separate identities of each of the peninsular states and the distant Borneo states. The common status of the myriad peoples of the country is Malaysian citizenship, but it takes more than this shared status to transcend the separate identities of diverse cultures. Until the end of the Second World War, the various ethnic communities in Malaysia were separated—partly out of circumstance, partly out of preference—by differences of language, religion, residence, economic activity, and dietary habits. These differences persist and will continue to be significant.

Historical Background

The establishment of a settlement at Malacca by the Sumatran prince Parameswara early in the fifteenth century marked the beginning of recorded history in the Malay Peninsula. But the region was not bereft of cultural activity before that time. The Peninsula, strategically placed at the crossroads of maritime trade between China and India, had long been a place where Hindu and Buddhist influence intersected. It had also become an area of Islamic influence, certainly by the fourteenth century and possibly earlier. When Parameswara adopted

Islam and the name Sultan Iskandar Shah, he changed the course of indigenous cultural development in the entire region. His conversion established Islam as the religion of those living on the Peninsula and a social hierarchy that would survive to the modern era: a royal aristocracy comprising the sultan, his family, and his court; a class of local leaders comprising district chiefs and village headmen; and a peasant class.

In 1511 the Portuguese conquered Malacca, which by this time was the capital of a kingdom that controlled most of the Peninsula and much of Sumatra. Because the Portuguese were more interested in trade than in subjugation, the effect of their conquest was to disperse the Malays, not to convert or contain them. The same was true after the Dutch took over Malacca in 1641. They were interested in maintaining a permanent base for purposes of strategy and trade, not in dominating the local populace or mobilizing it to produce goods for the markets at home. Even after the British established their presence in the region by settling in Penang in 1786, Malacca in 1795, and Singapore in 1824, their chief concern was the expansion of trade. The settlements provided the required ports of call for ships of the East India Company making the long voyage between China and India.

During the entire period, sultanates prospered in Johore, Pahang, and Perak. Bugis from the Celebes established the Selangor Sultanate, Minangkabaus from Sumatra the Negri Sembilan Sultanate. In the early nineteenth century the sultanates of Kelantan, Trengganu, Kedah, and Perlis reverted to the suzerainty of Siam. On Borneo, meanwhile, the long-established sultanates of Brunei and Sulu began to be fragmented. Much of modern Sarawak became the personal domain of the Brooke family, starting with James Brooke in 1841; parts of modern Sabah became the property of a private company, the North Borneo Chartered Company, in the late 1870s.

The discovery of rich tin deposits in Perak and Selangor in about 1850 began the transformation of economic activity on the Peninsula. Chinese had mined tin there at least as early as the sixteenth century, but on a small scale. With the new discoveries the expansion of Chinese mining settlements was rapid. In the Larut Valley of Perak, for example, the Chinese population rose from nearly zero in 1850 to an estimated 40,000 in 1870. Many of them came from South China as the indentured laborers of Chinese merchants who supplied labor in the straits settlements of Penang, Malacca, and Singapore and elsewhere in the Peninsula. Clan wars among the Chinese led the Sultan of Perak to ask the British to intervene and restore order. This intervention marked the start of the extension of British influence inland from the straits settlements. A pattern of indirect rule was established: in exchange for British protection, a British agent was made responsible for administration, law, and taxation in Perak. The Sultan continued to be responsible for matters of custom, religion, and land. By the late 1880s the British had established indirect rule in Selangor, Negri Sembilan, and Pahang as well. They subsequently extended the pattern to Kelantan, Trengganu, Perlis, and Kedah, which Siam transferred to Britain in 1909, and to Johore, which accepted a British adviser in 1914.[1] British commercial interests followed on the heels of British colonial administration, and the Malay Peninsula quickly became the main supplier of tin and rubber to the world.

In the late nineteenth century British planters had tried various strains of rubber trees in the Peninsula without much success. But with the introduction of *Hevea brasiliensis* seeds, nurtured at Kew Gardens in London and multiplied in the botanical gardens of Singapore, the plantations carved out of the lowland forests began to flourish. Financed by British companies, they expanded rapidly. To man the estates, plantation owners brought in hundreds of thousands of indentured workers from South India during the early decades of the twentieth century. During the same period, new technology—notably the gravel pump and the tin dredge—made tin mining possible on a much larger scale and therefore more efficient. The entry of the British into mechanized mining displaced many Chinese mine laborers, but the opportunities in estates, urban commerce, and small-scale industry continued to encourage the flow of immigrants from China.

The Malays had little contact with the burgeoning tin and rubber industries or with the new commercial activities in towns. Some of them nevertheless established smallholdings in rubber. Generally they preferred their traditional style of rural life and were disinclined to subject themselves to the exceedingly harsh living conditions in the mines and on the plantations. British colonial policy reinforced this preference and kept Malays separate from the modern sector. The immigrant population continued to grow rapidly until the 1930s, when colonial authorities, recognizing the potential problems associated with a large immigrant population, encouraged the immigration of Malays from Sumatra and Java. Although most Chinese and Indians came with

1. Perak, Selangor, Negri Sembilan, and Pahang constituted the Federated Malay States; Kelantan, Trengganu, Perlis, Kedah, and Johore the Unfederated Malay States. The straits settlements of Penang, Malacca, and Singapore were a crown colony.

the intention of making what they could and returning to their home-
land, it was becoming apparent that many of them would take up permanent residence in the Peninsula.

The Second World War brought the destruction and deterioration of
much of the physical plant built up in preceding decades. But the effect
of the Japanese occupation was more than economic. It punctured the
myth of British invincibility and unleashed nationalist sentiments. The
political awakening in the Peninsula did not, however, revolve around
Malayan nationalism. It revolved around Malay nationalism, Indian nationalism, and Chinese nationalism—each fragmented and decidedly
separate. To join the movements in a combined effort would prove to
be difficult.

Postwar Constitutional Development

The British instituted the Malayan Union in April 1946 to replace
the patchwork of four federated Malay states, five unfederated Malay
states, and two straits settlements.[2] The thinking must have been that
the Malayan Union, in addition to simplifying and centralizing administration, would engender loyalty to a larger nation-state that subsequently would be granted independence. But three provisions of the
Union grated upon Malay sensibilities: the loss of identity by individual states; the loss of sovereignty over the Malay states by their hereditary rulers; and, not least, the offer of citizenship to non-Malays on
fairly liberal terms. The Malay response led to the formation of the
United Malays National Organization (UMNO) which used the traditional Malay political structure to marshall widespread opposition to Britain and the Union.

The colonial government agreed in July 1946 to negotiate another
constitution in conjunction with the Malay rulers and the representatives of UMNO. To accommodate Malay demands concerning citizenship, the identity of states, and the sovereignty of rulers, the British
established the Federation of Malaya in February 1948 to replace the
Malayan Union. Among its chief features were a federal legislative

2. For strategic and economic reasons the British did not include Singapore, the third
straits settlement, in the Malayan Union. Great Britain, Colonial Office, *Malayan Union
and Singapore: Summary of Proposed Constitutional Arrangements* (London: His Majesty's Sta-
tionery Office, 1946).

council and an executive council presided over by the high commissioner. These bodies were forerunners of the parliament and cabinet that would govern after independence. They nevertheless were appointive, not elective, and the high commissioner retained real power. Legislative assemblies replicated this structure in each of the states, where chief ministers headed executive councils but British residents and advisers retained real power.

Political turmoil did not subside with the adoption of the new constitution. The Malayan Communist Party (MCP), an outgrowth of the Malayan Peoples Anti-Japanese Army formed during the War to resist the Japanese occupation, was active in the labor movement after the resumption of British colonial rule. Most of its members were Chinese. Rejecting the legitimacy of the colonial government, the MCP chose in 1948 to go underground and foment revolution that would lead to independence and the formation of a communist state. Several thousand of its members withdrew to the jungle and began a long campaign of guerrilla warfare against all those opposing their aims. The emergency declared in June 1948 in response to this renewal of violence had one lasting consequence: To cut off lines of sympathy and support, whether voluntary or exacted, hundreds of thousands of rural Chinese were resettled in new villages, mostly on the fringes of towns and cities. Although the curfews and fences erected to curtail movements were to disappear after a few years, this pattern of residence was to continue. Whereas most Chinese had not been urban dwellers, the Chinese suddenly became almost exclusively urban. In addition, the emergency pitted government forces, mostly British and Malay, against guerrilla forces and supporters, mostly Chinese. The character of this conflict threatened to undermine progress toward communal harmony.

The political development of the Peninsula continued during the emergency, particularly after 1952, when the security situation had for the most part been brought under control. Indeed the emergency probably forced the pace of political development. As part of the hearts-and-minds campaign to turn sentiment against the MCP, the British held elections for seats on local councils that were to acquire increasing responsibility for local matters. And just as Malays formed UMNO as a communal party, Indians formed the Malayan Indian Congress (MIC) and Chinese formed the Malayan Chinese Association (MCA). In the first federal elections in 1955, UMNO, the MCA, and the MIC joined to form the Alliance Party, which swept into power by taking fifty-one of the fifty-two seats on the legislative council.

From the beginning political negotiation was essentially conducted by the top leaders of these three parties. Each of the major parties has had competitors that have been more radical in communal orientation. For example, the Pan-Malayan Islamic Party has challenged UMNO by insisting on even greater rights for Malays than were provided for in the federal constitution and by propounding the formation of a theocratic state based on Islam. Competitors of the MCA and the MIC have espoused equal rights for all Malaysians and the adoption of Chinese and Tamil as official languages. Other parties have tried to muster pancommunal support, invariably without success. Their lack of appeal indicates the extent to which communal issues were, and would continue to be, the dominant political issues in the country.

When the Federation of Malaya secured its independence from Britain on 31 August 1957, it set itself three main objectives in addition to solving the conventional problems of social, political, and economic development. The first was to have Malays, who saw the country as being essentially Malay, participate more broadly in the economy without depriving non-Malays of their property or unduly restricting their opportunities. Whereas British commercial interests controlled the plantations, the larger tin mines, and industries, and whereas Chinese controlled urban commerce, Malays worked almost exclusively in traditional agriculture and the government services. The second objective was to have non-Malays, in exchange for citizenship and the right to participate in the political process, accede to the Malay language, special privileges for Malays, and broader economic participation by Malays. The third objective was to foster and maintain communal stability. None was to be easily accomplished.

Constitutional provisions were made for citizenship in various categories: by operation of law, registration, or naturalization. Most Malays and many non-Malays automatically became citizens. Others, mainly non-Malays, could become citizens subject to the fulfillment of certain qualifications. Citizenship was automatic for all persons born in the country after independence, but a constitutional amendment subsequently limited such citizenship to those with at least one parent who was a citizen or permanent resident. Other important provisions had to do with language and religion, which for all ethnic groups represented the embodiment of their ethnic cultures. Malay and English were to be official languages for ten years, after which the policy would be reviewed. Islam became the religion of the federation, but the practice of other religions was to be freely permitted.

In addition, the constitution safeguarded the special position of Malays. Non-Malays wanted to have equal rights with Malays. Malay leaders felt that if non-Malays had equal rights, Malays would be at an economic disadvantage and ultimately a political disadvantage. By granting special privileges to Malays, the constitution created the context for their broader participation in the economy. The privileges include the continuing reservation to Malays of large areas of land, with the proviso that such land not be transferred to non-Malays. They also include, in proportions deemed reasonable by the Supreme Head of State, the reservation to Malays of positions in the public services, particularly at higher levels; places and scholarships at educational institutions; and permits and licenses that are required to conduct certain types of trade and business. Parallel to these special privileges, the constitution safeguarded the interests of the other communities.

The constitution maintained the position and prestige of the sultans and the identity of the states. Together the hereditary rulers and governors constitute the Conference of Rulers. The hereditary rulers elect one of their number to serve a term of five years as the Supreme Head of State, or *Yang di-Pertuan Agung*. The constitution also created a strong central government responsible for most matters, including health, education, finance, external affairs, internal security, and civil and criminal law. Certain powers nevertheless are within the purview of the states, notably those over land, agriculture, and forestry. Other items, such as social welfare and drainage and irrigation, are the concurrent responsibility of state and federal governments. In the event of any conflict, however, the federal authority is supreme.

The country is ruled by a bicameral parliament comprising the *Agung* (Supreme Head of State), the *Dewan Negara* (Senate), and the *Dewan Rakyat* (House of Representatives). The *Dewan Rakyat* is the principal lawmaking body; its 154 seats are elective. The *Dewan Negara* can initiate legislation and has certain ratificatory powers. Its fifty-eight seats are in part appointive and, insofar as each of the thirteen state assemblies nominates two members, in part elective. The prime minister is the member of the *Dewan Rakyat* who commands the confidence of that house; ministers constituting the cabinet may, with the consent of the *Agung*, be appointed from either house. Unicameral legislative assemblies of elected representatives govern the states. A chief minister is drawn from each assembly to appoint an executive council, which manages those state affairs within its purview.

Because the states have authority over land, they receive the proceeds from the sale or rental of state land and from mining and forestry licenses and royalties. Within the system of land tenure, more than 4 million acres are designated as Malay reservation land that cannot be transferred to non-Malays. The reservation of land to Malays, first legislated under the Malay Reservations Enactment of 1913, has had four main effects: keeping in Malay hands land that might otherwise have gone to non-Malays; denying Malay holders of reservation land access to many sources of credit because of their inability to use their land as collateral for loans from non-Malays; impeding development of reservation land by government and non-Malay interests; restricting the use of reservation land to residential, agricultural, and small commercial purposes. The Islamic system of inheritance, by fragmenting holdings into smaller and smaller parcels, also affects the use of land.

Sabah, Sarawak, and Singapore joined with the Federation of Malays to form Malaysia on 16 September 1963. Brunei, on the north coast of Borneo, was also to join in the formation of the new nation, but its leaders withdrew from the negotiations because of disagreement over the position of the Brunei sultan and the disposition of Brunei's oil revenue. The change in constitutional status of these states was not well received by neighboring countries. The Philippines renewed their dormant claim to Sabah in the international courts and broke off diplomatic relations with Kuala Lumpur. In an attempt to crush the nascent political entity of Malaysia, Indonesia initiated an armed confrontation that lasted for more than three years.

The essential circumstances surrounding the formation of Malaysia would appear to be these. Singapore had for years been excluded from the constitutional developments in the Peninsula because of its predominantly Chinese population. To have incorporated Singapore alone would have reduced the proportion of Malays to less than half and made the numbers of Malays and Chinese approximately equal. This prospect was not acceptable to Malay political leaders. Incorporating Sabah and Sarawak along with Singapore, however, preserved the majority of indigenous people and better assured the viability of the Borneo states. The level of political and economic development in these two states lagged far behind that in the Peninsula. As British colonies after the Second World War, they were not encouraged to develop politically, and their economic efforts were directed toward reconstruction. Because of their different level of development, political leaders in Sabah and Sarawak wanted constitutional provisions that would protect the interests of these two states and their substantial wealth of natural resources.

The solution was a confederation, an enlarged federal structure with special provisions for the new states. Sabah and Sarawak obtained greater control over local affairs than was enjoyed by peninsular states—notably over immigration, education, and civil service. This special status satisfied leaders in both states who were concerned lest Kuala Lumpur return them to colonial status by taking the best jobs and exploiting the best opportunities. Singapore obtained autonomy in such matters as language and education and was permitted to retain a substantial share of the revenue that it earned from trade. But questions about the precise meaning of special terms for the new states caused tensions from the outset, and differences over the style of political debate and the negotiability of political and economic issues led to the separation of Singapore from Malaysia in August 1965. Federal loyalties occasionally wavered in the Borneo states as well, largely because of their natural wealth and the autonomy given them in their political affairs, but these states have increasingly come into the federal ambit.

Changes in Ground Rules after 1969

Economic changes during the 1950s and the early part of the 1960s were less dramatic than political and constitutional changes. True, progress was being made toward solving the conventional problems of national development. Social services were expanding; infrastructure was improving; growth in national output was steady. But little progress was being made toward solving the special problems of Malaysia. Exports continued to depend on the performance of a few primary commodities, and when government formulated Malaysia's first plan in 1966, manufacturing constituted only 10 percent of the GNP. Substantial dualism between agriculture and other sectors continued to characterize the economy. Within agriculture there was another kind of dualism: a modern estate sector featuring high productivity; a traditional smallholder sector featuring low productivity and low incomes. Added to this, foreign commercial interests continued to dominate the modern sector. The principal structural change was the conversion of large acreages of rubber to oil palm in response to the decline in the price of rubber.

Along with these somewhat discouraging economic trends, disenchantment was growing among all segments of the population. With urban unemployment rising and with education and language again looming as issues, non-Malays began to question the extent to which their interests were being safeguarded. At the same time the economic position of Malays seemed not to have improved substantially, as was promised, in the years after independence. This perception contributed to the frustration of Malay sensibilities about what really was being done for them. As a result, increasing currency was attached to the Malay word *bumiputra*, which distinguishes indigenous Malaysians from nonindigenous Malaysians.

A study of income distribution confirmed that the economic position of Malays at the end of the 1960s was still significantly inferior to that of non-Malays.[3] In Peninsular Malaysia the average per capita income of Malays was half that of the Chinese. Although Malays accounted for slightly more than half the peninsular population, almost 80 percent of the Malays worked in rural areas, primarily in traditional agriculture. Only half the non-Malays worked in rural areas. In urban areas, where about a third of total employment was to be found, the non-Malay share of jobs exceeded 75 percent. Moreover the representation of Malays in most economic sectors—particularly in managerial, professional, and supervisory occupations—was poor. Imbalances in the ownership of assets were a further source of communal disparities. Malay agricultural landholdings outside traditional agriculture were negligible. Chinese landholdings were on the average twice the size of Malay landholdings. In the corporate sector the proportion of share capital of limited companies held by Malays was only about 2 percent. The Chinese community held about a third of share capital, foreigners most of the remainder. Consequently the inequality of income in Peninsular Malaysia was substantial. The bottom 40 percent of the populace received only 12 percent of total income; the top 5 percent received 28 percent. The inequality within the main communal groups was only marginally less than that for the entire population.

In the wake of federal elections in May 1969, the fragile communal stability was shattered. Opposition parties championing the interests of non-Malays performed better than expected, and Malays regarded that performance as a strong challenge to Malay political supremacy. As tensions rose and uncertainty abounded, riots and reprisals racked the capital and left hundreds of Malaysians dead. A state of emergency was declared. Parliament was suspended. Civil order was restored by the army and police. And the National Operations Council was formed to assume responsibility for governance.

Malaysian political leaders, spurred by the requirement to eliminate conditions seen as causes of the communal riots, decided that several of

3. The data were for 1970, but they serve as a proxy for conditions in the late 1960s. Department of Statistics, "1970 Census Post Enumeration Survey" (Kuala Lumpur, n.d.; unpublished computer tapes).

the ground rules for governance had to be changed. First, the discussion of sensitive constitutional issues was removed from public debate. When parliamentary government was restored in February 1971, the constitution was amended to make seditious the public discussion of constitutional provisions for language, citizenship, the special position of Malays, and the status of the rulers. The passage of this amendment was in fact among the preconditions for the restoration of parliamentary rule. Second, economic planning assumed new criteria and objectives. Under the two Malayan five-year plans and Malaysia's first plan, for 1966–70, the criteria for planning had largely been financial and administrative. Under Malaysia's second plan, for 1971–75, economic planning was to be explicitly based on social criteria as well. Third, government began to pursue the policies for Malay language and education with greater resolve. Beginning in late 1969 Malay became the language of instruction in the first standard of primary school. Each year thereafter it was to become the language of instruction of the next higher level, so that by 1982 all education up to the sixth form of secondary school would be in Malay.

Perhaps most important, government formulated the New Economic Policy in mid-1970 and incorporated it into the second plan. The overriding aim of that policy is to promote national unity by pursuing two objectives: the eradication of poverty and the restructuring of society so as to eliminate the identification of race with economic function. For the first objective, government set ambitious long-term targets for the reduction of poverty among the entire population. For the second objective, policymakers established long-term targets for the Malay ownership of share capital in limited companies and for the proportion of Malays employed in manufacturing, enrolled in institutions of higher learning, and installed in managerial positions.

Success in attaining the twin objectives of reducing poverty and increasing the Malay participation in the economy will depend as much on social and political management as on economic management. In some countries, including those in East Asia which showed sustained high rates of growth during the 1960s and 1970s, economic concerns are in many ways separate from social and political concerns. In others—and Malaysia is among them—social, political, and economic concerns are inextricably intertwined. The Malaysian government realizes that national unity, the prerequisite for continuing economic progress, has many aspects and cannot be achieved by economic means alone. It also realizes that the formulation of a program to attain the basic goals of the New Economic Policy is the most important economic challenge. The riots in 1969 highlighted the dangers inherent in a multiracial society when ethnic prejudices are exacerbated by economic disparities. The long-term political and communal stability of Malaysia will depend on progress toward correcting these disparities.

Growth, Structural Change, and Social Progress

THE AVERAGE GROWTH RATE OF REAL GNP in Malaysia was about 7 percent a year during 1961–76 (table 2.1). The economy recorded this growth despite the sharp fluctuations in prices of principal exports and the uncertainties created by the confrontation with Indonesia in the first half of the 1960s, the separation of Singapore in 1965, and the riots in 1969. These political factors clearly affected the level of private investment in the 1960s: the growth of public investment remained sluggish, and the rate of gross fixed capital formation remained stagnant at about 16 to 17 percent of GNP. Nevertheless the growth in GNP for that decade averaged about 6 percent a year; it then fluctuated widely between 1970 and 1976, averaging 7.7 percent a year. This improved performance was the result of sharply higher levels of investment, the emergence of sizable output of crude oil, and the slowing down of the deterioration in the terms of trade. The rate of gross fixed capital formation, although falling from the peak of almost 27 percent in 1974 to 22 percent in 1976, was substantially higher during 1970–76 than 1961–70. In addition, the terms of trade, which declined nearly 20 percent during 1960–70, declined only 4 percent during 1970–76. The secondary income and demand effects of a given increase in output were thus considerably greater in the later period.

For 1960–76 the average growth of per capita GNP in Malaysia was about 4 percent a year, well above that for middle-income developing countries (table 2.2). The sustained high growth in Malaysia basically was the result of the country's wealth in natural resources, especially its untapped reserves of cultivable land; an outward-oriented growth strategy; good, albeit cautious, economic and financial management; and, not least, stable social and political institutions. Three specific factors were important: sharp rises in productivity in the rubber sector—rises which cushioned the effects of steep price declines and helped maintain the Malaysian share in the world rubber market; a big push for export diversification through rapid expansion of the production of palm oil

Table 2.1. *Expenditure on Gross Domestic Product, 1961–76*
(percent)

Item	Share of gross national product in current prices			Average annual rate of growth in constant 1970 prices		
	1961	1970	1976	1961–70	1970–76	1961–76
Consumption	80.4	77.8	70.1	4.7	6.8	5.4
Gross investment	17.1	20.5	21.9	6.7	9.4	8.7
Fixed investment	15.6	17.3	22.2	6.4	11.6	9.8
Exports	50.3	45.1	54.0	6.0	7.9	6.4
Imports	44.7	40.4	42.4	2.9	6.9	4.7
Gross domestic product in market prices	103.0	103.0	103.5	6.3	7.8	6.8
Gross national product in market prices	100.0	100.0	100.0	6.4	7.7	6.7

Note: Growth rates were calculated by the least squares method.
Source: World Bank estimates linking the Department of Statistics' old series of national accounts for 1961–70 to the new series for 1971–76 and deflating by the United Nations' deflators for Malaysia for 1961–70. See tables C.5 and C.6 in appendix C.

Table 2.2. *Gross National Product per Capita, Malaysia and Selected Groups of Countries, 1960–76*

Country or group of countries	Gross national product per capita, 1976 (U.S. dollars)	Average annual rate of growth, 1960–76 (percent)
Malaysia	860	3.9
Low-income countries	150	0.9
Middle-income countries	750	2.8
Industrial countries	6,200	3.4
Countries having centrally planned economies	2,280	3.5

Note: Figures for groups of countries are median values.
Source: World Bank, *World Development Report, 1978* (New York: Oxford University Press, 1978).

and the extraction of timber; and rapid manufacturing growth, which averaged about 13 percent a year during 1968–76 and was increasingly oriented toward exports.

Despite the impressive performance of the economy, as measured by GNP growth, the improvement in the income situation of a substantial part of the population was modest before the 1970s. Because of the sizable loss in the terms of trade, average per capita income in Peninsular Malaysia increased only 2 to 3 percent a year during 1960–70. The growth of average per capita income in the traditional agricultural sector probably was only 1 to 2 percent a year. The employment situation remained difficult under the impact of a rapidly growing labor force. In the first half of the 1970s, however, the living standard of a majority of Malaysians significantly improved, reflecting the acceleration of the rate of GNP growth, the leveling of the terms of trade, and the maturation of investments related to poverty eradication.

Export Growth and Diversification

With a ratio of merchandise exports to gross domestic product (GDP) of almost 50 percent, Malaysia is heavily dependent on the export sector. Trends in its exports therefore display the strength of the economy and the structural change over time. The value of Malaysian exports rose from M$3.2 billion in 1961 to M$13.4 billion in 1976, a more than fourfold increase (table 2.3). The volume of exports during this period expanded at the average annual rate of 6 to 7 percent, a rate roughly in line with the real growth in GNP.

Although nearly half of Malaysia's earnings from merchandise exports were derived from rubber in 1961, less than a quarter originated from this source in 1976 (table 2.4). The share of tin, the other principal export in the early 1960s, declined from 16 percent to 11 percent over the same period because of stagnant output and despite a sharp price rise. The increases were substantial in the shares of timber, oil palm, petroleum, and manufactured goods. The decline in relative earnings from rubber was mainly the result of a long-term decline in the international price of rubber. Despite a doubling of the export price of rubber between 1972 and 1976, the unit value of exports in 1976—M$1.91 a kilogram—was no higher in nominal terms than the average for 1960–62. The index of international inflation, measured by the export prices of manufactured goods from developed countries, showed an increase of 125 percent over the period. As mentioned earlier, productivity gains enabled the expansion of rubber production and exports in the face of falling prices. The acreage under mature rubber increased only 13 percent during 1960–75, but production doubled, indicating an average improvement in yields of 4 percent a year. The principal factor in yield increases was the massive replacement of old rubber trees by new,

Table 2.3. *Volume and Value of Exports, by Commodity,*
1961, 1970, and 1976

Commodity	1961	1970	1976	Average annual rate of growth (percent)		
				1961–70	1970–76	1961–76
Volume (thousands of metric tons)						
Rubber	785	1,345	1,620	4.9	3.2	4.2
Tin	76	94	82	2.4	−2.3	0.5
Petroleum[a]	1,910	4,970	7,219	11.2	6.4	9.3
Timber[b]	3,036	10,329	15,227	14.6	6.7	11.3
Palm oil	95	402	1,339	17.4	22.2	19.3
Value (millions of Malaysian dollars)						
Rubber	1,567	1,724	3,117	1.1	10.4	4.7
Tin	533	1,013	1,527	7.4	7.1	7.3
Petroleum	107	202	1,766	7.3	43.5	20.5
Timber	188	842	2,326	18.1	18.5	18.3
Palm oil	61	264	1,215	17.7	29.0	22.1
Manufactured goods[c]	146	333	2,036	9.6	35.2	19.2
Other[d]	636	784	1,432	2.4	10.6	5.6
Total	3,238	5,162	13,419	5.3	17.3	9.9
Share of commodity exports in gross national product (percent)	50	43	50	—	—	—

— Not applicable.
Sources: Bank Negara, *Quarterly Economic Bulletin*, vol. 9, no. 4 (December 1976); Ministry of Finance, *Economic Report, 1977–78*.
   a. Includes re-exports from Brunei.
   b. In thousands of cubic meters.
   c. Groups 5 through 8 of the standard international trade classification (SITC), excluding tin.
   d. Calculated as a residual item.

technologically improved varieties in rubber estates and smallholdings. Malaysia was thus able to increase its share in the world production of natural rubber to nearly 50 percent.

   The strong push for productivity in the rubber sector was accompanied by a rapid diversification to oil palm, a high rate of exploitation of forest resources, the expansion of petroleum exports, and a sharp increase in exports of manufactured goods. In 1961 exports of these

Table 2.4. *Structure of Exports, by Commodity, 1961, 1970, and 1976*
(percent)

Commodity	1961	1970	1976
Rubber	48	33	23
Tin	16	20	11
Petroleum	3	4	13
Sawlogs	4	12	11
Sawn timber	2	4	6
Palm oil	2	5	9
Manufactured goods	5	7	15
Other	20	15	12
Total	100	100	100

Sources: Same as for table 2.3.

four commodity groups totaled about M$500 million and constituted 16 percent of Malaysian exports. By 1976 these exports amounted to M$7.3 billion, or 54 percent of all exports. Thus more than two-thirds of the increment in merchandise exports during 1961–76 was provided by relatively new exports. Starting almost from scratch, Malaysia became the world's leading producer and exporter of palm oil; it accounted for 45 percent of world output in 1976. Three factors were instrumental in the rapid expansion of oil palm plantations in Malaysia: the soil and climate are ideal for the cultivation of oil palms; estates and land development schemes provided the management necessary to achieve high yields; the rubber price declined during the 1960s. The competitiveness of Malaysian production of palm oil has been a factor underlying the expected increase in share of palm oil in world production of oils and fat from less than 5 percent in 1960 to more than 10 percent in 1985. Largely because of these factors, Malaysian production of palm oil remains quite profitable.

The volume of timber exports from Malaysia increased from 3 million cubic meters in 1961 to more than 15 million cubic meters in 1976, when timber exports were second in value only to rubber. The East Asia and Pacific region accounted for 75 percent of the world's exports of tropical hardwood in the mid-1970s; Malaysia accounted for 20 percent of those exports (see chapter nine). On a per capita basis, however, Malaysian exports of timber were six times those of Indonesia and five times those of the Philippines, the other principal producers in East Asia. Peninsular Malaysia was able to increase its exports of processed woods and thus increase the value added in exports. But 63 percent of the value of timber exports from Malaysia still arose from log exports.

Between 1974 and 1977 the Malaysian output of crude oil more than doubled to nearly 200,000 barrels a day; gross exports of petroleum and partly refined products rose to more than M$2 billion. On a per capita basis Malaysia's crude oil output in 1977 was higher than Indonesia's, about the same as Mexico's, and between 50 and 60 percent of Nigeria's. Most of the oil is in Sabah and Sarawak and produced by Shell and Esso under production-sharing arrangements that were finalized in 1976.

Although primary exports still constituted nearly 85 percent of Malaysian exports in 1976, the growth of manufactured exports, at an average real rate of 24 percent a year during 1970–76, was faster than any other principal commodity group, except petroleum. Malaysian exports of manufactured goods of US$800 million in 1976 were a small fraction of those, say, from Taiwan, Hong Kong, Singapore, or Korea. But on a per capita basis they were substantially higher than those from Brazil, Mexico, India, Pakistan, Thailand, and the Philippines, the other developing countries leading in the export of manufactured goods (table 2.5). A large part of the expansion in manufactured exports from Peninsular Malaysia has been in electronics, garments, textiles, and footwear. Between 1970 and 1976 exports of these products in current

Table 2.5. *Manufactured Exports from Leading Developing Countries, 1975*

Country	Manufactured exports (millions of U.S. dollars)	Share in total exports (percent)	Manufactured exports per capita (U.S. dollars)
Malaysia	667	17.7	56
Brazil	2,192	25.8	21
Hong Kong[a]	4,464	96.5	1,015
India	2,089[b]	45.9[b]	3
Korea	4,136	82.7	117
Mexico	1,967	56.8	33
Pakistan	589	56.3	8
Philippines	258	11.4	6
Singapore[a]	1,286	25.5	571
Taiwan	4,303	81.1	268
Thailand	498	22.9	12
Yugoslavia	2,781	68.3	130

Source: Country data compiled by the World Bank.
a. Excludes re-exports.
b. For the statistical year ending 31 March 1976.

Table 2.6. *Exports of Manufactured Goods, by Selected Commodity Groups, 1970 and 76*

Commodity group	1970	1976	Percentage increase
Electronics and miscellaneous manufactures	12	191	1,490
Textiles and footwear	10	120	1,100
Wood products	29	130	348
Rubber products	5	18	260
Chemicals and chemical products	10	23	130
Nonmetallic mineral products	6	11	83
Iron and steel and metal manufactures	6	20	233
Machinery and transport equipment	7	223	3,086
Petroleum products	52	58	12
Total[a]	137	794	480

Source: Ministry of Finance, *Economic Report, 1977–78*.

a. Because of differences in the definition of manufactured goods, the numbers here differ somewhat from those in table 2.3

prices showed a nearly twelvefold increase to more than US$300 million (table 2.6). A substantial part of this expansion was from free trade zones, where multinational corporations dominate. Electronics assembly firms accounted for at least 90 percent of exports from free trade zones in 1974.[1]

The share of labor-intensive export industries in total export earnings, industrial output, and manufacturing employment significantly increased in the first half of the 1970s. Analysis with an input-output model, which included indirect effects, suggests that 45 percent of industrial expansion during 1970–75 was attributable to exports.[2] Although it is difficult to make precise estimates, manufactured exports apparently accounted for about 20 percent of gross manufacturing output in 1976. Comparable figures are about 30 percent for Korea and 5 percent for the Philippines. There also is little doubt that the expansion of manufacturing for export was responsible for a substantial portion of the 108,000 additional jobs created in the manufacturing sector during 1971–75, the period of Malaysia's second plan. The continued satisfac-

1. Most of those exports were subassemblies, such as circuit fittings, office machine parts, and television and radio parts. There also were assemblies of air conditioners and electric calculators.

2. World Bank, "Malaysia: Second Plan Performance and Third Plan Issues," report no. 1177a-MA (a restricted-circulation document), 2 vols. (Washington, D.C.: World Bank, 1976; processed), vol. 2, annex V.

tory development of manufactured exports will thus be a crucial factor in sustaining high rates of growth in manufacturing employment and output.

The foregoing review of the principal developments in exports shows the importance of rapid export expansion in economic growth. It also highlights the strong push to diversify primary exports and manufactures. Without that diversification, growth in the real purchasing power of exports would have been limited. Rubber exports, traditionally the principal foreign-exchange earner, doubled in volume between 1960 and 1977, but their real purchasing power declined 15 percent. Malaysia not only adjusted to the challenge of a secular decline in the international prices of rubber; it developed important new lines of production to prevent the momentum of growth from slowing down.

The push for diversification and improvements in productivity was made possible by the availability of land and, later in the period, by the discovery of new petroleum reserves; it was facilitated by the significant foreign interests in the estate and manufacturing sectors. But the role of government and the domestically owned private sector should not be minimized. The establishment of free trade zones by government was important in the rapid growth of manufactured exports in the 1970s. The support of government was also instrumental in spurring the production of rubber and palm oil. Estates did take the lead in replacing old rubber trees by replanting new varieties, but rubber growers with smallholdings of fewer than 100 acres also replanted at fairly high rates as a result of a vigorous government program.

Since the early 1960s, and possibly before, the yield increases of more than 5 percent a year for smallholders have been much faster than those in the estate sector. Total production of smallholders grew three times as fast, and by 1976 exceeded, that of estates. Nevertheless the average yields of smallholders still were about 70 percent of those on estates, partly because of differences in replanting. Smallholders had replanted 68 percent of their acreage by 1975; estates more than 90 percent. Estates similarly led the diversification into oil palm, but the output of palm oil from land development schemes administered by the Federal Land Development Authority (FELDA) and other agencies has been rapidly catching up with that of estates.

Agriculture

During 1961–76 the growth rate of agricultural output was about 6 percent a year, among the highest rates anywhere. The expansion in the production of palm oil and rubber, which now account for about half the agricultural output, has been the principal factor in agricultural growth. The doubling of rice output between 1960 and 1976 was another source of growth, even though rice now accounts for less than a tenth of the value added in agriculture. The high rate of forest exploitation also contributed significantly. The trend of agricultural growth has been fairly constant, but the trend in agricultural incomes for the 1970s is different from that for the 1960s.

Although the rate of growth of agricultural production was high, the growth of real agricultural incomes during the 1960s was not more than 1 to 2 percent a year. The real income from growing rubber declined between 1960 and 1970 as the sharp fall in prices totally offset the growth in rubber output of more than 5 percent a year.[3] That decline hit the estate sector especially hard because, even by 1970, more than 70 percent of the value added in estates was from rubber. Nevertheless the estate sector was able to earn profits by making impressive increases in the productivity of land and labor. Despite a nearly 50 percent rise in production, the number of workers employed on rubber estates declined by 10 percent during the 1960s. Because wage rates either stagnated or rose only slightly, wage costs in relation to the gross value of output were reduced. In the traditional sector, which includes land development schemes, real incomes expanded 2 to 3 percent a year during the 1960s. Because employment increased 1.5 percent a year during that period, the increase in average real earnings per worker was modest.[4]

Thus, despite the apparent success of the policies of government for small-scale agriculture, the income disparity between the traditional agricultural sector and the rest of the economy in Peninsular Malaysia widened from about 1:2.5 in 1960 to more than 1:3 in 1970. It probably was not fully understood that this outcome was mainly a result of external factors and the inevitably long gestation periods of land development and irrigation projects. It was clear, however, that the worsening relative position of the traditional sector hit the Malays hardest: more than 50 percent of the Malay labor force employed in Peninsular Ma-

3. In agriculture the modern estate sector should be distinguished from the traditional sector. The modern estate sector in 1970 accounted for only about 18 percent of the agricultural labor force, but 50 percent of rubber production and 90 percent of palm oil production in Peninsular Malaysia. The lower-income traditional sector mainly consists of rice farmers and rubber growers and accounts for three-quarters of agricultural employment. The remainder of the agricultural labor force engages in forestry and fishing.

4. The higher estimate of the expansion of real incomes is based on five-year moving averages of agricultural prices.

laysia was in the traditional agricultural sector in 1970; fewer than 20 percent of non-Malays were in that sector. Consequently there was a certain disillusionment with the programs of rural development toward the end of the 1960s. The riots in 1969 compounded this disillusionment. Whatever the immediate cause, the riots probably had their roots in tensions arising from the widening income disparity between the Malay and Chinese communities—the one predominantly rural, the other predominantly urban.

The definite shift by government toward providing greater job opportunities for Malays in the urban sector—a shift embodied in the New Economic Policy—can thus be linked to the disappointing effect of rural development on living standards of rural Malays. But as the following discussion shows, there has been nothing inherently wrong with Malaysia's agricultural strategy. If there had not been a sharp, and to some extent unforeseen, deterioration in the terms of trade, rural incomes per worker would have significantly increased, even in the 1960s. And if government had been less vigorous in pursuing its rural development programs, rural poverty would have become even more critical.

The trend of rural and agricultural incomes in the first half of the 1970s, in part reflecting the payoff of past investments, was more favorable than that in the 1960s. The rate of growth of the smallholder sector accelerated; the deterioration in the agricultural terms of trade, despite rather wide year-to-year fluctuations, halted. Precise figures are not available, but per capita real incomes of smallholders were at least 25 percent higher in 1976 than in 1970.[5] Thus, in sharp contrast with the 1960s, there was little, if any, widening of disparities between rural and urban areas. In addition, the lag in rural incomes probably was no longer a source of widening income differences between ethnic groups.

Manufacturing

The concerted effort to industrialize in Malaysia only got going with incentives legislation and increased tariff protection at the end of the 1950s.[6] Under more conducive policies the 1960–70 period was a suc-

5. The improvement would probably have been greater if the Malaysian dollar had not appreciated.

6. The discussion in this section primarily centers on Peninsular Malaysia, which accounts for more than 90 percent of the manufacturing output of the country. It generally excludes off-estate processing activities, which are considered to be part of the primary sector.

Table 2.7. *Composition of the Output and Growth of Manufacturing, by Commodity Group, Peninsular Malaysia, Selected Years and Periods, 1959–73*

Commodity group	Percentage composition of output				Percentage composition of incremental output		
	1959	1963	1968	1973	1959–63	1963–68	1968–73
Food, beverages, and tobacco	36.7	28.5	29.2	23.8	−3.9	29.8	21.1
Wood products	16.1	13.2	11.8	13.1	2.6	10.6	13.7
Rubber products	7.5	6.2	6.4	9.5	1.3	6.6	11.2
Textiles, footwear, and clothing	—[a]	2.2	3.4	5.9	—[a]	4.5	7.2
Chemicals	7.5	11.3	9.9	7.5	26.3	8.7	6.3
Metal products	4.3	4.9	4.9	4.9	6.6	4.9	4.9
Machinery and transport equipment	6.7	5.6	5.5	6.4	1.2	5.4	7.0
Electrical machinery	—[a]	1.3	2.6	8.1	—[a]	3.8	10.9
Other	21.2	26.8	26.3	20.8	65.9	25.7	17.7
Total[b]	100.0	100.0	100.0	100.0	100.0	100.0	100.0

Source: Department of Statistics, *Census of Manufacturing*, 1959, 1963, 1968, 1973.
a. Included in the group of other commodities.
b. Excludes off-estate processing.

cessful decade of growth based mainly on the substitution of imports and the processing of raw materials. Average annual growth in manufacturing output during the 1960s was about 11 percent. The share of manufacturing output in GDP at factor cost increased from less than 10 percent in 1960 to 17 percent in 1970.[7] Given the adverse trends in the prices of agricultural exports, the manufacturing sector was particularly important as a source of growth in incomes. Output continued to grow rapidly, until the recession that set in by the middle of 1974. The recession in industrial countries and sluggish domestic demand resulted in a considerable decline in manufacturing growth in 1975. In the following year, however, there was a complete recovery back to the trend level of output. During 1970–76 manufacturing growth averaged 13 percent a year. By 1976 manufacturing value added exceeded 23 percent of GDP at factor cost. The performance of the sector has thus been crucial for sustaining high rates of growth in the economy.

Given Malaysia's favorable resource endowment, the structure of manufacturing has been dominated by the processing of such domestic raw materials as rubber, wood, and food (table 2.7). Although there

7. These shares are based on the system of national accounts recently instituted in Malaysia. Under the old system the shares of manufacturing in GDP would be significantly lower.

was some decline in the shares of wood and food products, value added in these three subsectors still accounted for almost half the manufacturing value added in 1973. Perhaps the most notable shifts in the structure of output were the increasing shares of textiles, footwear, and clothing and of electrical machinery, mainly electronics: their combined share increased from a negligible level in 1959 to 14 percent in 1973. That increase appears to have been mainly at the expense of food processing; its share fell from 37 percent of manufacturing value added in 1959 to 24 percent in 1973.

Rapid industrial growth in the 1970s can be linked to an apparent shift in the relative importance of the domestic market, import substitution, and export growth. In the 1960s growth in domestic demand and import substitution were dominant as direct sources of industrial growth, though exports became more significant toward the end of the decade. Looking at Peninsular Malaysia alone, which most past analyses have done, nevertheless conceals an important change in the direction of exports. The reason is that Peninsular Malaysia's trade figures include trade with Sabah and Sarawak. Manufactured exports in the 1960s were heavily concentrated on Sabah and Sarawak, which became part of a customs union with the peninsular states when they joined Malaysia in 1963. Thus, until the late 1960s, the real impetus for the growth of output in Peninsular Malaysia appears to have been import substitution in the federation at the expense of exports outside the federation. After this time, particularly from 1972 onward, the share of such exports grew significantly (table 2.8).

Table 2.8. *Market Shares for Manufacturing Output, Peninsular Malaysia, Selected Years, 1963–74*

| | Percentage of total output | | |
Year	Peninsular Malaysia	Sabah and Sarawak	Exports outside Malaysia
1963	72	1	27
1968	77	5	18
1969	77	6	17
1970	76	7	17
1971	76	7	17
1972	73	9	18
1973	64	9	27
1974	57	10	33

Sources: Department of Statistics, *Peninsular Malaysia Monthly Statistics of External Trade*, various issues; unpublished working tables supplied by the Economic Planning Unit.
   a. Excludes sawmilling and food, beverages, and tobacco.

In relation to per capita income and population, the degree of industrialization in Malaysia probably was still low in the mid-1970s. Part of the reason for Malaysia's deviation from a "normal" level of industrialization lies in the character of the economy, which has specialized in the production of primary commodities and allowed the internal demand for manufactured goods to be met from imports rather than domestic production. The openness of the economy is illustrated by the fact that Malaysia's manufacturing industry was relatively unprotected, whether measured by nominal protection or effective protection, until the early 1960s. Although this lack of excessive protection probably dampened manufacturing growth, Malaysia generally was able to avoid the pitfall of overprotected industries catering solely to the domestic market. Industrial growth initially relied heavily on import substitution, but after the late 1960s export expansion became a leading factor.

Reflecting the labor intensity of manufactured exports and the avoidance of serious factor-price distortions, the growth of manufacturing employment has been high. It averaged about 5 percent a year during 1960–70 and accelerated to about 7 percent a year during 1970–76. Even though manufacturing employment represented only 10 percent of total employment in 1976, it provided nearly one of every five jobs created during 1961–76. Furthermore there were some gains in restructuring the racial composition of employment toward the end of this period. For example, it has been estimated by government that Malay employment in the secondary sector increased from 31 percent to 37 percent during 1970–75. The country thus is fortunate in having developed a reasonably strong base of industrial employment before the reserves of land have been exhausted.

Nature and Control of Inflation

The size of the Malaysian export sector has made the task of short-term economic management difficult; it also has increased the susceptibility of the Malaysian economy to imported inflation. Between 1972 and 1974 the general price level, as measured by the consumer price index for Peninsular Malaysia, increased 30 percent. This increase was directly attributable to a sharp rise in import costs and the expansionary impact of the rise in export demand. The real purchasing power of exports rose more than 60 percent in the short period between 1972 and 1974 (table 2.9). In 1970 and 1971 there had been a reduction of 16 percent. The expansionary impulse, equal to more than 30 percent of GNP in 1973 and 1974, obviously was too large to be counteracted by

Table 2.9. *Purchasing Power of Exports, 1960–76*

Year	Export earnings (millions of Malaysian dollars)	Index of import prices (1970 = 100)	Purchasing power of exports (millions of 1970 Malaysian dollars)	Percentage change in purchasing power
1960	3,600	95.0	3,789	—
1961	3,208	95.0	3,377	−10.9
1962	3,232	95.0	3,402	0.7
1963	3,296	95.0	3,469	2.0
1964	3,346	96.0	3,485	0.5
1965	3,752	96.0	3,908	12.1
1966	3,808	97.0	3,926	0.5
1967	3,679	95.0	3,873	−1.3
1968	4,070	99.0	4,111	6.1
1969	4,921	100.0	4,921	19.7
1970	5,020	100.0	5,020	2.0
1971	4,884	104.1	4,692	−6.5
1972	4,736	113.0	4,191	−10.7
1973	7,263	122.2	5,944	41.8
1974	9,991	146.3	6,829	14.9
1975	9,042	162.4	5,568	−18.5
1976	13,265	172.5	7,690	38.1

— Not applicable.

Sources: Bank Negara, *Quarterly Economic Bulletin*, various issues; World Bank estimates based on figures supplied by the Department of Statistics.

stabilization measures, whether conventional or unconventional. Except for this relatively short period, however, Malaysia has enjoyed remarkable price stability. During the 1960s the average rise in consumer prices was only 1 percent a year. The rate of price increase again slowed down to an annual rate of 3.5 percent between 1974 and 1976. The average rate of inflation in Malaysia during 1970–76 of 6.7 percent a year, though much higher than the 1960s, was lower than that in most countries. Among countries belonging to the Organization for Economic Cooperation and Development (OECD), only Germany and the United States had inflation rates of less than 7 percent a year during 1970–76.

Several factors explain why the rate of inflation in Malaysia, a very open economy, has been lower than even the international rate of inflation, as measured by the developed countries' index of U.S. dollar prices of manufactured exports. First, the secular deterioration in the Malaysian terms of trade, especially the sharp reduction in the real price of rubber, had a dampening effect on money incomes and demand. Second, the Malaysian dollar appreciated in relation to the U.S.

dollar. Until 1971 the exchange rate was M$3.06 to the U.S. dollar. The exchange rate was adjusted in successive steps to M$2.40 to the U.S. dollar by the middle of 1973, when a floating rate was adopted. In relation to a trade-weighted basket of currencies, the Malaysian dollar appreciated 13.6 percent between 1971 and 1976. Upward revaluation, especially that in 1973, definitely was an anti-inflationary measure. Third, during the 1960s Malaysia also cushioned the impact of imported inflation by successfully shifting to cheaper sources of imports. The adjustment was facilitated by the fact that Malaysia, because of its financial strength, did not have to rely on the use of foreign loans tied to import credits. In addition, Malaysia's sources of imports have generally been diverse.

On the domestic front, government scrupulously avoided recourse to inflationary means for financing its budget deficits. Public sector revenue grew rapidly during 1966–76, partly as a result of taxation efforts and partly as a result of the accretion of substantial oil revenue. The ratio of government revenue to GNP exceeded 26 percent in 1976. During 1970–76 public saving averaged 2 percent of GNP. Although the deficit in the public sector during this period was large, averaging 8 percent of GNP, it was almost entirely financed by nonbank borrowing. Even so, the reliance of the public sector on the banking system became greater after the 1960s, when there was hardly any increase in the net claims of the banking sector on federal and state governments. During 1970–76 these claims increased M$1.8 billion, constituting about 17 percent of the public sector deficit and 20 percent of the monetary expansion. Nevertheless, because of the substantial increase in oil revenue, government deficits will continue to have limited significance as a source of inflationary pressure.

A more powerful source of expansion has been the foreign sector. Net external reserves, which changed very little in the 1960s, increased from US$800 million at the end of 1969 to US$2.4 billion at the end of 1976. The increase in net foreign assets was responsible for more than 40 percent of the expansion in the supply of money and quasi money from M$4.7 billion at the end of 1971 to M$12.8 billion at the end of 1976. The average annual rate of monetary expansion of more than 22 percent during 1971–76 also reflected a nearly threefold expansion in private sector credit. Most of that expansion was related to the increase in value of foreign trade and thus was largely the result of exogenous circumstances.

The increase in the supply of money narrowly defined—currency in circulation and demand deposits—at the average annual rate of 19 percent during 1971–76 was somewhat faster than the growth of GNP in current prices. Quasi money—time and savings deposits—grew considerably faster. Whereas quasi money constituted less than 30 percent of the broad money supply in 1960, the proportion rose to nearly 60 percent in 1975. Some of these assets belong to the public sector corporations, which have been rapidly growing. Nevertheless the activities of the Malaysian banking system in mobilizing private saving appear to have grown tremendously and now correspond more closely to those in some of the neighboring East Asian countries. As a result of the large inflow of time and savings deposits into commercial banks, the liquidity position of those banks has generally remained comfortable. In addition, except for the period from mid-1973 to mid-1975, interest rates have remained low. The prime interest rate, which was raised in steps to 10 percent by April 1974, gradually came down by mid-1977 to 7.5 percent, the same level as that in the early 1970s. The rate on fixed deposits of twelve months' maturity, which rose to the peak of 8 percent in April 1974, was by mid-1977 down to 6.5 percent, only marginally higher than the rate a decade before.

Thus the position in the mid-1970s was characterized by a fair degree of monetary stability. That stability could be easily disturbed, however, if there were a resurgence of international inflationary pressure or an outburst of export demand for Malaysia's principal primary exports. Although a boom in export incomes can be partly moderated by an increase in saving, it is almost impossible to neutralize completely an expansionary impulse equal to more than 30 percent of GNP, as was the case in 1973 and 1974. That expansion probably was exceptional. Malaysia will nevertheless continue to be faced with substantial fluctuations in its export earnings. Given the size of its export sector, short-term economic management will continue to pose special problems. Even a 10 percent change in the relative prices of exports would increase or decrease its gross national income by 5 percent. With a 20 percent change, the real increase or decrease in national income resulting from changes in terms of trade could swamp the influence of domestic factors on demand and output.

What are the implications of these new conditions for policy? Because Malaysia will often have to contend with changes in the purchasing power of its exports equal to 5 to 10 percent of GNP, the limits of monetary policy should be recognized. Fiscal policy must play a greater anticyclical role: government must be more active in designing expenditure programs and adjusting taxes, especially export taxes, to prevent wide swings in economic activity and ensure the orderly growth of incomes of the rural masses. In a period of rapidly rising prices, the distribution of gains between traders and producers is uneven. For example, real earnings from rubber, a principal source of income for many smallholders, increased 60 to 70 percent between 1972 and 1974. The export duties levied were modest, and they were not imposed until April 1974. Nevertheless the system of progressive rates of export duty on rubber is a built-in stabilizer and should be extended to other primary products. Government intervention cannot and should not be limited to upswings. Malaysia should be willing to run relatively large deficits on government and balance-of-payments accounts in periods of recession. A system of compensating payments, partly through adjustments of arrears and taxes due to government, needs to be devised along with expenditure programs that can be instituted or cut back depending upon the needs of the situation.

High levels of international reserves are an important prerequisite for flexibility in short-term economic management. The level of external reserves in 1977, equal to more than seven months of imports, cannot be considered too high in the light of Malaysia's heavy export dependence. Indeed the reserves might grow somewhat faster than imports until investment picks up sharply. Any undue growth in external reserve levels would nevertheless exercise a sharp expansionary influence on money supply. That could endanger monetary stability, a prospect which further reinforces the argument for stepping up investment.

Trends of Saving and Investment

As the foregoing discussion suggests, Malaysia's resource position has remained comfortable since independence, reflecting the inherently strong export position, an adequate and fairly elastic tax system, and cautious monetary and economic management. Because external reserves have been adequate, foreign borrowing has been limited. Total public debt outstanding at the end of 1977 was US$1.6 billion; debt service payments during 1976 represented only about 4 percent of exports of goods and nonfactor services. For the entire 1960–76 period, the current account of the balance of payments was approximately in balance. Meanwhile the rate of national saving increased from about 19 percent of GNP in the early 1960s to an average of 25 percent during 1974–76 (table 2.10). During 1962–75 the marginal rate of saving was about 28 percent.[8]

8. Calculated from three-year averages centered on 1962 and 1975.

Table 2.10. *Rates of Saving and Investment, 1961–76*
(percentage of GNP)

Year	Gross saving	National saving	Foreign saving[a]	Fixed investment	Public investment	Private investment
1961	17.1	19.6	−2.5	15.6	5.6	10.0
1962	19.7	20.1	−0.4	17.1	7.3	9.8
1963	19.2	18.7	0.5	17.0	7.1	9.9
1964	19.0	17.3	1.7	16.8	7.4	9.2
1965	18.8	20.4	−1.6	16.6	6.7	9.9
1966	18.7	20.2	−1.5	17.0	6.0	11.0
1967	19.0	20.3	−1.3	16.5	5.9	10.6
1968	19.0	21.3	−2.3	16.2	5.7	10.5
1969	16.4	24.0	−7.6	15.0	5.2	9.8
1970	20.5	22.2	−1.7	17.3	5.5	11.7
1971	21.3	19.9	1.4	21.4	6.4	15.0
1972	22.9	18.1	4.8	24.0	8.4	15.6
1973	23.5	25.7	−2.2	23.0	6.7	16.3
1974	29.8	25.4	4.4	26.5	7.5	19.0
1975	23.3	20.2	3.1	25.0	9.8	15.2
1976	21.9	29.9	−8.0	22.3	8.5	13.8

Note: All rates were calculated from data in current prices.
Source: World Bank estimates linking the old series of national accounts of the Department of Statistics for 1961–70 to the new series for 1971–76. The breakdowns of public and private investment for 1971–76 are estimates based on calculations by the Economic Planning Unit and the Department of Statistics to derive a breakdown of investment that is consistent with the definitions for the new series of national accounts. The estimates for 1961–70 are based on the old series of national accounts but linked so that the entire series is consistent with the new definitions.
   a. Equivalent in definition to the deficit in the current account.

The high rates of saving demand some explanation because they have been a significant factor in Malaysia's development. One researcher has cited a number of reasons for Malaysia's exceptional savings performance: the unequal distribution of income; the traditional attitudes of the Chinese community toward saving; the well-developed system of social security, combined with the custom of taking a job after retirement; and the long record of price stability.[9] The structure of the economy and the effort to increase government revenue enabled the public sector to contribute to this savings performance. In addition, the substantial vulnerability of Malaysia's income to fluctuations in a few international prices may have resulted in a reluctance to spend windfall income when export prices were high.

   9. Wolfgang Kasper, *Malaysia: A Study in Successful Economic Development* (Washington, D.C.: American Enterprise Institute for Public Policy Research, 1974), pp. 14–17.

Given that resources were not a major constraint on development, the rate of investment expansion in Malaysia in the 1960s was disappointing. The rate of gross fixed-capital formation of 15 to 16 percent of GNP in 1968–69 was no higher than the level in 1961. Investments in perennial crops by the estate sector and in tin mines, which represented more than a third of private investment in the early 1960s, tended to stagnate because of structural factors. Although incentives for planting oil palms remained strong—they resulted in a doubling of the acreage under oil palm on estates between 1965 and 1970—rubber replanting declined from 304,000 acres in 1961–65 to 128,000 acres in 1966–70. The reason for the decline was that 90 percent of the acreage under rubber on estates had been replanted with high-yielding varieties by the late 1960s. The main constraint on further large-scale investment by the estate sector, more than 60 percent of which is owned by foreign interests, was the availability of land. Land development has, as a matter of government policy, been largely reserved for the development of smallholdings by government agencies. This policy made good sense for promoting employment, overcoming rural poverty, and diversifying the gains from growth. But it did mean, in contrast with the past, that greater responsibility for sustaining a high rate of agricultural investment shifted to government agencies in charge of diversification, land development, and agricultural modernization. Given this growing role of government in agricultural development, the virtual stagnation of the rate of public sector investment at about 6 percent of GNP throughout the 1960s is not easy to understand. Part of the explanation is attributable to the modest targets of Malaysia's first plan, for 1966–70, which projected a financial constraint; part to government's inadequate capacity for planning and implementation capacity, which led to shortfalls in investment programs. In the private sector the general business uncertainty following the separation of Singapore in 1965 may also have dampened investment demand. In 1969 the rate of fixed private investment—at about 10 percent of GNP—was no higher than in the early 1960s.

Since 1971, the first year of the second plan, the growth in public investment has been sharp and sustained. In constant prices, fixed public investment more than doubled between 1970 and 1976; it grew at an average annual rate of more than 15 percent. Public investment was about 9 percent of GNP during 1976. That expansion reflected the goals of the New Economic Policy and significantly contributed to accelerating the growth rate and the direct attack on poverty.

The expansion in private investment also was substantial after the late 1960s, but the trend is less clear-cut. Between 1969 and 1974, there was a big jump, estimated at 120 to 150 percent, in real private fixed investment. In relation to GNP, private fixed investment reached a peak of 19 percent in 1974. But the decline was sharp, as private investment fell in absolute terms by about a fifth between 1974 and 1976; its ratio to GNP dropped to less than 14 percent in 1976. That level of private investment included substantial investments in the oil sector in Sabah and Sarawak and in housing construction. Although official data are lacking, it appears that the decline between 1974 and 1976 was considerably greater—perhaps as much as 50 percent greater—for manufacturing investment than for all private investment. The importance of stimulating a recovery in manufacturing investment, a subject discussed in chapter three, had therefore become critical for overall growth.

Progress toward Eradicating Poverty

In addition to achieving impressive growth, Malaysia has given special attention to rural development and the eradication of poverty. The initial thrust of government policies in the mid-1950s was toward rural infrastructure, so as to improve living conditions in rural areas.[10] In the 1960s emphasis was increasingly placed on providing land to the rural poor and raising the productivity of small-scale farmers. Given these efforts, a substantial reduction in poverty might have been anticipated. There is little evidence, however, that such a reduction occurred, at least during the 1960s. Furthermore some observers have claimed, one on the basis of a comparison of data for 1957 and 1970, that the distribution of income worsened and the absolute incomes of the poor substantially declined.[11] But another observer, on the basis of an analysis of data previously unavailable, has shown that systematic biases in the surveys for those years could explain the apparent deterioration in incomes and income distribution and that the decline in incomes, if there was a decline, cannot be determined.[12] Although it is uncertain wheth-

10. For a discussion of programs for rural development see Government of Malaya, *First Malaya Plan, 1956–1960* (Kuala Lumpur: Government Press, 1956); idem, *Second Malaya Plan, 1961–1965* (Kuala Lumpur: Government Press, 1961); and David Lim, *Economic Growth and Development in West Malaysia, 1947–70* (Kuala Lumpur: Oxford University Press, 1973).

11. See for example E. L. H. Lee, "Rural Poverty in West Malaysia, 1957 to 1970," in *Poverty and Landlessness in Rural Asia* (Geneva: International Labour Organisation, 1977), pp. 185–203.

12. Sudhir Anand, *Inequality and Poverty in Malaysia: Measurement and Decomposition* (New York: Oxford University Press, forthcoming), ch. 4.

er incomes of the poor deteriorated during the 1960s, there is no evidence to suggest they increased. Thus the incidence of poverty has remained high. Government has estimated that 49 percent of households in Peninsular Malaysia in 1970 had incomes below the poverty line—the income required to provide basic nutritional and other non-food requirements—and that 86 percent of those households were in rural areas.[13] During the period of Malaysia's second plan, however, government estimates that the incidence of poverty declined to 44 percent. This estimate may understate the improvement, because 1975 was an abnormally poor year for the prices of many of Malaysia's primary commodities, especially rubber and palm oil. If 1976 were used as the terminal year, it is probable that the incidence of poverty declined to 40 percent.

The continued widespread existence of poverty, despite high growth rates and a strong political commitment to programs for eradicating poverty, points to the substantial inequality in the initial income distribution and to such special factors as the deterioration in the terms of trade of rubber growers and the relatively long gestation period of rural investments. These special factors dampened the effect of essentially well-conceived efforts at rural development, at least in the medium term. The relatively high rate of population growth since the Second World War, averaging 2.8 percent a year in Peninsular Malaysia, further hampered the task of substantially improving the living standards of low-income groups. These difficulties have undoubtedly been responsible for the disappointing progress toward poverty alleviation. But most of the difficulties—the strong demographic pressure, the extremely uneven pattern of income distribution in the preindependence period, the declining rubber prices, and the inherently long gestation periods of investments in tree crops—were outside the control of government policies.

Despite these limitations, there definitely has been progress. It would thus be a pity if the preponderance and the persistence of the problem of poverty were to obscure the solid achievements of the

13. According to official figures, all households having an annual income of US$265 per capita in 1975—equivalent to M$180 a household a month in 1970 prices—were below the minimum standard. The corresponding figures for rural areas in Indonesia, Thailand, and the Philippines were respectively estimated by the World Bank to be US$95, US$95, and US$155. To some extent the higher income requirement in Malaysia is attributable to the higher domestic price of rice, the staple foodgrain. But the difference still is too large to be explained by this factor alone. Thus the official Malaysian figures exaggerate the problem of absolute poverty, at least in relation to international comparisons.

Malaysian efforts at rural development. It can still be reasonably argued, given Malaysia's favorable resource position, that much more could have been done to alleviate poverty, particularly among such groups as fishermen, new villagers, estate workers, and farm laborers, who appear to have gained little from public programs. Nevertheless few other developing countries have achieved as much as Malaysia during this period. These achievements are typified by the sustained average rate of output growth in smallholder agriculture of close to 6 percent a year over the 1960–75 period, by at least some reduction in the incidence of poverty during the later part of this period, and by the sustained increase in access of those living in rural areas to such social services as education, health, roads, water supply, and electrification.

A basic reason for poverty and income inequality in Malaysia is the ownership of land. Although the area under crops per capita compares favorably with some neighboring countries, landholdings are very unequal, partly because of the dominant estate sector. In 1960 that sector accounted for 36 percent of the 5.9 million acres under crops in Peninsular Malaysia and 50 percent of the 3.9 million acres under rubber. During the 1960–76 period the acreage in the estate sector remained stable at around 2.2 million acres; the acreage under crops in Peninsular Malaysia increased to 7.6 million acres. Outside the new land settlement schemes, 45 percent of about 400,000 rubber smallholders had holdings of less than 5 acres in 1976; the average size of holding for this group was 3 acres. The average size of rice holding was 2.8 acres. Roughly half the agricultural labor force either was landless or had uneconomic holdings. Because of the strong relation between poverty in agriculture and the large proportion of agricultural workers having no land of their own or holdings too small to provide full-time productive employment and income above the poverty line, government has invested heavily in land development, selecting settlers from among the landless poor. Between 1955 and 1975 nearly 1.5 million acres were developed in Peninsular Malaysia alone; the Federal Land Development Authority (FELDA) developed about half of this acreage.

Land Development

Land development schemes were responsible for a large proportion of job creation in agriculture during the 1966–76 period; they were expected to be responsible for a third of the incremental output of principal agricultural crops, in constant prices, between 1970 and 1980. Several criticisms have nevertheless been leveled against those schemes.

The criticisms center on the high cost of land settlement, the high proportion of total allocations for agricultural development to new settlement, the limited participation of settlers in the early stages of development, and the limitation of direct benefits to a relatively small number of farm households. These criticisms have some justification, but they must be seen in perspective. During 1960–75, for example, FELDA settled only 33,000 families; of these families 13,700 were settled during 1971–75. But the low settlement level is largely a problem of time lags. During the period of the second plan about 1 million acres of land were developed by all agencies, with a potential for settling about 75,000 families and providing about 110,000 jobs. Because of time lags, however, only about 39,000 families were settled during this period. In the present mode of settlement, settlers are not brought into the schemes until the second year for oil palm or the third for rubber. Even with these lags, however, land development accounted for more than a third of the additional jobs in agriculture during this period. The cost of creating these jobs was substantial: it is estimated that the average expenditure for each family settled in schemes recently developed by FELDA was US$15,000.

The costs of land development have been high, in part because the holdings are to provide settlers with an eventual income in the median range. Nevertheless the economic rates of return of FELDA schemes have been satisfactory at 14 to 16 percent. The benefits of a given level of land development could be more widely spread by reducing the size of holdings. Naturally that would result in less employment and lower relative incomes for each settler family. The decision about the size of holdings or the income level of settlers is a matter of judgment. The current objective of FELDA is to ensure that settlers remain within a reasonable relative income range for two or three decades. A much smaller holding would not be economically viable in the long run. But because the long-run prospects for the prices of rubber and palm oil are more favorable now than a few years ago, the current income objective could be achieved with somewhat smaller holdings. Government therefore reduced the size of holdings in future FELDA schemes from 12 acres for oil palm and 14 acres for rubber to 10 acres for both crops.

The current rate of land development by all agencies in Peninsular Malaysia is about 170,000 acres a year. Under FELDA's reduced allotments, that acreage would eventually provide settlement on an annual basis for about 17,000 families and jobs for about 25,000 persons. The numbers are small in relation to the number of agricultural households below the poverty line—more than half a million. But in relation to the current growth of about 25,000 jobs a year in agriculture, job creation through land development obviously is significant. Land development accelerates the rate of employment creation and contains the number of households in the traditional smallholder sector. Moreover a continuing high rate of land development offers opportunities for eradicating poverty directly, by distributing assets to the poor, and indirectly, by stimulating the growth of the economy.

Past attempts at low-cost settlement in Malaysia have sometimes proved disappointing in the land use and income levels achieved. Despite such problems as poor infrastructure and little extension assistance, there is cause for encouragement in the achievements of settlers who developed their own land in some of the early land schemes. Many of the difficulties that plagued earlier efforts could be avoided with more supervision during the initial stages of development and with a strong system of agricultural support services to provide technical advice and supervision. Increased settler participation should also result in less stringent repayment terms, which would also reduce the required size of holding in relation to income objectives. Various alternatives should be fully explored in the large schemes to increase the number of settlers who benefit and to reduce the capital cost for each family settled. In addition, efforts to design alternative types of land development scheme should continue with a view to spreading the benefits of land development more widely. For example, increasing settler involvement through a "farm enterprise" scheme merits consideration, at least on an experimental basis. The development of the settler's entrepreneurship and self-reliance would be valuable in itself. Increased settler participation should also help to reduce financial outlays for each acre settled.[14]

Programs to Assist Traditional Smallholders

In addition to giving special attention to land development as an important long-run solution to poverty, government has undertaken a broad range of programs to assist farmers working holdings that have been in operation for some time. Rubber smallholders, excluding those on the land development schemes, increased their output at an average

14. It was stated in Malaysia's third plan that FELDA would carry out pilot projects with greater settler participation and self-help. Government of Malaysia, *Third Malaysia Plan, 1976–1980* (Kuala Lumpur: Government Press, 1976), p. 299.

annual rate of about 7 percent during 1960–75, considerably faster than the rate of growth of 2.4 percent on estates.[15] What is more important, their rate of yield increases during this period—5 percent a year—was higher than that in the estate sector. By 1976, however, only 67 percent of traditional smallholders had replanted their rubber, indicating the considerable scope for further productivity gains.[16] Contrary to widespread impressions, there is no hard evidence that smallholders with very small plots lagged in replanting. Indeed, of registered smallholders with plots of less than 5 acres, 59 percent had replanted their rubber by 1974, a figure higher than average; 37 percent of the largest holdings had been replanted (table 2.11). But for Malays, who had an average holding half the size of the average Chinese holding, the proportion who had replanted their rubber was substantially lower than that for Chinese: 44 percent compared with 66 percent.

It would thus appear that the impressive productivity improvement in the smallholder sector was widely shared, but that the number of rubber smallholders in poverty decreased little, if at all. The underlying reason for this pattern was the sharp decline of rubber prices in real terms. The price in 1976 was half that in 1956 (table 2.12). Thus for many rubber smallholders the decline in relative prices offset their gains in productivity. That should not detract from the importance of rural development efforts in this area. If productivity had not improved, the real incomes of rubber smallholders would have sharply declined; because few of them had alternative opportunities, the number of poor would have increased. But the decline in rubber prices has clearly frustrated the efforts of government to alleviate poverty. Fortunately the outlook for rubber prices is good. With the prospective increases in rubber production, a substantial reduction in poverty among smallholders can be expected.

15. See table 8.7 in chapter eight. The estimate of production on land development schemes, an estimate which is excluded from total smallholder production in table 8.7, refers only to FELDA schemes. From no production in 1960, rubber output from FELDA schemes is estimated to have reached 68,000 tons a day in 1976. Ministry of Finance, *Economic Report, 1976–77* (Kuala Lumpur, 1976), p. 87.

16. This figure is for smallholders registered with the Rubber Industry Smallholders Development Authority (RISDA); the figure for all smallholders would be lower. It should be added, moreover, that to the extent some estates are subdivided into holdings of less than 100 acres, the improvement in productivity and the progress in replanting may be only statistical. Ministry of Finance, *Economic Report, 1977–78* (Kuala Lumpur, 1977), p. 94.

Table 2.11. *Registered Smallholdings of Rubber, by Ownership and Acreage of Holding, Peninsular Malaysia, 1974*

Ownership and acreage of holding[a]	Thousands of smallholders	Thousands of acres	Average acreage of holding	Percentage of new planting or replanting[b]
Malay	270.64	1,134.71	4.19	43.7
0–5	202.52	558.03	2.76	53.2
5–10	56.35	389.37	6.91	36.0
10–15	7.62	89.46	11.74	33.5
15–30	3.50	65.42	18.69	31.0
More than 30	0.65	32.43	49.89	25.4
Chinese	129.42	1,088.23	8.41	66.4
0–5	47.87	180.18	3.76	77.9
5–10	53.17	389.54	7.33	73.7
10–15	16.56	184.01	11.11	70.6
15–30	8.50	170.80	20.09	59.0
More than 30	3.32	163.70	49.31	39.2
Other	5.50	51.74	9.41	53.1
0–5	2.54	8.89	3.50	58.6
5–10	1.69	12.64	7.48	65.7
10–15	0.52	6.27	12.06	58.7
15–30	0.45	8.58	19.06	50.9
More than 30	0.30	15.36	51.20	38.4
Total	405.56	2,274.68	5.61	54.8
0–5	252.93	747.10	2.95	59.2
5–10	111.21	791.55	7.12	55.0
10–15	24.70	279.74	11.33	58.4
15–30	12.45	244.80	19.66	51.3
More than 30	4.27	211.49	49.53	37.1

Note: As of 31 December 1974 registered smallholdings excluded schemes developed by land development authorities, as well as the holdings of smallholders who did not have their holdings registered, such as those who did not hold a valid title to the land they cultivated.

Source: Figures supplied by the Rubber Industry Smallholders Development Authority (RISDA).

a. Acreage categories are based on the acreage planted in rubber.

b. For new planting and replanting after 1953.

Large increases in output have also been recorded in rice, the second most important smallholder crop. Rice output rose at an average rate of 4.1 percent a year during 1960–75. The main source of the increase in output was the increase in the proportion of rice land that is double-

Table 2.12. *Rubber Prices on the New York Market, Selected Years, 1956–76*
(U.S. cents a kilogram)

Year	In current prices	In constant 1975 prices
1956	75.4	175.3
1961	65.0	145.7
1966	52.0	111.1
1971	39.9	72.2
1976	87.2	86.8

Source: World Bank, "Commodity Trade and Price Trends," (Washington, D.C., 1976; processed).

cropped from a negligible level in 1960 to 57 percent in 1975; the annual yield increases of 1.2 percent a cropped acre have been modest.[17]

The increased double-cropping of rice was made possible by two major irrigation projects, the Muda and Kemubu projects. Financed in part by World Bank loans, the projects were the first applications of large-scale irrigation for double-cropping rice in Malaysia. They approximately doubled the incomes of nearly 75,000 padi farmers in three of the poorest states—Kedah, Perlis, and Kelantan. They also were largely responsible for reducing the country's dependence on imports from more than 40 percent of domestic rice requirements in 1967 to 13 percent of the increased requirements in 1975.[18] The areas served by these two projects now account for 60 percent of the production of rice in Malaysia. In the Muda area on the west coast of Peninsular Malaysia, the average farm size is 4 acres; more than 40 percent of the 51,000 farmers are tenants. With a substantial increase in employment resulting from the project, together with a decline in seasonal migratory labor from Thailand and Kelantan, where the Kemubu project is located, opportunities were greatly improved for local landless and underemployed persons. Although there is no direct evidence for the precise number of jobs created, rapidly rising wages are indirect evidence that the employment situation improved. Much of the success of the Muda project has been attributed to the preparatory work undertaken in conjunction with participating farmers, to a program for seed multiplication, and to the formation of farmers' associations for the provision of

17. See table 8.6 in chapter eight.
18. Poor growing conditions temporarily increased the need for imports to 18 percent of domestic consumption in 1977.

credit, inputs, and marketing and extension services. The Kemubu project, although less successful than the Muda project, has also had a significant impact on rice farmers.

Even with fairly dramatic increases in rice output and a 75 percent increase in the purchase price between 1970 and 1975, the incidence of poverty among rice growers in Peninsular Malaysia remains high—77 percent of them have incomes below the poverty line described earlier. The main reason for this high incidence is the small size of holdings: 55 percent of all holdings are less than 3 acres; 80 percent are less than 5 acres.[19] Estimates in the third plan indicate that an owner-operated, double-cropped holding of about 3 to 4 acres is needed if a rice farmer is to earn an income above the poverty line. Reductions in tenancy, increases in irrigation, and a continuing review of the policy for rice prices are needed to ensure significant further reductions in this large poverty group.[20]

Few new irrigation investments were initiated in the mid-1970s; only modest growth in rice output can be expected to come from further increases in double-cropping during the late 1970s and early 1980s. In any case, no additional areas are suitable for large-scale irrigation schemes, and future projects will be relatively small in scale.[21] Yield improvements and the resettlement of excess labor from poor rice-growing areas on newly developed land have been promoted under the third plan. In the long run, however, market limitations will also tend to impede the growth in rice output. Because Malaysia's comparative advantage does not lie in export of rice, any expansion of production would have to be limited to increases in domestic demand.

The incidence of poverty among the smaller groups of agricultural workers—fishermen, coconut farmers, agricultural laborers, and estate workers—also is high. More than 60 percent of agricultural households other than rice farmers and rubber smallholders, or 230,000 households,

19. Part of this high incidence of poverty among rice smallholders may be attributable to the possibility in the survey that own-consumption of rice, which obviously is significant for rice farmers, may have been valued at farmgate prices, whereas the poverty-line income was determined at retail prices. Figures on the incidence of poverty among rice farmers and the size of holdings were supplied by the Economic Planning Unit.

20. Between 30 and 40 percent of rice farmers are tenants. The problem of tenancy is to some degree mitigated by the facts that some tenants also are landlords and that some landlords often are close relatives of tenants. See chapter eight for a discussion of issues associated with reducing poverty among rice smallholders.

21. It was targeted in the third plan that the double-cropped acreage would expand 16 percent during 1976–80.

had incomes below the poverty line in 1975. The problem of poverty for these groups came into sharp focus only in the early 1970s. In addition, the policies and programs required to improve their incomes might be more difficult to formulate and execute than those for rice farmers and rubber smallholders. These groups are heterogeneous, and their racial composition is distinct. Most rice farmers and rubber smallholders are Malay; most residents of new villages are Chinese; most estate workers are Indian.[22]

Employment Growth

Employment growth in the economy is a particularly important source of poverty alleviation. In the traditional agricultural sector the need for reasonable growth in incomes puts an upper limit on labor absorption. Adequate job creation outside the agricultural sector assumes even greater significance when, as in Malaysia, the labor force is rapidly growing. Given the lagged effect of high rates of population growth after the Second World War, the growth of the labor force increased from less than 2 percent a year in the 1950s to 3.2 percent a year during 1971–75, the period of the second plan. It was expected to increase to 3.3 percent a year during 1976–80.[23]

Although there is considerable uncertainty about the growth rates of employment and labor force during the 1960s, there is general agreement that employment did not keep pace with the growth in labor force.[24] As a result, the open unemployment rate in Peninsular Malaysia increased from about 6 percent in 1960 to 8 percent in 1970. This increase suggests that the 6 percent annual rate of GNP growth recorded in the 1960s was insufficient, even with heavy emphasis on agriculture, to generate an adequate number of jobs. It should be stressed, however, that this was in part the result of the deterioration in the terms of trade, which is estimated to have been more than 20 percent during the 1960s.

22. During the communist insurgency in the 1950s, hundreds of thousands of Chinese were moved from rural areas to "new villages" on the outskirts of towns and cities.

23. *Third Malaysia Plan, 1976–1980*, pp. 140 and 147.

24. The basic problem in estimating rates of employment growth in the 1960s is the lack of comparable cross-sectional data. Depending on the end years compared in official estimates, rates of labor force growth range from about 2.2 to 2.8 percent a year, those of employment growth from 1.9 to 2.5 percent a year. But irrespective of the combination of end years used, labor force growth was faster than employment growth. It therefore is reasonably certain that unemployment increased during the 1960s.

This deterioration meant that the growth of real income during that period was substantially less than the growth of output. The growth of income and consumption per capita was less than 2 percent a year in Peninsular Malaysia during 1961–70 and, as mentioned earlier, less than 1 percent in the traditional agricultural sector. Thus the relatively slow growth of agricultural employment—1.1 percent a year during 1961–70 in Peninsular Malaysia—was partly attributable to stagnating real incomes.

Although the growth of the labor force further accelerated in the 1970s, the growth of employment opportunities was at least as rapid. The rate of job creation for Malaysia during 1970–75 averaged 3.3 percent a year, which was slightly faster than labor force growth; the open unemployment rate declined from 7.9 percent to 7 percent. There also was some evidence of a decline in underemployment: the average number of hours worked in the rural areas increased; the number of hardcore unemployed decreased.[25] Although the evidence is inconclusive, there may also have been some increase in the real wage rate during this period.

A basic cause of this improvement was the acceleration in the growth rates of investment and GNP during 1970–76. Furthermore the deterioration in the terms of trade over this period was moderate at 4 percent. Real per capita income increased 4.5 percent a year, compared with less than 2 percent a year in the 1960s. In addition, real per capita income in agriculture increased at roughly the same pace as that in the rest of the economy. The number of families settled on newly developed land also increased. Thus the growth in agricultural employment, which constitutes nearly half of total employment, increased to 1.6 percent a year. If the growth in nonagricultural employment had not increased to 4.8 percent a year, reflecting the strong push for labor-intensive manufacturing and the further expansion of public investment and administration, the improvement in the employment situation would have been limited.

The foregoing discussion supports the general impressions that the incidence of poverty has been reduced mainly in recent years and that the reduction has been closely linked to the rate of economic expansion. In the future, therefore, the need is clear for sustaining high rates of economic growth and maintaining the momentum of the smallholder sector.

25. *Third Malaysia Plan, 1976–1980*, p. 26.

Progress toward Restructuring Society

The second objective of the New Economic Policy is to restructure society: that is, to reduce and eliminate the identification of race with economic function by redressing racial imbalances in income, employment, and the ownership of corporate assets. It is targeted that the pattern of employment will reflect the racial composition of the population by 1990. It also is targeted that the share of bumiputras in the ownership of the corporate sector will increase to at least 30 percent by 1990; their share was 2 percent in 1970. Because these targets are to be reached in the context of rapid economic growth and because most of the poor are Malay, the programs associated with this objective will concurrently contribute to the eradication of poverty.

Restructuring Employment and Ownership

Traditionally Malays have predominated in the agricultural sector, non-Malays in the secondary and tertiary sectors. Although systematic efforts to increase the share of Malays are relatively recent, some restructuring of employment has proceeded under the momentum of growth and the structural change in output. For example, the proportion of Malays employed in the primary sector came down from 75 percent in 1957 to less than 60 percent in 1975. At the same time, the proportion of Malays employed in the secondary and tertiary sectors respectively increased to 15 percent and 26 percent in 1975, compared with 9 percent and 16 percent in 1957. There is no doubt, however, that the shifts were accelerated during 1971–75 under the impetus of the New Economic Policy.

More than half of the new jobs in the secondary and tertiary sectors went to Malays during the period of Malaysia's second plan. It is interesting to note, however, that the number of Malays in agriculture increased more than 35 percent between 1957 and 1975; the number of non-Malays in agriculture hardly changed. Thus the share of Malays engaged in primary activities—as distinct from the proportion of Malays—actually increased from 60 percent in 1957 to 67 percent in 1975. The share of non-Malays correspondingly declined. The respective shares of Malays in the secondary and tertiary sectors also rose—from 26 percent and 31 percent in 1957 to 37 percent and 42 percent in 1975. The apparently paradoxical increase in the share of Malays in all sectors over 1957–75 is partly explained by the increase in the Malay share in total employment from 47 percent in 1957 to 53 percent in 1975. That increase was a reflection of the faster growth of the Malay population and labor force; what is more important, it was also a reflection of the shifts in employment toward secondary and tertiary sectors.[26] Two variables will continue to govern the rate of restructuring employment. The first is the growth rate of the secondary and tertiary sectors. The higher this rate of growth, the greater will be the possibility for absorbing Malays into the urban sector. The second is the trend in the number of non-Malays in the agricultural sector. If the number of non-Malays in agriculture remains unchanged, as in the past, there will be greater competition for jobs in commercial and industrial sectors. There will thus continue to be a tradeoff between the availability of land to non-Malays and the opportunities for the employment of non-Malays in the nonagricultural sector.

The underlying causes for imbalances in the ownership of assets differ from those for imbalances in incomes and employment. The open character of the Malaysian economy and its historical development on the basis of exploiting natural resources for export have led to substantial foreign ownership of the economy. In 1970 foreigners owned almost two-thirds of the share capital of limited companies; Malays only 2.4 percent. To remedy this imbalance government set long-term goals to increase Malay ownership and reduce foreign ownership (see chapter three). During the period of the second plan, government policies led to a substantial restructuring of ownership. By 1975 Malay ownership of the share capital of limited companies, including that held by Malay interests, increased to almost 8 percent; foreign ownership declined to 55 percent. The main instrument for achieving this restructuring was the purchase of shares by public trust agencies on behalf of Malays. Such public agencies as Perbadanan Nasional Berhad (PERNAS, the National Trading Corporation), Majlis Amanah Rakyat (MARA, the Council of Trust for Indigenous Peoples), the Urban Development Authority, and the state economic development corporations purchase shares and hold them in trust with the intention that they will be gradually transferred to pri-

26. This increasing share of Malays in the employment in all sectors is a statistical phenomenon often observed when the weights are changing over time. The decline in the share of agriculture in total employment, combined with the stagnation of non-Malay employment in agriculture, made it possible for Malays to increase their share in agricultural employment with only a small increase in the number of Malays employed in the sector. This in turn made it possible for most of the increase in Malay employment to go to the industrial and service sectors. Because of the low initial share of Malays in employment in industry and services, their share in these sectors increased as well.

vate Malays. More than three-quarters of the 5.5 percentage point increase in ownership by Malays and Malay interests was accomplished by these agencies. In line with the stated policy of government, the restructuring was achieved at the expense of foreigners rather than non-Malays, whose share increased from 34 percent to 37 percent during this period.

Restructuring Education

Since independence in 1957 a principal goal of the educational system has been to redress the lag in the education of Malays. In 1957 the country had four separate streams of education at the primary level: one for each of the three largest ethnic groups, plus one in English. The streams varied in content and quality. The structure of the system now is virtually unified. Minor variations in Sabah and Sarawak are gradually being phased out. Headway has also been substantial in introducing the Malay language as the medium of instruction in all schools. Although only 38 percent of students in Peninsular Malaysia were enrolled in Malay-medium schools in 1970, this proportion increased to 67 percent in 1977. Except in Sarawak, the English language stream was phased out of public primary schools in 1976.

During 1970–75, the Malay share of enrollment increased at every level. It increased most at the tertiary level, where the Malay share in domestic enrollment rose from 50 percent to 65 percent (table 2.13). Because Malays make up only slightly more than half the population of Peninsular Malaysia, it may appear that the opportunities of non-Malay cohorts are now being restricted to make up for unequal opportunities in the other direction in the past. But many Malaysians are being educated abroad, especially at the tertiary level, and the racial composition of tertiary students abroad still is substantially weighted toward non-Malays. Consequently the total shares in tertiary enrollment—that is, the domestic and foreign shares combined—are much closer to the composition of the population. In addition, the shares in domestic enrollment must be viewed against the substantial increase in domestic enrollment. Again the largest jump was at the tertiary level, where enrollment increased 140 percent. This increase, which enabled a 15 percentage point increase in the share of Malays, also accommodated a 64 percent increase in the number of non-Malays enrolled in tertiary education in Malaysia.

More disaggregated data on enrollment nevertheless show that the growth in non-Malay enrollment in certain key areas was much less than the 64 percent increase for all tertiary institutions. Non-Malay

Table 2.13. *Enrollment by Race and Level of Education, Peninsular Malaysia, 1970 and 1975*

Level of education	1970			1975		
	Malay	Non-Malay	Total	Malay	Non-Malay	Total
	Thousands of students					
Primary	759.0	662.5	1,421.5	876.0	710.9	1,586.9
Lower secondary	193.1	185.4	378.5	305.7	255.8	561.5
Upper secondary	43.6	45.8	89.4	101.5	65.6	167.1
Postsecondary	4.6	6.0	10.6	8.8	7.5	16.3
Tertiary[a]	6.6	6.7	13.3	20.5	11.0	31.5
	Percentage composition					
Primary	53.3	46.7	100.0	55.2	44.8	100.0
Lower secondary	51.0	49.0	100.0	54.4	45.6	100.0
Upper secondary	48.7	51.3	100.0	60.7	39.3	100.0
Postsecondary	43.3	56.7	100.0	53.9	46.1	100.0
Tertiary[a]	49.6	50.4	100.0	65.0	35.0	100.0

Source: Third Malaysia Plan, 1976–80.
a. For all Malaysia.

enrollment in degree courses, as distinct from diploma and certificate courses and preliminary and preuniversity courses, increased only 25 percent during 1970–75; it declined in some faculties. Thus, while the enrollment of non-Malays grew substantially at the tertiary level, there was a significant change in the structure of enrollment. That change substantially limited the growth of domestic educational opportunities in certain areas for non-Malays. In addition, it has gradually become more difficult for Malaysian students to study abroad, and this difficulty has primarily affected non-Malays. As a result, education has become a primary concern to many non-Malays. This concern can be seen as one cost of the policies followed, but the benefits should not be overlooked. The main benefit is that the Malays are catching up with non-Malays at all levels of education. It would thus be consistent with national objectives if future educational opportunities, including those abroad, were to be more equally shared by non-Malays.

Despite the progress in education, substantial disparities in educational opportunities remain between the various regions and social strata. These disparities can be traced to the lower secondary cycle: enrollment ratios for a sample of youths over fifteen showed a wider range of variation for location (28–47 percent) and socioeconomic class (16–65 percent) than for the principal racial groups (30–38 percent).[27] A

27. Ministry of Education, *Kajian Ketitiran* [*Drop-out Study*] (Kuala Lumpur, 1973).

national survey has shown that almost all primary school leavers in some districts can proceed to secondary schools; in other districts only a third of these children have that chance.[28] The main cause of this difference is the lack of lower secondary school facilities in rural areas. And despite past emphasis on training for employable skills, the balance remains skewed toward academic training. Of the 166,000 students completing their ninth year of schooling in 1976, 63 percent continued with further education or training, but only 4 percent were in occupationally oriented programs. This proportion of occupational training is low in relation to the sectoral composition of the job creation projected and the number of job openings for production workers. Although occupational training is rapidly expanding at 23 percent a year, the number of students enrolled in such training will remain small in relation to the output of lower secondary schools and the new openings for jobs. A long-term plan for occupational training, including rural nonfarm training, remains to be developed. More must be done to orient the educational system toward national manpower needs and to improve the capacity of government agencies to implement programs by expanding the training for public administrators.

Public Sector Planning

Malaysia's public sector has contributed to the success of the Malaysian economy. One of its most important contributions has been in directing development through economic planning, which is well established. The first attempt at planning began in 1950, and the sophistication of planning has considerably increased since then, from the determination of little more than broad targets, to the expansion of government departments, to the preparation of comprehensive multisector plans. Planning is undertaken in the context of five-year plans, which are reviewed and revised midway into the period to allow for changes in external and domestic conditions not originally anticipated. Two aspects of planning in Malaysia are noteworthy: both the public and private sectors take the plans seriously; and policies and programs, in addition to being reflected in the planning documents, appear to be largely determined during planning itself.

28. World Bank, "Malaysia: Fifth Education Project Staff Appraisal Report," report no. 2082b-MA (a restricted-circulation document) (Washington, D.C.: World Bank, 1979; processed), p. 12.

Table 2.14. *Development Programs of the Public Sector, 1961–80.*

Sector	Percentage composition of expenditure			
	1961–65	1966–70	1971–75	1976–80[a]
Agriculture and rural development	17.0	31.2	24.2	29.0
Drainage and irrigation	4.0	9.6	3.1	3.8
Land development	5.0	10.2	13.0	12.3
Other	8.0	11.4	8.1	12.9
Industrial development and mining	2.5	3.9	18.4	10.6
Transport	26.7	15.2	20.4	17.2
Communications	4.6	5.7	6.8	7.3
Utilities	21.0	19.1	10.3	13.1
Education	9.9	9.2	7.7	10.2
Health and housing	7.3	9.6	4.7	6.6
Other social services	4.5	2.2	3.0	2.1
Administration	6.3	3.9	4.0	3.7
Other	...	...	0.5	0.2
Total[b]	100.0	100.0	100.0	100.0
Total in relation to gross national product	8.3	6.7	10.0	10.4

... Zero or negligible.
Sources: Ministry of Finance, *Economic Report*, various years; 1976–80 from *Third Malaysia Plan, 1976–1980.*
 a. Targeted.
 b. Excludes defense and security.

A central feature of the plans is the development program proposed for the public sector. A large and increasing share of development expenditure has gone to the agricultural sector in the years since independence, reflecting in part the high priority that the ruling government has given to improving the welfare of the rural poor. The content of Malaysia's development programs shifted after the early 1960s, with greater emphasis on agriculture and industry, less emphasis on basic infrastructure. In the five-year plan for 1961–65 agriculture and industry received less than 20 percent of development expenditure; transport, communications, and utilities more than 50 percent.[29] In Malaysia's third plan for 1976–80 it was proposed that agriculture and industry would receive about 40 percent and that basic infrastructure would receive almost the same (table 2.14). In agriculture the principal in-

29. The first two five-year plans covered the 1956–60 and 1961–65 periods and pertained only to the Federation of Malaya. Plans introduced after the formation of Malaysia in 1963 were resequenced, with the First Malaysia Plan covering 1966–70; the Second Malaysia Plan, 1971–75; and the Third Malaysia Plan, 1976–80.

crease has been in the expenditure for land development, which was to rise from 5 percent of the total in 1961–65 to more than 12 percent in 1976–80.

The allocations for industry also increased markedly, from 2.5 percent in 1961–65 to a targeted 10.6 percent in 1976–80. This pattern reflects the emphasis of the New Economic Policy on improving the economic position of Malays. A number of public enterprises—PERNAS, MARA, the Urban Development Authority, and the state economic development corporations—received large allocations to expand their activities and thereby increase Malay participation in commerce and industry. In addition to these institutions, allocations were increased for such publicly owned enterprises as the national airline and the national shipping company. As a result, the direct involvement of the public sector in production activities has been considerably expanded.

Two key factors explain the contribution of planning to development in Malaysia, a contribution much greater than in other developing countries. First, the development program has been well funded. Second, the implementation of proposed programs has been good. With the preparation of annual budgets closely linked to the development plan, projects generally have been funded in accord with their economic priority. The original targets of plans for financing projects have generally been fulfilled: the implementation ratio was 114 percent in 1961–65, 94 percent in 1966–70, and 143 percent in 1971–75. Although part of this performance can be explained by unanticipated inflation, physical implementation has also been high, especially in relation to other countries in the region.

In summary, the process of planning and the programs of investment have made a considerable contribution to Malaysia's development. They established the basic infrastructure required for growth; they increased the output of many of the rural poor through large investments in irrigation and land development. In addition, the plans and economic management of government have provided an economic atmosphere conducive to maximizing the contribution of the private sector. Despite the significant increase of government expenditure in industry, government has not significantly taken over the traditional activities of the private sector. Tariff policies appear to have created some distortions and inefficiencies, but these do not appear to have been excessive. Perhaps most important, government has been a significant agent in maintaining the openness and price stability of the economy.

THREE   Kevin Young

𝕝𝕝𝕝𝕝𝕝𝕝𝕝𝕝𝕝𝕝𝕝𝕝𝕝𝕝𝕝𝕝𝕝𝕝𝕝𝕝𝕝𝕝𝕝𝕝𝕝𝕝𝕝𝕝𝕝𝕝𝕝𝕝𝕝𝕝

The New Economic Policy and Long-term Development Issues

DESPITE MALAYSIA'S RAPID RATE OF ECONOMIC GROWTH in the years after independence, two fundamental problems persist: widespread poverty and serious racial imbalances. In response to these problems, government adopted the New Economic Policy in 1971 "to eradicate poverty among all Malaysians and to restructure Malaysian society so that the identification of race with economic function and geographical location is reduced and eventually eliminated, both objectives being realized through rapid expansion of the economy over time."[1] To make these objectives specific, ambitious numerical targets were established for reducing poverty and achieving a better racial balance by 1990. Repeatedly reemphasizing its commitment to these targets, government has fashioned its five-year plans as the building blocks for realizing basic objectives.

In this chapter Malaysia's development problems and prospects are reviewed with particular reference to the New Economic Policy. First, the detailed objectives of that policy are presented, and the strategy proposed by government to attain them is reviewed. Next, the prospects for ensuring the availability of resources, sustaining rapid growth in manufacturing, and expanding the public programs to alleviate poverty are examined in turn. Last, the investment requirements to achieve rapid growth are evaluated. What emerges from this analysis is that the government's strategy for development—sustaining rapid industrial growth and focusing public programs on the poor—can enable Malaysia to meet the targets for reducing poverty and restructuring society. Given the internal consistency of the government's plan, the question is whether that strategy can be successfully pursued. Although Malaysia has many things in its favor, the discussion suggests that meeting the targets of the New Economic Policy will require vigorous government

---

1. Government of Malaysia, *Third Malaysia Plan, 1976–1980* (Kuala Lumpur: Government Press, 1976), p. 7.

efforts in promoting rapid industrial growth and implementing more effective programs that reduce poverty directly.[2]

Targets of the New Economic Policy

According to government estimates for 1970, almost half the households in Peninsular Malaysia were in poverty: that is, their incomes were not sufficient to provide an adequate diet and four essential non-food items—housing, clothing, utilities, and transport.[3] The income line used to define poverty was a monthly household income of M$180 in 1970 prices.[4] As the discussions in chapters two and four indicate, this poverty line, when compared with international standards, may overstate to some degree the extent of absolute poverty in Malaysia. It nevertheless falls between a quarter and a third of average per capita income, the criterion often used for relative poverty. The official estimate of poverty thus provides a reasonable guideline for establishing targets to reduce poverty.

The vast majority of the poor—86 percent in 1970—live in rural areas. The Malaysian population still is largely rural, and the incidence of poverty among households is twice as high in rural areas as in urban areas. The two largest groups in poverty in 1970 were rubber smallholders and rice cultivators, who together constituted 44 percent of the poverty households (table 3.1). Among the racial groups, the incidence of poverty is highest among Malays; nearly two-thirds of Malays were below the poverty line in 1970. Poverty is also substantial among the other racial groups: 39 percent of Indians and 26 percent of Chinese were below the poverty line in 1970.

The government's target is to reduce the incidence of poverty from 49 percent of households in 1970 to 17 percent by 1990. Given the rapid rate of population growth expected over this period—the number of households is projected to increase 3.3 percent a year—attaining this target will be a formidable task. To achieve such a reduction implies

2. Many of the arguments in this chapter are drawn from the principal issues and conclusions identified in subsequent chapters.

3. Because of the lack of income data on Sabah and Sarawak, poverty estimates are only for Peninsular Malaysia.

4. In 1975 prices this poverty line is about equal to the annual per capita income of US$265 referred to in chapter two.

that the number of poverty households in 1990 would be a third of what it would be if there were no reduction in the incidence of poverty: that is, about 1 million fewer households would be in poverty. Although the targets show a reduction in the incidence of poverty in both rural and urban areas, there would be an absolute increase of 45 percent in the number of poor households in urban areas. The basis of this increase is the assumption that there will be a continuing flow of labor from rural to urban areas. It is projected that the number of rural households will grow at the rate of 1.7 percent a year, compared with 6.4 percent for urban households. This difference implies a net migration of about 600,000 households from rural to urban areas during 1970–90. In other words, rural-urban migration will make possible much of the reduction in poverty targeted for rural areas. This projected migration, as well as the simultaneous decline in the incidence of urban poverty, is based on the assumption of rapid growth of employment opportunities in the modern sector.

Table 3.1. *Incidence and Composition of Poverty Households, by Location and Sector or Occupation, Peninsular Malaysia, 1970, Estimates for 1975, and Targets for 1980 and 1990*

Location and sector or occupation	All households	Poverty households	Percentage incidence of poverty households	Percentage composition of poverty households
		1970		
Rural	1,203.4	705.9	58.7	89.2
Agriculture	852.9	582.4	68.3	73.6
Rubber smallholders	350.0	226.4	64.7	28.6
Oil palm smallholders	6.6	2.0	30.3	0.3
Coconut smallholders	32.0	16.9	53.8	2.1
Rice farmers	140.0	123.4	88.1	15.6
Other agriculture[a]	285.9	185.6	64.9	23.5
Fishermen	38.4	28.1	73.2	3.5
Other industries	350.5	123.5	35.2	15.6
Urban	402.6	85.9	21.3	10.8
Mining	5.4	1.8	33.3	0.2
Manufacturing	84.0	19.7	23.5	2.5
Construction	19.5	5.9	30.2	0.7
Transport and utilities	42.4	13.1	30.9	1.7
Trade and services	251.3	45.4	18.1	5.7
Total	1,606.0	791.8	49.3	100.0

The other objective of the New Economic Policy—to restructure society—covers three principal areas: employment by sector, employment by occupation, and ownership of the share capital of limited companies.

The targets for employment by sector call for a pattern of employment that more closely reflects the racial composition of the population (tables 3.2 and 3.3). Because of the very large initial shares of Malays in agriculture and Chinese in secondary and tertiary employment, the objectives imply a rising Malay share in the secondary and tertiary sectors and a rising Chinese share in agricultural employment. For example, the share of Malays in the secondary sector is to increase from 31 percent in 1970 to 52 percent in 1990; that of Chinese is to decrease from 60 percent to 38 percent over the same period. The shifts implied for Indian employment are much less severe because the Indian share in employment in each sector currently is roughly proportional to their share in the population.

All households	Poverty households	Percentage incidence of poverty households	Percentage composition of poverty households	Location and sector or occupation
		1975		
1,348.5	729.9	54.1	87.4	*Rural*
915.1	576.5	63.0	69.0	Agriculture
396.3	233.8	59.0	28.0	Rubber smallholders
9.9	0.9	9.1	0.1	Oil palm smallholders
34.4	17.5	50.9	2.1	Coconut smallholders
148.5	114.3	77.0	13.7	Rice farmers
284.4	183.8	64.6	22.0	Other agriculture[a]
41.6	26.2	63.0	3.1	Fishermen
433.4	153.4	35.4	18.4	Other industries
553.0	105.2	19.0	12.6	*Urban*
5.3	2.0	37.7	0.2	Mining
120.4	21.0	17.4	2.5	Manufacturing
25.5	6.1	25.9	0.7	Construction
64.4	13.8	21.4	1.7	Transport and utilities
337.4	62.3	18.5	7.5	Trade and services
1,901.5	835.1	43.9	100.0	*Total*

(table continues on the following pages)

Table 3.1 (*continued*)

Location and sector or occupation	All households	Poverty households	Percentage incidence of poverty households	Percentage composition of poverty households
		1980		
Rural	1,500.7	646.7	43.1	84.2
Agriculture	957.5	471.8	49.3	61.4
Rubber smallholders	423.4	169.4	40.0	22.0
Oil palm smallholders	24.5	2.0	8.2	0.3
Coconut smallholders	34.0	16.0	47.1	2.1
Rice farmers	150.1	109.6	73.0	14.2
Other agriculture[a]	283.0	152.7	54.0	19.9
Fishermen	42.5	22.1	52.0	2.9
Other industries	543.2	174.9	32.2	22.8
Urban	769.8	121.6	15.8	15.8
Mining	5.4	1.7	31.5	0.2
Manufacturing	181.1	25.4	14.0	3.3
Construction	33.8	6.8	20.0	0.9
Transport and utilities	84.5	14.6	17.3	1.9
Trade and services	465.0	73.1	15.7	9.5
Total	2.270.5	768.3	33.8	100.0

Note: The poverty line income used to distinguish poverty households from other households is, according to the official definitions, the monthly income necessary to cover minimum nutritional requirements and essential nonfood expenses. The statistical bases for the estimates and projections include: the postenumeration survey of the 1970 Population Census; the labor force surveys of the Department of Statistics; and socioeconomic surveys on specific poverty groups undertaken by various agencies, including the mini-

Two things are especially noteworthy in these targets. First, the degree of restructuring is substantial. Second, no group is to experience an absolute decline in employment. Indeed, for all three main groups, the growth of employment in industry and services is to be no less than the growth of the labor force. Thus the gains by Malays are to be made through a redistribution of growth, and this redistribution is to be considerable. For example, almost 65 percent of the additional jobs in the secondary sector would go to Malays; more than 60 percent of the new employment in agriculture would go to non-Malays. To achieve this restructuring will require rapid and sustained growth of employment in the secondary and tertiary sectors. It is projected that the annual rate of

All households	Poverty households	Percentage incidence of poverty households	Percentage composition of poverty households	Location and sector or occupation
		1990		
1,689.7	388.9	23.0	75.6	*Rural*
908.8	241.5	26.6	46.9	Agriculture
417.2	100.1	24.0	19.5	Rubber smallholders
22.8	0.7	3.0	0.1	Oil palm smallholders
28.4	7.7	27.1	1.5	Coconut smallholders
133.4	40.0	30.0	7.8	Rice farmers
266.2	77.1	29.0	15.0	Other agriculture[a]
40.8	15.9	39.0	3.1	Fishermen
780.9	147.4	18.9	28.7	Other industries
1,381.1	125.0	9.1	24.4	*Urban*
5.5	1.0	18.2	0.2	Mining
406.2	31.0	7.6	6.0	Manufacturing
56.7	7.1	12.5	1.4	Construction
128.5	11.1	8.6	2.2	Transport and utilities
784.2	74.8	9.5	1.6	Trade and services
3,070.8	513.9	16.7	100.0	*Total*

stries of Agriculture, Primary Industries, Labor and Manpower, and Housing and Village Development, as well as the General Planning Unit of the Prime Minister's Department.

Source: *Third Malaysia Plan, 1976–1980.*

a. Includes agricultural households in urban areas, agricultural laborers, estate workers, and part-time farmers.

employment growth will be about 5 percent in both these sectors.[5]

The restructuring of employment by occupation is also to be substantial. The targets call for gains by Malays in all occupations except agricultural workers (table 3.4). The increase is to be particularly large for administrative and managerial workers, for which category the Malay share of employment is projected to increase from 22 percent in 1970 to 49 percent in 1990. Significant gains in the Malay share are also targeted for clerical and production workers. As for the employment

(text continues on page 69)

5. *Third Malaysia Plan, 1976–1980,* p. 68.

Table 3.2. *Population, Labor Force, and Employment, by Race, Peninsular Malaysia, 1970, Estimates for 1975, and Projections for 1990*

Year and item	Malay	Chinese	Indian	Other	Total
1970		*Thousands*			
Population	4,822.0	3,274.0	978.0	73.0	9,147.0
Labor force	1,563.0	1,111.6	334.4	26.0	3,035.0
Employment	1,436.6	1,034.3	297.6	25.2	2,793.7
Unemployment	126.4	77.3	36.8	0.8	241.3
		Percent			
Population	52.7	35.8	10.7	0.8	100.0
Labor force	51.5	36.6	11.1	0.8	100.0
Employment	51.4	37.0	10.7	0.9	100.0
Unemployment rate	8.1	7.0	11.0	3.1	8.0
1975		*Thousands*			
Population	5,510.0	3,687.0	1,105.0	83.0	10,385.0
Labor force	1,873.1	1,297.9	389.0	30.0	3,590.0
Employment	1,744.8	1,204.1	341.7	26.6	3,317.2
Unemployment	128.3	93.8	47.3	3.4	272.8
		Percent			
Population	53.1	35.5	10.6	0.8	100.0
Labor force	52.2	36.2	10.8	0.8	100.0
Employment	52.6	36.3	10.3	0.8	100.0
Unemployment rate	6.9	7.2	12.2	11.3	7.6
1990		*Thousands*			
Population	8,163.0	5,230.0	1,599.0	108.0	15,100.0
Labor force	3,042.0	2,003.5	589.5	41.0	5,676.0
Employment	2,920.9	1,923.0	565.8	39.4	5,449.1
Unemployment	121.1	80.5	23.7	1.6	226.9
		Percent			
Population	54.1	34.6	10.6	0.7	100.0
Labor force	53.6	35.3	10.4	0.7	100.0
Employment	53.6	35.3	10.4	0.7	100.0
Unemployment rate	4.0	4.0	4.0	4.0	4.0

Source: *Third Malaysia Plan, 1976–1980.*

Table 3.3. *Employment, by Race and Sector, Peninsular Malaysia, 1970, Estimates for 1975, and Targets for 1990*

Year and sector	Malay	Chinese	Indian	Other	Total
1970		*Thousands of workers*			
Primary	951.1	300.9	142.0	12.0	1,406.0
Secondary	173.1	335.1	51.7	2.9	562.8
Tertiary	312.4	398.3	103.9	10.3	824.9
Total	1,436.6	1,034.3	297.6	25.2	2,793.7
		Percentage composition			
Primary	67.6	21.4	10.1	0.9	50.3
Secondary	30.8	59.5	9.2	0.5	20.2
Tertiary	37.9	48.3	12.6	1.2	29.5
Total	51.4	37.0	10.7	0.9	100.0
1975		*Thousands of workers*			
Primary	1,032.6	317.6	170.3	13.8	1,534.3
Secondary	265.0	386.9	71.1	3.3	726.3
Tertiary	447.2	449.6	100.3	9.5	1,056.6
Total	1,744.8	1,204.1	341.7	26.6	3,317.2
		Percentage composition			
Primary	67.3	20.7	11.1	0.9	46.2
Secondary	36.5	53.3	9.8	0.4	21.9
Tertiary	42.3	47.3	9.5	0.9	31.9
Total	52.6	36.3	10.3	0.8	100.0
1990		*Thousands of workers*			
Primary	1,091.4	503.2	170.6	12.4	1,777.6
Secondary	782.7	575.3	143.1	7.0	1,508.1
Tertiary	1,046.8	844.5	252.1	20.0	2,163.4
Total	2,920.9	1,923.0	565.8	39.4	5,449.1
		Percentage composition			
Primary	61.4	28.3	9.6	0.7	32.6
Secondary	51.9	38.1	9.5	0.5	27.2
Tertiary	48.4	39.0	11.7	0.9	39.7
Total	53.6	35.3	10.4	0.7	100.0

Note: The primary sector includes agriculture; the secondary sector, mining, manufacturing, construction, utilities, and transport; the tertiary sector, wholesale and retail trade, banking, public administration, education, health, and defense.
Source: Third Malaysia Plan, 1976–1980.

Table 3.4. *Employment, by Occupational Category and Race, Peninsular Malaysia, 1970, Estimates for 1975, and Targets for 1990*

Occupational category	Percentage composition				Thousands of workers
	Malay	Chinese	Indian	Other	
1970					
Professional and technical[a]	47.2	37.7	12.7	2.4	129.6
Administrative and managerial	22.4	65.7	7.5	4.4	22.8
Clerical	33.4	51.0	14.3	1.3	140.0
Sales	23.9	64.7	11.0	0.4	316.0
Agricultural	68.7	20.8	9.6	0.9	1,364.5
Production	31.3	59.9	8.6	0.2	358.4
Service and other	42.9	42.5	13.4	1.2	462.4
Total	51.4	37.0	10.7	0.9	2,793.7
1975					
Professional and technical[a]	48.5	37.1	12.5	1.9	171.1
Administrative and managerial	32.4	55.2	9.9	2.5	33.4
Clerical	38.7	48.3	12.0	1.0	180.6
Sales	25.0	65.2	9.6	0.2	318.4
Agricultural	68.3	20.3	10.5	0.9	1,463.2
Production	37.0	53.5	9.2	0.3	474.0
Service and other	48.3	40.9	9.9	0.9	676.6
Total	52.6	36.3	10.3	0.8	3,317.2
1990					
Professional and technical	50.0	37.2	11.5	1.3	387.0
Administrative and managerial	49.3	39.4	9.8	1.5	73.9
Clerical	47.9	38.7	12.5	0.9	372.2
Sales	36.9	51.8	11.0	0.3	445.9
Agricultural	62.3	27.8	9.2	0.7	1,700.9
Production	52.0	38.0	9.6	0.4	1,072.1
Service and other	52.3	35.4	11.4	0.9	1,397.2
Total	53.6	35.3	10.4	0.7	5,449.1

Source: Third Malaysia Plan, 1976–1980.

a. The dominance of Malays in the teaching profession explains the high proportion of Malays in this category in 1970 and 1975. For other occupations in this category—such as chemists, scientists, architects, surveyors, engineers, and legal and medical personnel —the Malay proportion in employment is much lower.

Table 3.5. *Ownership of Share Capital of Limited Companies, Peninsular Malaysia, 1970, Estimates for 1975, and Targets for 1980 and 1990*

Ownership	Millions of Malaysian dollars	Percentage of total	Millions of Malaysian dollars	Percentage of total	Average annual rate of change (percent)
	1970		1975		1971–75
Malays and Malay interests	125.6	2.4	768.1	7.8	43.6
Malay individuals	84.4	1.6	227.1	2.3	21.9
Malay interests[a]	41.2	0.8	541.0	5.5	67.4
Other Malaysians[b]	1,826.5	34.3	3,687.3	37.3	15.1
Foreign[c]	3,377.1	63.3	5,434.7	54.9	10.0
Total private sector[d]	5,329.2	100.0	9,890.1	100.0	13.2
	1980		1990		1976–90
Malays and Malay interests	3,284.3	16.0	24,009.7	30.0	25.8
Malay individuals	695.4	3.4	5,914.2	7.4	24.3
Malay interests[a]	2,588.9	12.6	18,095.5	22.6	26.4
Other Malaysians[b]	8,290.5	40.4	32,012.9	40.0	15.5
Foreign[c]	8,952.2	43.6	24,009.7	30.0	10.4
Total private sector[d]	20,527.0	100.0	80,032.3	100.0	15.0

Note: The figures for 1970 differ from those presented in the second plan and its mid-term review because of the exclusion here of government, the reclassification of trust agencies as Malay interests, and the reallocation of most shares previously categorized as being held by other companies to the shareholders of those companies.
Source: Third Malaysia Plan, 1976–1980.
   a. Agencies considered to hold shares in trust for Malays, such as MARA, PERNAS, Bank Bumiputra, Bank Pembangunan, the Urban Development Authority, and the state economic development corporations.
   b. Includes nominee companies and third-company minority holdings.
   c. Nonresidents.
   d. Excludes government and its agencies, except trust agencies.

targets by sector, those by occupation are to be attained through rapid growth that will facilitate absolute gains by all racial groups.

The third principal area of restructuring is the ownership of share capital. In 1970 about 63 percent of the share capital of limited companies was foreign-owned. Malays owned less than 1 percent; public trust agencies 1.6 percent; non-Malays the remaining 34 percent. The targets for restructuring equity are twofold: to increase the domestic ownership of equity to 70 percent by 1990; and to increase the Malay share—that is, the share of Malay individuals and public trust agencies—to 30 percent (table 3.5). As with the other areas, all groups, including foreigners, would experience an absolute increase in their equity holdings. The restructuring would nevertheless reduce the foreigners' share to 30 percent. The share of non-Malay nationals is to increase from 34 percent to 40 percent.

A central feature of these targets is that three-quarters of the increase in Malay ownership would come from the acquisition of shares by government agencies. These agencies include Majlis Amanah Rakyat (MARA), Perbadanan Nasional Berhad (PERNAS), Bank Bumiputra, Bank Pembangunan, the Urban Development Authority, and the state economic development corporations. These agencies are to transfer shares to Malay individuals as their incomes and savings increase. It has not been specified, however, how that transfer would take place. The financial implication of this proposed share acquisition is that public trust agencies would purchase share capital equivalent to about 1.5 percent of GDP over the 1975–90 period. To ease the financial burden on these agencies and to help meet the targeted Malay share of 30 percent, government could expand the definition of trust agencies to include such national public corporations as Petroliam Nasional Berhad (PETRONAS, the National Petroleum Corporation) and the Malaysian International Shipping Corporation.

Some observers of the Malaysian scene have argued that the equity restructuring proposed is more apparent than real, because most of it will be accomplished by increasing the public sector's ownership of limited companies. Although this argument is correct as far as it goes, it does not take fully into account other important factors that government confronts. Few observers would deny that there is a pressing political need to increase significantly the Malay share in ownership of the economy. It also is clear, given the high incidence of poverty among Malay households, that any attempt to shift ownership in a dramatic way to Malay individuals would imply a real loss for non-Malays and possibly worsen the distribution of income among Malays by creating a new class of wealthy corporate owners. As a result, government has been pursuing a more moderate course—a course which recognizes the need to restructure equity and the danger of redistributing equity before Malays have the means to purchase it. Although this course should not be faulted, it is important that investments not be held up because of the lack of Malay counterpart funds. It also is important to dispel the fear among non-Malays that equity will one day have to be transferred at less than market value. In addition, the achievements in this area, while fulfilling social and political needs, should not be confused with the need to build an entrepreneurial class of Malays. A more complete discussion of this last point is in chapter seven. Finally, the measures of

Table 3.6. *Growth Targets of the Outline Perspective Plan,*
by Sector, 1976–90
(percent)

Sector	Average annual rate of growth, 1976–90
Agriculture	5.3
Mining	5.0
Manufacturing	12.7
Construction	8.3
Utilities	9.7
Services	8.4
Gross domestic product	8.2

Source: Third Malaysia Plan, 1976–1980.

government for restructuring equity call for a significant increase in domestic control of the economy. That control is a principal aim of the measures.

Imperatives for Rapid Growth

Government has emphasized in its plans that rapid economic growth is essential to attaining the goals of the New Economic Policy. Only through rapid growth can enough employment be generated in industry and services—the higher income sectors—to reduce poverty substantially. Furthermore rapid growth is essential to enabling simultaneously a substantial relative improvement in the economic position of Malays and a substantial absolute improvement in that of non-Malays. In this context, the target of the perspective plan covering the period to 1990 is for a long-term rate of real GDP growth of more than 8 percent a year (table 3.6).[6] The manufacturing sector is projected to be the leading growth sector with a growth rate of close to 13 percent a year. The services sector is to grow at about the same rate as GDP; agriculture is to grow at the rate of about 5 percent a year. On the basis of this pattern of output growth, it is projected that almost 90 percent of the 2.4 million jobs to be created between 1975 and 1990 will be in industry and services. Given the structure of employment in 1975, this pattern of job

6. The Outline Perspective Plan, 1970–1990—referred to in this volume as the perspective plan—was incorporated in the third plan.

Table 3.7. *Population and Labor Force, Malaysia, 1970, Estimates for 1975, and Projections for 1980 and 1990*

| | Millions of persons | | | | Average annual rate of growth (percent) | | |
Item	1970	1975	1980	1990	1970–75	1976–80	1981–90
Population	10.8	12.2	14.0	18.1	2.6	2.7	2.6
Labor force	3.6	4.2	5.0	6.6	3.2	3.3	2.9

Source: Third Malaysia Plan, 1976–1980.

creation implies a net shift out of agriculture of almost a million jobs.

Overlying these ambitious targets for reducing poverty and restructuring society, and further necessitating a rapid rate of economic growth, are the rapid projected rates of growth in population and labor force. Growing at an annual rate of about 2.7 percent since 1970, Malaysia's population reached 12.3 million in 1975. The population density was about 37 persons per square kilometer, although Peninsular Malaysia, which had 84 percent of the population, had a density eight times higher than Sabah and Sarawak: 79 persons per square kilometer, compared with 10 persons per square kilometer. Because of rapid population growth in the past, about 43 percent of the population in 1970 was under 15; the dependency ratio was 0.9.[7] The population growth rate for the second half of the 1970s was projected in the third plan to continue at about 2.7 percent a year.

An essential element in Malaysia's prospects for long-term development is the number of additional jobs the economy must provide to keep unemployment from rising. As a result of a high population growth rate during 1957–75, the number of persons of working age will increase considerably during 1976–90. What is significant is that this increase cannot now be influenced by policy. Even if Malaysia achieves a substantial reduction in the rate of population growth during this period, the number of persons who will be of working age has essentially been predetermined by population growth during the preceding fifteen years. According to the third plan the labor force was projected to grow at the average annual rate of 3.3 percent during 1976–80 and 2.9 percent during 1981–90 (table 3.7).[8] The labor force in Peninsular

7. The ratio of those under 15 and over 65 to those 15–64 years of age.

8. The third plan anticipated some changes in participation rates during 1975–80 because of an increase in female participation and the effects of longer periods of enrollment in schools. These effects appear to offset each other, and the participation rate was pro-

Malaysia is estimated to have increased 2.7 percent a year during the 1957–67 period.[9]

The discussion of alternative growth strategies, presented in appendix A and summarized in a subsequent section of this chapter, affirms the necessity for government to pursue a strategy of rapid growth if the targets of the New Economic Policy are to be attained. For example, if the manufacturing growth rate were significantly lower than the 13 percent targeted and a GDP growth rate of only 5 to 6 percent were achieved, the rates of employment growth in industry and services would be significantly lower than those forecast in the perspective plan, and the possibility of restructuring employment would be severely limited.[10] To achieve the restructuring targets in the modern sectors, the growth of non-Malay employment in those sectors would then have to be held to about half of the growth of the non-Malay labor force. That would imply either a substantial shift of non-Malays to the agricultural sector or a significant increase in their unemployment. Because government has emphasized that employment restructuring will not be undertaken at the cost of unemployment among non-Malays, the restructuring targets would clearly be seriously jeopardized.

The effect of a GDP growth rate of 5 to 6 percent on efforts to reduce poverty would also be significant. Slower growth would severely restrict the opportunities for migration out of agriculture. Given the likelihood of somewhat reduced growth of agricultural output, per capita household income in agriculture would probably increase no more than about 1.5 percent a year. Under these circumstances it is likely that the incidence of poverty could not be reduced much below 30 percent by 1990 and that the number of families in poverty in 1990 would be almost twice the number projected in the perspective plan. Although these estimates are rough approximations, they clearly indicate that rapid economic growth is essential to achieving the long-term targets of the New Economic Policy.

---

jected to change only slightly, from 63.4 in 1975 to 63 in 1980. The estimates for 1981–90 imply an average rate of growth during 1976–90 of 3 percent a year and are close to recent estimates by the World Bank of labor force growth for Peninsular Malaysia. The World Bank estimates assume constant age- and sex-specific participation rates and lead to labor force growth of 3.1 percent a year during 1976–90.

9. "Methodology Used in West Malaysian Labor Force and Employment Analysis," an unpublished technical appendix to Donald R. Snodgrass, "The Growth and Utilization of Malaysian Labor Supply," *Philippine Economic Journal*, vol. 15, nos. 1 and 2 (1976), pp. 276–313.

10. This pattern of growth is referred to as the moderate growth path in a subsequent section of this chapter and as alternative I in appendix A.

Role of the Public Sector

In addition to pursuing a strategy of rapid growth, government proposes to meet its targets through more direct means. To reduce poverty it is focusing public investment and development programs on the poor. To restructure society it is introducing quotas and controls. With a public development program, excluding defense and security, equivalent to about 10 percent of GDP, the potential effect of government programs is substantial. Furthermore, government estimated that about 40 percent of the development program in the third plan would be directed toward reducing poverty. In general the agricultural sector was to account for about 29 percent of planned expenditure, social services for 19 percent, transport for 17 percent, utilities for 13 percent, and other sectors for the remaining 22 percent (see table 2.14 in chapter two).

Because most of the poor live in rural areas and receive the bulk of their income from agriculture, the principal antipoverty programs of government are directed toward rural households. Agricultural programs fall into two basic categories: those for assisting traditional farmers on their existing smallholdings and those for developing additional land for agriculture. Programs in the first category were given much more emphasis in the third plan than in the second plan. They increase the productivity of small-scale farmers by teaching better farming practices and by supplying irrigation and drainage, subsidies for replanting tree crops, improved inputs, and better access to credit. Programs in the second category develop previously uncultivated land for settlement by families with little or no land of their own. They provide settlers with the means of earning a better living and relieve the pressure of population on agricultural land that is already occupied.

For the 1975–90 period the perspective plan projects a reduction in the incidence of poverty among agricultural households in Peninsular Malaysia from 63 percent to 27 percent. As noted earlier, the principal means of reducing poverty among agricultural households is through rapid employment growth in industry and services. That growth would require a substantial transfer of labor from rural to urban areas and imply that the agricultural labor force would grow only 1 percent a year, which is equivalent to creating about 245,000 jobs in agriculture in Peninsular Malaysia during the 1976–90 period. Given this growth of employment in agriculture, the reduction of poverty among agricultural households would mainly be the result of the land development program proposed in the perspective plan. That program alone would provide incomes above the poverty line to about 200,000 families in Peninsular Malaysia during this period. Assuming no significant changes in the agricultural terms of trade, the remainder of the poverty reduction would have to come largely from government programs to increase productivity in areas traditionally cultivated. In addition to its agricultural programs, government is mounting urban and country-wide programs to provide the poor with better access to housing, water, sewerage, electrification, health care, and family planning.

Government efforts to achieve a better racial balance are diverse: directly regulating private sector enterprises; establishing public bodies to purchase or create corporate assets on behalf of Malays; expanding programs of education, training, and technical assistance for Malays; favoring Malays in admission to tertiary educational institutions under a system of quotas and preferences; introducing Bahasa Malaysia, the Malay language, as the principal language of instruction in schools; giving Malays preference in public sector jobs; providing credit to Malay enterprises; giving price preferences to Malay suppliers; and setting quotas for public construction contracts to be awarded to Malay firms. The most controversial and potentially far-reaching policy is embodied in the Industrial Coordination Act. Passed in 1975, it will enforce targets for restructuring equity and employment through a system for licensing firms having a number of employees and an amount of paid capital above a specified minimum.

Under these policies some notable progress appears to have been made during 1971–75. The number of Malay graduates from higher level institutions increased more than threefold. The Malay share in institutional credit increased from 14 percent to 30 percent. In the context of accelerated economic growth, the Malay share in manufacturing employment increased from 29 percent to 33 percent; that in administrative and managerial employment from 22 percent to 32 percent. The Malay share in corporate equity increased from 2.4 percent to 7.8 percent, though the bulk of this increase was the result of an increase in the shares held by Malay interests, not Malay individuals.[11]

Availability of Resources

When the third plan was being drafted, the world recession was having serious adverse consequences for Malaysia. Output stagnated in 1975, and there were substantial declines in the world prices of Malaysia's principal exports—rubber, palm oil, tin, and timber. As a result, the terms of trade fell from 102 in 1974 to 87 in 1975 (1970 = 100). In

11. *Third Malaysia Plan, 1976–1980,* tables 4-15, 4-16, and 8-2.

addition, negotiations with the oil companies over production-sharing were stalled, and major increases in oil production were not foreseen. It is understandable in this context that planners were cautious in projecting resource availability for the 1976–80 period. The projections foresaw a further deterioration in the terms of trade, deficits of more than 3 percent of GNP in the current account of the balance of payments, and a very small current surplus in the public sector—all of which would constrain the public program of development.

Subsequent performance showed that 1975 deviated from the trend and was not an appropriate base year for forecasting. In 1976 there was a substantial recovery in most areas of economic activity. Output growth rebounded to 10 percent. The world prices for Malaysia's principal export commodities registered substantial gains—palm oil was the exception—and the terms of trade rebounded to their 1974 level. In addition, following the settlement of the production-sharing agreement with the oil companies, the production of oil increased from about 100,000 barrels a day in 1975 to 170,000 barrels a day in 1976. Combined with the more moderate import growth that resulted from sluggish investment activity, there was a current account surplus equal to more than 6 percent of GDP, one of the highest external surpluses in history. Consequently Malaysia's reserves, including holdings of foreign exchange by PETRONAS, increased by about M$2.5 billion to a level equivalent to seven months of imports. Furthermore, because of the improvement in the terms of trade, the almost 10 percent increase of GNP in 1976 was amplified into a 17 percent increase in national income. That gain represented more than a third of the increase in national income projected by the plan for 1976–80 and about half of the projected increase in national income per capita. As a result of these and other factors, the resource position of the public sector in 1976 also improved over the previous year and was markedly better than had been forecast when the third plan was prepared. The current surplus of the public sector, excluding PETRONAS, rose from M$471 million in 1975 to M$1,273 million in 1976, substantially above the M$100 surplus that had been forecast for 1976. In addition, the current surplus of PETRONAS in 1976 was about M$525 million.

The recovery of output and world demand in 1976, together with the better prospects for oil production, thus suggested the adoption of a much higher base for resource projections than was used for the third plan. The following examination of likely price trends, longer-term prospects for the growth of physical output of primary resources, and implications for export earnings and public sector revenue therefore takes 1976 as a base year. In assessing the implications of these projections for the availability of resources for development, it should be kept in mind that 1976 was a year of substantial surplus in the current account of the balance of payments and the public sector. Thus, with that year as a base, resource use could increase more rapidly than resource availability.

Physical Resources

Although Malaysia's land resources are abundant in relation to its population, questions remain about exactly how much land still is available for cultivation. In 1975 about 15 million acres were under cultivation: 9.4 million acres were under permanent cultivation; 5.6 million acres in Sarawak were under shifting cultivation (table 3.8). Government estimates that another 19 million acres could eventually be developed for agriculture. Of this total, 8.2 million acres are in Peninsular Malaysia, where more than 85 percent of the population lives.

The estimates of the availability of land in Peninsular Malaysia may nevertheless be exaggerated. First, infrastructure and various types of wastage, which are not taken into account, may require discounting the estimates by as much as 20 percent. Second, it is likely that much of the land is marginal and would require substantial inputs of fertilizer to make it suitable for sustained agriculture. It probably includes a considerable area of slopes, which would make erosion a serious problem for some crops. Third, part of the suitable land is likely to be relatively inaccessible and in much smaller blocks than land developed in the past. Fourth, some part of this land should be conserved for environmental reasons. Therefore, until more detailed studies of land availability are completed, it would be safer to assume that no more than 4

Table 3.8. *Availability of Land, 1975*
(thousands of acres)

Region	Total land area	Land under cultivation in 1975	Undeveloped land suitable for cultivation	Other land
Peninsular Malaysia	32,467	7,400	8,200	16,867
Sabah	17,750	900	4,400	12,450
Sarawak	30,750	6,700[a]	6,400	17,650
Malaysia	80,967	15,000	19,000	46,967

Source: Third Malaysia Plan, 1976–1980.
a. Includes 5.6 million acres under shifting cultivation.

Table 3.9. *Production of Principal Primary Commodities, 1960–76, and Projections for 1976–90*
(percent)

Commodity	Average annual rate of growth	
	1960–76	*1976–90*
Palm oil	18.1	9.6
Petroleum	36.0	6.3
Rubber	4.8	3.9
Sawlogs	10.1	−1.0
Sawn timber	8.8	...
Tin	1.1	1.1

... Zero or negligible

Note: The decline in the growth of production of primary commodities will be mitigated by the production of natural gas, which is to begin in the 1980s.

Sources: 1960–76 from Bank Negara, *Quarterly Economic Bulletin*, vol. 10, no. 4 (December 1977) and Ministry of Finance, *Economic Report, 1977–78* (Kuala Lumpur, 1977); 1976–90 from World Bank estimates (see chapter nine).

million additional acres could be brought under cultivation in Peninsular Malaysia.

Government plans that about 2.4 million acres in Peninsular Malaysia are to be developed during 1976–90. This figure is well below even the lower estimate of 4 million acres of available land and indicates that new land in Peninsular Malaysia will not be exhausted at least until the end of the century. The amount of land projected for new development in Sabah and Sarawak during 1976–90 is about 1 million acres, or less than 10 percent of the official estimate of land available in those states. Even if this official estimate is optimistic, it is clear that land availability will not become a constraint in Sabah and Sarawak in the foreseeable future. For all of Malaysia, the projected development of about 3.2 million acres of land during 1976–90 implies an average annual growth rate of about 1.8 percent a year in the cultivated agricultural land, compared with about 1.7 percent a year during 1966–75.[12] Thus, solely on the basis of additional land, and assuming that land fertility does not decline, agricultural output should increase almost 2 percent a year.

Malaysia's other principal natural resources are tin, oil, natural gas, and forests. With the exception of natural gas, the prospects for increas-

12. This growth is based on the estimated 9.4 million acres of land under permanent cultivation and a quarter of the land under shifting cultivation.

es in the rate of exploitation of these resources are not as promising as in the past (table 3.9). For tin, given the lack of prospecting in recent years, a significant increase in production is unlikely. Production therefore is tentatively projected to increase at the average rate of about 1 percent a year during 1976–90. For oil, given the current official estimate of proven reserves of 1 billion barrels, substantial increases in production over the level of about 180,000 barrels a day achieved toward the end of 1976 would be unlikely. Under the assumption that some small additional finds will be made, the output of oil is projected to grow about 6 percent a year, or substantially slower than the rate of 36 percent a year during 1960–76. Because the current official estimate of reserves will probably prove to understate Malaysia's true reserves, this forecast is, if anything, on the cautious side. For sawlogs and sawn timber, given the increasing environmental concern over the rate of forest exploitation and the large expansion of production in 1976, it seems unlikely that production will increase significantly beyond the high 1976 levels. The exception to these trends is the production of liquefied natural gas, (LNG), which is to begin in 1983. The potential production of gas, though substantial, is small in relation to that of oil. By 1985, when an LNG plant is to be operating at full capacity, the value of LNG exports will probably be less than a fifth of the value of oil exports.

The growth of rubber and palm oil production, which can be projected with some certainty on the basis of past investments and the expected rate of new land development, is also likely to be less in the future. The production of palm oil was expected to continue to increase during the period of the third plan because of plantings undertaken in the past. The growth rate will nevertheless fall sharply in the 1980s, given the much larger base of production and the reduction of palm oil's share in land development. Although the growth rate of rubber production will not decelerate as much as that of palm oil production, some decline in growth is likely because the benefits from replanting with high-yielding clones will become smaller in relation to the area already replanted.

Exports

The further development of Malaysia's natural resources is a key element in the country's export prospects. In 1976 tin, rubber, petroleum, palm oil, and forest products constituted 71 percent of Malaysian exports. Because detailed projections of commodity exports are discussed in chapter nine, only some of the principal conclusions are presented

Table 3.10. *Projections of Exports, 1976–90*
(percent)

Item	Average annual rate of growth		
	Prices	Volume	Total
Principal primary commodities	7.6	3.8	11.7
Palm oil	5.5	9.2	15.2
Petroleum	7.3	6.3	14.1
Rubber	7.0	3.4	10.7
Sawlogs	9.8	−0.9	8.7
Sawn timber	11.1	0.0	11.1
Tin	7.8	−0.3	7.5
Natural gas	7.3	—	—
Manufactured goods	7.2	12.0	20.0
Miscellaneous exports and services	7.2	6.6	14.1
Total goods and nonfactor services	7.3	6.2	13.9
International inflation	7.2	—	—

— Not applicable.
Source: World Bank projections (see chapter nine).

here. The prices of the main export commodities are expected to maintain or possibly improve their relative positions over the long term. During 1976–90 the prices of the seven principal primary exports should increase at an average annual rate of 7.6 percent, or slightly faster than the rate of international inflation of 7.2 percent (table 3.10).[13] Only the prices of rubber and palm oil are expected to deteriorate in real terms. This prospect for prices, together with average annual growth of 3.8 percent in the exports of these commodities, means that primary products will continue to dominate Malaysian exports. Their share in total exports will of course depend on the performance of manufactured exports, about which there is considerable uncertainty.

As the discussion in chapter nine indicates, manufactured exports from Malaysia increased about 24 percent a year during 1970–75, compared with about 15 percent a year for all developing countries. This performance is largely explained by Malaysia's participation in the rapid growth of world trade in electronics and textiles. But a number of

13. Those seven principal exports are tin, rubber, petroleum, palm oil, sawlogs, sawn timber, and natural gas. The index of import prices is assumed to increase at the same rate as the World Bank index of international inflation: that is, at 7.2 percent a year on the average between 1976 and 1990.

factors suggest that the growth of manufactured exports may slacken in Malaysia. First, World Bank projections, which assume no substantial changes in current trade barriers, indicate some slackening in the growth of manufactured exports from developing countries during the coming years. During 1975–85 the manufactured exports of developing countries are projected to increase at an average annual real rate of 12 percent, which is the same as that during 1960–75 but significantly less than the 15 percent rate during 1970–75. Although this projected growth rate for manufactured exports is speculative, it is a useful benchmark for projecting Malaysia's performance. Second, the base of manufactured exports in Malaysia now is much larger than it was in 1970. Between 1970 and 1976, for example, the share of manufactured exports in merchandise exports more than doubled from less than 7 percent to 15 percent. Thus the absolute increases needed to sustain rapid growth have become much larger. Third, the outlook for continuing rapid growth in exports of clothing and textiles from developing countries is doubtful. If the quantitative restrictions on imports of clothing and textiles by developed countries are strictly enforced, it is estimated that the annual growth of these exports could be significantly less than 10 percent, compared with almost 20 percent during 1970–75. Because a significant part of Malaysia's past export growth has been in this category, some damping down of the growth of manufactured exports is likely.

In the light of past performance, there is no obvious reason to expect Malaysia to do worse than the average for developing countries. In fact, if it is assumed that Malaysia will do as well as the average in each of the main categories of manufactured exports—clothing, textiles, chemicals, iron and steel, machinery and equipment, and other—Malaysia would achieve an average growth of manufactured exports of about 12 percent a year, given its composition of those exports (see table 2.4 in chapter two). If this growth rate were sustained, the share of manufactured exports in merchandise exports would increase to almost a third by 1990.

If an annual growth rate of about 6.6 percent is assumed for other exports and services, the real growth of exports through 1990 would be 6.2 percent a year. If the prices of manufactured exports keep pace with international inflation, the index of export prices would increase at almost the same pace as that of import prices. As a result, the terms of trade would be roughly constant through 1990. The projected growth of manufactured exports also implies that primary commodities would constitute 53 percent of exports in 1990, compared with 69 percent in 1976. Malaysia's export receipts would thus continue to be vulnerable to fluctuations in the prices of primary commodities. Nevertheless the vulnerability of the country will be much less than in the past. For example, two commodities constituted almost 60 percent of merchandise exports in 1970; six commodities would constitute 60 percent in 1990. Furthermore, although rubber will still be Malaysia's largest export in 1990, it is expected to represent only 14 percent of exports, compared with 20 percent in 1976.

The purchasing power of Malaysian exports is projected to grow at 6.2 percent a year during 1976–90. But the future capacity to import should include not only the power of future exports to purchase imports, but also the import capacity not used in the past. As is evidenced by the large current account surplus in 1976, that unused capacity is substantial. Therefore the projected growth of exports, together with the substantial surplus of 1976, would enable a real growth of imports during 1976–90 of about 8 percent a year, compared with less than 6 percent during 1970–76.

Public Sector Resources

Because of recent developments, especially the increased prospects for revenue from oil, the constraint of resources on the public sector is likely to be much less than was foreseen when the third plan was drafted. Chapter six provides a more detailed assessment of the public sector's prospects for revenue. That assessment indicates that public sector revenue, including that of PETRONAS, will be significantly greater than in the past. Even if there are significant increases in current expenditure, public sector saving during 1976–85 is expected to be equal

Table 3.11. *Current Account of the Public Sector, 1971–75, and Projections for 1976–80 and 1981–85*

	Percentage of gross national product		
Item	1971–75	1976–80	1981–85
Current revenue[a]	25.8	31.9	32.8
PETRONAS revenue	...	2.2	2.2
Current expenditure	23.4	26.2	26.2
Public saving	2.4	5.7	6.6

... Zero or negligible
Source: Table 6.10 in chapter six.
a. Includes current surpluses of public authorities and PETRONAS revenue.

to about 6 percent of GNP, compared with 2.4 percent during 1971-75 (table 3.11). In assessing these estimates, it is important to keep in mind that the increase of public revenue in relation to GNP has already been substantial.

During the period of the second plan, government borrowed the equivalent of about 8 percent of GNP from domestic and foreign sources. With its current surplus and a small drawdown of assets, it financed a development program equal to about 11 percent of GNP. The analysis in chapter six makes it clear that Malaysia could easily borrow at the same relative levels as in the past without endangering the financial position of the public sector or the external creditworthiness of the country. For its financial resources, the public sector is projected to have more saving available—the equivalent of at least 3 to 4 percent of GNP more saving— during 1976-85 than 1971-75.

An important element in these projections is PETRONAS. It has been estimated that the current surplus of PETRONAS would provide more than half of the additional saving available during 1976-85, or the equivalent of about 2 percent of GNP (see chapter six). This estimate is important because there may be a tendency to earmark such funds for further petroleum-related investments. Although developing the petro-chemical industry in Malaysia may turn out to be a sound investment, the size of the investment should not be determined by the amount PETRONAS receives in oil revenue. The obvious danger of tying oil reve-nue to the development of the petrochemical industry is over-investment in petrochemicals and underinvestment elsewhere. One way to ensure that this does not happen is to include PETRONAS revenue in the normal review and allocation procedures of the public sector. That would not only help determine the appropriate level of invest-ment in petrochemicals; it might also prevent a situation in which some parts of the economy would have surplus resources but others would not be able to undertake worthwhile projects because of shortages in resources.

Summary

Two conclusions emerge from the foregoing review of Malaysia's prospects for physical and financial resources. First, significantly more resources are likely to be available than were expected in 1975, when the third plan was drafted. Second, the slower physical growth of a number of primary agricultural commodities will make it difficult for Malaysia to maintain the historical rate of agricultural growth of 6 per-cent. Although the production of other agricultural commodities could offset this possible slowdown to some extent, it will be difficult, even with a further expansion of public investment in agriculture, to achieve a growth rate of 6 percent. This likely slowdown reinforces the need for rapid expansion in the manufacturing sector. As will be shown in more detail later in this chapter, the initial resource surplus, together with the prospective revenue from exports and the public sector, will enable the financing of such a rapid expansion.

Rapid Growth in Manufacturing

Malaysia has provided a fundamentally attractive environment for investors. The stability of government, the freedom in politics, the minimal interference by government, the ample availability of finances, the financial creditworthiness of the country, the substantial base of infrastructure and natural resources, the plentiful supply of relatively well-educated labor, the comparative honesty and efficiency of government administration—all these factors were significant in Malaysia's rapid industrial growth during the 1966–75 period.

The continuation of rapid industrial growth, particularly in labor-intensive manufacturing, is essential to attaining the objectives of the New Economic Policy. This growth will nevertheless have to be achieved in a somewhat different context from that in the past. First, although the shift from import substitution to export-led manufacturing growth has begun, further shifts in the pattern of growth will become increasingly necessary as the more obvious areas of import substitution are exhausted. Second, the growth of manufactured exports will be from a much larger base than in the past. Given the signs of increasing protectionism in developed countries, particularly in textiles, achieving rapid growth of exports will require an increasingly aggressive export strategy. Third, substantial technological changes are taking place in electronics, one of Malaysia's principal export industries. Fourth, the industrial sector will be required to accommodate much greater Malay participation than in the past. This sector thus deserves the continuing attention of government to ensure that the policy framework promotes vigorous growth. [14]

Rapid growth in the manufacturing sector—say, 12 to 13 percent a year—will require a substantial increase in investment in manufactur-

14. A more detailed discussion of issues meriting attention is presented in chapter seven.

ing. Government does not collect and publish data on manufacturing investment alone, but such indicators as investment approvals by the Federal Industrial Development Authority and imports of capital goods destined for the manufacturing sector strongly suggest that manufacturing investment significantly declined after 1974. On the basis of these indicators, it is estimated that manufacturing investment may have dropped from an average rate of about 4.5 percent of GDP during 1970–74 to about 3 percent by 1976. Because the manufacturing sector was growing faster than GDP during the 1970–76 period, the decline in manufacturing investment relative to manufacturing output was greater. Manufacturing investment fell from an average of more than 30 percent of value added in manufacturing during 1971–74 to less than 18 percent in 1976.

The reasons for this decline cannot be precisely determined. The international recession in 1975, the uncertainty engendered by the introduction of the Industrial Coordination Act and the Petroleum Development Act in 1975, the possible deterioration in the competitive edge of Malaysia's manufacturing industry, and the cyclical decline following the abnormally high level of investment in 1974—all these factors may have acted, in isolation or in concert, to depress investment. Whatever the reasons for the decline, it is clear that a substantial recovery in manufacturing investment is needed to achieve the planned growth rate in manufacturing of 12.6 percent a year through 1990. For example, if it is assumed that the incremental capital-output ratio were to remain unchanged, the continuation of the 1976 level of manufacturing investment at about 3 percent of GDP would generate annual growth in manufacturing output of less than 8 percent. Alternatively, to achieve the 12.6 percent target for growth of manufacturing output, investment would have to recover quickly to about 5 percent of GDP.

In this light a high priority will have to be given to ensuring a favorable climate for private investment. One element of such a climate is maintaining Malaysia's competitive international position in external and domestic markets. The manufacturing sector in Malaysia, as in other resource-rich countries, faces an exchange rate that tends to be largely determined by exports of such natural resources as tin, rubber, and petroleum. Those exports clearly exert an upward pressure on the exchange rate. That may be desirable for controlling inflation, but the risk is that other exports, such as manufactured exports, may be put at a competitive disadvantage. This possible tradeoff must be considered in the implementation of policies designed to promote rapid employment growth in manufacturing and to move simultaneously toward external equilibrium. Expansionary fiscal measures, designed to accelerate development programs and stimulate private investment, are possible mechanisms for circumventing that tradeoff without artificially controlling the movements of exchange rates. Such measures would increase the demand for imports, reduce external surpluses, and improve employment prospects.

It also is important that the enforcement of restructuring objectives does not undermine business confidence and profits. Aware of this problem, government acted in 1976 and 1977 to strengthen the confidence of investors. Foremost among these actions were amendments to the Petroleum Development Act and the Industrial Coordination Act. Government also emphasized that it will be flexible in implementing the programs for restructuring. Such flexibility is essential because the targets for restructuring employment and equity are ambitious. As is indicated later in this chapter, they can be achieved only if the growth of the manufacturing sector is rapid.

Policymakers are in a precarious situation in this regard. Rapid growth is essential to a successful program of restructuring. At the same time the trickling down of the benefits of unfettered rapid growth to Malays is unlikely to satisfy social demands for racial equity. Government is thus in the position of having to steer growth so that Malays derive substantial benefits and concurrently to maintain an attractive environment for investors, many of whom are non-Malay. The dangers inherent in this process are considerable. Attempts to force the pace of restructuring could result in less investment by non-Malays and in slower growth, which would be self-defeating. On the other hand, government has a clear mandate to achieve substantial restructuring in the economy by 1990. To a large extent government will have to proceed by trial and error, because there are few, if any, successful precedents to follow. There nevertheless appears to be some potential for softening the costs of restructuring to non-Malays and for simultaneously pursuing the principal restructuring objectives. For example, it may be possible to give poor non-Malays greater access to land in development schemes and to institute a system of fiscal incentives geared to promoting the restructuring of equity and employment.

As the discussion in chapter seven indicates, it may be appropriate for government to modify the current system of fiscal incentives to encourage labor intensity and promote the restructuring of employment. A study of fiscal incentives by the Economic Planning Unit concluded that tax holidays are perverse because they are worth more the higher the level of pretax profits: that is, the less they are needed.

It also concluded that the alternative forms of fiscal incentives introduced in 1968 are largely ineffective because under most conditions they are less attractive than the tax holiday to investors.[15] In that same study is a proposal for a new form of incentive that would base tax relief partly on the value and partly on the labor-intensity of investment. Such an incentive would have neither the perversity nor the strong capital-using bias of the tax holiday; it also would provide a suitable basis for experimentation. This reform could go even further. Because protection makes fiscal incentives largely redundant, the tax holiday could be restricted to the encouragement of export promotion and regional location. Government might also design fiscal incentives to promote more strongly the restructuring of employment.

Associated with the restructuring effort is the need to encourage Malay entrepreneurship. Entrepreneurial development requires increasing emphasis on the development of small-scale industry: the smallest firms, particularly Malay firms, must be helped to grow larger; entrepreneurs in rural areas, where the Malay population is concentrated, must be helped to develop. The public agency having the broadest mandate in this area is MARA, which is involved in lending, purchasing equity "in trust," and providing technical assistance and professional services to Malay small-scale businesses. A study by the Economic Planning Unit on bumiputra participation in business recommended, among other things, the strengthening of loan programs, technical assistance, and advisory services.[16] The general development of small-scale industry could also benefit from efforts to minimize the adverse impact of the direct controls of the Industrial Coordination Act on smaller firms—larger firms always are more capable of dealing with red tape and influencing administrative decisionmaking. Government has already moved in this direction by substantially increasing the minimum size of firms that must restructure their equity. The development of Malay small-scale industry requires striking a balance: if preferences to Malays in interest rates and lending conditions are too great, lending programs may fail in their aim to create Malay small-scale businesses that are viable in the long term. Moderate margins of preference, together with an intensified program of technical assistance, are thus to be preferred.

---

15. Economic Planning Unit, "Tax Incentives for Industry" (Kuala Lumpar, 1974; processed).

16. Economic Planning Unit, "Bumiputra Participation in Business: Report on a Research Project" (Kuala Lumpur, 1975; processed).

Public Programs to Reduce Poverty

In addition to ensuring rapid growth in the private sector, the public sector has an essential role in achieving the objectives of the New Economic Policy. First, by virtue of the public sector's large size—it now is spending the equivalent of more than a third of GDP—it will continue to have an important effect on the performance of the economy. Second, a large part of the additional resources available, beyond those forecast in the third plan, will accrue directly to the public sector. Third, the flexibility of the public sector to attack directly the problems of poverty and racial imbalances is much greater than that of the private sector.

Expanding the Development Program

One possible response to the greater availability of resources in the public sector is to expand the development program. At first glance, there is a strong justification for such an increase, because the development program provides one of the most direct ways to assist groups in poverty. The emphasis on such assistance in the third plan is evident in the allocation of 38 percent of expenditure to programs directed toward groups in poverty, the increased allocations to assist traditional smallholders in agriculture and to housing, and the relative increases in allocations to the poorest states. Some of the additional resources available to government could also be devoted to enlarging the programs for infrastructure. Those programs, in addition to providing the basic infrastructure for a rapidly growing economy, can have a significant effect on poverty by providing such services as rural roads, water supply, and rural electrification and by creating jobs in the construction stage. Furthermore the expansion of public spending can have some significant second-order effects on the growth of incomes.

Projects that directly benefit the poor obviously deserve high priority in any expansion of the development program. In view of the substantial amount of undeveloped land in Malaysia, an expansion of the land development program would ease the problems of unemployment and poverty. According to the third plan, government is to develop about 3.2 million acres of land during 1976–90. If the average allotment to each family settled is 10 acres, this land would eventually accommodate about 300,000 families. But because of lags between development and settlement and the higher acreages allotted to settlers during 1971–75, actual settlement during 1976–90 would be closer to 235,000 families and would provide employment to about 350,000 persons. Those jobs are equivalent to about 15 percent of the new employment projected for the period.

Expanding the program of land development would therefore have a significant effect. For example, a 50 percent increase in the current rate of development could create an additional 150,000 jobs and directly reduce the number of poor households by about 100,000, a figure equivalent to about 10 percent of households in poverty in 1975. The indirect effects would also be significant. Although an expansion of this magnitude would appear within the overall estimate of land available in Peninsular Malaysia, it is not certain what the quality of this land is or whether an even larger expansion could be accommodated. The land survey government is currently conducting—to determine precisely the amount and carrying capacity of land still available—should answer these questions. An expansion of the program and its benefits might also be achieved through other types of settlement arrangements—for example, by increasing settler participation, which government is now trying on a pilot basis.

Land development will remain an important vehicle for raising rural incomes, but expanded programs to assist traditional smallholders are essential for raising the incomes of the large number of poor in households that will not be resettled. One of the principal means of reducing the high incidence of poverty among rubber smallholders is the government program to replant rubber trees with high-yielding clones. The target in the third plan for rubber replanting is 450,000 acres. If this target is reached, about 300,000 acres would still be under old, low-yielding trees in 1980. If the Rubber Industry Smallholders Development Authority (RISDA) were able to expand its capacity to undertake a larger program, the added reduction in poverty could be significant. Other programs to assist traditional smallholders appear to warrant expansion as well: providing extension services and credit, particularly in rice production; developing and promoting suitable intercrops for coconut farmers; creating small-scale systems of irrigation; improving research for the development of better seeds and planting material.

An important complement to these efforts would be an expanded program of family planning. Although little can be done to alter the growth of the labor force during the 1976–90 period, further reductions in fertility would reduce the dependency burden of the population during this period. In the longer term, when Malaysia begins to encounter constraints on land available for development, such reductions in fertility would lessen the pressure of absorbing a rapidly growing labor force into productive employment. Malaysia has already made progress in reducing fertility; the birth rate declined from 39 per thousand in 1960 to 31 in 1975. The effect of this reduction has nevertheless been muted by successful efforts to reduce mortality. As a result, although Malaysia's birth and death rates are substantially lower than those for the average of "middle-income countries," its population growth rate of about 2.6 percent a year is only slightly lower than that average.[17] Even though Malaysia has a low death rate, the young age structure of the population and the fairly high rates of infant and toddler mortality imply that continuing socioeconomic development, particularly the expansion of programs for health, nutrition, and education, could accelerate the rate of population growth. Thus, if the targeted reduction to a 2 percent rate of population growth is to be achieved by 1985, an expansion of the program to reduce fertility is warranted, particularly in disadvantaged communities and regions.

In addition to accelerating the programs to increase the productivity and incomes of the poor, government might consider more direct measures to improve the access of the poor to services satisfying their basic needs. Substantial progress has already been made in this regard, in large part through government efforts to increase food output and the physical supply of basic services. For example, most observers generally agree that hunger is not a significant problem in Malaysia. The public school system provides ready access to all students at the primary level, and attendance essentially is universal. Compared with other developing countries, secondary school enrollments in Malaysia are high at 40 percent. In health care, standards of preventive health are high compared with other developing countries, and the need for curative care of most of the population is largely met through the public system at little private cost. Despite these achievements, serious problems persist. At every level of education, especially at higher levels, the enrollment ratio of the poor is less than that of the rest of the population. In addition, the costs of education borne by the poor constitute a burden on their limited incomes. For such public utilities as electricity, water supply, and sewage disposal, the access of the poor is minimal, and low income appears to be a principal constraint on consumption.

Housing is another basic need not being adequately provided to the poor. In urban areas the pressing problem is overcrowding. The third plan thus set an ambitious target of providing about 115,000 low-cost

17. World Bank, *World Development Report, 1978* (New York: Oxford University Press, 1978), table 15.

units. An important element of the housing program is the objective of reducing the unit cost of houses financed through the Ministry of Housing and Village Development from M$17,700 during the period of the second plan to M$7,700 during the period of the third plan. But even this reduction would still leave houses substantially beyond the means of the lower 40 percent of the population—they cannot even afford houses that cost M$3,000. Although it is essential that government continue its efforts to reduce the unit cost of housing, the provision of capital subsidies for low-cost housing could also be considered.

Such housing projects and programs would primarily affect the urban poor. In rural areas, where most of the poor live, providing housing is not as important. The 1970 census showed that, in relation to the number of units and overcrowding, there was little problem. Instead the issue is upgrading quality by improving access to water, electricity, and toilet facilities: 69 percent of dwellings in rural areas were found to be substandard in 1970. The discussion in chapter five indicates that low income seriously constrains the consumption of utilities and that some element of subsidy would be required for the poor to have real access to these services. By providing some type of financial assistance to defray part of the cost, government could substantially improve the access of the poor to basic services. The illustrative calculations in chapter five indicate that significant improvements could be achieved at a cost that is within the financial scope of government.

Expanding Implementation Capacity

Although a strong case can be made for a general increase in the development program and for particular emphasis on projects to reduce poverty, serious constraints are likely to arise in identifying, preparing, and implementing certain kinds of project. Government has been investigating the general implementation capacity for construction and building projects, which constitute about 45 percent of the public development program under the third plan. It has identified problems in financial and manpower planning at the state level and in the supply of material resources. Because the scarcity of qualified manpower in the public sector appears to be a serious constraint on expanding the development program, government might consider short-term measures to break this bottleneck. One possibility, which would not conflict with policies for restructuring in the public sector, would be to make more use of the private sector, in which the skill shortage may not be as acute. That could be done, for example, through fixed-term consultan-

cy contracts until vacancies in the public sector could be filled by qualified Malays.

The Implementation and Coordination Unit in the Prime Minister's
Department is responsible, as its name suggests, for coordinating development activities, identifying deficiencies, and overseeing the implementation of the New Economic Policy. Toward this end, the unit is
setting up a computerized system to monitor the physical and financial
performance of projects and public corporations. The monitoring of
scarce resources, such as skilled manpower, is not included, but it may
be in the future. Although these are steps in the right direction, the
importance of expanding the public development program warrants the
introduction of measures to overcome problems already identified.
When the immediate expansion of programs is impossible, it is important that a concrete, phased plan be developed to increase the capacity
for planning and implementation. Plans for the various areas and sectors should then be integrated with a national plan for the expansion of
development planning and implementation capacity in the public sector, a plan which should be monitored as closely as the financial plans.
If this is not done, implementation capacity may remain indefinitely as
the binding constraint. Meanwhile it is important to inform the implementing agencies when additional funds are available so that they can
immediately begin to increase their capacity for larger programs.

Feasibility and Effectiveness of Alternative Growth Strategies

To assess the feasibility of sustained rapid growth, a simple macroeconomic model was constructed to attempt to capture the main economic relations in the Malaysian economy.[18] Three growth paths were considered: moderate growth, rapid growth, and accelerated growth. The
moderate growth path was introduced earlier in this chapter to sketch
the effect on the New Economic Policy's objectives of a lower growth
rate than forecast in the third plan. The central assumption in this path
is that manufacturing investment would not recover from its estimated

18. A more detailed discussion of the possible effects of alternative investment scenarios on growth, employment, and the objectives of the New Economic Policy is presented in appendix A. In that discussion the path of moderate growth is referred to as
alternative I, that of rapid growth as alternative II, and that of accelerated growth as
alternative III.

low level in 1976. The rate of GDP growth of about 5 to 6 percent a year under this path would make it virtually impossible to attain the targets of the New Economic Policy. Consequently the growth paths that merit consideration as alternatives for government are rapid growth and accelerated growth.

Under the rapid growth path, income would increase about 8 percent a year. The principal investment assumption in this alternative is that manufacturing investment would recover by 1980 and continue to grow vigorously thereafter. In addition, government would accelerate its current and development expenditures, such that public consumption in 1990 is 30 percent higher, and public investment is 20 percent higher, than the levels implied in the perspective plan. This alternative would imply growth of manufacturing output of 10 to 11 percent a year during 1976–90. The rate is somewhat lower than that specified in the perspective plan, but it would be compensated for by the effects of higher public spending and better terms of trade. The growth of employment would also be somewhat lower than that specified. Although not enabling full achievement of the numerical targets of the New Economic Policy, this alternative would provide for a considerable degree of racial restructuring and poverty reduction.

The accelerated growth path projects income growth of 9 percent a year and assumes even faster growth in manufacturing investment and output than that under the rapid growth path. Rough calculations in appendix A indicate that it is probable under this alternative that the targets for reducing poverty and restructuring society would be fully met. Manufacturing output would grow at 13 percent a year, or about the same as the rate targeted in the perspective plan. Achieving this output would require an acceleration in manufacturing investment to an average growth rate of 17 percent a year during 1976–90. This task is formidable. It may be constrained by an insufficient demand for output, because it assumes that Malaysian manufactured exports will perform somewhat better than the average for developing countries over the period to 1990. Although this alternative requires a favorable international environment, and therefore is generally beyond the control of domestic policies, its resource implications are discussed here because of the uncertainties in projecting world demand, because unforeseen opportunities may arise, and because this alternative comes closest to the growth rate targeted for manufacturing in the perspective plan.

The detailed projections for the three alternatives are presented in appendix A. A principal conclusion to be drawn from the projections is that resources should be sufficient to finance a high rate of economic growth. This comfortable resource position is largely a result of the resource surplus in the base year, 1976. Under the rapid growth path, which projects an income growth rate of almost 8 percent a year, the estimated investment requirement in 1990 would be about 28 percent of GDP, compared with about 21 percent in 1976.[19] Generally an increase of this magnitude in the investment rate would imply a substantial increase in domestic saving which, if not forthcoming, would constrain the achievement of rapid growth. In Malaysia, however, this constraint is not serious because the domestic rate of saving in 1976 was almost 30 percent of GDP, more than enough to finance the higher level of investment. The model projects a further small increase in domestic saving, largely because of an anticipated increase in the saving by the public sector, including PETRONAS. But this increase clearly is not necessary to finance the targeted investment level. In fact, considering Malaysia's excellent potential for raising external loans, even a significant fall in domestic saving would not require cutting back investment, because that fall could, if necessary, be compensated for by making greater use of foreign resources.

Malaysia should also have enough foreign exchange to finance the imports required for rapid growth in income and investment. This conclusion, as that for saving, is primarily based on the large surplus in the current account of the balance of payments in 1976, a surplus equivalent to more than 6 percent of GDP. Under the rapid growth path, this large initial surplus, together with a projected rate of export growth of about 6.5 percent a year, would allow imports to grow slightly faster than GDP and still enable the current account to be in approximate balance in 1990. The implied import elasticity should allow for the needed shift in expenditure toward investment, which usually is more import-intensive than other expenditure. Judging by Malaysia's historical import elasticities, however, this estimate, if anything, is high. Thus the rapid and accelerated growth paths should not be constrained by a deficiency either of saving or of foreign exchange to purchase the required imports.

The effect of the rapid and accelerated growth paths on the numerical targets of the New Economic Policy is also discussed in detail in appendix A. In general, the calculations confirm the importance of rapid growth, particularly in manufacturing, for achieving those targets. The analysis of the moderate growth path in the first part of this chapter indicated that low rates of manufacturing and GDP growth would

---

19. That investment requirement is in constant 1970 prices.

result in a substantial shortfall in meeting the targets in the perspective plan for reducing poverty and restructuring society. On the other hand, the opportunities for income growth and employment under an aggressive growth strategy would enable substantial reductions in poverty and substantial restructuring. The rough calculations in appendix A indicate that the rapid and accelerated growth paths would result in the approximate achievement of the targets. The somewhat higher projections for growth in manufacturing, GDP, and income under accelerated growth would result in a somewhat better performance in reducing poverty and restructuring society than those under rapid growth and in some respects those under the perspective plan. The character of the calculations—they are approximate—would argue against reading too much into small differences between the various estimates. Nevertheless these estimates clearly confirm the need for achieving growth and investment rates of this broad order of magnitude to meet the targets of the New Economic Policy. They thus confirm that the government's development strategy of sustaining rapid economic growth is appropriate.

Summary Assessment

Given the internal consistency of the government's plan, the logical question is, Can it be achieved? Answering this question with certainty is difficult. The prospects for achieving rapid growth are in many respects favorable. Resources should be sufficient to finance rapid growth. The prospects for agricultural growth of 4 to 5 percent a year are relatively firm, given the past investments, the continuing availability of land, and the government's proposed investment program. The prospects for manufacturing growth, the linchpin of rapid economic growth, nevertheless are mixed. Malaysia does provide a fundamentally attractive economy for investment. As a result, an excellent record of manufacturing growth was established during the 1966–75 period. But new elements may somewhat alter the prospects for continuing this record. Although Malaysia's manufacturing growth will increasingly have to shift from import substitution to the expansion of exports and domestic demand, the external environment appears to be less hospitable than in the past. There is, moreover, evidence that the rate of manufacturing investment declined in the mid-1970s, though it is not clear whether cyclical or structural factors have been at work. Cyclical factors are largely beyond Malaysia's control. But certain domestic factors, in part responsible for the downturn in investment, can be ameliorated by appropriate government action.

What might constitute such appropriate government action? Suggestions have already been made about maintaining the competitiveness of Malaysia's external position, flexibly implementing the restructuring policies, and possibly offering financial incentives for the restructuring of employment. But a thorough analysis of the manufacturing sector—more thorough than that undertaken here—is needed to design a policy framework that facilitates the greatest exploitation of opportunities. Such an analysis would cover infrastructure requirements, restructuring policies, financial and other incentives, the possibility of an expanded public role for the sector, and disaggregated trends of wages, prices, and investment.

Regardless of the future performance of the manufacturing sector, an expanded public program is warranted, especially in areas that directly reduce poverty. First, even under the more optimistic scenarios for manufacturing growth, there still will be 2 to 3 million persons in poverty in 1990. Second, resources will be available to the public sector for undertaking such an expansion. Third, public investment offers greater potential than private investment for reducing poverty among certain hardcore poverty groups unlikely to share in the benefits of rapid growth.

What, then, can government do? Again, a number of suggestions have been offered about promising areas for expanding the programs to reduce poverty. These include accelerating the program of land development, increasing the participation of settlers in that development, broadening the program of rubber replanting by smallholders, expanding the extension and credit services for rice cultivators, and intensifying the efforts to promote intercropping by coconut smallholders. In addition to investments intended to raise incomes by increasing productivity, a significant reduction in poverty could be achieved by improving the access of the poor to such basic services as housing, education, electricity, and water supply. The analysis in chapter five suggests that access could be considerably improved by providing subsidies to reduce the income burden of such services on the poor. Extending the physical availability of such services is also needed, particularly in the Northeast. Clearly a systematic analysis of strategies and programs for eradicating poverty and restructuring society is needed to provide a solid basis for expanding the long-term investment program. At the same time, however, a concerted effort must be made to improve the capacity of the public sector to identify, prepare, and implement projects to reduce poverty.

FOUR

Willem Bussink

Employment
and Income Distribution
in Peninsular Malaysia

MOST OF THE DEVELOPMENTS underlying Malaysia's problems with poverty and the identification of race with economic function occurred during the later part of British colonial rule. With the expansion of tin
mining and rubber cultivation in the late nineteenth and early twentieth centuries, the immigration of Chinese and Indians accelerated. The
importance of this immigration shows up in rapid population growth:
the peninsular population is estimated to have been 250,000 in 1800, 2
million in 1900, and 3.7 million in 1930. Immigration slowed down
only during and after the depression of the 1930s. Consequently the
proportion of Chinese residents born in the Peninsula increased from
30 percent in 1931 to 76 percent in 1957; that of Indian residents from
21 percent to 66 percent.

The large-scale immigration of workers was encouraged by the British because Malays generally did not participate in the emerging modern economy. Various reasons have been suggested to explain this lack
of participation: they range from low motivation among Malays to bad
conditions in the tin mines and rubber estates. Whatever the reasons,
the result was a concentration of Malays in rural areas, especially in
smallholder agriculture. In contrast, non-Malays came to dominate the
urban sector. And as smallholder agriculture increasingly lagged behind the modern sector, poverty increasingly became a phenomenon
affecting the Malays.

Low rates of immigration and natural increase during the depression
and the Second World War brought the population growth rate down

This chapter discusses issues of employment and the distribution of income in Peninsular Malaysia alone; limitations of data preclude a similar review of the situation in
Sabah and Sarawak. Because the literature on these subjects already is substantial, no
comprehensive review is attempted here. Instead the chapter summarizes work by the
World Bank in these areas over the last several years.

substantially. After the war, mortality rates in Peninsular Malaysia began to drop dramatically, fertility rates to increase. Thus, by the mid-1950s, the population's rate of natural increase probably was about 3.5 percent. Only then did fertility begin to decline and the natural growth of the population to subside. Because such demographic changes determine the natural growth of the labor force with a time lag of some fifteen to twenty years, that natural growth accelerated in the 1960s and most of the 1970s.

Against this demographic background, international economic developments were not favorable for Malaysia in the 1960s. Although the production of rubber grew rapidly, there was a substantial fall in rubber prices. The modern rubber sector was able to compensate for this by rapidly replacing old rubber trees with new, high-yielding varieties. For smallholders this replanting was more difficult because of their meager resources and poor access to credit. In addition, because of the price squeeze, rubber estates substantially cut back their work forces. That cutback, together with accelerated growth of the labor force and only moderate growth in real incomes, led to rising unemployment, which in turn must have kept real wage levels down. It is widely believed that these unfavorable developments led to substantial emigration. Because average real incomes in the low-income agricultural sector showed little growth and because the overrepresentation of Malays in agriculture increased, the distribution of income may have become less equal during the 1960s.

The direct evidence for such a deterioration is not conclusive. To identify broad trends in the distribution of income, a number of researchers have compared the household budget survey of 1957–58 and the postenumeration survey conducted in conjunction with the 1970 census.[1] If comparability were not a problem, it would be clear that the distribution of income deteriorated substantially between 1957 and

1. Of two other principal surveys, the 1967–68 sample survey of households counted only cash incomes, making it wholly uncomparable. The 1973–74 survey of households had not been fully analyzed at the time of this writing, but preliminary analysis of this source has shown patterns that are broadly similar to those of the postenumeration survey. Within this broad similarity, the distribution of income appears to have become somewhat more equal by 1973, probably as a result, at least in part, of substantially higher real prices for rubber. Department of Statistics, *Household Budget Survey of the Federation of Malaya 1957–58, Report* (Kuala Lumpur, n.d.); idem, *Socio-Economic Sample Survey of Households—Malaysia, 1967–68* (Kuala Lumpur, 1970); idem, "1970 Census Post Enumeration Survey" (Kuala Lumpur, n.d.; unpublished computer tapes); idem, "Malaysia Household Income and Expenditure Survey, 1973–74" (Kuala Lumpur, n.d.; processed).

1970: the Gini coefficient increased from 0.37 to 0.51. Because the lack of comparability has not been easy to establish—the published report on the earlier survey is deficient in such information as sample coverage and the definition of income—this conclusion has been widely drawn. But on the basis of a detailed review of unpublished files on the 1957–58 survey, Anand concludes that there was a substantial bias toward equality in that survey.[2] In his view the direct evidence is insufficient either to accept or reject the contention that the distribution of income deteriorated in Peninsular Malaysia between 1957 and 1970.

Structure of Employment and Income in 1970

The World Bank, in close cooperation with the Malaysian govern- ment, constructed a social accounting matrix for Malaysia for 1970. This accounting framework integrates conventional national accounts with data on the creation and distribution of income.[3] Although the data have limitations, a principal one being that information on the distribution of income has been forced into consistency with the nation- al accounts, it is safe to assume that the sketch of the economy they provide roughly conforms to reality.

For a number of principal sectors, table 4.1 provides information on employment and value added, which is disaggregated into labor and two kinds of capital. This information enables, among other things, a comparison of value added and labor incomes per worker in various sectors.[4] The sectoral differences are clear. For example, agriculture provided nearly 50 percent of total employment, but less than 30 per- cent of value added and less than 25 percent of labor incomes. As would be expected, incorporated business capital was concentrated in some agricultural subsectors, mainly in estates, and in the modern sectors of the economy. Labor incomes per worker, including the self-employed, show great variations, which persist even if unincorporated business income is added. It also is clear that Malay workers in the private sector

2. For a detailed account see Sudhir Anand, *Inequality and Poverty in Malaysia: Measure- ment and Decomposition* (New York: Oxford University Press, forthcoming), ch. 2.

3. The discussion in this section centers on the distribution of value added, by sector and factor, and its link to employment and labor incomes. For a full discussion of the method and results, and much more detail on the material presented here, see Graham Pyatt and Jeffrey I. Round, "The Distribution of Income and Social Accounts: A Study of Malaysia in 1970" (Washington, D.C.: World Bank, 1978, processed).

4. The study of Pyatt and Round provides information on labor incomes by educa- tional level and sector for rural and urban areas, and a breakdown over more sectors.

Table 4.1. *Structure of Employment and Income, by Sector, Peninsular Malaysia, 1970*

Sector	Thousands of workers	Value added (millions of Malaysian dollars)			
		Total	Labor	Unincorporated business capital	Incorporated business capital
Rubber	724	1,168	743	237	188
Palm oil	44	245	74	6	165
Rice	296	303	159	144	—
Other agriculture	229	573	330	174	68
Forestry and fishing	113	471	161	64	246
Mining	85	579	326	24	229
Manufacturing	265	1,124	644	77	403
Utilities and construction	94	579	273	29	277
Trade, transport, and private services	595	2,021	1,386	493	142
Health and education	109	585	567	18	—
Defense and other government services	240	727	727	—	—
Total or average	2,794	8,375[b]	5,390	1,267	1,718

— Not applicable.

Source: Graham Pyatt and Jeffrey I. Round, "The Distribution of Income and Social Accounts: A Study of Malaysia in 1970" (Washington, D.C.: World Bank, 1978; processed).

were heavily concentrated in the low-income agricultural sectors; non-Malays dominated the other sectors. There was some compensation for Malays in their heavy representation in the public sector, in which incomes were higher than average. But that sector provided only an eighth of employment.

Characteristics of the Distribution of Personal Income in 1970

A basic though somewhat outdated source on the distribution of income in Peninsular Malaysia is the postenumeration survey of 1970, a large sample survey covering about 25,000 households.[5] It is not specif-

5. The discussion in this section is primarily based on Anand, *Inequality and Poverty in Malaysia.*

| Value added per worker[a] (Malaysian dollars) | | | | |
Total	Labor	Labor and unincorporated business capital	Percentage of Malay workers in total	Sector
1,610	1,030	1,350	56	Rubber
5,570	1,680	1,820	61	Palm oil
1,020	540	1,020	84	Rice
2,500	1,440	2,200	82	Other agriculture
4,170	1,420	1,990	60	Forestry and fishing
6,810	3,840	4,120	23	Mining
4,240	2,430	2,720	29	Manufacturing
6,160	2,900	3,210	26	Utilities and construction
3,400	2,330	3,160	28	Trade, transport, and private services
5,370	5,200	5,370	61	Health and education
3,030	3,030	3,030	65	Defense and other government services
3,230	1,930	2,380	48	Total or average

a. Rounded to the nearest ten dollars.
b. Value added in the economy was M$9,038 million; it included M$663 million for housing, a separate category (without employment) in the social accounting matrix.

ically an income survey, and that may have affected the accuracy of information on incomes. The data were collected in interviews and may therefore suffer from lapses in recall, especially for income components which vary seasonally. Although data for eleven components of income were entered on the questionnaire, this detail was lost in transferring the data to tape. In addition, the prices at which payments in kind and own-consumption of produce were converted into income were largely left to the discretion of respondents. That may have led to significant errors in measurement. Furthermore the average household income falls short of the estimate in the national accounts by some 25 to 29 percent, depending on the way household incomes are derived from those accounts. It is not clear whether this difference biases the income distribution or, if it does, in what direction. The postenumeration survey therefore is not an ideal source for estimating the income distribution in Peninsular Malaysia, but at the time of this writing it was the best source available. It also was the most analyzed.

Distribution of Household Income and Household per Capita Income

Although the household is the unit which spends income, the distribution of household income clearly is not the best indicator for the distribution of economic welfare. Given the variations in household size, household per capita income is a better indicator. It still has some drawbacks, however, because needs can vary according to the age and sex composition of the household and because economies of scale can occur in satisfying such needs as housing. No attempt has been made to correct for these factors, and income inequality may be exaggerated as a result.[6] Nor has an attempt been made to estimate the distribution of real incomes by taking into account the possibility that different groups of consumers, such as those in rural and urban areas, may be paying different prices for their consumption goods.[7]

With the foregoing caveats in mind, the figures in table 4.2 give the main characteristics of the income distribution for households and, by assigning the same average income to all individuals in a household, for individuals. It is clear from the table that the inequality of income in Peninsular Malaysia was substantial in 1970. The richest quintile received about 55 percent of income; the ratio of the income of the richest quintile to that of the poorest was 16 to 1 for households and 13 to 1 for individuals. Chinese households on average had 2.3 times the income of Malay households; Indian households were in between; the small group of other households, comprising such groups as Europeans, Thais, and other Asians, on the average had more than twice the income of Chinese households. The divergence in average income between Chinese and Malays was smaller for individuals than households—2 to 1 compared with 2.3 to 1—because average household size was smaller for Malays. More generally, the correlation between household income

6. There is a negative correlation between the number of small children in a household and its per capita income. Dividing total household income by the number of "adult equivalents," not the number of persons in the household, would lead to a relative improvement of the position of the ppor in the income distribution.

7. No data were available to estimate price differences between various markets in 1970. Data supplied by the Economic Planning Unit suggest that price differences between urban and rural areas may have been as high as 10 percent in the mid-1970s. If this difference existed in 1970, the conclusions of this chapter would need some modification. But given the large weight of the rural sector in the total, rural prices would not differ much from average prices. Consequently the conclusions for rural areas, where most poverty in Malaysia is concentrated, would not materially change.

and household size was strong and positive, and this tended to make the income distribution for individuals somewhat less unequal than that for households.[8]

Although there was significant disparity in average incomes between the racial groups, that disparity was only a fraction of the income ratios between the higher and lower strata of the income distribution. It logically follows, and the figures in table 4.2 confirm, that inequalities were great in the distribution of income within each racial group: the Gini coefficient for Peninsular Malaysia was 0.51, but it still was more than 0.45 for Malays and Chinese, 0.50 for Indians, and 0.70 for others. In other words, although the per capita incomes of Chinese were twice those of Malays, the spread within each racial group was much larger than that between racial groups. This finding leads to another important conclusion. Even if differences in average incomes between racial groups—or between-race inequality—were completely eliminated but relative differences within each group remained the same, the overall income inequality would be only slightly lower.[9] This conclusion in no way diminishes the significance of income inequality between the races, but it does place that inequality in the perspective of a broader problem of general income inequality.

The technical properties of the Gini coefficient do not allow a mathematically consistent decomposition into the components of overall inequality attributable to inequality within groups and that between groups.[10] But an alternative index of income inequality, the Theil index, can be decomposed in a consistent manner.[11] This index indicates that 13 percent of the income inequality in Peninsular Malaysia was attributable to between-race inequality (table 4.3). Within states and within urban and rural groupings, the component of income inequality attributable to between-race inequality also was relatively small.[12] In interpreting such components, however, the large overall income in-

8. This is a tendency, not a rule. For example, the data in table 4.2 show that for Indians and other groups the income distribution for individuals was more unequal than that for households.

9. As Anand has shown, the Gini coefficient of a composite group is at least equal to the weighted average of Gini coefficients of subgroups—in this case 0.46. Anand, *Inequality and Poverty in Malaysia*, ch. 3.

10. A mathematically consistent decomposition is one in which all components are calculated in the same manner, without leaving a residual.

11. Other methods of decomposing income inequality give roughly the same results.

12. The larger component in Negri Sembilan probably is not significant because of the sample size of eleven households for "others" in that state.

Table 4.2. *Indicators of the Distribution of Income, Peninsular Malaysia, 1970*

Category of households or individuals	Sample size (households or individuals)	Average monthly income (Malaysian dollars)	Average household size	Gini coefficient
Household income				
All households	25,025	264	5.34	0.513
Malay households	13,864	172	5.07	0.466
Chinese households	8,004	394	5.82	0.466
Indian households	2,936	304	5.42	0.472
Other households	221	813	4.42	0.667
Household per capita income[a]				
All individuals	134,186	50	—	0.498
Malays	70,474	34	—	0.455
Chinese	46,726	68	—	0.454
Indians	16,010	57	—	0.500
Others	976	185	—	0.707

— Not applicable.
Source: Anand, *Inequality and Poverty in Malaysia.*
a. Calculated by assigning the same average income to all members of a household.

equality should be kept in mind. As for the case in the preceding paragraph, the small component of between-race inequality in overall inequality does not imply that income differences between races are necessarily small in an absolute sense.

The figures in table 4.3 on the level and distribution of income by race and state clearly indicate the relative poverty in Kelantan and Trengganu in the northeastern part of the Peninsula and the relative prosperity in the more urbanized states. In general, the higher the average income in a state, the greater the inequality. Nevertheless the Theil breakdown again shows that only a small component of overall income inequality—about 9 percent—was attributable to between-state inequality; within the main racial groups, an even smaller component was attributable to between-state inequality.[13] The equalization of income among races and states, particularly if focused on poverty groups, would no doubt have an effect on the lower income groups. By itself,

13. The exception was the "others" category. At least part of the large regional effect for that category is a statistical artifact caused by the small sample size.

Income share of poorest 20 percent (percent)	Income share of poorest 40 percent (percent)	Income share of richest 20 percent (percent)	Income share of richest 5 percent (percent)	Category of households or individuals
		Household income		
3.5	11.5	55.7	28.3	All households
4.3	13.2	51.6	24.0	Malay households
4.8	13.8	52.6	25.5	Chinese households
5.0	14.8	54.0	28.2	Indian households
0.5	2.2	68.2	26.0	Other households
		Household per capita income[a]		
4.3	12.3	54.8	28.5	All individuals
5.2	14.8	52.2	24.6	Malays
5.3	14.3	52.8	26.8	Chinese
5.0	13.7	56.7	29.5	Indians
0.5	2.3	75.5	31.0	Others

however, such an equalization would not lead to a substantial reduction in overall income inequality.

A breakdown by rural and urban residence and by race yields the same general results: less than 14 percent of overall income inequality was attributable to rural-urban differences in income; for Chinese the proportion was only 6 percent. Of equal significance, interracial disparities were much less in metropolitan towns than elsewhere: average per capita incomes of Chinese and Indians were the same; those of Malays were only 16 percent lower. Over all, the between-race component of inequality was rather small in metropolitan towns—6 percent. It was even less in smaller towns, but it was somewhat larger, about 11 percent, in rural areas. Within the main racial groups, inequality increased from rural areas to towns and metropolitan towns.

Distribution of Income among Earners

When concentrating on the welfare aspects of income, the focus has to be on the household, for it is the unit which spends income. To forge the link to the economy, the emphasis has to shift to earnings—that is, to the number of earners in a household and the distribution of incomes

Table 4.3. *The Distribution of Household per Capita Income, by State, Size of Community, and Race, Peninsular Malaysia, 1970*

State or size of community[a]	Malays	Chinese	Indians	Others	All communities	Between-race component of income inequality (percent)[b]
	Mean monthly income (Malaysian dollars)					
Perlis	26	40	16[c]	10	26	—
Kelantan	25	86	88	24	28	—
Trengganu	29	95	59	294[c]	32	—
Kedah	28	54	38	36	35	—
Johore	33	55	51	210	44	—
Perak	32	62	41	299	47	—
Malacca	35	64	51	77[c]	49	—
Negri Sembilan	33	80	59	854[c]	53	—
Pahang	40	77	74	50[c]	53	—
Penang	37	59	59	341	54	—
Selangor	57	89	73	369	78	—
Average for Peninsular Malaysia	34	68	57	185	50	—
Metropolitan towns[d]	77	92	92	328	92	—
Towns[e]	50	70	56	122	62	—
Rural areas[f]	30	55	44	124	38	—
	Gini coefficient					
Perlis	0.38	0.26	0.07[c]	0.45	0.39	8
Kelantan	0.43	0.47	0.50	0.63	0.47	14
Trengganu	0.42	0.51	0.56	0.66[c]	0.46	16
Kedah	0.40	0.43	0.43	0.50	0.44	12
Johore	0.43	0.39	0.41	0.60	0.44	13
Perak	0.44	0.43	0.42	0.52	0.47	13
Malacca	0.44	0.44	0.48	0.38[c]	0.47	9
Negri Sembilan	0.43	0.43	0.46	0.19[c]	0.49	26
Pahang	0.44	0.38	0.45	0.42[c]	0.46	14
Penang	0.40	0.47	0.48	0.52	0.48	15
Selangor	0.49	0.48	0.56	0.53	0.52	9
Average for Peninsular Malaysia	0.46	0.45	0.50	0.71	0.50	13
Metropolitan towns[d]	0.45	0.49	0.56	0.53	0.51	6
Towns[e]	0.44	0.44	0.49	0.68	0.46	5
Rural areas[f]	0.43	0.40	0.41	0.79	0.45	11

(table continues on the following page)

Table 4.3 *(continued)*

State or size of community[a]	Malays	Chinese	Indians	Others	All communities	Between-race component of income inequality (percent)[b]
Between-state component of income inequality[b] (percent)	8	5	6	48	9	—
Between-community component of income inequality[b] (percent)	12	6	11	13	14	—

— Not applicable.
Source: Anand, *Inequality and Poverty in Malaysia*, ch. 3.
a. States are arranged by average income.
b. According to the Theil index.
c. Based on sample of fewer than fifty households.
d. Metropolitan towns are those with a population of 75,000 or more.
e. With a population between 10,000 and 74,999.
f. With a population of 9,999 or fewer.

among earners. An earner is defined as any person who receives income from any source. Because the postenumeration survey did not differentiate income by source, the number of earners includes those who work, as well as those who receive income from investment, transfers, entrepreneurship, and other sources.

If the inequality of household per capita income is decomposed—into the inequality of income among earners and the inequality of the proportion of earners in the household—it appears that the inequality of income per earner was the larger component of the inequality of household per capita income. Together the two components could "explain" more than the total inequality, but the two components are negatively correlated: higher incomes per earner were generally associated with a lower proportion of earners in the household. This effect was particularly pronounced among Malays. Nevertheless Malays as a group had a lower-than-average proportion of earners, despite their lower-than-average incomes.[14] In any case, the possible secondary effect of an im-

14. This finding may be related to the high proportion of own-account workers, mainly poor farmers, in Malay households and to the possibility that family workers in farm households may not have been classified as income earners.

proved distribution of income among earners on the proportion of earners would nowhere be strong enough to offset a greater equality among
earners. Thus the policy actions that mitigate the inequality of income
among earners should also mitigate the inequality of household per capita income.

The principal characteristics of the distribution of income among
earners were in many ways similar to those of household income or
household per capita income (see table 4.2). The Gini coefficients for

Table 4.4. *Monthly Income per Earner, Gini Coefficient, and Percentage of
Income Inequality Attributable to Income Difference between Groups,
by Race, Size of Community, Employment Status, Occupation,
and Industrial Sector, Peninsular Malaysia, 1970*

Item	Malays	Chinese	Indians	Others	All commu- nities
	Mean monthly income (Malaysian dollars)				
Average for Peninsular Malaysia	118	209	180	574	163
Size of community					
Metropolitan towns	243	256	285	928	267
Towns	170	214	204	419[c]	201
Rural	104	177	137	394	128
Employment status					
Employers	422	769	720	1,772[d]	739
Employees	143	179	168	843	167
Own-account workers	89	235	225	88	134
Others	83	150	160	361[c]	118
Occupation[b]					
Professional and technical workers	319	459	567	1,026	424
Administrative and man- agerial workers	574	740	411	2,659[c]	669
Clerical workers	238	292	289	266[c]	272
Sales workers	118	269	206	316[c]	220
Service workers	172	167	149	665[c]	169
Farmers	84	214	160	55	101
Farm laborers	74	108	99	35[c]	87
Production workers	132	171	180	464[c]	160

racial groups were about the same, as were the proportions of income accruing to those at the top of the income range. Nevertheless the income share of the poorest 20 percent of earners was only 3.3 percent for Malays and 4 percent for Chinese, shares significantly lower than those for household income and household per capita income. This pattern reflects the negative correlation noted earlier between income and the proportion of earners in the household. Another characteristic of the distribution of earnings is that the divergence in the average income of

Malay	Chinese	Indians	Others	All commu-nities	Between-race component of income inequality[a] (percent)	Item
			Gini coefficient			
0.48	0.49	0.47	0.70	0.51	9	Average for Peninsular Malaysia
						Size of community
0.46	0.52	0.52	0.59	0.53	5	Metropolitan towns
0.48	0.49	0.45	0.58[c]	0.49	2	Towns
0.45	0.45	0.39	0.78	0.47	9	Rural
						Employment status
0.68	0.49	0.56	0.33[d]	0.52	3	Employers
0.48	0.45	0.44	0.63	0.48	7	Employees
0.40	0.43	0.51	0.54	0.48	24	Own-account workers
0.51	0.50	0.52	0.62[c]	0.54	11	Others
						Occupation[b]
0.34	0.38	0.49	0.51	0.42	13	Professional and technical workers
0.52	0.48	0.50	0.31[c]	0.53	17	Administrative and managerial workers
0.37	0.36	0.39	0.36[c]	0.37	2	Clerical workers
0.47	0.51	0.52	0.72[c]	0.53	8	Sales workers
0.40	0.49	0.43	0.52[c]	0.46	4	Service workers
0.37	0.43	0.48	0.36	0.42	22	Farmers
0.37	0.31	0.22	0.34[c]	0.33	8	Farm laborers
0.40	0.40	0.30	0.62[c]	0.40	4	Production workers

(table continues on the following pages)

Table 4.4 (*continued*)

Item	Malays	Chinese	Indians	Others	All communities
Mean monthly income (Malaysian dollars)					
Industrial sector[b]					
Agriculture	82	163	124	50	95
Agricultural products	81	139	114	997[c]	103
Mining	220	221	183	1,640[d]	223
Manufacturing	104	190	178	762[c]	165
Construction	200	212	181	194[d]	205
Public utilities	194	302	243	787[d]	232
Commerce	129	290	231	637[c]	238
Transport	185	225	230	512[c]	211
Services	242	266	278	951	268
Between states	—	—	—	—	—
Between communities of different size	—	—	—	—	—
Between employment status	—	—	—	—	—
Between occupations	—	—	—	—	—
Between industrial sectors	—	—	—	—	—

— Not applicable.
n.a. Not available.
Source: Anand, *Inequality and Poverty in Malaysia*, ch. 6.
a. According to the Theil index.

earners between Chinese and Malays was less (1.8 to 1) than that for household per capita income (2 to 1) and household income (2.3 to 1). Again, this pattern is related to the relatively low proportion of earners reported in Malay households. As a result, the component of inequality attributable to between-race inequality was smaller for earners' incomes than for household per capita income—9 percent compared with 13 percent. In fact, the components of between-group inequality for all the breakdowns in table 4.3 were smaller for earners's incomes than for household per capita income: those for earners' incomes seldom reached 10 percent. For metropolitan towns there was only a 5 percent divergence in average earnings between Chinese and Malays (table 4.4). The divergence just noted—1.8 to 1 between Chinese and Malay earners— therefore was principally linked to the larger proportion of Chinese in urban areas, where income levels are higher.

Malay	Chinese	Indians	Others	All communities	Between-race component of income inequality[a] (percent)	Item
				Gini coefficient		
						Industrial sector[b]
0.39	0.45	0.44	0.38	0.43	13	Agriculture
0.36	0.38	0.30	0.67[c]	0.38	17	Agricultural products
0.36	0.41	0.28	0.29[d]	0.40	7	Mining
0.49	0.51	0.40	0.57[c]	0.52	8	Manufacturing
0.41	0.41	0.25	0.14[d]	0.39	0	Construction
0.23	0.244	0.36	0.27[d]	0.34	10	Public utilities
0.47	0.52	0.53	0.68[c]	0.54	9	Commerce
0.34	0.30	0.32	0.55[c]	0.33	6	Transport
0.43	0.50	0.55	0.59[c]	0.39	7	Services
				Between-group component of income inequality[a] (percent)		
9	3	5	n.a.	8	—	Between states
9	3	11	9	10	—	Between communities of different sizes
8	18	7	28	12	—	Between employment status
37	25	35	60	32	—	Between occupations
27	7	14	32	16	—	Between industrial sectors

b. Because of incomplete information, some observations had to be excluded from these breakdowns.

c. Based on sample of ten to forty-nine earners.

d. Based on sample of fewer than ten earners.

If location, even in combination with race, cannot contribute much to the explanation of income differences among earners, the question naturally arises, Can factors more directly related to employment or occupation provide more of an explanation? Table 4.4 also gives data for breakdowns by employment status, occupation, and industrial sector, all combined with race. As mentioned earlier, the information on income is not broken down by source. The earnings of each income recipient thus reflect, in addition to receipts for labor, the ownership of assets and other income-earning capabilities. Consequently any match between total income and the characteristics analyzed in table 4.4—characteristics which broadly reflect the work situation—cannot be expected to be good. It can perhaps be assumed that the incomes of employees come closest to reflecting payments for labor. Nevertheless the Gini coefficients indicate that, within the employee category and within each racial group, incomes still were rather unequally distributed. In contrast, the divergence in average incomes between employees of various races was rather small. Thus the component of income inequality attributable to between-race inequality was similarly small among employees—it was only 7 percent.

On the other side of the spectrum are employers, for whom returns to capital probably constituted a substantial part of total income. On the average, employers' incomes were more than four times as large as employees' incomes. As would be expected, they were unevenly distributed, even within racial groups and especially among Malays. Conversely the component of income inequality attributable to between-race inequality was even smaller among employers than among employees. Only among own-account workers was that component relatively large, as was the divergence in average incomes between races. But this divergence probably was largely a reflection of occupational and sectoral differences. Most Malay own-account workers are poor rural farmers; most Chinese and Indian own-account workers belong to the urban middle class.

Of all the characteristics of income earners, occupation was most closely related to the distribution of their incomes. This relation shows up in table 4.4 in several ways. First and most directly, the component of income inequality attributable to between-occupation inequality was about a third for Peninsular Malaysia and roughly the same for the main racial groups. Second, when earners are grouped by occupation, and within occupation by race, the inequality of income within each subgroup, as measured by Gini coefficients, becomes much lower. Third, within a number of important occupations, the divergence in average incomes between racial groups was relatively small. For occupations for which that divergence was large, as for farmers and to a lesser extent the higher occupations, much of the remaining inequality was associated with race. For the occupation of farming, data on rubber smallholdings suggest that the divergence in average incomes was at least partly caused by disparities in the size of holding.

The breakdown by industrial sector contributes much less to "explaining" the inequality in earners' incomes than the breakdown by occupation. Over all, the component of income inequality attributable to income differences between industrial sectors was about a sixth, or half that of the occupational breakdown.[15] It can therefore be con-

15. Within the principal racial groups the component of income inequality attributable to income differences between industrial sectors was substantial only for Malays. Within those sectors, inequality was associated with race mainly in agriculture.

cluded that differences in earners' incomes were associated primarily with occupation and to some extent with race. The racial association was probably caused by racial differences in asset ownership, at least in part. The influence of investment income can be reduced by looking specifically at urban employees, who presumably have limited assets, to see what influences the distribution of incomes within occupational-racial groups. It appears that the education, experience, and sex of workers "explain" a significant part of the inequality not attributable to occupation and race, especially for occupations in which training is important, such as the professional-technical and administrative-managerial groups.

Profiles of Poverty

Another way of characterizing the distribution of income is to describe a profile of poverty. Poverty is usually defined by drawing a poverty line and classifying those with incomes below this cutoff point as poor. It generally is recognized that the choice of a poverty line, dependent as it is on the definition used, always is somewhat arbitrary. Problems of interpretation and measurement also are significant. Furthermore, by applying a single poverty line, much detail is lost. For example, there can then be no distinction between the poor and the very poor. These considerations point to the use of several poverty lines. One poverty line can be linked to absolute poverty, defined as the minimum income necessary to obtain sufficient food and satisfy other essential needs. Again, this definition depends on the interpretation of the terms, "sufficient" and "essential."[16] Other poverty lines can distinguish relative degrees of poverty.

Anand considered three poverty lines: M$15, M$25, and M$33 per capita a month in 1970 prices.[17] For those three definitions of poverty, and for the richest 5 percent of Malaysians having incomes of more than M$185 a month, table 4.5 provides breakdowns by racial group and by urban and rural location. The main findings are:

• Poverty was more widespread in rural areas than in urban areas.[18]

16. It should also be remembered that the data from the postenumeration survey significantly underestimate total incomes, that they may consequently underestimate the absolute incomes of the poor, and, to the extent this is so, that they may overestimate the incidence of poverty.

17. Anand, *Inequality and Poverty in Malaysia*, ch. 4.

18. To the extent that rural prices may have been lower or that home consumption may have been valued at lower than retail prices, the incidence of rural poverty may be overestimated.

Table 4.5. *Poverty and Affluence: The Distribution of All Households, Rural Households, and Urban Households, by Race and Income, Peninsular Malaysia, 1970*

Location of household or race	Monthly household income per capita (Malaysian dollars)							
	0–15	15–25	0–25	25–33	0–33	33–185	More than 185	All incomes
	Percentage of households in income group by race							
All households								
Malays	85	78	78	58	73	40	22	55
Chinese	8	17	13	28	17	46	56	32
Indians	5	10	8	13	9	14	17	12
Others	—[a]	—[a]	1	—[a]	1	—[a]	6	1
Total	100	100	100	100	100	100	100	100
Rural households[b]								
Malays	90	79	84	66	80	50	33	67
Chinese	5	12	9	21	12	35	45	22
Indians	4	8	6	13	8	14	16	11
Others	—[a]	—[a]	1	—[a]	1	—[a]	6	—[a]
Total	100	100	100	100	100	100	100	100
Urban households[c]								
Malays	43	35	37	29	35	25	15	26
Chinese	35	45	42	56	47	62	62	58
Indians	22	19	20	15	18	13	17	15
Others[a]	1	1	1	—[a]	1	—[a]	6	—[a]
Total	100	100	100	100	100	100	100	100
	Percentage of households in racial group by income							
All households								
Malays	24	28	51	13	65	33	2	100
Chinese	4	11	15	11	26	65	9	100
Indians	7	18	25	14	39	54	7	100
Others	25	15	40	5	45	22	34	100
Average	16	21	37	13	49	46	5	100
Rural households[b]								
Malays	26	30	56	14	70	29	1	100
Chinese	5	14	18	13	32	63	5	100
Indians	7	20	27	17	44	52	4	100
Others	40	19	60	5	65	15	20	100
Average	20	25	45	14	59	39	3	100
Urban households[c]								
Malays	8	15	23	11	34	60	7	100
Chinese	3	9	12	9	21	67	12	100
Indians	7	14	21	10	30	56	13	100
Others	4	9	13	3	16	32	52	100
Average	5	11	16	10	26	63	11	100

Table 4.5 (*continued*)

Note: Figures may not reconcile because of rounding.
Source: Anand, *Inequality and Poverty in Malaysia,* ch. 3.
  a. Between 0.3 and 0.7 percent of households—a distinction felt to be necessary because of the potentially large rounding errors for this small group.
  b. Rural households accounted for 71.6 percent of all households.
  c. Urban households accounted for 28.4 percent of all households.

- Among the three main racial groups, the incidence of poverty was by far the highest among Malays.[19] More than a quarter of rural Malays were below the low poverty line of M$15 a month.
- The more restrictive the definition of poverty—that is, the lower the poverty line—the clearer are racial differences in the incidence of poverty.[20] Conversely the more inclusive the definition of poverty, the more the profile of poverty resembles that of the general population. For the low poverty line, 85 percent of all the poor were Malays; in rural areas this proportion was 90 percent. For the high poverty line, M$33 a month, these proportions still were 73 percent and 80 percent. In urban areas the incidence of poverty of Malays under all three poverty lines was also higher than that of the other races. But because the Chinese urban population was more than twice as large as the Malay urban population, the absolute number of urban poor was higher for Chinese than Malays under the two higher poverty lines.

The official poverty line adopted in Malaysia's third plan was equivalent to the highest of Anand's poverty lines—a monthly income of M$33 per capita in 1970 prices.[21] Compared with absolute poverty lines estimated for other countries in Southeast Asia, and given the lack of widespread hunger and the relatively good health conditions in Malaysia, this official estimate, which classifies 50 percent of the population as poor, appears to be high. On the other hand, the significantly more skewed distribution of income and generally higher cost of living in Malaysia in relation to other countries in the region would tend to result in greater poverty than would be expected solely on the basis of

19. The heterogeneous group of others had an even higher proportion in poverty, but it also had a high percentage in affluence.
20. This finding also is true for the other correlates of poverty discussed in the following paragraph.
21. That poverty line amounts to US$265 per capita in 1975 prices and exchange rates.

Malaysia's relatively high per capita income.[22] The Economic Planning Unit in 1978 revised the official poverty line downward from M$33 to M$29 per capita a month in 1970 prices.[23] The basis for the revision was the use of a less generous diet than was used in the earlier estimate. Under the revised poverty line, it is roughly estimated that about 43 percent of the population was in poverty in 1975 and about 38 percent in 1976.[24] Although it can still be argued that the conditions of life for the poor in other Southeast Asian countries are harsher, it is clear that poverty is a serious problem in Malaysia and that the low incomes of a substantial portion of the population deny full access to the goods and services necessary to meet basic human needs.

Poverty, in addition to being largely a rural and Malay phenomenon, is also correlated with other characteristics of the head of household: agriculture, especially independent farming; low education; female sex; and middle or old age.

In rural areas in 1970 the incidence of poverty apparently was largest among farmers and farm laborers in rice farming and mixed agriculture; the incidence of poverty generally was higher among farmers than farm laborers (table 4.6). This pattern reflects the prevalence of laborers in the relatively well-paid plantation sector; farmers include owner-operators as well as sharecroppers. As would be expected, most poverty is located in the northern states, and the separation is clear between the states oriented toward rubber and those oriented toward rice. All these findings are roughly consistent with the findings of the Economic Planning Unit.

In aggregate, the urban poverty group was only a seventh of the size of the rural group. In urban areas, as in rural areas, the relative incidence of poverty among employees was lower than that among own-account workers. But because the employee group in cities and towns was larger, more than half the urban poor were in this group. About 20 to 25 percent of urban poor were classified as farmers or farm laborers; most of the others were in commerce and services or in other activities in the traditional sector.

22. In 1970 the poorest 40 percent of households in Malaysia received only 11.2 percent of private income. In the East Asia and Pacific region the poorest 40 percent of households received 17.3 percent of private income; in countries at the same income level, they received 13.4 percent.

23. That income is equivalent to US$230 per capita a year in 1977 prices.

24. The significant reduction in poverty in 1976 over 1975 was largely caused by the significant improvement in the terms of trade and the resulting increase in income.

Table 4.6. *Percentage of Rural Poor and Relative Incidence of Poverty, by Sector and Occupation, Peninsular Malaysia, 1970*

Sector or occupation	Percentage of rural poor	Relative incidence of poverty[a]	States in which the rural poor are concentrated[b]
Rice and mixed agriculture			
Farmers	41	1.50	Kelantan and Kedah
Farm laborers	6	1.45	Kedah and Kelantan
Rubber			
Farmers	17	1.25	Perak, Johore, and Kelantan
Farm laborers	20	1.05	Perak and Johore
Coconut			
Farmers and farm laborers	3	1.25	n.a.
Fishermen	6	1.15	Perak, Kelantan, and Johore

n.a. Not available.
Note: The poverty line used in this table is M$25 per capita a month.
Source: Anand, *Inequality and Poverty in Malaysia*, ch. 5.
a. Percentage in poverty divided by 44.6, the average percentage of the rural population in poverty.
b. States together containing at least 50 percent of rural poor in the occupation indicated.

Labor Market Trends and Issues

The share of agriculture in employment has been large but declining. The reasons for this decline probably were different for the 1957–67 and 1970–75 periods. In the earlier period, as already mentioned, estate employment dropped steeply and, though traditional agriculture absorbed more workers, agriculture as a whole accounted for about 30 percent of the increase in employment. The secondary sectors contributed nearly a quarter of all new jobs, but by far the largest absorption—more than 45 percent—was in the tertiary sector, which in 1957 accounted for only a quarter of employment (table 4.7).[25]

25. As in most developing countries, there are conceptual and statistical problems in assessing labor market trends in Malaysia. Table 4.7 presents the best available data on

(note continues on page 120)

Table 4.7.   *Employment, by Sector and Race, Peninsular Malaysia, 1957,*
1967, 1970, Estimates for 1975, and Targets for 1990

Year or period	Agriculture				Mining, manufacturing, construction, utilities, and transport			
	Malays	Chinese	Others	Total	Malays	Chinese	Others	Total
	Thousands of persons employed							
1957[a]	747	300	176	1,223	96	213	69	378
1967	866	348	180	1,394	149	305	67	521
1970	951	301	154	1,406	173	335	55	563
1975	1,033	318	184	1,535	265	387	74	726
1990	1,091	503	183	1,778	783	575	150	1,508
Growth, 1957–67	119	48	4	171	53	92	−2	143
Growth, 1970–75	82	17	30	129	92	52	19	163
Growth, 1975–90	58	185	−1	243	518	188	76	782
	Percentage composition of sectoral employment by race							
1957	61	25	14	100	25	56	18	100
1967	62	25	13	100	29	58	13	100
1970	68	21	11	100	31	59	10	100
1975	67	21	12	100	37	53	10	100
1990	62	28	10	100	52	38	10	100
Growth, 1957–67	70	28	2	100	37	64	−1	100
Growth, 1970–75	64	13	23	100	56	32	12	100
Growth, 1975–90	24	76	0	100	66	24	10	100
	Percentage composition of racial employment by sector							
1957	73	40	47	57	9	28	18	18
1967	65	34	49	51	11	30	18	19
1970	66	29	48	50	12	32	17	20
1975	59	26	50	46	15	32	20	22
1990	37	26	30	33	27	30	25	28
Growth, 1957–67	38	17	—	30	17	33	—	25
Growth, 1970–75	27	10	67	25	30	31	42	31
Growth, 1975–90	5	26	0	11	44	26	32	37

— Not applicable.

Note: Growth figures are not shown for 1967–70 because the data for those two years are from different sources.

Sources: 1957 and 1967 from "Methodology Used in West Malaysian Labor Force and Employment Analysis," an unpublished technical appendix to Donald R. Snodgrass,

Services and public administration				Total				Year or period
Malays	Chinese	Others	Total	Malays	Chinese	Others	Total	
Thousands of persons employed								
178	242	129	549	1,020	756	374	2,150	1957[a]
316	378	118	812	1,331	1,031	365	2,727	1967
312	398	114	825	1,437	1,034	323	2,794	1970
447	500	110	1,057	1,745	1,204	368	3,317	1975
1,047	845	272	2,163	2,921	1,923	605	5,449	1990
138	136	−11	263	311	275	−9	577	Growth, 1957–67
135	102	−4	232	308	170	45	523	Growth, 1970–75
600	345	162	1,106	1,176	719	237	2,132	Growth, 1975–90
Percentage composition of sectoral employment by race								
32	44	24	100	47	35	17	100	1957
37	49	14	100	48	39	13	100	1967
38	48	14	100	51	37	12	100	1970
42	47	11	100	53	36	11	100	1975
48	39	13	100	54	35	11	100	1990
52	52	−4	100	54	48	−2	100	Growth, 1957–67
58	44	−2	100	59	33	9	100	Growth, 1970–75
54	31	15	100	55	34	11	100	Growth, 1975–90
Percentage composition of racial employment by sector								
17	32	35	26	100	100	100	100	1957
24	36	33	30	100	100	100	100	1967
22	38	35	30	100	100	100	100	1970
26	42	30	32	100	100	100	100	1975
36	44	45	40	100	100	100	100	1990
45	50	—	43	100	100	100	100	Growth, 1957–67
44	60	−9	44	100	100	100	100	Growth, 1970–75
51	48	68	52	100	100	100	100	Growth, 1975–90

"The Growth and Utilization of Malaysian Labor Supply," *Philippine Economic Journal*, vol. 15, nos. 1 and 2 (1976), pp. 276–313; other years from *Third Malaysia Plan, 1976–1980*.

a. Total experienced labor force.

Despite the difficulties associated with interpreting unemployment statistics in developing countries, it is clear that open unemployment in Malaysia increased during the 1960s.[26] This increase, together with the heavy accretions to the labor force in traditional agriculture and services and the indications of outmigration, strongly suggests that the employment situation was unfavorable in the 1960s. An important unfavorable element in the labor market in the late 1960s was the high unemployment rate among educated persons, especially school-leavers. The lack of opportunities was especially severe for Malays; the unemployment rate of Malay graduates of secondary schools was more than 25 percent. Also during this period, the relative concentration of Malays in the low-productivity agricultural sector further increased.

The emphasis of the New Economic Policy on growth and the international economic boom during 1972–74 led to improvements in the labor market in the first half of the 1970s. Despite the recession in 1975, employment increased 3.5 percent a year during 1971–75. Moreover the secondary sector increasingly contributed to the creation of new jobs. Unemployment showed a tendency to fall, and the share of Malays in agricultural employment decreased for the first time, albeit slightly. It therefore appeared, at least until the international recession in 1975, that the more aggressive development policy of government was starting to pay off in an improvement in the labor market.

Although the foregoing conclusion is fairly robust, it is not yet clear how the labor market functions in the economy—that is, how developments in the economy and the labor market influence each other. A number of aspects of the urban labor market have nevertheless been investigated.[27] An important finding is that there has been substantial "friction" in the labor market: differences in labor earnings have not been quickly eliminated by adjustments in supply and demand. This conclusion, already suggested by the large sectoral differences in incomes in table 4.1, is confirmed in several ways. First, rural-urban mi-

---

the sectoral and racial breakdowns of employment for the 1957–75 period. Because the data are from different sources, they are not strictly comparable, but they do provide a reasonable indication of broad trends. In addition, the figures for 1970 in table 4.7 differ from those in table 4.1.

26. For example, Snodgrass estimates that between 1962 and 1967 the unemployment rate increased from 6.1 percent to 6.8 percent. The estimate of the unemployment rate for 1970 in the third plan is 8 percent. Donald R. Snodgrass, "The Growth and Utilization of Malaysian Labor Supply," *Philippine Economic Journal*, vol. 15, nos. 1 and 2 (1976), pp. 276–313.

27. See especially Dipak Mazumdar, *Urban Labor Markets and Income Distribution in Malaysia* (New York: Oxford University Press, forthcoming).

gration, especially by Malays, has not functioned as an effective equalizer of income. Most migrants appear to be better educated than persons born in urban areas; migrants from farming families are in the minority. Second, there appears to have been a segmentation in the urban labor market, whereby Malay and Chinese entrepreneurs largely hired workers of their own race. Third, there is substantial unemployment among secondary school-leavers, but that apparently has only gradually led to a downgrading of the jobs they accept.[28]

The substantial unemployment among the educated throws light on the relation between education and the distribution of income. As would be expected, given the experience of other countries, it generally is found in Malaysia that the correlation between education and income is strong. This correlation does not necessarily indicate, however, that a better education improves income; it may also indicate that the affluent get a better education. The existence of substantial unemployment among the educated makes it clear that improved education is not a sure way for individuals to increase their incomes; nor would large investments in education alone improve the distribution of income.

Policy Implications and Responses

The essence of the foregoing discussion can perhaps be best captured by one word: dualism. In Malaysia the dualism often found in developing countries is exacerbated by its existence not only in the modern sectors, but also in agriculture, and even in mining. It also is clear that, in addition to traditional economic dualism, there is racial dualism. Particular races are generally identified with particular economic functions. The outcome of such dualism has been substantial inequality in income. As already mentioned, that inequality can be linked to such factors as race, occupation, location, schooling, size of community, and household composition. Many of these correlates of income inequality overlap; they are not easily disentangled. Even so, a number of important points have emerged. The most important among these is the highly unequal distribution of income in Malaysia. In relation to this overall inequality, the income differences between races, between states, and between urban and rural areas, though significant in an absolute sense, are relatively small. Thus government policies to reduce racial and regional inequalities, though of high priority for other reasons, would by

28. Part of the problem for those school-leavers is that they still are too young, according to custom, to be fully employed.

themselves have only a limited equalizing effect on the distribution of income.

The discussion in this chapter has also brought out the fact that another group of correlates of the income distribution is not amenable, or is only indirectly amenable, to policy intervention. This group includes personal and family attributes. For example, although fertility and household composition are important factors in determining the welfare of a household, they can only be influenced in a general way, such as through the family planning program. Another factor in this category, the tradeoff between leisure and income, influences labor force participation rates as well as hours and intensity of work. For example, a study of rubber tappers has indicated that Malays show a higher preference for leisure time than Chinese. Other attributes, which can only be influenced over time because the annual additions are small in relation to the existing stock, include the education of the labor force.

It appears, then, that four important determinants of the distribution of income are amenable to policy intervention: education; occupation, linked to sector; the distribution of physical assets, including their productivity; and the provision of social services.[29] Because the occupational and sectoral structure of employment—except that associated with land development—is largely determined in the private sector, the function of government in this area will have to be to stimulate the private sector in the sectors more attractive from an occupational point of view. That would better enable the large numbers of new entrants into the labor force to find attractive occupations; it would also facilitate a gradual shift from the less productive sectors and occupations to the more attractive ones. To achieve these ends, upgrading education is a necessary but not sufficient condition. Policies for the distribution of assets and for improvements in the productivity of assets can also fulfill an important function in equalizing incomes. The data in table 4.1 nevertheless indicate the limitations of such policies: incorporated business capital is generally concentrated in sectors in which incomes already are high. Consequently, for this policy area, any improvement in the distribution of income will have to come largely from increased returns to unincorporated capital, especially in agriculture.

The government's New Economic Policy, although formulated to reduce poverty and restructure society, includes most of the elements

29. Government could also make the tax system more progressive. See chapter five for a discussion of the provision of social services in relation to the tax system.

necessary to improve the distribution of income. Such an improvement is not, by itself, a principal objective of that policy. But by aiming directly at the reduction of poverty, the first objective of the New Economic Policy also aims at the heart of the problem of income inequality. Furthermore government has formulated, again under the New Economic Policy, ambitious targets for employment growth in the attractive sectors and occupations. It has also identified distributing new assets, including land, and improving the productivity of the poor as important policy instruments. Clearly these elements of the New Economic Policy will, if successfully implemented, ameliorate the skewed distribution of income. The distributional implications of other elements—intended to reduce and eliminate the identification of race with economic function—are much less direct. These elements are to be implemented by restructuring employment and the ownership of corporate assets in the context of dynamic growth, not by substituting one race for another in a static situation. By strengthening the imperative for rapid economic growth, they will perhaps influence the distribution of income most. Although the effect of rapid economic growth on the distribution of income cannot be predicted with confidence, experience in other countries strongly suggests that its effect on reducing poverty will be substantial.

Among the elements of the New Economic Policy, the intention to restructure the ownership of corporate assets is most in danger of adversely influencing the income distribution.[30] With the ownership of corporate capital rather concentrated, and with Malay earners in the metropolitan towns already almost at par with the Chinese, the switch from foreign to Malay ownership of corporate assets could worsen the distribution of income, at least in the short run. This argument has been used by those who assert that the main effect of the New Economic Policy will be to create a few Malay millionaires. Much depends, however, on the way the policy is implemented. Certainly much more emphasis is being given to Malay control over important segments of the economy, through holding the assets "in trust" by trust agencies, than to the creation of private investment income for wealthy Malays. As long as undue private transfers are not instituted to force achievement of the targets for restructuring corporate equity, the outcome postulated by the critics can be avoided. Furthermore the tendency of entrepreneurs to hire employees of their own race is a potent argument for creating a Malay entrepreneurial class.

---

30. This danger is recognized in the third plan. *Third Malaysia Plan, 1976–1980*, p. 80.

In sum, the New Economic Policy, with its emphasis on reducing poverty and restructuring society in the context of rapid economic growth, provides a policy framework favorable to moderating income inequalities. In fact, it can be convincingly argued that the thrust toward modernization and the eradication of poverty, together with the insistence that no one should be left behind in development, already implies a policy to moderate income differences. It may thus be desirable to formalize this implicit policy, perhaps as a third objective of the New Economic Policy. To do so could help allay any lingering fears among the poor and among middle-income earners in non-Malay groups that they may not benefit, or may even lose out, under the New Economic Policy.

Prospects for Employment and its Restructuring

Of the New Economic Policy's specific quantitative targets for 1990, those for the growth in production and employment are most essential, because success in reducing poverty and restructuring employment will depend on success in these areas. According to the perspective plan for the period to 1990, the expansion of production is to be rapid: nearly 10 percent a year for the secondary sector, including 12 percent for manufacturing; about 8.5 percent for services; and 5.5 percent for agriculture.[31] The corresponding growth rates of employment are about 5 percent a year for the secondary and tertiary sectors and 1 percent a year for agriculture. Employment in Peninsular Malaysia is thus expected to grow at 3.4 percent a year, or well in excess of the growth in the labor force, which is estimated in the perspective plan at 3.1 percent a year. Achieving these targets would make it possible to minimize unemployment by 1990. That achievement, together with the significant shift toward more productive employment, would enable reducing the incidence of poverty from 44 percent in 1975 to 17 percent in 1990. It would also enable—without restricting too severely the new opportunities for Chinese in the modern sectors—a nearly complete restructuring of employment by race. The targets, summarized in table 4.7, indicate that few of the racial imbalances in employment in various sectors would remain in 1990.

31. *Third Malaysia Plan, 1976–1980*, ch. 4.

Notwithstanding the substantial room for restructuring under conditions of very rapid growth in aggregate employment over a fifteen-year period, the patterns into which new employment needs to be channeled are starkly different from those applicable in the past. The most sweeping changes targeted are in agriculture, which would absorb only 5 percent of the net addition of Malays to the labor force. This target implies that 76 percent of the new places in agriculture would be taken up by Chinese. Many observers have raised questions about the realism of these targets. One problem is that most, if not all, of the desirable new jobs to be created in agriculture will be in land development schemes. But as long as Malays continue to be in an inferior income position, it will be difficult to allocate much of the land newly developed to Chinese.

The foregoing discussion demonstrates that the targets for restructuring employment may not be easy to fulfill. This conclusion applies even if the employment targets by sector are realized. These targets are rather high, however, at least for the modern sectors. It is explicitly stated in the third plan that not much improvement in productivity has been assumed in some subsectors of the services and that some underemployment in these subsectors may persist. Because policy instruments have not yet been devised to induce workers to leave agriculture under these circumstances, the estimates may overemphasize the relative shift from employment in agriculture to that in services.[32] In addition, the employment estimates are based not only on rather high employment elasticities, but on high targets for production in the modern sector, especially in manufacturing. It was mentioned in chapter three that the recession in 1975–76 led to a severe decline in manufacturing investment. As a result, a substantial recovery must occur if the targets for investment and employment are to be attained. If employment in the modern sectors expands less rapidly than foreseen, more workers will remain in agriculture, and the restructuring targets, especially those for agriculture, will be even more difficult to attain without forcing them on reluctant segments of the population.

All this is not to say that the objective to restructure employment should be put aside as unrealistic or impractical. It does not appear to be desirable, however, to enforce the restructuring targets at any cost. Such enforcement could jeopardize economic growth, which is instru-

32. As table 4.7 shows, more than half of all new jobs during 1976–90 are to be created in the services sector, compared with a previous high of 44 percent during 1970–75.

mental to any reasonable effort at restructuring. To be guarded against, then, is the vicious circle that can develop between enforced restructuring and economic slowdown. Under these circumstances it seems appropriate to conclude that the objective and the process of restructuring are more important than the specific numerical targets set. The principal goal is to foster national unity, which will be jeopardized if that vicious circle is allowed to develop. Reducing the identification of race with economic function should be continued, but as government has stipulated, it should be continued in a way that enables all groups in society to feel that they are participating significantly and continuously in economic development. If fostering this perception were to involve softening some of the numerical targets—for example, by including the Malays benefiting from land development schemes among those whose jobs have been restructured—the cost of retaining the objective and process of restructuring would be relatively small. In addition, given the more comfortable resource position Malaysia now enjoys, greater use can be made of incentives to attain the restructuring objectives than of regulations, which could dampen business activity and the growth context in which restructuring must take place.

In summary, the rapid expansion of the labor force expected over the 1975–85 period makes it imperative that the momentum of economic growth be sustained. This means that the economy must continue to grow at least at the 8 percent annual rate projected by government. If this growth can be attained without significant capital deepening, the outlook for a large-scale restructuring of employment would be good.[33] There would then be a gradual tightening of the labor market, which would facilitate the shift to more remunerative jobs and the full participation by the poor in the benefits of development. This tightening could also halt the tendency for rural-urban disparities to widen. Malaysia clearly has the natural and human resources to implement such a strategy and to attain the targets set by government for the improved economic and social welfare of all Malaysians.

---

33. For example, large investments in petrochemicals will not contribute much to employment creation.

FIVE

Jacob Meerman

Public Services
to Meet Basic Needs

THE PERSISTENT INTEREST IN ECONOMIC GROWTH springs from its strong
association with human welfare. At its root, growth is the fundamental
means of increasing human welfare. Of late the conviction has spread
that growth by itself is not enough. There is much stress on reaching
hitherto neglected millions by satisfying their basic needs directly —
providing food to meet the physical requirements of a productive life,
shelter and clothing to ensure reasonable protection against the rigors of
climate, and public services that make available the education, clean
water, and health care that all need if they are to become fully productive.[1] Meeting the basic needs of the poor for food, shelter, and clothing
must rely for the most part on increases in income and changes in relative prices. Improving the access of the poor to basic services, on the
other hand, requires an expansion of the function of government in
providing these services directly. This chapter is limited to a discussion
of basic services of the latter type.

In essence the question addressed is, Who gets what and why? Such
an assessment also illuminates the other side of the provision of services, Who does not get what and why? with all the implications this has
for policy and planning to remedy shortfalls. To make the assessment
two sets of data were gathered: information on the kinds and costs of

The discussion in this chapter is restricted to Peninsular Malaysia. An article similar to
this chapter appeared as Jacob Meerman, "Public Services to Meet Basic Needs," *World
Development*, vol. 7 (1979), pp. 615–34.

1. Robert McNamara, "Address to the Board of Governors" (Washington, D.C.:
World Bank, 26 September 1977).

government services and a sample survey of the use households made of these services.[2]

The analysis of data for 1974 shows that the poorest categories of Malaysians in the Peninsula—the Malays, rural dwellers, and those living in the North—were the least well served by the public utilities. But they were well represented in the use of public medical care and primary education.[3] What also emerges is that many of the poor were unable to avail themselves of certain services because their incomes were too low. If more of the poor are to have their children educated to higher levels, the out-of-pocket costs that constitute such a heavy burden for them will probably have to be subsidized. If the poor are universally to have pure water and electricity, it appears that fundamental changes must be made in policies for pricing these services to reduce their costs to the poor.

Identifying the Poor

What needs emphasis in identifying the poor is the basic concept of household per capita income, which for each household is total income divided by the number of members in the household. This measure avoids the error suggested by using household income alone—that the welfare of a household is independent of the number of its members and that a three-person household, for example, is economically no better off than a nine-person household with the same income.

2. The sample survey included 1,465 households in Peninsular Malaysia; it was partitioned according to income, ethnicity, region, and other variables. It was a random sample, in two stages, developed in cooperation with the Malaysian Department of Statistics. The survey, called the Distributive Effects of Public Spending Survey, was conducted by a private firm in 1974; the mean rate of response was 80 percent. (Only 4 percent of the sample refused to be interviewed; the other failures to respond were the result of failure to locate the respondent.) The size of the sample was sufficient for most parameters to be estimated with reasonable sampling accuracy. In general, analysis of the sample data indicates that they are of high quality, with small response errors and few coding errors. For more detailed treatment of the access to public services and the underlying method and arithmetic on which the conclusions in this chapter are based, see Jacob Meerman, *Public Expenditure in Malaysia: Who Benefits and Why* (New York: Oxford University Press, 1979).

3. As discussed ibid., public expenditure for agriculture and for settlement of new lands also was substantially in favor of the poor.

Table 5.1. *Monthly Household per Capita Income, Household Income, and Household Size, by Population Quintile of Household per Capita Income, Peninsular Malaysia, 1974*

Quintile	Percentage of households	Average number in household	Mean household per capita income (current Malaysian dollars)	Range of mean household per capita income (current Malaysian dollars)	Percentage of total income	Mean household income (current Malaysian dollars)
1	17.6	6.6	19.82	0–29	4.8	129.3
2	18.6	6.3	35.72	29–43	8.8	223.4
3	19.1	6.1	51.81	43–61	12.4	315.5
4	20.1	5.8	80.60	61–103	19.8	460.8
5	24.5	4.8	253.87	103–2,500	53.4	1,037.0
Total or mean	100.0	5.8	94.09	—	100.0	471.8

— Not applicable.
Source: Distributive Effects of Public Spending Survey.

When the population of Peninsular Malaysia is partitioned into quintiles of equal population, the two poorest quintiles—the poorest forty—are found to have received 13.6 percent of income in 1974 (table 5.1). The cutoff point for this group is household per capita income of M$43 a month (US$215 a year).[4] In this chapter households with monthly per capita incomes below M$43 are defined as being below the poverty line. Bacause average household size is a negative function of household per capita income, the number of households in each quintile steadily increases with income.[5] Thus the poorest forty, with 40 percent of the population, accounted for 36 percent of the households in 1974. The rate at which they generated income was only 34 percent of the mean rate for all households and a mere 13 percent of the mean rate for house-

4. This cutoff point is very close to the official poverty line used in the third plan, which in 1974 prices and rates of exchange was about US$223 per capita.

5. Two additional points should be made. First, the lack of correlation between household income and household per capita income is substantial; their R^2 is only 0.66. Second, in each quintile the product of household per capita income and number in household is not equal to average household income; mean household per capita income exceeds per capita income.

Table 5.2. *Percentage Distribution of Poverty Households, by Race, Region, Size of Community, and Sex of Head of Household, Peninsular Malaysia, 1974*

Race, region, size of community, or sex of head of household	Percentage in poverty within partition	Percentage of total households in poverty, by partition	Percentage of total households, by partition	Relative incidence of poverty
Race				
Malay	46	73	58	1.26
Chinese	17	15	31	0.48
Indian	42	12	10	1.20
Other	46	1	1	1.00
Region				
North[a]	46	37	29	1.28
Other[b]	37	53	54	0.98
Selangor[c]	19	3	17	0.53
Size of community				
Metropolitan[d]	13	6	16	0.38
Large urban[e]	29	12	15	0.80
Small urban[f]	36	12	12	1.00
Rural[g]	45	70	56	1.25
Sex of head of household				
Male	37	84	83	1.01
Female	35	16	17	0.94
All poverty households	36	100	100	1.00

Source: Distributive Effects of Public Spending Survey.
a. Kedah, Perlis, Kelantan, and Trengganu.
b. Penang, Perak, Negri Sembilan, Johore, Malacca, and Pahang.
c. Includes the Federal Territory.
d. Population of 75,000 or more.
e. Population between 10,000 and 74,999.
f. Population between 1,001 and 9,999.
g. Population of 1,000 or fewer.

holds in the top quintile, which received more than the other four quintiles combined.

When the population is partitioned by race, region, and residence, it is apparent that the incidence of poverty in Peninsular Malaysia was greatest among Malays, in the North, and in rural areas (table 5.2). For all three variables the probability of being in poverty was about 0.45.

Table 5.3. *Public School Enrollment Rates and Current Expenditure per Household by the Federal Government, by Educational Level and Quintile of Household per Capita Income, Peninsular Malaysia, 1974*

Item	Enrollment rates (percent)			Total current expenditure per household (Malaysian dollars)
	Primary level	Secondary level	Postsecondary level	
Quintile				
1	0.85	0.33	0.031	450
2	0.86	0.33	0.012	396
3	0.93	0.40	0.023	454
4	0.99	0.44	0.026	384
5	0.90	0.48	0.055	370
Mean	0.90	0.40	0.031	411
	Malaysian dollars			
Current federal subsidy per student-year	238	299	3,197	—

— Not applicable.
Source: Distributive Effects of Public Spending Survey.

Seventy-three percent of poverty households were Malay; 70 percent were in rural areas. In addition, 78 percent of Malay households were rural. The rural, poor Malays tended to be rubber tappers, laborers, fishermen, and farmers. Together the four poverty occupations accounted for 73 percent of poverty households and slightly more than half of all households. For this combined occupational group, the probability of being in poverty was 0.51.

Education

The public school system of Malaysia is readily accessible to all students at the primary level. Although attendance is not compulsory, the enrollment rate was 90 percent in 1974 (table 5.3).[6] Primary education

6. The enrollment rate is defined as the number enrolled at a given level, corrected for underage and overage students, divided by the number of children of suitable age for that level in the population.

thus was essentially universal. Compared with those in other developing countries, secondary enrollment rates were also high: the mean rate was 40 percent. At the postsecondary level the enrollment rate was 3 percent. The country has succeeded in moving from traditional underrepresentation of Malays in higher education to an ethnic balance. By 1974 more than half the postsecondary students were Malay. This is an impressive achievement in developing a comprehensive system of public education. At all three levels of education, enrollment rates increased with income. The current subsidy per household from the federal government—that is, the current expenditure by the federal government on education per household—roughly decreased with income, because household size and the number of school-age children per household decline with rising income.

Although schools are "free" in Malaysia, the out-of-pocket cost to a household of keeping children in school is substantial. The principal components of this cost are books, informal school fees, snacks, uniforms, shoes, transport, and supplies. These costs increase with educational level and place a large burden upon poor households: in 1974 the mean out-of-pocket cost to a household having one student in secondary school was equal to 13 percent of household income in the first quintile and 11 percent in the second quintile. For many of the poor, such burdens preclude putting children through secondary school.[7] The mean burden of these out-of-pocket educational costs is presented in table 5.4, by quintile of household per capita income and race, for households with children in school. For the first quintile the mean burden was 18 percent of household income; for the second it was 10 percent. It is clear that those in the poorest forty could ill afford the out-of-pocket costs of maintaining even two students, particularly if one was in secondary school.[8]

7. The data concerning out-of-pocket costs generated in the sample survey were nearly identical with the estimates developed by the Ministry of Education in 1973 on the basis of information obtained from schoolmasters. In 1973 the Ministry mean was M$114 a pupil at the primary level and M$295 at the secondary; in the survey the comparable means were M$123 and M$283 respectively. The problem is not that these costs are high; it is that the incomes of the poor are so low. On the average the out-of-pocket costs of a single student at the secondary level amounted to less than 5 percent of average household income, as measured in the survey. In the school year 1974–75 government began to distribute free textbooks to all students in assisted schools. This program probably reduces out-of-pocket costs by about a sixth.

8. Other factors are the increased cost of transport and maintenance for rural students without nearby secondary schools; the poorer quality of rural schools with the poorer preparation in those schools for the lower secondary examination; and a home atmosphere in which educational achievement is not emphasized.

Table 5.4. *Out-of-pocket Costs for Households with Students, by Quintile of Household per Capita Income and Race, Peninsular Malaysia, 1974*

Partition	Out-of-pocket costs in relation to income	Percentage of households with children in school
Quintile		
1	0.180	79
2	0.104	69
3	0.096	71
4	0.075	60
5	0.055	50
Mean	0.104	65
Race		
Malay	0.115	66
Chinese	0.087	64
Indian	0.088	62
Other	0.109	45

Source: Distributive Effects of Public Spending Survey.

To reduce the burden of out-of-pocket costs for education, state and federal governments provide assistance of various kinds, such as free books, payment of examination fees, and payment for board and lodging in residential schools. Of this assistance in 1974, 55 percent was for students at the postsecondary level and 37 percent was for those at the secondary level. The concentration of assistance at the postsecondary level, where few students are from poverty households, explains why public aid toward these costs increased rapidly with income. Such public aid was M$52 a household in the fifth quintile and M$21 in the first (table 5.5). To estimate the capital service costs shown in table 5.5, the flow of services was imputed from the public capital used in producing the various student-years of education at primary, secondary, and postsecondary levels. Including the results of such imputation by quintile of household per capita income, increases the federal subsidy by 24 percent.[9]

9. In addition to calculating current unit costs, flows of services were imputed from public capital—schools, equipment, and so forth—used in producing the outputs. This imputation has not been attempted in other studies, even though it is apparent that the failure to impute a return to government capital is an error in national accounting. When such services as education, medical care, transport, and police protection are privately provided, the capital stock involved commonly brings a return equivalent to that brought

Table 5.5. *Outlays per Household for Education, by Component of Expenditure, Peninsular Malaysia, 1974*
(Malaysian dollars)

Quintile of household per capita income	Current public subsidy		Capital service costs	Total public costs	Out-of-pocket costs per household	Total	Public costs as percentage of household income
	Student places	Aid for out-of-pocket costs					
1	450	21	112	583	221	804	38
2	396	23	108	527	215	742	20
3	454	29	102	585	295	880	15
4	384	35	92	511	288	799	9
5	370	52	91	513	291	804	4
Mean	411	33	100	544	265	809	13

Source: Distributive Effects of Public Spending Survey.

One fact emerging from this analysis is the sacrifice that the poor make to keep their children in school. Average spending for education was nearly a fifth of the income of the 79 percent of households in the first quintile that had children in school (table 5.4). Even allowing for some bending of the truth, this is impressive. And even this ratio is an understatement of the burden: 18 percent of income is a far greater sacrifice for a poor family than for a wealthy family, because far more of the goods and services sacrificed by the poor are necessary to physical well-being. Perhaps more than any other variable, this sacrifice expresses the aspiration of the poor of Malaysia for a better life—if not for themselves, then for their children. This desire raises two questions: How likely are the poor to achieve high levels of education? Even with high levels of achievement, how likely is there to be a serious gap between expectation and realization?

The answer to the first question is unambiguous. At every level the highest drop-out rate was that of the poor. At the primary level their

---

by other privately owned capital. It must be conceded that there is a flow of services from government capital as well and that underestimation of the size of the public sector would be substantial if these capital service costs were not taken into account. Capital service costs for Malaysia were imputed on the basis of data on the costs of new facilities, which permitted estimating the average cost of replacing the capital used per unit of output. Imputed to this average cost was a gross rate of return of 14 percent a year, which is defined as the cost of the flow of services from capital in place. The rate is below what the private economy earns in Malaysia and is perhaps similar to gross pretax returns of many public utilities.

enrollment rate was below the mean; at the secondary level the discrepancy was even greater; at the postsecondary level the enrollment of the poorest forty was a fifth of the average. There are many factors in this outcome. Schools in rural areas, where most of the poor live, have facilities that are poorer and teachers who are not as highly qualified as those in urban areas. Because parents are poorly educated, the home environment does not offer motivation for success in school. But meager financial resources must also be a factor—far more so than in developed countries. Adding earnings forgone to the burden only makes the conclusion more convincing.

The disparity in opportunity could be reduced by the channeling of additional resources to the poor, particularly to primary and secondary school students. It may make sense in rural schools to provide transport, to eliminate covert fees, and to grant books, paper, pencils, and other supplies. Alternatively government could consider providing assistance in kind or in cash on the basis of a test of financial means. However it is done, reducing the educational burden of the poor appears to be desirable. If government expects great benefits to accrue to the community at large—positive externalities—from a population educated at least through lower secondary school, the case for doing this is even stronger.

Estimates of the aggregate cost of such a grant program are presented in table 5.6. The following assumptions were made in computing these estimates: government instituted a policy of cash grants to meet house-

Table 5.6. *Hypothetical Grants for Out-of-pocket Costs of Education, by Size of Grant, Number of Households Assisted, and Aggregate Resource Costs, Peninsular Malaysia, 1974*

Item	Lowest quintile	Next-lowest quintile
Grant per household (Malaysian dollars)		
Primary level	80	40
Secondary level	200	100
Number of households participating		
Primary level	425,727	390,998
Secondary level	134,814	150,143
Aggregate costs (millions of Malaysian dollars)		
Primary level	34.0	15.6
Secondary level	27.0	15.0
Total	61.0	30.6

Source: Calculated by the author.

hold costs of keeping children in school in 1974; for primary and secondary levels government would have covered about two-thirds of mean out-of-pocket costs for those in the lower income quintile and about a third for those in the next-lowest quintile; as a consequence of the grants, enrollment rates in both quintiles rose to the 1974 mean level—that is, to 90 percent in primary school enrollments and to 40 percent in secondary school enrollments. The total costs in 1974 would have been M$91.6 million, or 0.8 percent of gross domestic product (GDP) at factor cost and 2 percent of federal government expenditure.[10] Because of the great increase in government resources since 1974, a similar calculation for more recent years would indicate an even lower fiscal burden. Because the problem for households is more serious at the secondary level, the program could be restricted to that level and achieve commensurate savings. Alternatively the primary program could be reduced; the secondary program increased by a like amount. The point, given the resources of Malaysia, is that such a program need not be onerous. An enormous jump in enrollment in secondary school, which could be expensive, would presumably be precluded by the hurdle of the lower secondary examination, which is taken on completion of the third form. In the past that examination has restricted the number passing to the places available in the fourth form.

The answer to the second question, which is about the likelihood of a gap between the expected and actual consequences of educational achievement, is more complicated. In most countries the private return and presumably the social return from education at each level have substantially fallen as enrollment rates have risen. This phenomenon, along with the high open unemployment rate of those leaving secondary school and of university graduates, is well recorded. Similar phenomena are in evidence in Malaysia. In a recent study of returns from education in Malaysia, the conclusion was reached that "Malaysia is or soon will be overinvesting in education, from an economic point of view."[11] The criterion used for evaluating investment in education was social return, as measured by the total costs of education and the part of the wages of those who were educated which was attributable to increasing education. In this context overinvestment means a return from education that is lower than that from capital in general. Even in economic terms, this definition is restrictive. Education may, for example, affect

10. Administrative costs would increase the estimates somewhat.

11. O. Donald Hoerr, "Education, Income, and Equity in Malaysia," *Economic Development and Cultural Change*, vol. 21, no. 2 (January 1973), pp. 247–73.

production functions and generate additional returns from other factors. It often is argued that such externalities are important. Yet the decreasing employment and presumably decreasing wages associated with an expanding educational system suggest that the definition is useful. The misallocation of resources associated with this process might nevertheless be reduced by revising the curriculum away from the traditional academic program and emphasizing vocational and technical programs, from which social returns can be expected to be higher. There has been some movement in this direction—toward residential science schools and vocational schools, for example. More of such movement probably is desirable.

One reason for overinvestment is the discrepancy between private return and social return. Because a large share of the cost of education, particularly at the postsecondary level, is borne by the community, one way of reducing overdemand would be to increase the private component of the cost. But besides the question of externalities, doing this at the primary level and to some degree at the secondary level would conflict with distributive goals. In contrast, the beneficiaries at the postsecondary level overwhelmingly are the wealthy, which suggests the desirability of increasing the private share of their costs. This might be accomplished by student-loan financing, a method of financing that has not been emphasized in Malaysia. In any event it may make sense to restrict most postsecondary subsidies for out-of-pocket costs to students who are most in need of them.

At the postsecondary level it might also be desirable to vary subsidies according to the expected social return. This could mean drastically reducing the subsidies to students in the arts and social sciences. Students in these faculties now are extremely well supported. Of the seventy students in the survey who were in public postsecondary institutions, fifty-three were aided. Thirty-six of them were studying liberal arts or social sciences; they received mean assistance with out-of-pocket costs that was 40 percent higher than the average for the whole group of assisted students. But students of precisely these disciplines first present an employment problem. It might make more sense to attract students into programs in which serious shortages are expected to persist: engineering, science, medicine, technical education, and agricultural research and extension.[12]

12. R. Thillainathan, "Malaysia," in *The Role of Public Enterprise in National Development in Southeast Asia*, ed. Nguyen Truong (Singapore: Regional Institute of Higher Education and Development, 1976), p. 131.

Table 5.7. *Total Costs, Mean Unit Costs, and Frequencies of Use of Public Medical Services, Peninsular Malaysia, 1973–74*
(Malaysian dollars)

Component of cost	Total recurrent costs (millions)	Annual frequency per household	Unit current facility costs
Hospital inpatient day	86.5	2.53	20.32
Hospital outpatient visit	25.3	4.76	3.16
Rural clinic visit	22.6	3.23	4.17
Birth assisted by government midwife	2.8	0.04	37.42
Subtotal	137.2[a]	—	—
Central overhead	9.4	—	—
Stores and research	5.0	—	—
Total allocated, by output	151.6	—	—
Public health	18.9	—	—
Total	170.5	—	—

— Not applicable.
Source: Distributive Effects of Public Spending Survey.
a. Includes M$9.15 million in private payments for public care.

The problem with the foregoing suggestions is the predominance of Malays in the liberal arts and social sciences. In the survey thirty-four of the thiry-six assisted students were Malay. Concentration of Malays in these "surplus" faculties has been the principal means of raising the rate of their enrollment in universities.[13] One obvious suggestion is to encourage Malays at the secondary level to follow curricula that will prepare them for entrance into the shortage fields at the postsecondary level; another is to rethink the present policy of blanket support of Malays in the liberal arts and social sciences. At the very least this support should be restricted to Malays from poor households. Most Malays now supported are from higher-income groups.

To return to the original query, unless there is substantial change, the prognosis is this: substantially decreasing returns for those leaving secondary school and increasing mismatching of the predominantly Malay liberal arts graduates. This outcome may also have high costs of another kind: social discord, because some are favored by virtue of race, and unsatisfied and unsatisfactory employees. Widespread frustration of expectations is likely.

13. Ibid., p. 132.

Unit current overhead costs	Total unit current costs	Unit capital costs	Total unit costs	Component of cost
2.15	22.47	17.49	39.96	Hospital inpatient day
0.33	3.49	2.09	5.58	Hospital outpatient visit
0.44	4.61	1.47	6.08	Rural clinic visit
3.96	41.39	25.24	66.63	Birth assisted by government midwife
—	—	—	—	Subtotal
—	—	—	—	Central overhead
—	—	—	—	Stores and research
—	—	—	—	Total allocated, by output
—	11.25	—	11.25	Public health
—	—	—	—	Total

Medical Care

Curative, as opposed to preventive, medical care was the object of more than 85 percent of public spending for medical care in Peninsular Malaysia in 1973–74. This spending can be accounted for according to four basic curative procedures: hospital inpatient treatment, hospital outpatient treatment, rural clinic outpatient treatment, and assistance with births by a government midwife (table 5.7).[14] Generally the fees for public medical services were low, or no fee was charged. They were highest for such nonmedical services as food and accommodation in hospitals. The survey showed that more than two-thirds of hospital inpatients paid no fees; the same was true of more than three-quarters of outpatient treatments at all facilities. Regression analysis, with the various procedures as dependent variables, rejected income as an explanatory variable.

Consumption of each type of publicly financed procedure, by quintile of household per capita income and race, indicates a high degree of

14. As for education, the opportunity cost of capital investment for hospitals, clinics, and equipment can be estimated. The results suggest that medical care in Malaysia is best described as capital intensive. For example, adding the capital service cost of M$17.49 to the recurrent costs of M$22.47 per inpatient-day increases total costs per inpatient-day 78 percent. Similarly, increasing the costs of hospital outpatient care by the capital service cost raises their total 60 percent.

Table 5.8. *Distribution of Public Medical Services, by Quintile of Household per Capita Income and Race, Peninsular Malaysia, 1974*

Partition of households	Annual days in hospital		Hospital visits as outpatient[a]	
	Density	Frequency	Density	Frequency
Quintile				
1	0.14	2.40	0.19	5.33
2	0.18	3.47	0.19	4.90
3	0.11	1.30	0.24	5.46
4	0.20	3.00	0.20	4.46
5	0.12	2.50	0.18	3.96
Race				
Malay	0.13	2.08	0.19	4.24
Chinese	0.14	1.90	0.21	5.12
Indian	0.30	7.21	0.26	5.92
Mean	0.15	2.53	0.20	4.76

Source: Distributive Effects of Public Spending Survey.
a. Density is for a single month; frequency is for a year.

success on the part of government in providing medical care (table 5.8). Density refers to the proportion of households that used a given facility during a given period of time—a year for days spent as hospital in-patients and for midwife-assisted births, a month for outpatient visits to hospitals or rural clinics. From one household in six, some member stayed in a hospital during the preceding year; from one in five, some member visited a hospital as an outpatient during the preceding month; from one in eight, some member visited a rural clinic during the preceding month. Although detailed data concerning outpatient visits were collected for only a single month in the belief that not all households could accurately recall all outpatient visits during a twelve-month period, the use of clinics during a twelve-month period was also examined. From about 76 percent of all households there were one or more outpatient visits to government facilities during the year preceding the interview.

Frequency refers to the mean number of outputs consumed by households in the various partitions over the entire year. With respect to outpatient care, the rural clinic system, despite its having a far larger number of facilities for outpatients than hospitals, administered a smaller number of treatments than hospital clinics—3.23 per household in the rural clinic system and 4.76 in hospital clinics. This pattern

Rural clinic visits[a]		Rural midwife-assisted births	Partition of households
Density	Frequency	Density/Frequency	
			Quintile
0.20	4.67	0.09	1
0.20	4.50	0.06	2
0.13	3.10	0.07	3
0.13	3.29	0.02	4
0.04	1.31	0.01	5
			Race
0.16	3.69	0.06	Malay
0.07	2.04	0.01	Chinese
0.16	4.43	0.02	Indian
0.13	3.23	0.04	Mean

probably was the result, at least in part, of the small number of persons served by each rural clinic. With respect to inpatient care, income did not appear to be a strong determinant of consumption—a conclusion that holds even if data are converted to a per capita basis to correct for the decrease in number in household as income increases.

Unlike the hospital-based services, visits to rural clinics and births assisted by government midwives were strongly and negatively associated with income. In contrast, private outpatient visits were positively associated with household per capita income. The increase was monotonic: the fifth quintile purchased about five times as many as the first quintile. Probably reflecting differences in income, this pattern was carried over unambiguously to the partitions by ethnic group, region, and residence. Frequency of private treatment invariably increases as mean income of the cells within the partition increases. In addition, when private and public outpatient attendances are combined, a clear, positive, monotonic relation between attendances and income evolves.

The mean annual current expenditure of the federal government on health was M$156 per household in 1974; for poverty households it was M$184 (table 5.9). Rather striking is the finding that benefits to residents of Selangor and the Federal Territory were far lower than benefits to residents of other regions, notwithstanding the highly developed

Table 5.9. *Distribution of Subsidy for Combined Medical Services to Households, by Race, Size of Community, Region, and Quintile of Household per Capita Income, Peninsular Malaysia, 1977*
(Malaysian dollars per household)

Partition of households	Subsidy for preventive medical care	Subsidy for current outputs of medical care	Capital service costs	Total subsidy
Race				
Malay	10.71	76.32	52.17	139.20
Chinese	12.12	66.22	47.18	125.52
Indian	11.79	193.48	147.57	352.84
Size of community				
Metropolitan[a]	10.69	66.99	50.07	127.75
Large urban[b]	11.17	106.99	78.17	196.33
Small urban[c]	11.68	91.76	68.45	171.89
Rural[d]	11.32	82.02	56.18	149.52
Region				
Selangor[e]	11.19	35.94	26.10	73.23
North	11.29	97.87	71.10	180.26
Other	11.21	85.36	58.36	154.93
Quintile				
1	12.82	92.84	61.75	166.81
2	12.04	110.98	79.06	202.08
3	11.77	62.09	40.48	114.34
4	11.13	92.74	66.32	170.20
5	9.17	71.50	54.19	134.86
Mean	11.25	84.58	59.96	155.79

Source: Distributive Effects of Public Spending Survey.
a. Population of 75,000 or more.
b. Population between 10,000 and 74,999.
c. Population between 1,000 and 9,999.
d. Population of less than 1,000.
e. Includes the Federal Territory.

system of public medical care in Selangor and the Federal Territory.[15] The impoverished North received the highest public expenditure per household. In general, residents of metropolitan areas received less public care than those of rural or small urban communities. This pattern reflects the demand of metropolitan residents, who tend to be well off, for private medical care.

In comparison with those in other developing countries, standards of preventive medical care in the Peninsula are high. The benefits to both the rich and the poor have been substantial, as is borne out by the results of the survey. Premises of 76 percent of all households were sprayed against malaria or other disease in the twelve months preceding the interviews. Of children in school, 30 percent had received inoculations of some sort in school during the three months preceding the interviews. In the same period, 22 percent had had medical examinations and 41 percent had had dental examinations. These data are consistent with comprehensive coverage of the school population during a one-year period and indicate that the standards of preventive health in Malaysia are high by developing-country standards.

The basic conclusion to be drawn is that morbidity, not income, determines the demand for medical services. The need of the poor and most of the rest of the population for medical care is met through the public system at little private cost.

Having drawn such a sweeping conclusion, I must offer one caveat: The need for medical care can be met with a large range in quality of treatments and procedures. In this context, death rates are instructive. In 1973 such rates, by community, were unequal for infants, toddlers, and recent mothers (table 5.10). The mortality of Malays, who can be taken as a proxy for rural and poor households, was above average for these three categories. This finding suggests that the poor rural population receives care of lower quality than that received by the urban and rich, the proxy for Chinese. Nevertheless the poor quality of care accounts at best for only part of the discrepancy in mortality for these categories. Morbidity is another factor, particularly for toddlers. It clearly is affected by the purity of drinking water, which is a function of income and residence. In this context, note that waterborne diseases are an important reason for admission to hospitals in the Peninsula.

15. The sample survey showed that medical care was often administered in a state different from that of residence. This finding reflects in part the system of referring serious cases to the more comprehensive centers—from a rural clinic to a general hospital, for example.

Table 5.10. *Mortality Rates, by Race: Crude, Neonatal, Toddler, and Maternal, 1957, 1970, and 1973*

Category and year	Total	Race		
		Malay	Chinese	Indian
Crude				
1957	12.4	14.9	9.8	11.1
1970	7.3	7.6	6.6	8.5
1973	6.9	6.9	6.4	8.4
Neonatal				
1957	29.6	34.6	22.2	30.6
1970	22.9	24.1	19.7	28.0
1973	23.1	24.5	19.5	26.8
Toddler				
1957	10.7	14.1	6.6	9.0
1970	4.2	5.6	2.1	3.8
1973	3.7	4.8	2.0	4.1
Maternal				
1957	2.8	4.0	1.4	2.1
1970	1.5	2.2	0.5	1.2
1973	1.1	1.6	0.3	0.5

Source: Nwanganga Shields, "Population Change and Socio-economic Development in Peninsular Malaysia," (Washington, D.C.: World Bank, 1978), appendixes 6 and 7.

Education is another factor. It is a determinant of diet, hygiene, and fertility, all three of which affect mortality. In addition, the reaction of a household to disease or trauma tends to be more appropriate as income and educational level increase—that is, choices between traditional and modern procedures become more appropriate. This pattern of choice may be important in prenatal and postnatal care. In sum, the Malays are poorer and have less education than the other ethnic groups, conditions that imply higher morbidity and less appropriate response to situations requiring medical care.

Electricity, Water, and Sewage Disposal

To regard electricity as a basic need might at first glance appear to be stretching things, but the effects of electricity on the quality of life are considerable. As a household consumer good, it provides numerous opportunities for activities that would otherwise be difficult or impossible. As a means of production, it expands the range of opportunities of the household or firm. Nevertheless less than 12 percent of the rural population of developing countries in 1971 had electricity.[16] In contrast, 44 percent of all the rural households in the Peninsula had electricity.

Much of the interest in hygienic water stems from its importance to public health. In many developing countries, waterborne and water-related diseases are among the principal causes of death. The World Health Organization considers the provision of a safe and convenient water supply to be "the single most important activity that could be undertaken to improve the health of people living in rural areas."[17] The importance of its provision notwithstanding, "only about 15 percent of the rural population in developing countries had reasonable access to safe water."[18] In Peninsular Malaysia, however, 49 percent of the rural population, including residents of small urban concentrations, used piped and hygienically treated water in 1974.

Greater use of piped water implies greater probability of pollution from seepage of waste water and human waste into the system. Consequently the supply of piped and treated water—particularly in urban areas—creates a demand for flush systems to carry away wastes. Such systems also require large volumes of water, so piped water in the household is the fundamental requirement for access to flush systems.[19] In brief, piped water facilitates the supply of flush systems and creates the demand for them. But the lag is substantial between the installation of piped water and the ensuing demand for flush systems. Typically a country has far more households with piped water than with flush systems. In this respect, Malaysia is typical: 57 percent of the households in Peninsular Malaysia had piped and treated water in 1974; 26 percent of the households had flush systems.

The spatial distribution of these three household services in Peninsular Malaysia was similar to that in other countries (table 5.11). The

16. World Bank, *Rural Electrification*, a World Bank Paper (Washington, D.C., October 1975), p. 17.

17. World Bank, *Village Water Supply*, a World Bank Paper (Washington, D.C., March 1976), p. 5.

18. Ibid., p. 6.

19. Flush systems, as the term is used here, include means of disposing of wastes. The means range from public sanitary sewers to household cesspools with open drains.

Table 5.11. *Percentage of Households Supplied with Electricity, Piped and Treated Water, and Flush Sewage Disposal, by Quintile of Household per Capita Income, Race, Size of Community, and Region, Peninsular Malaysia, 1974*

Partition of households	Electricity	Pure piped water	Flush sewage disposal
Income quintile			
1	24	23	3
2	47	47	10
3	49	52	19
4	65	68	29
5	84	83	56
Race			
Malay	38	41	17
Chinese	84	83	39
Indian	74	68	34
Size of community			
Metropolitan[a]	90	88	62
Large urban[b]	69	58	28
Small urban[c]	72	63	26
Rural[d]	39	46	16
Region			
Selangor[e]	81	76	49
North	31	30	12
Other	62	65	26
Mean	56	57	26

Source: Distributive Effects of Public Spending Survey.
a. Population of 75,000 or more.
b. Population between 10,000 and 74,999.
c. Population between 1,000 and 9,999.
d. Population of less than 1,000.
e. Includes the Federal Territory.

proportion of households consuming the services greatly increased with community size, and rural areas lagged behind urban areas. But the discrepancy between town and country was less in Peninsular Malaysia than in the developing countries in general. In addition, the distribution of the services was congruent with other characteristics of the various partitions: the Chinese led in consumption of all three; the Indians followed; the Malays lagged far behind. Increasing income brought increasing consumption of each service, and the likelihood of effective demand increased with degree of development, as measured by per capita income. The underdeveloped and relatively rural North was below the mean in consumption of all three services.

It is tempting to conclude that income is the only variable operating to influence demand. Across all partitions, the correlation between the mean household per capita income of the partition and the proportion of households consuming the service is very high and positive. Such variables as region, race, and size of community usually exert their own impact on effective demand, independent of income. But in most cases, the effect of such independent variables is to reinforce the effect of income. This outcome probably is the result of the fact that utilities "chase" income. Malaysia offers utilities at prices that cover total cost; distribution networks have generally been installed in areas where effective demand is most concentrated. Hence the variables for region and size of community can be seen as measuring the availability of services largely as a function of income. Regression analysis, based on the distinction between access to a service and effective demand for that service, confirmed this view.[20]

Not all households have access to electricity or piped water, and not all households having access choose to purchase the output of the utility that is available. This state of affairs raises two interrelated questions: Which households have access to the utilities? Given access, who purchases the service and why?

Before moving to the empirical data gathered in the 1974 survey, I should like to amplify the concept of access. Electricity provides a good illustration. In the survey an attempt was made to divide the sample into households having access and those not having access. Households without electricity were asked two questions: Is electricity available in this area? Could you get it into your house if you wanted it? Of the 647 nonusers, 580 answered yes to both questions, thus claiming to have access. Presumably for many of these households access would mean connection to an autogenerator.[21] But 227 of the 580 nonusers also agreed that "The Authority would need to lead a line two or more miles

20. See appendix B for a discussion of the linear regression model used to analyze the supply, demand, and consumption of public utilities.

21. Autogenerators supply electricity for less capital but substantially higher operating costs. A small diesel motor lighting the village stores and the homes of village notaries is a typical example. Autogeneration accounted for 11 percent of all households with electricity in the sample. In some studies such households are defined as not having electricity.

to connect the house to the electricity supply." The necessity of a line two or more miles long nearly always implies that a household does not have access. After long consideration it was decided that the definition of households having access would be restricted to those who claimed access and needed connecting lines of one mile or less in length. Although this definition is more stringent than that implied by the house-holders' own perceptions, it still indicates that 80 percent of all house-holds in the Peninsula had access to electricity in 1974. This discussion suggests the difficulty of arriving at a workable definition of access. From the perspective of the household, the degree of access is measured by the cost to the household of connection. As range of access is increased, household costs increase. Households to which the cost of access is below a well-defined cutoff point should ideally be defined as having access. It was impossible to generate data consistent with such a criterion. As a substitute, the cutoff cost was defined in relation to the needed length of the line.

The results show clearly that utility supply is highest in areas in which incomes are high and populations are concentrated (table 5.12). In contrast, the low-income partitions—rural areas, the North, and the Malays—were least well supplied. Of interest are the circumstances under which households effectively demand a utility to which they have access. Rejections were substantial: Although 80 percent of all households had access to electricity, 70 percent of households with access demanded it. With respect to piped and treated water, the lower proportion of households that were supplied—69 percent—is offset by the higher proportion of households having access that demanded it—82 percent. Among the poorest forty the proportion demanding each service was below the mean. For this group, moreover, income turned out to be a more important determinant of demand for water and electricity than it was for the entire sample. In general the elasticity of demand for service was high with respect to income and to what might be called a modern life-style, which is associated primarily with the largest cities and the Chinese.[22]

From the analysis two partitions are seen to have had large deficiencies: the North and poverty occupation. This conclusion is reinforced by the findings presented in table 5.13, which shows the mean number of services supplied and consumed. A household receiving all three utilities would have the maximum score of 3. The table shows

22. The analysis underlying these conclusions is in appendix B.

Table 5.12. *Access to, Demand for, Given Access, and Consumption of Public Utilities, All Malaysia, Poorest Forty, and Those Living in the North, Peninsular Malaysia, 1974*
(percentage of households)

Utility and partition	Access	Demand, given access	Consumption
Electricity			
All Malaysia	80	70	56
Poorest forty	70	51	36
Residence in the North	62	49	31
Urban residence[a]	n.a.	81	n.a.
Piped and treated water			
All Malaysia	69	82	57
Poorest forty	52	67	36
Residence in the North	36	84	30
Flush systems			
All Malaysia	56	46	26
Poorest forty	34	21	7
Residence in the North	37	32	12
Mean percentage, all three services			
All Malaysia	68	66	46
Poorest forty	52	46	26
Residence in the North	45	55	24

n.a. Not available.
Source: Regression analysis of data from Distributive Effects of Public Spending Survey.
a. Includes only those residing in metropolitan and large urban communities.

Table 5.13. *Combined Supply and Consumption of Utilities, by Region and Poverty Partition, Peninsular Malaysia, 1974*

Variable	Poverty occupation	North	Poorest forty	Mean	Other region	Selangor[a]
Combined supply	1.29	1.34	1.56	2.05	2.25	2.59
Combined consumption	0.56	0.72[b]	0.78	1.38	1.52	2.06
Household per capita income (Malaysian dollars)	57	61	28	94	88	171
Percentage of total households	34	29	36	n.a.	54	17

n.a. Not available.
Source: Distributive Effects of Public Spending Survey.
a. Includes the Federal Territory.
b. By state, combined consumption in the North was 0.89 in Kedah and Perlis, 0.64 in Trengganu, and 0.57 in Kelantan.

Table 5.14. *Supply of the Combined Utilities, by Region and Size of Community, Peninsular Malaysia, 1974*

		Size of community			
Region	Metropolitan[a]	Large urban[b]	Small urban[c]	Rural[d]	Total
Selangor[e]	2.70	—	2.38	2.40	2.59
North	—	1.72	1.10	1.18	1.34
Other	2.94	2.84	2.63	1.91	2.25
Total	2.84	2.16	2.39	1.72	2.05

— Not applicable.
Source: Distributive Effects of Public Spending Survey.
a. Population of 75,000 or more.
b. Population between 10,000 and 74,999.
c. Population between 1,000 and 9,999.
d. Population of less than 1,000.
e. Includes the Federal Territory.

that combined supply for the North and for poverty occupation was far below the mean. In fact, the combined supply of these two partitions was even less than that of the poorest forty. This is true despite the fact that household per capita income in the North considerably exceeded that of the poorest forty. This is but another facet of the earlier conclusion: The North, independent of such other variables as race, income, and size of community, had a unique and negative regional effect. Because of the congruence of access and demand, the ranking of the three partitions persists when combined consumption is compared.

As a target for remedial action, the North is superior to poverty occupation. It is a well-defined area, and the supply of utilities necessarily is area-specific, not household-specific. In contrast, although poverty occupation is well defined, with 93 percent in rural and small urban locations, poverty households are dispersed throughout the Peninsula. Although only 6 percent are in Selangor and 46 percent are in the North, there still are 49 percent in the "other" region.

For rural residence the combined mean supply of 1.72 is 84 percent of the aggregate mean of 2.05 (table 5.14). Some of this discrepancy is caused by the North. With the North out, variation between rural and urban residence diminishes and the rural mean rises to 87 percent of the aggregate mean. Thus the balance or equality in supply of utilities in Peninsular Malaysia suggests a primary focus on the North as a region, not on rural areas. This conclusion is reinforced by the fact that urban scores outside the North far exceed the scores in the North for both large urban and small urban communities. Because costs of providing utilities are lower in urban communities than in rural communities, while effective demand is higher, that reinforcement suggests that consideration should initially be given to improving the supply in the towns of the North.[23]

Implicit throughout this discussion is the notion that blanket provision of these utilities to all households should be public policy. As noted earlier, however, many households with access are not purchasing utilities because their incomes are too low. This pattern can be illustrated by pulling together the data on effective demand, which suggests that 34 percent of all households would not demand a service even if they were on the supply (see table 5.12). More than half this failure to demand would be concentrated among the poorest forty. The definition of access with respect to each service includes households over a range of costs of access. In some cases these costs are considerable. But failure to demand is substantial even when access is restricted to a tight definition. For example, for electricity in urban areas, where incomes are above average and life styles are modern, failure to demand still was nearly a fifth of the total in 1974.

What this implies is that subsidies are necessary if achievement of 100 percent demand is the goal. This conclusion is reinforced by the fact that, outside the cities in the North, the households to which the cost of supply is low—that is, the households in urban areas and developed regions—have already been included on the supply. Thus the mean costs of supply would rise as a necessary consequence of blanket supply. In such circumstances, requiring that households cover full costs, as is now done, would reduce the various demand percentages below the estimates shown in table 5.12.

Concluding Speculations

In closing, the principal conclusions are reviewed along with the policies they suggest. The suggestions are highly speculative and are intended to stimulate, not to prescribe. Of the basic services reviewed, the two closest to being universally provided are medical care and primary education. As a means of making education more widely accessible, the possibility arose of a system of grants to deal with the burden

23. The survey also included the question, What additional services do households want from government? In the North 15 percent of households gave assistance with the costs of education as the single most desired item, 15 percent gave pure water, 19 percent gave electricity, and 16 percent gave bridges and highways.

of out-of-pocket costs on poor households having school-age children at the primary and secondary levels. With respect to medical care, the relatively high newborn and maternal death rates of Malays suggest that there may be considerable room for improvement of rural prenatal and postnatal care, despite the already pronounced efforts of government in this direction. It would be worth while to find out the degree to which the discrepancy in death rates of the newborn among the various partitions is the result of socioeconomic variables or of the lack of adequate care.

Access to and demand for public utilities are not nearly universal. Most of the poor do without. The data on access reinforce what already is known: Rural areas and the North are areas where deficits are pronounced. What is surprising—at first glance—is the importance of costs in determining who will purchase a public utility. Conservative estimates show that subsidies would be necessary for more than a quarter of the population, unless the costs of the services could be greatly reduced. As a source of water supply, standpipes appear to be a possible low-cost alternative. No low-cost alternative source of electricity is apparent.[24] And with respect to sewage disposal, hygiene need not require sophisticated flush systems in areas in which the density of population is low. In any event, if all public utilities are to be universally supplied and demanded, a departure from present pricing policy will be necessary, unless there is a radical innovation in the ways of producing and distributing services.

This argument leads to the question of alternative uses of the resources involved in any such subsidy—improving rural roads or schools, for example. Another aspect is the question of externalities. The positive externalities of hygienic water supply might justify a subsidy. Relevant here is the amount of disease that could be prevented by broadening the supply of clean water in the Peninsula. Some unpublished data from the Ministry of Health are indicative: stomach disorders and worms are listed among the eleven principal complaints of patients in government outpatient clinics; patients with gastroenteritis rank third in frequency of admission to government hospitals. In this context it is noteworthy that effective demand for pure water is highest in the North, where it is scarcest. Multifamily standpipes might be a

24. One possible alternative for rural electricity is autogeneration, which in 1974 accounted for 11 percent of the households with electricity in the Survey. Autogeneration could presumably be included in the official program of rural electrification, particularly where it is not feasible to tie villages into the national grid or to develop a large, independent generating capacity.

way of reducing unit costs. Similarly, public health externalities suggest the desirability in urban areas of providing flush systems, or at least a hygienic bucket or pit system.[25] The survey found that 14 percent of those living in large urban areas and 2 percent of those in metropolitan areas simply deposited their wastes on the ground or over streams.

Expansion of utility networks is greatly facilitated by the degree to which they generate financial returns, because the proceeds are generally used to finance investment in expansion of the network. Consequently any subsidy program would need to be explicitly discussed in conjunction with its effect on investment programs. Obviously the central government would need to provide the resources to meet the cash deficit and to provide for depreciation and, above all, expansion. If there are to be subsidies for the provision of public utilities, another question is, Who is to benefit? Blanket subsidies would clearly benefit those already consuming, which means that benefits would be negatively correlated with income. They would also be expensive. A better alternative would be a sliding tariff, with initial consumption of the utility at a very low rate, but with rates increasing as consumption goes up. Presumably the poor would consume very little, the rich a great deal. The poor would thus have access to a basic good at a very low cost.

One possible approach to surmounting these difficulties, and the problem of basic needs, might be a system of quasi-cash grants pegged to household per capita income and restricted to certain purposes—to cover the costs of school, of water, or possibly of certain foodstuffs, for example. In other words, a restricted kind of money, which could be used solely to meet basic needs of the poor, would be distributed.

---

25. In the bucket or pit systems a truck or cart moves human wastes from a pit or other container. Ultimate disposition is frequently to cultivated fields. It is possible to decontaminate such wastes before final disposition. In 1974 this mode was used by 56 percent of households in the Peninsula.

SIX

John Tillman

Stabilization and Public Finance

SUSTAINED ECONOMIC DEVELOPMENT in Malaysia did not begin until the 1960s. The Korean War had generated a major economic boom, but that boom was followed by a period of more modest growth. As economic growth accelerated in the 1960s, it was accompanied by an increase in gross capital formation as a proportion of GNP. For Peninsular Malaysia, investment averaged 18 percent of GNP in 1960–65; it was about 12 percent in 1955–59.[1] Much of this increase came from the growth of public investment. After a period of consolidation in the late 1960s, development expenditure was further expanded during the period of Malaysia's second plan, 1971–75, when public investment is estimated to have averaged 9.7 percent of GNP. The economy nevertheless continued to be prone to export-induced fluctuations because of the continuing importance of exports and the predominance in exports of a few primary commodities, which are subject to large variations in price.

A stronger savings effort facilitated the increases in investment. The average level of gross national saving rose from 15 percent of GNP during 1961–65 to 22 percent during 1971–75, but variation around the trend, largely generated by fluctuations in export earnings, was considerable. During the 1960s domestic saving was sufficient to finance investment and enable Malaysia to maintain a resource surplus. The surplus increased as the development effort was consolidated in the second half of the 1960s, but the expansion of the development program under the New Economic Policy altered the resource balance during 1971–75. Because of Malaysia's good credit standing, the emerging gap was financed without difficulty, and surpluses in 1976 and 1977 more than compensated for the current account deficits incurred in the preceding five years.

1. Historical data in this chapter are from Ministry of Finance, *Economic Report*, various years; Bank Negara, *Quarterly Economic Bulletin*, various issues; and International Monetary Fund (IMF), *International Financial Statistics*, various issues.

Although Malaysia continues to encourage private enterprise and maintain liberal policies for trade and payments, the public sector has grown in importance because of the expansion of the development program. During the period of Malaysia's second plan, public expenditure averaged 35 percent of GNP, well above the level for most developing countries. Government nevertheless introduced measures to ensure that current revenue did not lag too far behind total expenditure. New taxes were introduced; the rates of existing taxes were increased. The growth of revenue was also helped by the strong tax base created by the export sector. Even so, the absolute size of the gap in public financing more than tripled between 1966–70 and 1971–75. When measured as a proportion of GNP, however, the gap less than doubled, increasing from 4.8 to 9.3 percent. To finance that gap, government increased its foreign borrowing, both project and market, and its domestic borrowing from both the social security system and the financial sector.

Stabilization

The fluctuation of export earnings has been the principal cause of instability in the Malaysian economy. Dependence on a few primary exports, the prices of which are subject to large variations, makes it unrealistic to expect domestic policies to offset completely the effects of external changes. As is outlined below, however, the authorities have increasingly used a combination of monetary and fiscal policies in response to such fluctuations. The principal instruments of monetary policy have been regulating interest rates on commercial bank loans and deposits and varying the statutory reserve ratio. The federal government has used the budget countercyclically by controlling the rate of growth of government expenditure and, to a lesser degree, by changing taxation. In addition, a large part of federal tax revenue is derived from export and income taxes, both of which are sensitive to fluctuations in export prices. But the effectiveness of income tax as a countercyclical device has been limited by the lag between the receipt of income and payment of tax.

There have been two major export-led booms in the postwar period: the Korean War boom in 1950–51 and the commodity boom in 1973–74. Both tested countercyclical policy. In the first boom the policy response was limited to a small increase in the rates of export duty on rubber, the relaxation of certain import restrictions, the introduction of price controls, and the rationing of rice, sugar, and certain other commodities. Countercyclical policy nevertheless had become more active by the early 1970s. In the two decades between these booms, export earnings went through a number of cycles, with troughs in 1953–54, 1957–58, 1961–62, 1966–67, and 1971–72. In the two recessions of the 1950s, government reacted procyclically to declining revenue and increasing budget deficits by either restraining expenditure or scaling down plans for increased outlays. The acceleration in the government's development effort during 1961–65 began when export earnings and revenue collections were depressed. The budgetary response to the 1966–67 depression in exports was less marked, but the increased development efforts of the second plan coincided with the period of depressed export earnings in 1971 and 1972.

The export boom that began in late 1972 was superimposed on the expansionary fiscal and credit policies adopted in 1971 and 1972. Government responded with a series of monetary measures, increasing both the required reserve ratio and interest rates. Government also removed certain import restrictions and allowed the exchange rate to appreciate during the first half of 1973. The nominal rate appreciated 13 percent against the U.S. dollar; the trade-weighted effective rate appreciated 7 percent. These measures proved insufficient to deal with the expansionary factors influencing the money supply, which rose nearly 40 percent in 1973, and further monetary and fiscal measures were introduced in 1973 and 1974, including a 20 percent ceiling on credit expansion in 1974. Although discretionary fiscal responses to the export boom of 1973 were delayed in part by the fear of reducing the momentum of the country's development program, the tax system had more built-in stabilizers than in the early 1950s.

Between mid-1974 and mid-1975 export earnings sharply declined, resulting in a marked slowdown in economic growth. The dominant concern in 1975 and 1976 was to revive the economy without generating fresh inflationary pressure, and countercyclical policies were adopted. Credit policy was eased by abolishing the ceilings on credit expansion and lowering statutory reserve ratios and bank lending rates. The federal budget deficit increased to about 9 percent of GNP in 1975; it was about 7 percent of GNP in 1974.

Development of the Monetary System

The operation and development of monetary institutions have reflected both the development of the economy and the fiscal and financial policies of government. At the beginning of the 1950s the monetary system comprised a currency board and commercial banks. The currency board was the sole issuer of domestic currency, which it issued in exchange for sterling. Its assets were largely kept in sterling assets, mainly U.K. assets. A central bank was formally established in January 1959. It was given powers to be the sole issuer of currency and to regulate commercial banks through the prescription of minimum reserve and liquidity requirements for commercial banks and through the regulation of interest rates for loans and deposits. Because of the prospects of a political union between the Federation of Malaya and the other members of the currency board—Singapore, Sabah, Sarawak, and Brunei—the central bank did not replace the currency board as the issuer of currency until June 1967.

With the establishment of the central bank, explicit monetary policy became possible. Initially reliance was placed on setting the minimum loan and maximum deposit rates of commercial banks. Subsequently use has also been made of the statutory reserve ratio to influence the growth of credit. Direct influence of the money supply through open market operations has been limited by the absence of an active secondary market in government securities. The central bank has not attempted to encourage the growth of a secondary market for government securities, and open market operations have not been developed as a monetary policy instrument. Since the floating of the Malaysian ringgit in 1973, exchange rate management has become an additional policy option.

In the absence of domestic financing of the public sector by monetary authorities, currency has been created by exchanging foreign assets for local assets. This exchange provides the basic link between the balance of payments and the money supply (currency and commercial bank deposits). In the 1950s commercial banks were largely oriented toward foreign trade. But with the growth of the economy and with encouragement from the central bank, they became increasingly oriented toward the domestic economy. Originally, and in keeping with their status as branches of foreign banks and their orientation to foreign trade, banks kept their liquid assets abroad. Since the mid-1960s they have been required to hold their liquid assets domestically, and government provides securities for this purpose. Thus, from the mid-1960s onward, commercial banks have provided significant financing to government. Despite these changes, the basic characteristics of money supply have remained similar throughout the postwar period: the increase in net foreign assets of the central bank has provided the basis for the growth of the money supply.

Table 6.1. *Factors Influencing the Money Supply,*
1961-65, 1966-70, and 1971-75

	Average annual percentage change			Change in net foreign and domestic assets as proportion of change in monetary base[b]	
Period	Money supply[a]	Monetary base	Multiplier	Net foreign assets	Net domestic assets
1961–65	5.3	4.8	0.1	1.16	0.02
1966–70	6.7	6.3	0.3	1.30	−0.12
1971–75	16.6	18.1	−0.1	1.60	−0.26

Source: Calculated from IMF, *International Financial Statistics,* various issues.

a. The instantaneous percentage change in the money supply should be exactly given by the sum of the percentage change in the monetary base and the multiplier. Because data exist only for discrete points in time, the factoring here is approximate.

b. The monetary base is equal to net foreign assets (net international reserves of the central bank) plus net domestic assets (central bank holdings of government securities less government deposits) plus other items net.

In table 6.1 the growth of the money supply is approximately factored between the change in the monetary base—that is, the net foreign and domestic assets of the central bank—and the change in a multiplicative factor that depends upon the portfolio behavior of commercial banks and the public. That growth was almost entirely the result of the growth in the monetary base. Because the central bank has not provided finance for government, the dominant influence in the growth of the money supply has been the surplus in the balance of payments. Nevertheless the monetary effect of the expansionary fiscal policies pursued in 1971–75 came through the impact on the balance of payments of the foreign market borrowing by government. During 1971–75 that borrowing was responsible for more than half the increase in the net foreign assets of the central bank.

Monetary Impact of Public Sector Financing

The development of the monetary system and the financing requirements of the public sector have been closely related. The monetary system encouraged certain patterns of public sector financing; the government's financing needs over the years influenced the growth of the monetary system. But because government has had access to growing tax revenue and growing social security surpluses, the financing needs of the public sector have not been beyond the resources of the financial sector and the feasible limits of foreign borrowing. Thus the monetary system and the money supply have not been drastically changed by the financing needs of government. The monetary system evolved without actively having to be the lender of last resort to government.

The extent to which the cautious fiscal policies of government were the result of the original structure of the financial sector—a structure which encouraged government to rely on tax revenue and social security surpluses for meeting growing expenditure, not on domestic and foreign financial borrowing—is conjectural. For most of the postwar period, foreign borrowing has been the residual component in the government budget. Expenditure has been adjusted to keep such borrowing needs within bounds. Although federal government expenditure increased from 17 percent of GNP in 1955–60 to 29 percent in 1976, revenue also increased. Social security contributions financed a large part of the budget deficit, leaving a residual deficit to be financed from foreign and domestic sources, a deficit that has risen from about zero in 1955–60 to 5 percent of GNP in 1971–75. The need for inflationary financing has been limited. Net borrowing from the central bank has not been a feature of Malaysian financial policy, and recourse to foreign market loans has been restrained. The bulk of domestic borrowing, other than that from the Employees' Provident Fund, has been from the virtually captive market of commercial banks, insurance companies, and other private financial institutions.

In this examination of the effect of the public sector on the monetary system and the money supply, the focus is on the federal government. Not only is the federal government the largest element of the public sector, accounting for the bulk of public sector revenue and deficits; federal loans and grants are the principal source of finance for state government deficits. Until the mid-1970s the recourse of state governments to other borrowing was limited to loans of up to one year in maturity from approved domestic banks. Public authorities either borrow directly from the federal government or receive foreign project loans under the auspices of the federal government. Foreign project loans are generally tied to financing specific imports and therefore do not have the monetary effect of foreign market loans or the use of foreign assets.

The development of federal government financing is given in table 6.2. In this table the financing of the deficit is split into monetary and nonmonetary financing. Monetary financing comprises financing from the central bank, commercial banks, foreign market loans, and the use of foreign assets. Other domestic financing, mainly social security sur-

Table 6.2. *Federal Government Financing, 1956–75*

Item	Millions of Malaysian dollars				Percentage of gross national product	
	1956–60	*1961–65*	*1966–70*	*1971–75*	*1956–60*	*1961–65*
Revenue	4,002	6,366	9,897	18,546	15.7	18.5
Grants	154	106	196	74	0.6	0.3
Expenditure	4,419	7,916	12,437	24,998	17.3	23.0
Overall budget deficit	−263	−1,444	−2,404	−6,378	−1.0	−4.2
Financing	263	1,444	2,404	6,378	1.0	4.2
Monetary financing	n.a.	369	945	2,063	n.a.	1.1
Central bank	n.a.	−35	−221	31	n.a.	−0.1
Commercial banks	n.a.	93	657	990	n.a.	0.3
Foreign[a]	n.a.	311	509	1,042	n.a.	0.9
Nonmonetary financing	n.a.	1,075	1,459	4,315	n.a.	3.1
Public funds	n.a.	0	364	221	n.a.	0
Social security	424	591	1,008	1,958	1.7	1.7
Other domestic	n.a.	75	53	820	n.a.	0.2
Foreign project borrowing	n.a.	48	240	809	n.a.	0.1
Unidentified	n.a.	361	−206	507	n.a.	1.0

Note: Figures for 1956–63 are for Peninsular Malaysia.
— Not applicable.
... Zero or negligible.
n.a. Not available.

pluses, and foreign project loans are classified as nonmonetary financing. To a large extent, nonmonetary financing represents a transfer of private sector savings to government; foreign project loans are usually related to the foreign costs of a particular project and do not represent any addition to domestic demand. Monetary financing of the overall deficit grew from 1.1 percent of GNP in 1961–65 to 2.4 percent of GNP in 1971–75. Part of the increase during 1971–75 was the result of countercyclical policies designed to offset the slowdown in export-induced growth in 1974–75.

During the 1950s budget deficits were frequently more than met by the surpluses of the Employees' Provident Fund, a social security institution started in 1951. The social security system continues to be an important source of financing; it contributed 31 percent to the financing of deficits during 1971–75. The expanded development program in the

Percentage of gross national product		Financing as a percentage of the budget deficit			
1966–70	1971–75	1961–65	1966–70	1971–75	Item
19.3	21.1	—	—	—	Revenue
0.4	0.1	—	—	—	Grants
24.2	28.5	—	—	—	Expenditure
−4.7	−7.3	—	—	—	Overall budget deficit
4.7	7.3	100	100	100	Financing
1.8	2.4	26	39	32	Monetary financing
−0.4	...	−2	−9	—	Central bank
1.3	1.1	6	27	16	Commercial banks
1.0	1.2	22	21	16	Foreign[a]
2.8	4.9	74	61	68	Nonmonetary financing
0.7	0.3	0	15	3	Public funds
2.0	2.2	41	42	31	Social security
0.1	0.9	5	2	13	Other domestic
0.5	0.9	3	10	13	Foreign project borrowing
−0.4	0.6	25	−8	8	Unidentified

Sources: Ministry of Finance, *Economic Report*, various years; Bank Negara, *Quarterly Economic Bulletin*, various issues; IMF, *International Monetary Statistics*, various issues.

a. Market loans plus use of foreign assets; excludes foreign project borrowing.

1960s increased the budget deficits, which averaged 4.5 percent of GNP during the 1960s. Beginning in 1965–67 a significant part of the deficits were financed by the financial sector through the requirement that the holdings of government securities by the financial sector be related to its assets. The liquidity requirements for commercial banks were changed to make only domestic assets eligible as required liquid assets; in practice these assets consist largely of government securities, including treasury bills. Previously, banks held the bulk of their liquid assets as balances with foreign banks. Insurance companies have also been required to invest 20 percent of their assets in government securities.

During much of the 1960s the use of the foreign assets accumulated in the 1950s amounted to as much as half of the foreign monetary financing; foreign project financing remained limited. Only limited foreign borrowing was needed during the period of Malaysia's first plan, 1966–70; part of the foreign monetary financing was the transfer of government assets to the central bank, accounting in part for the decline in central bank financing.

As a consequence of the way in which public debt was financed, more than half the debt of the federal government has been held by the Employees' Provident Fund, other social security institutions, and official funds. The remaining domestic debt has been almost entirely held by the financial sector; commercial banks held three-quarters of this debt during 1971–75. Despite increased foreign borrowing in the first half of the 1970s, the external public debt remains modest. A portion of recent commitments is not scheduled to be disbursed for some years. The debt-service ratio for external public debt—that is, the ratio of annual payments of principal and interest on that debt in relation to annual exports of merchandise and services—remains low. It increased from only 1.3 percent in 1965 to 4.3 percent in 1976.

Price Developments

During most of the postwar period, Malaysia has maintained a high degree of price stability. Rapid inflation has occurred only in two periods: during the Korean War boom in 1950–51, when the consumer price index rose by nearly 40 percent; and during the export boom in 1973–74, when that index rose by 30 percent. Between these two periods, any increases in prices were isolated events, as in 1957, 1963, and 1967. From 1956 to 1972 the price level increased only 16 percent; the average annual increase was 0.9 percent. Malaysia's experience with prices compares favorably with other developing countries and with many industrial countries. Inflation in the industrial countries averaged 3.2 percent a year during 1956–72—it averaged 2.7 percent a year in the United States, 3.9 percent in the United Kingdom, and 4.9 percent in Japan. Although inflation in Malaysia in 1973–74 was higher than that in the industrial countries as a group, it has since been lower. Among Malaysia's partners in the Association of the South-East Asian Nations, only Singapore has had a comparable price record; Thailand, Indonesia, and the Philippines have had more rapid inflation.

What accounts for such price stability? A salient feature of the Malaysian economy is its openness to foreign trade, and the stability of import prices, except in 1950–51 and 1973–74, has contributed to domestic price developments. Not only do exports and imports each account for nearly half of GNP; trade and capital flows are subject to relatively few restrictions. Because the economy of Malaysia is relatively small, the country is a price taker for imports: that is, the prices of Malaysian imports, expressed in a foreign currency, are largely independent of domestic developments. Changes in export prices have only a limited direct impact on the consumer price index because the domestic consumption of most export commodities is small. Thus domestic price developments would be expected to follow import price developments if the exchange rate is fixed.

Until the early 1970s the only import price index available from Malaysia was a unit value index, which does not fully distinguish between changes in quality and changes in price. An alternative index of import prices is the World Bank index of international inflation, which is calculated on the basis of prices of manufactured exports from developed countries. Because manufactured goods constitute a large proportion of Malaysian imports—64 percent in 1976—this alternative index, when expressed in Malaysian currency, provides some indication of import price developments. The import price index, the international inflation index, and the consumer price index are shown in figure 6.1. For much of the postwar period, including the periods of rapid inflation in the early 1950s and the 1970s, movements of consumer prices followed those of import prices. Nevertheless changes in aggregate demand must at times have had a short-run effect on domestic prices, particularly the prices of goods and services not entering into international trade.

In the long run, inflationary pressure is reflected in balance-of-payments developments. Thus, if domestic policies generate domestic demand beyond that which could be financed by sustained capital inflows, a deterioration would be expected in the balance of payments, and the result would be a loss of reserves. If, as has happened in some countries, the authorities react to the loss of reserves by introducing import controls and other restrictive measures, the openness of the economy would be reduced. This reduction would increase the extent to which domestic price developments could deviate from those of external prices. But Malaysia has not been subject to periodic balance of payments crises. Indeed the rise in net reserves has been virtually uninterrupted. This has been partly the result of the satisfactory performance of exports. Another reason has been the cautious monetary and fiscal policies followed by the authorities.

The prospects for inflation in Malaysia during the period to 1985 are closely linked to international price developments. The index of international inflation on the average rose 1 percent a year during 1951–70; the prospects through 1985 are for an annual rate of 6 to 7 percent. As

Figure 6.1.   *Price Indexes, Peninsular Malaysia, 1950–76*
(1970=100)

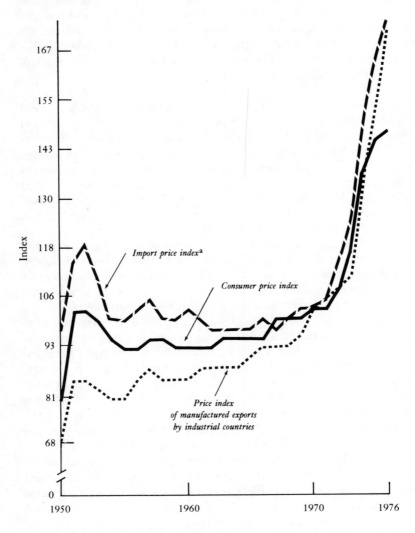

Note: The import price index and the price index of manufactured exports by industrial countries are in relation to Malaysian currency.

Sources: Price index of manufactured exports from World Bank, "Price Prospects for Major Primary Commodities" (a restricted-circulation document), various years; other indexes from data supplied by the Malaysia Department of Statistics.

a. A unit value index before 1970.

argued above, if the exchange rate continues to be fixed, inflation in Malaysia can be expected to be close to the international rate. Appreciating the exchange rate would tend to reduce domestic inflation but, if the appreciation were not well timed, it could have adverse effects on the export sector and, through its impact on domestic prices of rubber and palm oil, on the incomes of the smallholder sector.

If inflation in Malaysia were to be 6 to 7 percent on a continuing basis, it would sharply contrast with the rate prevailing during the twenty years before 1973, when Malaysian prices were virtually stable. If Malaysian authorities are unwilling to accept such a rate of inflation, they might wish to use monetary and fiscal policies to reduce aggregate demand. Given the openness of the Malaysian economy, however, a major contractionary effort would be needed to reduce inflation well below the international level. Such a policy, continuously in force, could have an adverse effect on growth. Although it might be possible to combine acceptable adjustments in the exchange rate with monetary and fiscal measures to reduce domestic inflation to a level somewhat below the international rate, that level would still be well in excess of the rate prevailing during the 1950s and 1960s. The Malaysian authorities will thus need to plan to minimize the disruptions and losses incurred by sectors of the economy that have difficulty dealing with continuing inflation.

Patterns of Public Expenditure and Revenue

The growth of public expenditure in relation to GNP has been rapid. Such expenditure rose from 28 percent of GNP in 1966–70 to 35 percent in 1971–75; it peaked at 38 percent in 1975, when GNP was depressed. These ratios are exceptionally high for a developing country and comparable to the ratios for many developed countries.[2] The expenditure for economic development showed the largest relative increase (table 6.3). That expenditure comprises federal development expenditure and investment by public entities and such publicly owned cor-

---

2. There are difficulties in obtaining consistent data for international comparisons of the relative sizes of public sector expenditure. For differing two-year periods during 1972–75 the ratio of central government expenditure to GDP was 30 percent for Malaysia, 35 percent for the United States, 36 percent for the United Kingdom, and 37 percent for the Federal Republic of Germany. It was 11 percent for the Philippines, 14 percent for Thailand, 18 percent for Indonesia, and 26 percent for Singapore. These figures were calculated from data in IMF, *International Monetary Statistics*, various issues.

Table 6.3. *Distribution of Public Sector Expenditure,*
1966–70, 1971–75, 1976, and Estimates for 1976–80

Item	Percentage of gross national product			
	1966–70	*1971–75*	*1976*	*1976–80*
Current expenditure[a]	20.9	24.6	26.1	27.5
Federal	17.2	20.6	22.5	23.0
Security[a]	5.4	6.5	6.1	n.a.
Social services	5.6	6.9	6.7	n.a.
Economic services	1.4	1.6	1.7	n.a.
General administration	1.9	2.1	2.1	n.a.
Debt, pensions, and other	2.9	3.5	5.9	n.a.
State	3.7	4.0	3.6	4.5
Development expenditure	6.9	10.0	10.6	9.9
Social	1.3	1.6	n.a.	1.7
Economic	5.6	8.5	n.a.	8.1
PETRONAS investment	—	—	n.a.	0.8
Total	27.8	34.6	36.7	38.2

— Not applicable.
n.a. Not available.
Sources: Ministry of Finance, *Economic Report*, various years; World Bank estimates based on revised expenditure in the third plan.
a. Includes development expenditure for security: 1.2 percent of GNP in 1971–75 and 1.3 percent of GNP in 1976–80.

porations as Perbadanan Nasional Berhad (PERNAS), the Urban Development Authority, and the state economic development corporations. The increased current expenditure for social services largely reflects rising wages and employment in health and education. About 90 percent of current expenditure on those services has been for the compensation of employees, compared with 50 percent for economic services.

During the period of the third plan, public expenditure was expected to average 37.4 percent of GNP.[3] The increase was to be the result of higher federal current expenditure, which was planned to rise to 23 percent of GNP in 1976–80 from 21 percent in 1971–75. Much of this increase had already occurred by 1976, when federal current ex-

3. The figure for 1976–80 excludes the investments by Petroliam Nasional Berhad (PETRONAS) in the oil sector; those investments were expected to be equivalent to 0.8 percent of GNP.

penditure, including total security expenditure, amounted to 22.5 percent of GNP. The share of development expenditure in GNP was to remain about the same as that for 1971–75, as was the distribution of this expenditure between social and economic programs.

During 1971–75 public revenue in Malaysia averaged 26 percent of GNP, a high percentage relative to other countries at a similar level of development. Also during 1971–75 the tax revenue of the federal government averaged 19 percent of GNP, a level possible because of the character of the economy and because of the government's efforts to raise taxes.[4] Early in the postwar period, taxes on international trade provided more than three-quarters of federal tax revenue. But as new taxes were introduced, taxes on international trade declined in importance. Income tax was introduced on a permanent basis in 1947; it has since become the largest source of tax revenue, contributing nearly 30 percent of tax revenue in 1971–75. Export earnings now are taxed implicitly through the corporate income tax and explicitly through export duties.

Import duties were originally concentrated on a few commodities, principally tobacco, liquor, and petroleum. During the mid-1960s the revenue from these duties was adversely affected by import substitution. To offset this effect, excise taxes were imposed on domestically produced goods. The base of indirect taxes was further widened with the introduction of the import surtax in 1967 and the sales tax in 1972. These two taxes contributed 11 percent of tax revenue in 1976. In addition, to capture the diversification of exports, taxes were extended to exports of palm oil and timber in 1968, although the latter was restricted because timber extraction is taxed by the state governments. Increased oil production and higher oil prices have provided a new source of federal revenue. In 1976 about 7 percent of federal taxes were derived from oil production, an amount equal to 1.5 percent of GNP.

Given the introduction of new taxes, the increase in the rates of existing taxes, and the built-in elasticity of the tax system, federal tax revenue increased from 13 percent of GNP in 1964 to 20 percent in 1976

---

4. For the ratio of tax to GNP during 1972–76, Malaysia ranked fifth in a sample of forty-seven countries. Its high ratio was the result of a high level of domestic income and the importance of exports in GNP, two factors contributing to the lending capacity of any country. One study has shown that Malaysia's high ratio was about what would be expected when these two factors are taken into account. Alan A. Tait, Wilfrid L. M. Grätz, and Barry Eichengreen, "International Comparisons of Taxation for Selected Developing Countries, 1972–76," *International Monetary Fund Staff Working Papers*, vol. 26, no. 1 (March 1979), pp. 123–56.

Table 6.4. *Buoyancies and Elasticities of Revenue, Estimates for 1964–76*

Item	Proxy for tax base	Average buoyancies	R^2	Average built-in elasticities	R^2
Federal taxes[a]	GNP	1.26	0.99	—	—
Personal income tax	GDP	—	—	1.55	0.98
Company tax[b]	Exports	—	—	1.45	0.97
Indirect taxes[c]	GNP	—	—	0.88	0.99
Federal nontax revenue	GNP	0.73	0.74	—	—
State government revenue[a]	GNP	0.83	0.80	—	—
Public authority surpluses	GNP	0.44	0.28	—	—

— Not applicable.

Sources: Elasticities from John P. Hutton, "Income Tax and the Distribution of Income in Malaysia" (Kuala Lumpur: Ministry of Finance, 1977; processed); buoyancies calculated from Treasury, *Estimates of Federal Government Revenue,* various years.

a. Excludes oil revenue. Including oil revenue gives a buoyancy of 1.3.

b. Excludes oil revenue.

c. Excludes export taxes.

(table 6.4). For the 1964–76 period the average buoyancy of federal taxes in relation to GNP is estimated to have been 1.4. Tax buoyancies measure not only the relation of actual tax collections to the tax base or its proxy, but the effect of discretionary changes made in the tax schedules. To forecast future tax revenue, an estimate is required of the built-in tax elasticity—that is, the relation of tax revenue to the tax base. The elasticities of various taxes in Malaysia have been estimated in a number of studies. One of those studies estimated tax elasticities for income taxes on individuals, income taxes on companies (excluding oil revenue), and indirect taxes other than export taxes (table 6.4).[5] For personal income tax, nominal GDP lagged by one and two years was used as the tax base. For company income tax, the most satisfactory proxy for the tax base was found to be the value of exports of goods and nonfactor services in current prices lagged by one and two years. The lags are the result of basing current-year tax liabilities on income earned in the previous year. The finding that export earnings are the most appropriate proxy for the tax base can be explained by the importance of export earnings in company profits and taxes. For indirect taxes, the

5. John P. Hutton, "Income Tax and the Distribution of Income in Malaysia" (Kuala Lumpur: Ministry of Finance, 1977; processed).

tax base was nominal GNP, split into a real income component and a price component to capture the effects of specific taxes.

The elasticity of the personal income tax for 1964–76 is estimated to have been 1.55, which means that revenue from this source could be projected to grow 1.55 times faster than GDP. The long-run elasticity of company income tax is estimated to have been 1.45. For indirect taxes the elasticities in relation to real GNP and the price level were found to be virtually identical—0.88. The results indicate that revenue from personal and company income taxes should more than keep up with the growth of income and exports, but that increases in tax rates will be necessary for indirect taxes to maintain their relative yield. The tax buoyancies for federal nontax revenue, state government revenue, and public authority surpluses were found to be less than unity—that is, these sources of revenue have not grown as fast as nominal GNP.

Budgetary Prospects for 1976–85

Malaysia's favorable prospects for growth in exports, real income, and oil production indicate that public sector resources, including domestic borrowing and foreign project loans, are likely to increase substantially during the 1976–85 period.[6] These resources could reach 39 percent of GNP during 1981–85; their rate of increase will probably be faster than that of public sector expenditure. There consequently would be a substantial reduction in the gap to be financed by foreign market borrowing. If this reduction materializes, government may wish to increase its expenditure beyond the predicted level, particularly in a way that affects households in poverty. Certain expenditures on education, health, and utilities could be increased, and additional resources could be raised by maintaining indirect taxes at their existing level of GNP or by allowing the full progressiveness of direct taxes and export taxes to take effect. Alternatively, if it appears likely that the projected increase in public sector resources will have an adverse effect on private investment, appropriate reductions should be considered in corporate income taxes or in domestic borrowing. Because the recent large increases in oil production and the more favorable prices for primary commodities have made the outlook for public sector resources

6. Public sector resources comprise government revenue, public authority surpluses, PETRONAS surpluses, domestic borrowing, and foreign project borrowing.

appear much brighter than was expected at the time the third plan was drafted, the resource prospects for the periods of the third and fourth plans are examined in detail in this section to determine whether a more ambitious development plan is financially viable. Projections of public sector revenue, potential domestic borrowing, and foreign project borrowing are compared with proposed public expenditure.[7]

Public Revenue

Revenue from oil production and export taxes is estimated directly from production and export forecasts; other revenue is estimated by using the buoyancies and elasticities in table 6.4. Projections of export tax revenue for the principal exports were based on the forecasts of exports given in chapter nine. The forecasts of tax revenue appear in table 6.5. Tax revenue is considerably less than would have been obtained by applying the current tax schedules to the forecasts of export volumes and values. Over the longer term, the prices of rubber and palm oil are expected to increase significantly and the progressiveness of the tax schedules would cause these export taxes to increase in relation to the value of exports. The progressiveness of these tax schedules was intended as a countercyclical device to capture part of the increased export earnings resulting from temporarily high prices, not to increase export tax receipts because of a secular increase in prices. It thus seems plausible to assume that some adjustments will be made in the export tax schedules.

For rubber it is expected that the real price will be maintained. It may therefore be plausible to assume that the proportion of export revenue collected as tax can remain at the high level of 18 percent expected in 1978 and not adversely affect profitability. For 1976–80 and 1981–85 it is therefore assumed that 18 percent of the value of rubber exports will be collected as tax. If no adjustment were made to the tax schedule, tax revenue would equal nearly 30 percent of the value of rubber exports by 1985, yielding an additional M$4 billion during 1979–85. For palm oil the real price is expected to be lower in 1978–85 than in recent

---

7. The macroeconomic framework of this analysis uses a 1976 base and assumes an average annual GDP growth rate of 6.7 percent in real terms and 15 percent in nominal terms for 1976–85. In accord with the analysis in chapter three and appendix A, this growth is broadly consistent with an assumption that private investment would recover, but that government expenditure would not markedly expand beyond what is forecast in the third plan.

Table 6.5. *Revenue from Export Taxes, by Principal Commodity, 1971–75, and Projections for 1976–80 and 1981–85*

	1971–75		1976–80		1981–85	
Commodity	Millions of Malaysian dollars	Revenue as a percentage of export value	Millions of Malaysian dollars	Revenue as a percentage of export value	Millions of Malaysian dollars	Revenue as a percentage of export value
Rubber	837	8	3,670	18	6,535	18
Palm oil	620	17	1,471	16	3,205	16
Tin	850	16	1,660	19	2,520	20
Other[a]	161	—	215	—	372	—
Total	2,468	—	7,016	—	12,362	—

— Not applicable.
Sources: Data supplied by Malaysian authorities and World Bank estimates.
a. Mainly timber and pepper. Oil is separately treated in table 6.6.

years, making some reduction in tax-to-exports ratio appropriate. Because the profitability of palm oil is thought to be somewhat higher than that for rubber, the tax burden on palm oil could remain at the 1977 level of 16 percent of export value. If no adjustment were made to the tax schedules, this revenue would come to nearly 25 percent of the value of palm oil exports, yielding an additional M$1 billion during 1979–85. For tin the situation is more complex. The projected decline in the volume of tin exports is in part the result of the current economic difficulties of the tin industry, suggesting that some reduction in the export tax rate would be appropriate. But if the tin industry's problems of access to previously unmined tin deposits are resolved, the present ratio of tax revenue to export value may prove acceptable. The current tax schedules are therefore assumed to remain unchanged, and tax revenue to be equal to 20 percent of export value.

Export taxes on pepper and on timber exported from Peninsular Malaysia form a large part of the remaining export taxes. Tax revenue from pepper is assumed to grow 14 percent a year because of increases of 7 percent in both volume and price. Export duties on timber are restricted to the 15 percent tax on logs exported from the Peninsula, but such exports are being rapidly phased out. Most timber exports are from Sabah and Sarawak and are not subject to federal tax. The principal tax on timber is the royalty on the extraction of forest products that accrues to state governments; in 1973 such royalties amounted to about 17 percent of the value of timber exported.

The production of oil will be a large source of revenue during the periods of the third and fourth plans. In addition, the production of liquefied natural gas, which is covered by agreements similar to those for oil, is scheduled to begin toward the end of the fourth plan period. Although this production will substantially boost public sector revenue, no estimate of revenue from liquefied natural gas is included in this forecast. Thus revenue prospects are even more favorable than those given here for oil alone. Projections of oil revenue are based on official forecasts that oil production would increase to 240,000 barrels a day by 1980 (table 6.6). For the 1981–85 period, oil production is assumed to increase 5 percent a year, implying some further increase in known oil reserves. Through a 10 percent royalty and a 45 percent tax on income derived from the production of oil, government collects more than 40 percent of the value of oil production as tax. In addition, the after-tax income of PETRONAS is available to the public sector. But in making projections of public sector resources, it is assumed that PETRONAS will finance its share of the cost of various petroleum-related

Table 6.6. *Oil Revenue, Projections for 1976–80 and 1981–85*

Item	1976–80	1981–85
Average price, (Malaysian dollars a metric ton)	282	404
Average volume (thousands of barrels a day)	207	280
	Millions of Malaysian dollars	
Federal oil revenue .	4,973	9,751
Royalties	720	1,375
Income tax	4,253	8,376
PETRONAS	3,167	6,051
Oil companies[a]	1,086	2,325
State oil revenue	720	1,375
Net revenue of PETRONAS after tax	3,885	7,424
Investments	1,330	4,320
Surplus	2,555	3,104
Gross public revenue[b]	9,578	18,550
Net public revenue[c]	8,248	14,230

Source: World Bank estimates.
a. The basis is previous year's production.
b. Before PETRONAS investments.
c. Net of PETRONAS investments.

investment out of its oil income. During the 1976-80 and 1980-85 periods, it is assumed that PETRONAS will finance 65 percent of the M$3.6 billion project for liquefied natural gas, as well as its share of a fertilizer plant, oil refinery, and other investments. Thus only half of its M$11.3 billion in income from oil will be available for public sector financing.

Projections of revenue from personal and corporate income tax and from indirect taxes were made by using the tax elasticities given in table 6.4 and the growth assumed for income and exports during 1976-85 (table 6.7). Real income is assumed to grow at an average annual rate of 6.7 percent during 1976-85; in nominal terms the growth rate is assumed to average 15 percent. Because of the growth in incomes and exports, in both real and nominal terms, the progressiveness of personal and corporate income taxes, as measured by the tax elasticity, would generate an increase in the burden of these taxes. Revenue from personal income taxes would rise from 2 percent of GNP in 1976 to 4 percent in 1985; revenue from corporate income tax, excluding that derived from oil production, would rise from 4 percent of GNP in 1976 to 8 percent in 1985.

It is assumed that government will take steps to moderate these increases, adjusting the tax schedules so that only part of the effects of the nominal and real rise in the tax base are captured. Thus revenue from personal income tax for 1981-85 is assumed to average 3 percent of GNP; that from corporate tax 7.5 percent of GNP. The tax buoyancies given in table 6.4 were also used to project nontax revenue, state government revenue, and public authority surpluses. Public sector revenue is projected to increase from 26 percent of GNP in 1971-75 to about 32 percent during 1976-85; revenue was already at this high level in 1977, when it amounted to 32.4 percent of GNP. Higher direct and export tax revenue and oil sector revenue, which more than offset the decline in indirect taxes and nonoil revenues of state government, were responsible for the increase.

Domestic Borrowing

Under existing institutional arrangements, the principal sources of domestic borrowing during 1976-85 will continue to be the social security system, principally the Employees' Provident Fund, and the financial sector. To project the resources expected to be available from that fund during 1976-85, gross contributions, withdrawals, and the interest on accumulated assets were forecast. Withdrawals are a func-

Table 6.7. *Public Revenue, 1971–75, and Projections for 1976–80 and 1981–85*

Item	Millions of Malaysian dollars			Percentage of gross national product		
	1971–75	1976–80	1981–85	1971–75	1976–80	1981–85
Federal revenue	18,641	45,238	90,437	21.2	25.4	26.6
Personal income tax	4,915	4,528	10,182	5.6	2.5	3.0
Corporate income tax		9,860	25,500		5.5	7.5
Oil[a]	746	4,973	9,751	0.9	2.8	2.9
Export taxes	2,468	7,016	12,362	2.8	3.9	3.6
Other indirect taxes	8,308	15,198	26,894	9.5	8.5	7.9
Nontax	2,204	3,663	5,748	2.5	2.1	1.7
State revenue	3,330	6,202	10,853	3.8	3.5	3.2
Nonoil	3,152	5,495	9,478	3.6	3.1	2.8
Oil	178	707	1,375	0.2	0.4	0.4
Total government revenue	21,971	51,440	101,290	25.0	28.9	29.8
Public authority surplus	705	1,354	2,582	0.8	0.8	0.8
Surplus of PETRONAS (net of investment)	—	2,555	3,104	—	1.4	0.9
Total public revenue	22,676	55,349	106,976	25.8	31.1	31.5

— Not applicable.
Sources: 1971–75 from Ministry of Finance, *Economic Report*, various years; other periods from calculations by the World Bank.
a. Income tax on oil.

tion of the growth of past contributions and retirement rates; gross contributions depend upon the growth of wages and the size of the employed labor force. In the past, expansion in the fund's coverage has caused the number of contributors to grow faster than employment. Although there may be some scope for further extending that coverage—for example, to self-employed persons—it is assumed the coverage will remain unchanged during 1976-85. The growth in the number of contributors is therefore assumed to be equal to the increase in employment. It was forecast in the third plan that the labor force would grow 3.3 percent a year. If the unemployment rate remains unchanged, this would also be the rate of growth of the labor force. The growth in real wage rates is assumed to be equal to the growth in productivity which, in those sectors of the economy covered by the Employees' Provident Fund, has been forecast to increase about 4.4 percent a year during the periods of the third and fourth plans. Thus wage payments are forecast to grow at an annual rate of 7.8 percent in real terms and 15.4 percent in nominal terms.

Regulations limit the growth in contributions to the Employees' Provident Fund to the increase in the wage bill of those employees whose wages are less than M$500 a month. Contributions are compulsory only on the first M$500 a month; beyond this wage level, payments are voluntary. During the period of the third plan, however, the wages of most earners in Peninsular Malaysia were likely to remain well below M$500 a month. If a substantial portion of wages exceed M$500, it seems likely that the limit would be raised. It therefore is reasonable to assume that the growth in gross contributions will be close to the growth in the nominal wage bill. Details of the projected increase in the fund's assets are given in table 6.8. During 1976-85 it is possible that the fund may be allowed to invest in publicly owned corporations. Such investment would not affect the total assets available to the public sector, because these corporations now receive their capital directly from the federal development budget.

Regulations covering commercial banks and certain other financial institutions ensure that the long-run demand of the financial sector for government securities, including treasury bills, is linked to the growth of the private sector's financial assets. The relation of the growth of national income to private financial assets can be approximated by the elasticity of real income in relation to the private sector's demand for real liquid assets—that is, currency plus the demand and time deposits of the private sector at commercial banks. That elasticity is estimated to

Table 6.8. *Increase in Assets of the Employees' Provident Fund, 1971–75, and Projections for 1976–80 and 1981–85*

Item	Millions of Malaysian dollars		
	1971–75	1976–80	1981–85
Gross contributions	1,504	3,436	6,991
Withdrawals	−405	−856	−1,386
Interest income	938	1,915	3,962
Administrative expenses	−44	−83	−134
Increase in assets	1,993	4,412	9,433

Sources: Data supplied by the Employees' Provident Fund and World Bank estimates.

be about 1.7. This estimate may tend, however, to be an understatement of the true relation, because there is some evidence that other financial assets have been growing faster than liquidity. Estimates of the financial sector's lending to government are given in table 6.9. The larger increase in the public sector's deposits with commercial banks during 1976–80 is the result of the rapid buildup of deposits during 1976 and 1977—a buildup caused by the increased public revenue in those years.

Implications of Additional Resources for Expenditure

The resources available to the public sector during 1976–85 are compared with estimates of the likely levels of public expenditure in table 6.10.[8] It is assumed that government current expenditure will be about 26 percent of GNP during 1976–85—M$47 billion in 1976–80 and M$89 billion in 1981–85. That expenditure was 23.4 percent of GNP during 1971–75. The allocation for development expenditure in the third plan was M$18.6 billion, with a provision for a higher target of M$20 billion in the event of the availability of additional resources. Given the subsequent improvements in the resource prospects of the public sector, it became probable that an even higher target would be set during the mid-term review of that plan. For the purposes of this analysis, how-

8. Domestic borrowing from the social security and financial system and foreign project borrowing are included in resource availability; domestic borrowing from the central bank is excluded.

Table 6.9. *Net Lending to Government by the Financial Sector, 1971-75, and Projections for 1976-80 and 1981-85*

| | Millions of Malaysian dollars | | |
Item	1971-75	1976-80	1981-85
Increase in government securities[a]	2,339	5,031	10,300
Increase in public sector deposits	544	1,140	750
Net lending to government	1,795	3,890	9,550

Note: Lending to government by the financial sector includes treasury bills.
Sources: 1971-75 from Bank Negara, *Quarterly Economic Bulletin*, various issues; other periods from calculations by the World Bank.
a. The projected growth in holdings is equal to the rate of inflation plus 1.7 times the rate of growth in real income.

ever, it is assumed that such expenditure would be M$20 billion, an amount equal to about 11.2 percent of GNP. Development expenditure was equal to 11.1 percent of GNP in the 1971-75 period. The growth rate of development expenditure projected by government for the 1980s will increase development expenditure during 1981-85 to 12 percent of GNP, or to M$41 billion in nominal terms. Investments by PETRONAS were roughly projected to be M$1.3 billion, or 0.8 percent of GNP, during 1976-80 and M$4.3 billion, or 1.3 percent of GNP, during 1981-85. Thus public expenditure has been projected to increase from 34.6 percent of GNP in 1971-75 to 38.2 percent in 1976-80 and 39.4 percent in 1981-85. The increase would be more than matched, however, by the growth of resources available to the public sector. Consequently the financing need to be met by foreign borrowing and other sources would decline from 1.7 percent of GNP in 1971-75 to 1.2 percent in 1976-80 and 0.3 percent in 1981-85.

As mentioned above, the reasons for the sharp rise in public sector resource availability, both in absolute terms and as a percentage of GNP, are the higher level of direct and export taxes and the revenue from oil during 1976-80. Moreover total resources during the period of the fourth plan will further increase by two percentage points and be equal to 39.2 percent of GNP. The reason for this rise is that increased domestic borrowing from the Employees' Provident Fund as well as the private financial sector will more than offset the small decline in project borrowing.

The importance of oil revenue in public sector resources has increased substantially. The oil revenue of government and PETRONAS

Table 6.10. *Public Sector Finance, 1971-75,*
and Projections for 1976-80 and 1981-85

	Millions of Malaysian dollars		
Item	1971–75	1976–80	1981–85
Public resource availability	28,347	65,833	133,000
Government revenue	21,971	51,440	101,300
Oil revenue	924	5,680	11,126
Domestic borrowing (net)[a]	4,629	8,300	19,000
Social security	1,958	4,412	9,433
Public authority surplus	705	1,354	2,600
PETRONAS revenue	—	3,885	7,400
Foreign project borrowing (net)	1,042	2,260	2,700
Public expenditure	30,316	67,958	133,950
Current expenditure[c]	20,542	46,630	88,900
Development expenditure	9,774	20,000	40,750
PETRONAS investments	—	1,330	4,320
Deficit	−1,969	−2,125	−950
Foreign market loans (net)	1,498[b]	2,125	950
Unexplained	471	—	—

— Not applicable.

Sources: Ministry of Finance, *Economic Report*, various years; Department of Statistics, "Preliminary National Accounts, Peninsular Malaysia 1970–75 and Malaysia 1971–75" (Kuala Lumpur, September 1977; processed); World Bank estimates.

was expected to average 5.4 percent of GNP during 1976–80—it averaged 1.1 percent of GNP during 1971–75—though an amount equal to 0.8 percent of GNP was scheduled for the oil-related investments of PETRONAS. In many respects the macroeconomic impact of oil revenue is similar to foreign market borrowing. The increased oil revenue of government and net surpluses of PETRONAS after investment do not represent a transfer of domestic purchasing power from the domestic private sector to government. When oil revenue is spent for general budgetary purposes, it represents a net addition to domestic demand. The oil-related investments of PETRONAS will have a large component of foreign costs and are therefore assumed to have little direct impact on domestic demand. During 1971–75 oil revenue and net foreign market borrowing were equal to 2.8 percent of GNP; during 1976–80 oil revenue alone was expected to be equal to 4.6 percent of GNP (government revenue of 3.2

Percentage of gross national product			
1971–75	*1976–80*	*1981–85*	*Item*
32.3	37.0	39.2	Public resource availability
25.0	28.9	29.8	Government revenue
1.1	3.2	3.3	Oil revenue
5.3	4.7	5.6	Domestic borrowing (net)[a]
2.2	2.5	2.8	Social security
0.8	0.8	0.8	Public authority surplus
—	2.2	2.2	PETRONAS revenue
1.2	1.3	0.8	Foreign project borrowing (net)
34.6	38.2	39.4	Public expenditure
23.4	26.2	26.2	Current expenditure[c]
11.1	11.2	12.0	Development expenditure
—	0.8	1.3	PETRONAS investments
−2.2	−1.2	−0.3	Deficit
1.7	1.2	0.3	Foreign market loans (net)
0.5	—	—	Unexplained

a. Assumes no change in the public sector's net position with the central bank during 1978–85.

b. Includes use of foreign assets.

c. Excludes expenditure on security.

percent plus PETRONAS revenue of 2.2 percent minus PETRONAS investment of 0.8 percent). This net addition to domestic demand was expected to lead to increased inflationary pressure on the nonoil sector, pressure that needs to be met by a continued openness of the Malaysian economy, if it is not to result in domestic inflation rising above international rates.

There should be no difficulty in financing the projected gap between public resources and public expenditure; the gap was projected to decline from 2.2 percent of GNP in 1971–75 to 1.2 percent in 1976–80 and 0.3 percent in 1981–85. Foreign market loans are being obtained on very favorable terms to cover the gap. Thus, given the public resources projected, there does not seem to be any budgetary problem in meeting the higher level of government expenditure. Indeed further resources could be generated from the tax system and other sources without too much difficulty. There are a number of possible ways of increasing public sector resources: increasing specific taxes, nontax revenues, and public authority surpluses in order to maintain their proportion of GNP; allowing the full progressiveness of direct taxes and export taxes to operate (the projections given in this section assume that this effect is moderated); putting the collection of income tax, particularly corporate income tax, on a current-year basis; minimizing the size of public sector deposits with commercial banks; increasing foreign project borrowing, which would depend upon further improvements in project preparation and implementation; financing oil-sector investments by increased foreign borrowing; and selling assets in publicly owned enterprises to the private sector. The choice that is made between the many options open to government will reflect the importance attached to various objectives. It may be desirable to direct increased resources toward dealing with the problems of poverty—for example, by increasing expenditure or by reducing certain taxes in such a way as to have a maximum impact on poverty groups. Alternatively, if the principal aim were to stimulate private investment, direct tax revenue or domestic borrowing could be reduced.

Increased expenditure on poverty-related programs would also be justified in the light of Malaysia's high incidence of poverty. Every effort should therefore be made to expand the public sector's capacity to design, prepare, and implement such projects. This expanded capacity is implicit in the increase in development expenditure to 12 percent of GNP during 1981–85. At the same time, government might consider the complementary approach of selectively reducing taxes in such a way as to have the maximum effect on low-income households. For example, because rubber smallholders constitute one large group of poor households, a reduction in the export tax on rubber would directly increase their incomes. Although it would be difficult to restrict the benefits of the reduction to smallholders alone, the increased profits of estates would be subject to corporate income tax. If necessary, a special tax on rubber profits could be introduced.

The resources now available to the public sector are the result of recent high rates of economic growth and the high prices for Malaysian exports. The added resources generated by the recent increases in production and prices of petroleum ensure that resources will keep pace with the growing demands being placed on the public sector. Further growth in the public sector—its resources rose from 29 percent of GNP in 1966–70 to 33 percent in 1976—thus seems possible. Although the public sector has an important role to play in providing the infrastructure necessary for the success of the New Economic Policy, the private sector is being called upon to step up investment and provide the employment opportunities for the rapidly growing labor force. Government will therefore need to continue to monitor the tax burden of the private sector to ensure that reduced profitability or a lack of funds does not constrain the growth of that sector.

Policies to Promote Industrial Development

MALAYSIA WAS LARGELY A FREE-TRADE ECONOMY until the late 1950s, an economy in which tariffs, generally low, were levied primarily for revenue.[1] In a report of the Industrial Development Working Party in 1957 it was urged that investment incentives and modest tariffs be made the basis of an industrialization effort. As a result, the Pioneer Industries Ordinance was enacted in 1958. The central feature of this legislation was a respite from corporation taxes for manufacturers whose production was new to Malaysia or insufficient in scale. The size of the manufacturer's investment was to determine the duration of this respite, which could be for as many as five years. In subsequent years moderate tariff protection began to be regularly granted to new industries that were deemed to require it.

To streamline the industrialization effort, government created two new independent agencies: the Tariff Advisory Board in 1963 and the Federal Industrial Development Authority (FIDA) in 1967. FIDA took over the functions of promoting industry and administering incentives within the Ministry of Trade and Industry. The independent Tariff Advisory Board took over the function of setting tariffs, which it did through open hearings, case by case; it also granted waivers of tariffs on imported inputs to selected firms. At the same time, a few quantitative restrictions, most of them temporary, were introduced. The Tariff Advisory Board was abolished in 1970, and its functions were transferred to FIDA.

In an attempt to hasten industrial growth, government replaced the Pioneer Industries Ordinance with the Investment Incentives Act in 1968. This act offered additional tax holidays on the basis of various

---

1. Several studies of Malaysian industrial policy appeared in the mid-1970s. See Kurt von Rabenau, *Trade Policies and Industrialization in a Developing Country: The Case of West Malaysia*, Economics Discussion Paper, no. 55 (Regensburg, Germany: University of Regensburg, 1975); C. B. Edwards, *Protection, Profits, and Policy: An Analysis of Industrialization in Malaysia*, 2 vols. (Norwich, England: University of East Anglia, 1975).

criteria—a firm's location, the type of product, the degree of local content, and export performance—or an investment tax credit equal to 25 percent of the value of investment. Subsequently, alternative concessions on the basis of labor use and location became available.

During the 1960s direct controls on investment, informally applied rather than legislated, were developed as a further instrument of industrial policy. All firms had to obtain approval from FIDA for new investment. This policy was made effective by the import-licensing system, which covers some industrial inputs, by controls on foreign exchange, and by controls on immigration. Although this licensing system did not appear to be a barrier to entry during the 1960s, except in industries deemed by government to be overcrowded, it did introduce bureaucratic delays. This system has since become increasingly important in enforcing the objectives of the government to restructure employment and equity. It consequently has been the subject of increasing criticism.

The industrial promotion effort came under a general strain in the late 1960s and early 1970s: coordination between agencies became increasingly difficult as a result of excessive paperwork; industrialization policies were felt to be too slow in getting results under the New Economic Policy. Many of these problems appear to have since been resolved by improved coordination. For tariffs, the speedup was achieved through the replacement of the Tariff Advisory Board by the Special Action Committee on Tariffs, which is served by a tariff unit that operates within FIDA.

Firms usually approach that committee for tariff protection once they are in production—that is, after they have applied, if they are going to, for fiscal incentives. One of the most important criteria for increased tariff protection is that the output of a firm, or its increment to production, should be sufficient to satisfy a given proportion of the domestic market. In principle this proportion should be 80 percent, but sometimes as little as 40 or 50 percent is acceptable. If this condition can be fulfilled, the degree of protection is apparently calculated by comparing the costs of production with the prices of imports. The tariff is based on the excess of the former over the latter, and the future possibility of dumped or marginally priced imports is generously taken into account. Under this case-by-case standard, the permissible price is related principally to costs of production plus what is seen to be an adequate return on capital; it is not related to the costs of imports or to other measures having efficiency as their basis.

The structure of nominal tariffs that has emerged from the gradual buildup of specifically protective rates still seems moderate by international comparison. Tariff rates generally range between 15 and 50 percent, but most are concentrated between 25 and 35 percent. In recent years new protective tariffs have been awarded in the range of 35 to 40 percent.

While a tariff application is pending, it has become customary for the Ministry of Trade and Industry, upon the recommendation of FIDA, to grant protection under temporary quotas. This protection typically is for six to nine months, but sometimes is longer. The general purpose of temporary quotas is to help local production get started and to avoid stockpiling by importers before the new tariff becomes effective. In 1974 some eighty items were imported under quotas.[2] Although the number of items has grown over the years, it has not grown dramatically. Of the eighty items under quotas in 1974, only about twenty were on the list in 1970. Only certain products, the most important among which are animal feeds, leather, automobiles, motorbikes, and bicycles, have enjoyed long-term protection. In addition, a few items, eight in 1974, are completely banned.

The Industrial Coordination Act, legislated in May 1975, gives legal sanction to the controls over entry. It also gives government, at least in principle, extremely broad authority to intervene, impose conditions of approval, and police these conditions. Under the act no person is allowed to engage in manufacturing activity without a license.[3] Existing and new manufacturers are required to apply for a license for each specific activity in which they engage. Government nevertheless foresaw automatic approval of licenses for most existing activities. The act is not intended to apply to firms employing fewer than twenty-five full-time paid workers and whose shareholders' funds are less than M$250,000. Its stated purpose is to see that optimum use is made of investment capital, land, and other scarce resources, such as trained manpower. A secondary purpose is the collection of information, which had formerly been required only of firms that were granted incentives. The act also stresses the need for conformity with the objectives of the New Economic Policy in trade and industry.

The Industrial Coordination Act became effective in May 1976, and firms were given a year to apply for their licenses. In its approval policy

2. Rabenau, *Trade Policies*, table A-1.
3. The Ministry of Trade and Industry attempted earlier to make certain that its permission was sought as a general requirement, but lacking the force of law the attempt had only limited success. An example cited in the explanatory note issued with the act was the plastic products industry, in which 62 of 266 establishments in Malaysia had official permission.

the Ministry of Trade and Industry has been concerned with fifteen aspects of the establishment and operation of a manufacturing operation, including the adequacy of its capacity, equity, employment, and management structure, its pricing policy, its export intentions, and its use of domestic inputs. Similar conditions are expected to be applied to new investments in manufacturing. Although the initial granting of licenses was to have been automatic for existing firms, maintaining the license depends upon progress in fulfilling certain conditions attached to it.

Many businessmen interpreted the Industrial Coordination Act as being primarily aimed at enforcing government policies with respect to racial participation. Because the New Economic Policy originally aimed to achieve its ultimate participation objectives by restructuring in new firms and activities, these businessmen feared that government intended to change the rules of the game by trying to alter the employment and ownership structure of existing firms. As a result, some members of the business community felt that the act, before its operating conditions were specified, affected the willingness of local businessmen to invest or reinvest and of new foreign investors to come to Malaysia. Concerned about this reaction, government repeatedly stressed that implementation of the act would be both reasonable and flexible and that government intended, through legislation, to remove the uncertainties surrounding its policies for restructuring.

The Effects of Industrial Promotion Policies

A substantial rise in average levels of effective protection of manufacturing between the early 1960s and the early 1970s was traced in a study made in 1975 by the Economic Planning Unit of Malaysia.[4] There was a growing concern in government, largely as a result of this finding, that high levels of protection had led—and might continue to

---

4. The rate of effective protection is an expression of the excess of domestic value added—the monetary costs of the local resources used—over world value added—the net foreign exchange saved or earned—in a given activity as a percentage of world value added. Estimates of effective protection provide a reasonable, if approximate, guide to the relative efficiencies, in the context of a static environment, of existing manufacturing activities, but with two provisos: these estimates must be based on reliable data, particularly for the relation of domestic prices to world prices; and the results should not be distorted by different rates of return on capital among the various activities. Economic Planning Unit, "Effective Protection and Industrialization Policies: Report on a Research Project" (Kuala Lumpur, 1975; processed).

lead—to an inefficient allocation of resources, in the sense that the foreign exchange saved or earned by the use of a given amount of local
resources might not be maximized. The effect of the system, according
to the study, had been to discriminate against agriculture and rural
income, to create distortions within the manufacturing sector that led
to the establishment of some high-cost industries, to favor products at
more finished stages of fabrication, and to create a bias against exports.
The implication of this analysis is that alternative investments—particularly in newer, demand-elastic activities in the primary sector or in
export activities in manufacturing—could have saved or earned foreign
exchange more efficiently.

Three independent studies of effective protection of manufacturing
in Peninsular Malaysia appeared in the same year as the study by the
Economic Planning Unit—those by Rabenau and Edwards already
cited and a third by Ariff.[5] The lack of harmony in the results is dis-
tressing. A significant reason seems to be that different means of relating domestic prices to world prices were used. In three of the studies,
including that of the Economic Planning Unit, the tariff schedule was
used; in the fourth, that of Edwards, price comparisons were extensive-
ly used. In the first three, the average levels of effective protection calculated for 1970 and 1973, weighted by world value added, range between 35 and 40 percent. In an international comparison of effective
protection in developing countries, these levels would be judged moderate to low. But by the use of tariffs, protection is overestimated to the
extent that there is water in the tariff and is underestimated to the extent that there are barriers other than tariffs. By Edwards's calculation,
the average level of effective protection in 1972 was 70 percent. This
appears to indicate that manufacturing in Peninsular Malaysia could
not be considered efficient, but his estimates of nominal protection often seem too high.

The truth about industrial efficiency in Peninsular Malaysia doubtless lies somewhere between the estimates of the Economic Planning
Unit and that of Edwards. Two general signs of efficiency, indicating
low rates of effective protection, can be cited: the growth of footloose
exports in recent years and the generally high rates of capacity use,
except in the 1974–75 period of recession. The rapid growth in the
manufacture of electronic assembly products, textiles, and garments in
recent years has been stimulated by competitiveness, not subsidies. Al-

    5. Rabenau, *Trade Policies;* Edwards, *Protection, Profits, and Policy;* K. A. M. Ariff,
"Protection for Manufactures in Peninsular Malaysia," *Hitotsubashi Journal of Economics,*
vol. 15, no. 2 (February 1975), pp. 41–53.

though most inputs are available free of duty, output is sold at unprotected world prices, and the subsidy element in tax incentives or possibly in the amenities of free-trade zones is not likely to be overwhelming. A preliminary finding in a research project of the World Bank was that in 1972 rates of capacity use in manufacturing in Peninsular Malaysia were high by the standards of developing countries. Equipment was found to run 75 percent of the total hours it was available in the year; the use of capacity was 65 percent in the Philippines, 81 percent in Colombia, and 47 percent in Israel.[6]

Effective protection in industry began to grow in the early 1960s, hence the discrimination against agriculture. According to the study by Edwards—the only such study in which time-series data are given for Peninsular Malaysia—effective protection grew most rapidly before 1966.[7] Growth thereafter, continuing into the 1970s, was slower (table 7.1). This trend corresponds to the shift observed at the end of the 1960s from import substitution to export-oriented growth. The finding of Edwards differs from that found in an earlier study—that effective protection was still low in the mid-1960s.[8] It also is not entirely consistent with claims that high levels of protection have been awarded to new investments in recent years automatically and with fair generosity.

In none of the various studies of effective protection were the authors able to establish a statistical relation between the level of effective protection by industry and the degree of import substitution achieved. Nevertheless the time-series data of Edwards enable him to assert that effective protection and growth are correlated.[9] However doubtful it may be that this relation is strong in a statistical sense, it can be illustrated by dividing industry into four segments, according to high or low growth of effective protection and output during each of two periods for which Edwards provides data. At this level of sectoral disaggregation, high growth of output is associated with a rapid development of effective protection (table 7.2).

6. The averages quoted are weighted by capital values. Helen Hughes and others, "Capital Utilization in Manufacturing in Developing Countries," World Bank Staff Working Paper, no. 242 (Washington, D.C.: World Bank, 1976; processed), p. 27.

7. In line with my earlier contention that the estimate of Edwards for 1972 is too high, I would argue that his time series represents somewhat of an exaggeration of the level and growth rate of effective protection.

8. Power found the average rate of effective protection to be −8 percent in 1963 and −4 percent in 1965. John H. Power, "The Structure of Protection in West Malaysia," in Bela Balassa and associates, *The Structure of Protection in Developing Countries* (Baltimore: Johns Hopkins University Press for the World Bank and the Inter-American Development Bank, 1971), p. 215.

9. Edwards, *Protection, Profits, and Policy*, pp. 100–01.

Table 7.1. *Effective Protection of Manufacturing in Peninsular Malaysia, Selected Years, 1962–72*
(percent)

Year	Including off-estate agricultural processing[a]	Excluding off-estate agricultural processing[a]
1962	15	25
1966	45	50
1969	45	65
1972	55	70

Source: C. B. Edwards, *Protection, Profits, and Policy: An Analysis of Industrialization in Malaysia*, 2 vols. (Norwich, England: University of East Anglia, 1975), vol. 1, p. 98.
a. Covers production for both domestic and export markets.

High effective protection has undoubtedly fostered the growth of some inefficient industries. Despite my having set forth earlier the general signs of efficiency, I must emphasize the economic inefficiency of certain industries. Many such instances of inefficiency are the result of moderate-to-high levels of nominal protection on output accompanied by waivers of tariffs on the imported inputs—principally textiles for the domestic market, some clothing for the domestic market, paper boxes, fertilizers, iron and steel, galvanized sheets and pipes, and components of motor vehicles and cycles for assembly.

This pattern reflects not only the creation of industries that serve a small market and are inefficient by virtue of their inability to capture economies of scale; it also reflects the tendency of the case-by-case tariff-setting system to discourage cost-consciousness in individual entre-

Table 7.2. *The Relation between Growth of Output and Effective Protection of Sixteen Groups in the Manufacturing Industry, 1962–67 and 1967–70*
(number of groups)

Period	Growth in effective protection	Growth in output High	Low
1962–67	High	6	2
	Low	1	6
1967–70	High	7	2
	Low	0	7

Source: Edwards, *Protection, Profits, and Policy*, table 78.

preneurs, primarily because they are protected on a cost-plus basis. It can be argued that the case-by-case method has a further effect on competition: Because a firm seeking tariff protection must be able to satisfy a given share of the domestic market for its product, the firm is encouraged to produce on a larger, not a smaller, scale. Inasmuch as fiscal incentives and protection both encourage large size, the result might be considered beneficial in industries in which economies of scale increase with size. On the other hand, these policies, together with direct controls on entry, generally tend to suppress competition.

Peninsular Malaysia risks developing a kind of dualism with respect to economic efficiency, with a highly efficient footloose export sector, most of it located largely in free-trade zones, and a somewhat inefficient domestic-market sector operating in a protected environment. One example of such dualism is in the textiles industry. A textile company in a free-trade zone exports fabrics that are identical with fabrics produced by another company in the local market at prices about 25 percent higher. Much of this inefficiency could be remedied. Many producers for the domestic market—of textiles and clothing, for example—could lower their prices. In such industries as motor vehicles, however, even reduced profits and increased technical efficiency would be unlikely to lead to economic efficiency because of the problems of fragmented and small-scale production. By the early 1970s, however, the trend of investment was moving away from these industries and toward some that were more efficient in producing goods for export—mainly footloose products and products processed from primary commodities. Continuation of this emphasis would be likely to increase economic efficiency among manufacturers of goods for export. Some attempt can also be made to improve economic efficiency in existing industries producing goods for the domestic market.

The manufacturing sector tends to produce finished, not intermediate, products. Tariffs characteristically rise with the stage of production. Thus it can be intuitively argued that the structure of protection has prevented a deepening of the pattern of industrialization. On the other hand, this situation may favor exports, such that the virtual absence in Peninsular Malaysia of industries producing intermediate goods and capital goods is by no means an unqualified negative factor. Indeed manufactured exports appear to have increased in the 1970s despite the high effective protection conventionally held to discourage such increases. This paradox is discussed further below. Until the end of the 1960s, however, import substitution, rather than export expansion, clearly predominated as a source of growth. This conclusion is consistent with Edwards's data, which show general rises in the levels of protection during the 1960s.[10]

Although evidence of the misallocation of resources into inefficient activities conventionally associated with protection can thus be found, the earlier conclusion bears repeating: Levels of effective protection, and thus inefficiency, probably did not grow during the 1970s. Although the protection system appears to be open-ended, tariff administrators seem to have shown a degree of moderation and to have avoided the worst excesses associated with protection.

What, then, of fiscal incentives, the array of measures typically coupled with protection to encourage domestic production? Despite the introduction in the early 1970s of labor-related tax incentives and investment tax credits, the tax holiday, or pioneer incentive, has remained dominant. Firms with pioneer status were responsible for only 1 percent of industrial output in 1959. By 1963 their share had risen to 17 percent, by the end of the 1960s to 30 percent—though these figures do include some firms whose pioneer status had expired. There subsequently was a further rise. Between 1970 and 1975 pioneer firms were responsible for more than 50 percent of the increase in employment in the formal sector—that is, the part of the manufacturing sector that is enumerated in industrial censuses and surveys and which accounts for about 70 percent of manufacturing employment. Pioneer firms have also tended to be significantly larger and more capital-intensive than other firms, though the differences in capital intensity significantly narrowed in the early 1970s.

A study of fiscal incentives by the Economic Planning Unit provides a thoughtful analysis of some weaknesses of the present system.[11] By means of a calculation of the capital-subsidy equivalent of fiscal incentives, the study demonstrates that there are three patterns.[12] First, the value to the investor of pioneer tax holidays rises with the level of profits, so the less an investor needs the incentive, the greater is that incentive. Second, the alternative investment tax credit is more attractive than the tax holiday only if the rate of return turns out to be very low in the long run. Third, the alternative concession on the basis of labor use is more attractive only if projects have very low capital-

10. See table 7.1.

11. Economic Planning Unit, "Tax Incentives for Industry" (Kuala Lumpur, 1974; processed).

12. The capital-subsidy equivalent is the ratio to equity of the net present value (using a 10 percent discount rate in this case) of the stream of tax benefits flowing from different long-run profit rates after a typical buildup of profits in the initial years of the project.

labor ratios. The point is also made that pioneer incentives penalize small investments and small-scale industry. In addition, because entrepreneurs have a choice between activities or techniques, such capital-related incentives encourage capital intensity in the industrial sector. The alternative concession on the basis of labor use appears to have been too weak to counteract this tendency.

In the study by the Economic Planning Unit, incentives are discussed largely in relation to their redundancy in the face of expected high levels of profit. More emphasis might be given to the issue of their redundancy in the many instances in which there is substantial protection of the domestic market. This apparent redundancy has been indicated in several surveys of individual firms.[13] It also is indicated by a comparison of the estimated value of fiscal incentives as subsidies to capital investment with the estimated effects of protection on the returns on capital. The Economic Planning Unit estimated, on the basis of observed rates of profits of pioneer firms, that the net present value of tax holidays could range between zero and 180 percent of the value of a firm's equity.[14] For example, an investment with a five-year tax holiday and an average rate of return after start-up of 30 percent would effectively receive a 23 percent subsidy. Edwards found that fourteen of thirty-nine industries would have incurred losses under free trade (assuming that they would not have been able to produce more efficiently), seven would have broken even, and eighteen would have made profits.[15]

Despite this evidence, the belief persists in some government circles in Malaysia, as it does in many developing countries, that tax holidays are essential if foreigners are to be attracted to import-substituting investments. The reason is that neighboring countries also provide incentives. Certainly, most foreign investors do profit from fiscal incentives in the sense that tax-sparing agreements between Malaysia and most of the countries having large investments there do relieve them of the requirement that they pay taxes to foreign treasuries on their un-

13. See, for example, Teh Kok Peng, "Protection, Fiscal Incentives, and Industrialisation in West Malaysia since 1957" (Ph.D. dissertation, Oxford University, 1975), p. 232.

14. The length of tax holidays could be between five and ten years; average long-run returns on equity—that is, profits after an initial start-up period of three years—were observed to range all the way from 0 to 100 percent. Economic Planning Unit, "Tax Incentives for Industry," ch. 3, p. 5.

15. In these eighteen profit-making industries, median values of effective protection of profits were 160–200 percent. Edwards, *Protection, Profits, and Policy*, table 12.

taxed Malaysian profits.[16] On the other hand, if the argument is correct that protection, not fiscal incentives, is the principal determinant of viability in production for the domestic market, foreign investors may seek pioneer status as much as a token of government support as for its subsidy value.

The substantial growth of exports in the 1970s appears to be at odds with the protection and fiscal-incentives policies, which provide a strong incentive to production for the domestic market. It has been pointed out that the boom in exports was dominated by a narrow range of products. In addition, the boom was aided by vigorous demand throughout the world, particularly for wood products, and by the coming of age of international subcontracting in electronics. In electronics particularly, the promotion of free-trade zones was a substantial factor. International subcontracting investment in electronics has taken place almost exclusively in free-trade zones or through bonded-warehouse arrangements. Some of the literature contains the implication that there is a substantial element of subsidization in industrial estates, but the evidence for this has not been well developed. Even if there is a subsidy element, it must have had only a small effect on total industrial production costs within these estates. Judged by other criteria—the rapid spread of these estates, the extent to which industrialists have chosen to locate on these estates, the apparent success of free-trade zones in recent years—the policy with respect to industrial estates might be considered very beneficial.

The significance of fiscal incentives in the growth of exports has been less obvious. Fiscal incentives—comprising tax deductions based on the ability of a firm to increase exports, deductions for promotional expenses, and accelerated depreciation—were introduced in the 1968 Investments Incentives Act. Because they are modest and cannot, except for the deduction of promotional expenses, be taken advantage of by firms already enjoying tax holidays, they have been of limited value and relatively little used.[17] The Malaysian government, through FIDA, has nevertheless been clearly aware in recent years of the need to promote exports, given the limitations to import substitution. Part of its effort has been in promotional activities, but it has sought increasingly to use

---

16. The United States taxes on repatriated dividends are an exception.

17. Hoffmann, in an interim report on a project surveying manufactured exports, indicates that these concessions apparently were important to small companies. Lutz Hoffman, "Interim Report on Methodology and Results of the HEX" (Regensburg, Germany: University of Regensburg, 1974; processed).

pioneer incentives in connection with export-oriented projects. A review by the World Bank of a sample of recent project approvals by FIDA
clearly indicates that, at least by 1975, export-oriented projects were
strongly represented in approvals of pioneer status; most import-
substituting projects received approval without incentives.[18]

A general case can be made that high levels of effective protection
discourage exports by making the domestic market far more attractive
and by raising the cost of inputs to some potentially exporting industries. Although positive effective protection undoubtedly makes exports relatively unattractive in general, there is little evidence to suggest
an inverse relation between export performance and the level of effective protection, industry by industry.[19] The probable reason is that
protection enables some firms to cover fixed costs in the domestic market and to export on the basis of variable costs.

The problem of high costs of inputs probably has not yet proved to
be a serious problem in the development of Malaysian exports. A widespread system of duty concessions on imported inputs, including the
system of free-trade zones, already exists, and the local production of
intermediate goods and capital goods has not yet proceeded very far.
Even so, many exporting firms consider duty-free imports an essential
condition for exporting, and many nonexporting firms regard the inability to acquire imports duty-free an important obstacle to the development of exports. This problem can be expected to grow worse as
local production of intermediate and capital goods increases.

Before passage of the Industrial Coordination Act in 1975, the direct
control of investment was informally administered in an effort to prevent the emergence of excess capacity and, in the 1970s, to press new
firms to comply with the objectives of the government under the New
Economic Policy of increasing the participation of bumiputras. Government has also controlled entry by limiting the number of approvals
of pioneer status in a given industry. On the other hand, it has tried to
foster competition by preferring to sanction more than one investment
in a given industry, even if doing so leads to built-in excess capacity or
to production in plants of smaller than optimal size. Nevertheless the
limitations to competition arising from the size of the market or from

18. In the sample 65 percent of approved investment with incentives—but only 16
percent of approved investment *without* incentives—was export-oriented.

19. The results on effective protection obtained by the Economic Planning Unit, for
example, show no clear relation between levels of effective protection and shares of exports in output from industry to industry.

barriers to entry have probably fostered the development of oligopoly as much as competition.

This characterization of the Malaysian incentives system—that excessive protection leads to significant inefficiencies and that tax incentives are unnecessarily generous—seems to be typical of many critical characterizations of the manufacturing sectors of developing countries. Yet it has also been asserted that industrial performance in Peninsular Malaysia has been impressive. These two seemingly contradictory assertions can be reconciled because the excesses of the Malaysian incentives systems are not extreme by the standards of many, if not most, developing countries and because these excesses do not characterize all sectors. They have, however, resulted in a certain dualism, as was suggested earlier. Government may find it tempting, perhaps under pressure from private industry, to continue to protect inefficient sectors oriented toward the domestic market and even to expand certain high-cost import-substitution sectors. But Peninsular Malaysia is industrially mature enough to be able to benefit from a reduction in protection in these sectors. Thus the essential objectives of policy reform would be to prevent industry in general from becoming less efficient as a result of creating new high-cost import-substitution sectors, to increase efficiency in existing high-cost import-substitution sectors, and to minimize the burden that may be imposed on the export effort by such sectors.

Reform of Industrial Incentive Policies

The studies of effective protection and tax incentives made by the Economic Planning Unit suggested fundamental reforms with the general object of reducing the level and economic cost of incentives. I will discuss tariff reform and fiscal reform in turn.

The study of effective protection suggested that future tariff-setting policy should be to allow a normal broad band of effective rates between 20 percent and 50 percent that would apply not only to new investments but also to existing industry. Reductions would be sought in the effective protection of those industries in which present rates were higher than 50 percent—approximately a third of all sectors. A regular review, industry by industry, was suggested to provide the basis for such reform. Export industries would receive moderate protection, probably at the lower end of the suggested 20 percent to 50 percent band. Over all, then, the retention of ad hoc tariffs, but the sharpening of criteria for protection and the reduction of the permissible band, were envisaged in the study. Finally, for the achievement of such objectives as regionalization, the creation of employment, and the transfer of technology, it was concluded that fiscal instruments should be preferred to the tariff.

A moderate degree of tariff protection of manufacturing—although what constitutes "moderate" is not precisely known—is justified on dynamic grounds. But the argument for "externalities" in manufacturing risks becoming a catchall that can be used to justify excessive protection. There are good reasons to argue that the greatest deficiency in the initial stage of industrialization is the shortage of managerial and labor skills, the acquisition of which constitutes a gain to the economy but not necessarily to the projects in which the skills are acquired. The danger of this argument is that industries incapable of becoming self-sufficient, even in the long run, will be encouraged.

In a subsequent study of tariff reform by the United Nations Development Program, ways were examined in which the concept of effective protection could be made effective.[20] The recommendation of the Economic Planning Unit that the case-by-case approach to tariff-making, combined with the effective-protection technique of cost-benefit analysis, be continued was accepted, and tariff inquiries covering all firms producing a given product were advocated. Tariffs would then be fixed on the basis of encouraging best-practice techniques. The 20 percent to 50 percent effective-protection band was accepted as reasonable initially, though it was considered to be somewhat high. Other important recommendations of the study were that tariff protection be considered at the time that approval of a project was being sought, that the combined effects of tariffs and fiscal incentives be taken into consideration, and that regular reporting by firms receiving protection be enforced.

One of the greatest dangers threatening the implementation of the proposed effective-protection ceiling may originate in arguments that the effective rate of protection does not take all the potential benefits of a project into account. It can be plausibly argued that in the fairly straightforward methodology proposed in the study by the Economic Planning Unit, adequate account is not taken, for example, of the social value of job creation in a labor-surplus economy. But if such unquantified benefits as job creation and externalities are allowed to override the effective-protection ceiling by means of the implicit argument that their

20. United Nations Development Program, "Tariff Reform in Malaysia: Project Findings and Recommendations" (n.p., 1975).

value is great, the effective-protection calculation may be reduced to the status of window-dressing. For this reason, it seems essential that a set of rules or guidelines be written, preferably with quantified elements, to deal with such benefits. In job creation, for example, a simple shadow-pricing exercise, such as valuing unskilled labor—or at least unskilled bumiputra labor—at 50 percent of the market wage, could easily be used to place some limit on the extent to which a labor-intensive project would be allowed to exceed the effective-protection ceiling.

The suggestion of the Economic Planning Unit that industries now enjoying effective protection of less than 20 percent be permitted to move up to 20 percent can be questioned. In some instances—shipbuilding, for example—higher rates might attract more resources into an industry suited to Malaysian conditions. In others, however, protection may already be sufficient, even at these low levels, to sustain the development of a local industry. The suggestion perhaps indicates that too much attention is being paid to removing distortions among manufacturing industries and too little to removing distortions between manufacturing and other sectors. If the long-term objective is to make protective rates uniform throughout the economy, it must be accomplished by attacking the higher rates, not by increasing the lower rates.

As government has recognized, the reform of effective-protection rates need not take only the form of lowering the nominal rates on the end product—or removing quantitative restrictions. There are a number of possible alternative steps, such as increasing tariffs or excise duties on inputs. In many instances, raising the cost of the inputs is a preferable alternative because it allows a degree of protection to industries that produce intermediate goods and capital goods.

Two further suggestions can be made about the execution of specific steps in reform of the protective system. First, particular attention should be paid to protection associated with the export of processed primary products. The data of Edwards suggested that at least two forms of processing for export, the processing of sawmill products and of coconuts, were economically unprofitable by virtue of the subsidy on purchases of raw material. This subsidy is derived from the imposition of export duties on raw, but not processed, materials. Processed exports, by design, are of great importance in the growth of manufactured exports, to the cost of which the government could usefully pay attention. A good sign in this respect is the emphasis on the upgrading of processed exports—from sawn wood to plywood, for example, and from rubber sheets to rubber products. Second, the relatively efficient export sector and the relatively inefficient import-substitution sector should be placed in closer competition by a selective modification of the policy with respect to free-trade zones, which now are allowed to supply the domestic market, if at all, only from small quotas and after payment of duties. For selected sectors, of which textiles is the prime example, a greater dose of competition could be provided by the abolition—or at least enlargement—of these quotas, or by tariff preferences.

One of several possible reforms suggested in the tax-incentives study of the Economic Planning Unit is the replacement of the present range of investment incentives with a single incentive combining a tax allowance equal to 50 percent of the value of investment, not more than 20 percent of which could be taken in any year, and another tax allowance of M$500 per employee per year for the first five years of operation. It was argued that the capital-using bias of the first part of the proposal would be offset by the labor-using bias of the second part. Although the size of the suggested incentive still seems large, the suggested formula is appealing and seems to provide a suitable basis for experiment. Its disadvantage is that any formula involving the valuation of investment and ratios of capital to labor will be more open to abuse and more costly to administer than the simple tax holiday. But Malaysia has already had some experience with this sort of undertaking in the investment tax credit and the alternative concession on the basis of labor use. Implementing an additional proposal to establish or reduce the minimum-size criterion, which is important to the development of successful small and medium-sized enterprises, would also increase the administrative burden on FIDA.

It has been argued that insufficient attention was paid in the tax-incentives study to the general redundancy of fiscal incentives in the face of tariff protection. The study does contain the suggestion that the list of products qualifying a firm for pioneer status is too long and should be shortened. Such reform could be even more fundamental. A good argument can be made for scrapping fiscal incentives and relying instead on tariffs alone, except in special cases. Clearly the more narrowly incentives are given, the more effectively government can achieve specific aims. The special cases could be projects engaged wholly or partly in exports, projects in selected development areas, and possibly a small number of other projects for which important externalities can be identified.

Although continuation of the case-by-case approach is acceptable, it should be coupled with a band of effective protection having a ceiling as high as 50 percent—an appropriate first step in a tariff reform whose ultimate goal should presumably be to achieve a uniformly low level of tariff protection for manufacturing.[21] Although the approach advocated in the study by the United Nations Development Program, involving the identification of least-cost techniques, may prove too sophisticated and demanding even for an enlarged tariff-setting body, a highly detailed approach should be adopted, although it would require considerably more resources than FIDA now has. Part of the approach should be to ensure that high protection, when given, is sufficient only to save the more efficient firms. Less efficient firms should be forced to improve or to cease production. The recommendation that required protection be considered at the time approval is sought is also well taken. It may prove politically impossible for government to withhold adequate protection after it has sanctioned the investment, particularly an investment in a large and highly visible project.

It often is argued that tax holidays and exemptions from duties on imports of capital equipment reduce the relative cost of capital and bias an investor in favor of capital-intensity. Several surveys have revealed a feeling among Malaysian businessmen in larger firms that they have little latitude to vary techniques, particularly when standards of quality are important. But this argument does not justify doing nothing about the incentives system with respect to the choice of technique. In certain microeconomic studies it is indicated that technical choices do exist in core and ancillary processes, even if businessmen are not always aware of them.[22] In addition, capital intensity is strongly correlated with the size of firms. Removing the size bias in the present incentives system would therefore remove some of the capital-intensity bias as well, other things being equal.

Finally the choice among different industrial activities is an aspect of the choice of technique. It can be argued that import substitution caused by protection, not fiscal incentives, leads to investments that become progressively more capital-intensive at the margin as the easier, more labor-intensive, import-substitution opportunities disappear. An export program can halt, if not reverse, this tendency. In Malaysia, this aspect of the choice of technique is illustrated in a comparison of the

21. Care should be taken in interpreting this ceiling. It is likely that there is redundancy in much of the industrial tariff because rates are set to exclude imports, not to equalize the competitive positions of local products and imports. In this sense it can be argued that the estimates of effective protection by the Economic Planning Unit represent *potential*, not *realized*, rates. By the same token, the proposed ceiling should generally be interpreted as a ceiling of potential, not realized, effective protection.

22. See, for example, publications of the World Employment Programme of the International Labour Organisation.

high degree of job creation that accompanied the export growth of the 1970s with the lower degree of job creation in the import-substituting 1960s.

Policies for Restructuring Ownership and Employment

The dual objectives of the New Economic Policy—general reduction of poverty through economic growth and specific restructuring with a view to eliminating the identification of race with economic function—both rely on rapid growth in the modern sectors of the economy. Three categories of restructuring can be considered: increasing the share of Malays in employment in the modern sector and, within this sector, improving the incomes of Malays by improving their skills; increasing the Malay share of corporate ownership; and increasing the number of Malay entrepreneurs and the degree of Malay managerial control. The first two policies have been translated into specific quantitative targets. The third is less quantifiable, but overlaps the first two. There nevertheless is a critical difference between the policy with respect to Malay ownership and that having to do with development of entrepreneurial and managerial skills. Ownership gives Malays the ability to enjoy the fruits of wealth. Entrepreneurial and managerial talents give them the ability to create wealth.

Despite the fact that they make up 52 percent of the labor force, Malays constituted only 29 percent of the labor force in manufacturing in 1970. Although the latter is the result of a steady improvement of their position in this sector during the 1960s, it reflects the fact that Malays continue to live predominantly in rural areas while Chinese Malaysians live predominantly in urban areas. In 1970, for example, 62 percent of the Malay labor force in manufacturing—but only 18 percent of the Chinese—lived in rural areas. In addition, the Malay share of wage income in manufacturing was significantly less than their share in the work force for two reasons. First, their living predominantly in rural areas tended to lead to lower wages: the average formal-sector wage in the four industrially advanced states—Selangor, Penang, Perak, and Johore—was more than twice that of the other seven states of Peninsular Malaysia. Second, employment of Malays was concentrated in unskilled and semiskilled occupations which are lower paid: only about 7 percent of industrial managers were Malay. On the other hand, there is no strong evidence that the employment of Malays was concentrated in small-scale industries. Indeed there is some evidence that the

Malay share in the labor force was greatest in the large firms.[23] If there was any sectoral concentration of Malay employment, it appears to have been in such industries as food processing and wood, in which rural location is an advantage.

Government policies to increase the rate of employment of Malays consist of policies with respect to regional location on the one hand and the attachment of conditions to the approval of new investments on the other. Partly as a result of these policies, the Malay share of employment in manufacturing continued to improve during the period of the second plan. The Malay share in employment is estimated to have grown from 29 percent in 1970 to 33 percent in 1975; this growth accounted for 43 percent of total growth in the labor force during that period. This performance, which surpassed the goals set forth in the second plan, was thus the result of a rapid change in overall growth rates and in the racial composition of employment in new firms, mainly in pioneer firms. It still allowed for a healthy, 6-percent annual growth in non-Malay employment. Efforts to improve the skills of Malay labor have proved to be less successful. In the 1974 annual report of FIDA only a marginal increase in Malay shares in professional, managerial, and technical occupations between 1971 and 1973 was noted.

The ownership and control of Malaysian manufacturing parallels that in other sectors insofar as it is characterized by the weakness of the position of the Malays and the strength of foreign investment. In 1970 Malays and Malay interests held only 2.4 percent of the share capital of limited companies in manufacturing; foreign interests held 63.3 percent.[24] By 1975 the proportion represented by their holdings had increased to 7.8 percent, but 80 percent of this increment was the result of an increase in the shares held by such trust agencies as Majlis Amanah Rakyat (MARA) and Perbadanan Nasional Berhad (PERNAS). Government policies and institutions to encourage Malay ownership, management, and entrepreneurship cover education and training, technical assistance, loan programs, industrial estate programs, and government purchase of equity in trust for Malays. One of the most important poli-

---

23. Chee Peng Lim, in a sample of manufacturing sectors, found the share of Malays in the labor force to be 29 percent in firms employing fifty or more persons; the average share was 24 percent. See Chee Peng Lim, "The Role of Small Industry in the Malaysian Economy" (thesis, University of Malaya, Kuala Lumpur, 1975), p. 72.

24. The percentage of the modern manufacturing sector as a whole that was foreign-owned was somewhat smaller because of the prevalence of nonincorporated firms. In 1970, for example, foreign investors controlled about 51 percent of the fixed assets of the firms covered in the Survey of Manufacturing for Industries.

cies, both to expand Malay ownership and to limit foreign ownership, has to do with the approval of new investments. In line with macroeconomic targets for 1990, at least 30 percent of the equity of most new investments must be from bumiputras, and no more than 30 percent can be from foreign sources.

The principal legislative effort directed at the participation of bumiputras and at local participation has been the Industrial Coordination Act, in which previously existing direct controls on new investments were codified and extended to firms already operating. The act is an important measure for changing the pattern of ownership. It is supplemented by informal but powerful administrative pressure, fiscal incentives and other locational incentives, lending programs, government purchases of equity in trust for bumiputras, government procurement policies, and programs of technical assistance and training. In addition to FIDA, some of the principal institutions involved in the execution of these measures are MARA, PERNAS, Malaysian Industrial Development Finance Corporation, Credit Guarantee Corporation, Bank Bumiputra, and the state economic development corporations.

From the lists of measures and institutions, it is obvious that the effort at restructuring the Malaysian economy has many sides. In addition, in many of the measures and institutions, this effort is mixed with, and often subordinate to, more general efforts to promote small business. Although certain overall objectives are clear, at least in a quantitative sense, the restructuring effort appears to be proceeding with little coherent planning or coordination.[25] Perhaps this cannot be completely avoided because the conventional wisdom, particularly that of economists, has far less to say on how to restructure an economy than on how to promote growth.[26] In the following paragraphs, some institutions concerned with the restructuring effort are briefly reviewed, and some concluding remarks on individual elements of the overall programs are offered.

- MARA and PERNAS are the two principal organizations having the purpose of developing enterprise among bumiputras. MARA, which

---

25. Recognizing the possible duplication of efforts in the small-business sector, the government set up an umbrella organization in 1973 called the National Advisory Council on Consultancy and Advisory Services for Small Industries and Businesses.

26. Both Chee Peng Lim, "Role of Small Industry," and Economic Planning Unit, "Bumiputra Participation in Business" (Kuala Lumpur, 1975; processed) provide useful reviews of programs intended for bumiputra businessmen and other owners and managers of small business enterprises, with suggestions for needed reform. See also World

has the broader mandate, is involved in lending, purchasing equity in trust, and providing technical assistance, technical education, and managerial and professional services. Lending is one of its most important activities. It lends at 7 percent, with liberal security conditions, for fixed capital and working capital. Its volume of lending has increased rapidly since 1970; so, too, has its rate of arrears, which in 1974 was almost 40 percent. This high rate is said to result from shortages of staff and failures to follow up. Most MARA loans are for commerce, construction, and transport; fewer than 10 percent are for manufacturing. Among its several non-lending activities, MARA has instituted an innovative entrepreneurial development program, the aim of which is to combine loans with intensive follow-up.

- PERNAS is the most important instrument of government for the purchase of equity in trust for bumiputras. It is a government-owned holding company with eight wholly-owned subsidiaries in a variety of sectors; some of the subsidiaries are also holding companies or companies engaged in joint ventures with large private concerns. Incorporated in 1969, PERNAS is considered to be part of the private sector, but it has a mandate to help increase the participation of bumiputras in the modern world of business and technology, as well as to develop profitable industries on its own. The main business of PERNAS, which was originally financed from government equity, is to engage in joint ventures, usually with a controlling share and mainly with foreign partners. The choice of investments, which cover activities in construction, engineering, steel, electronics, tires, palm oil, timber, tourism, trading, and insurance, is largely based on the criterion of profitability. Direct aid to bumiputras is secondary and takes the form of the creation of employment, which is small, preferential margins of 10 to 15 percent for supplier firms owned by bumiputras, and the use of bumiputra firms in distribution. Investment in bumiputra firms has been less important.
- Malaysian Industrial Development Finance Corporation, a private development finance company set up in 1960, is one of the principal suppliers of long-term credit, mostly in the form of large loans. In the late 1970s it began to increase the share of smaller loans and

Bank, "Industrial Growth and Economic Progress in Malaysia," report no. 861-MA (a restricted-circulation document) (Washington, D.C., September 1975; processed), ch. 9.

make a special effort, through its Bumiputra Assistance Unit, to increase lending to bumiputras. In 1973–74 about 12 percent of the number and value of its loans were to bumiputras. Malaysian Industrial Estates Limited, a subsidiary of Malaysian Industrial Development Finance Corporation, offers financial assistance for the purchase of factory sites. Both institutions offer loans to bumiputras on conditions that are modestly preferential.

- Credit Guarantee Corporation was formed by government in 1970 to encourage commercial banks to make loans to small businesses by guaranteeing 60 percent of the value of such loans. After a slow start, the volume of lending under the scheme dramatically increased when lending criteria were liberalized and lending quotas were set. It is not clear, however, to what extent this increase merely reflected a shift away from conventional bank credit. The scheme does not have a preferential element for bumiputras.

- Bank Bumiputra was established in 1966 to lend to bumiputras. The small average size of loan and high unit costs led the bank to extend its services to other clients, but lending to bumiputras continues to make up about 40 percent of its portfolio. Although Credit Guarantee Corporation has reduced the importance of Bank Bumiputra as a source of credit to bumiputras, Bank Bumiputra remains important for the widespread geographical location of its branches and the confidence of the bumiputra community that it enjoys.

- The state economic development corporations, most of which have quasi-independent status as the industrial-promotion arms of state governments, vary in quality. They nevertheless have generally displayed flexibility and resourcefulness and have played an important part in industrial development at the state level. For their operations they have relied heavily on federal loans, but they have also benefited from grants, interest-free loans, land grants for industrial and housing estates, and even from forest concessions from state governments. Their principal activities consist of the construction and operation of commercial-industrial accommodations, including industrial estates; low-cost housing projects in some states; direct investments, which take the form of complete ownership, joint ventures, and minority participations; and the operation of wholesale distribution facilities. In these activities, the participation of bumiputras appears to be promoted largely in informal ways—in preferences to Malays in the leasing of factory space, for example. Investment activities and wholesale operations are more directly aimed at fostering the business enterprises of bumiputras or helping ailing bumiputra firms.

- Like PERNAS, the Public Works Department, since 1972, and other government departments, since 1973, give preferences to supplier firms owned by bumiputras. These preferences typically take the form of a margin of 10 percent on small contracts and a smaller margin on larger contracts. Bumiputra firms apparently depend highly on public procurement.
- In addition to these institutions, the central bank, Bank Negara, initiated a system of granting priority to credit to Malays through the commercial banking system. Largely as a result of this system, the share of total bank credit extended to Malays and other indigenous persons in the private sector increased from 3.4 percent in 1970 to more than 12 percent in 1975.

All the institutions that have been discussed are involved in various aspects of promoting ownership by bumiputras or developing entrepreneurial and managerial ability. Two things should be highlighted: the limitations related to the ownership objective and the emphasis that needs to be placed on the entrepreneurial and managerial objective. To put it in language used earlier, the creation of wealth needs to be sustained before the enjoyment of its fruits can be sustained.

The policy of government to foster ownership by Malays has two principal elements: the rule that 30 percent of the equity in new investment be held by bumiputras; and the public purchase of equity in trust. Insofar as the absence of widespread ownership by Malays in the modern sector reflects the lack of means to acquire ownership, there is some risk that the requirements would be fulfilled in such a way that ownership by Malays is in name only. The acquisition of equity in trust, mainly by PERNAS, MARA, and the state economic development corporations, faces a similar problem of eventually generating sufficient real resources in the private hands of Malays to divest the government of the shares it holds. Another possible outcome, perhaps equally likely, is the development of a substantial public sector, despite the fact that this never was a specific policy objective. In the absence of private Malay funds, moreover, the public sector may be required to continue to grow in order to achieve the objectives of participation by bumiputras. Government must thus consider three fundamental issues: whether it wants an extensive public sector; if so, how the sector should be policed; and whether this particular means of achieving its objectives in ownership by bumiputras is appropriate.

The required emphasis on the objective of developing entrepreneurial and managerial skills leads naturally to emphasis on the promotion of small business, because small business is where entrepreneurship must begin. Such emphasis would also be an appropriate means of reaching many potential Malay businessmen who are located in rural areas or otherwise away from the largest cities. It may also be, in the natural sequence of entrepreneurial development, that manufacturing activities will at first take a place subordinate to that of activities in commerce, transport, and construction.

The use made by bumiputra businessmen of the services available to them from various institutions was examined in a study made by the Economic Planning Unit.[27] Some of its recommendations were related to financial assistance: loan staffs in lending agencies should be strengthened; lending agencies should adopt a clearer specialization by type of loan; credit terms should not be subsidized; efforts must be made to avoid defaults. Others were related to advisory services and business training: advisory services need to be extended and, where possible, coordinated with lending agencies; such services should be subsidized, though still charged at a nominal fee, and available throughout the country; training courses need to de-emphasize general motivational aspects and emphasize specific information and business skills; the number of qualified advisory personnel should be increased. Still others were related to policies for preferential public procurement: emphasis needs to be placed on smaller firms because such policies are designed to get firms started; a program should be started to encourage subcontracting between large suppliers and small firms; the frequent problem of late payments of contracts by government should be attacked.

These recommendations provide a useful basis for refining existing programs. One important question not directly tackled in these recommendations is delicate: How are Malays to be given preferences? The question is important because, without preferences, there is no reason to suppose that the rates of participation by Malays would be any higher than in the past.[28] Most programs—the principal exceptions being those of MARA and PERNAS—are not specifically related to restructuring. Increasing the participation of Malays largely depends on administrative preference. On the other hand, the experience of MARA, which has

27. Economic Planning Unit, "Bumiputra Participation in Business."
28. Indeed the participation of Malays shows some tendency to increase with size of firm.

had a high rate of arrears in its lending program, should be a salutary warning of the difficulties of trying to favor Malay entrepreneurs while still subjecting them to financial discipline. The recommendations of the Economic Planning Unit with respect to increasing loan staff and offering technical assistance, as forerunners of any increase in the volume of lending, are applicable to the problems encountered by MARA. For other agencies, a combination of light administrative preference with heavy doses of technical assistance and moderate margins of preference for Malays in lending may well represent a prudent middle path, for which some of the operations of Malaysian Industrial Development Finance Corporation could serve as a model.[29]

There is some cause for concern about attempts to expand small business in the manufacturing sector. The non-Malay business community may already have exploited many of the possibilities for efficient small-scale industry, and existing small enterprises may be capable of increasing their output through more intensive use of capacity. To the extent that this is so—something that is difficult to ascertain—programs for small businesses owned or managed by Malays could usefully have two emphases: the development of enterprises of any size in rural and regionally underdeveloped locations and the selection of existing small, self-sustaining Malay enterprises in urban areas for development into larger, say medium-sized, firms. More specifically, successful firms employing ten persons or fewer should be encouraged to grow to the point that they can employ, say, twenty to thirty persons. The idea that the Economic Planning Unit has of assisting the development of subcontracting by firms involved in public procurement could usefully be extended to the private sector as well. The development of a subcontracting exchange in FIDA, which already is being done informally, would complement some of the existing services of FIDA as an investment broker and would be a useful step in promoting both small and medium-size industry.

Although no minimum size is specified in the criteria for awarding investment incentives, smaller firms are at a disadvantage in obtaining incentives, primarily because the larger the firm, the better it is able to deal with red tape and to influence administrative decisionmaking. Fortunately the Industrial Coordination Act excludes from its system of controls firms with fewer than twenty-five full-time paid workers and

29. The technical assistance could cover special programs already under way, programs that are directed toward the development of entrepreneurial abilities among Malays, and specific assistance with the formulation and presentation of projects.

less than M$250,000 in shareholders' equity. But depending on the way
in which the incentives program is implemented, the act incurs the risk
of inhibiting the growth of a firm from small to medium size by suddenly imposing upon it a number of conditions, not all of which can be
fulfilled.

Postscript on Prospects

Can the manufacturing sector fulfill the high expectations held for it
in achieving the objectives of the New Economic Policy? A definitive
answer to this important question can only be arrived at after a comprehensive analysis of the prospects for growth of individual industries in
the Malaysian environment. Although no such analysis is attempted in
this chapter, a more general discussion can help to highlight some of the
issues affecting the prospects of the sector. Clearly, however, a thorough analysis of this question deserves the highest priority.

As has been emphasized in earlier reports on the manufacturing sector, the Malaysian economy holds a fundamental attraction for investors, both foreign and domestic. A significant factor in this attractive-
ness, especially to foreign investors, is the political stability that pre-
vails in Malaysia in an environment of political and economic freedom.
There is little fear of nationalization or constraints on the repatriation of
profits. Associated with this political stability has been the general efficiency and honesty of government. As the discussion in earlier chapters
makes clear, government has had a great deal to do with providing the
necessary infrastructure for economic development and has provided
incentives and protection to the manufacturing sector while avoiding
the excessive distortions and inefficiencies often observed in other developing countries.

Malaysia has formidable natural resources, and there is considerable
potential for investments in related processing activities. The commodities that appear to offer the most scope for further processing are
rubber, timber, and petroleum. Malaysia, in common with other East
Asian countries, also has an ample supply of unskilled labor. The projection is that the labor force will grow about 3 percent a year in the
foreseeable future—a rate that, under any reasonable assumptions, is
far in excess of the capacity of agriculture to absorb. Furthermore, the
nearly universal prevalence of primary schooling gives Malaysian labor
a certain advantage over many other developing economies. Access to
raw materials has been relatively good, because of the proximity of

Malaysia to international shipping routes and a well-developed system of internal transport. Finally, to the extent that accurate forecasts can be made, sufficient funds should be available to finance a high level of capital formation. Thus, as can be seen from the discussion in chapter three, even if a program of rapid growth is followed, domestic saving should be more than adequate to finance the required investment. If the need arises, the comfortable external position of Malaysia would allow substantial additional foreign borrowing.

Because many of the obvious areas of import substitution appear to have been exhausted, future growth of the manufacturing sector will have to rely increasingly on exports and expansion of domestic demand. As is discussed in chapter three, the prospects for sustained growth of domestic demand are good. The relatively favorable long-term prospects for the prices of the principal export commodities of Malaysia—combined with further exploration, production, and processing of petroleum products—should provide a substantial stimulus to domestic demand. Projecting international demand is much more hazardous. The 1978 World Development Report of the World Bank contains a projection that the exports of developing countries will grow somewhat more slowly between 1975 and 1985 than they did between 1970 and 1975—12.2 percent a year instead of 14.9 percent—assuming that trade barriers will remain roughly as they are now.[30] It thus is reasonable to expect some slackening in the growth of Malaysian exports. But in view of the past performance of Malaysia in export growth, which has been substantially better than the average performance of developing countries, it also is reasonable to assume that Malaysia would be able to achieve, at a minimum, a growth rate of 12 percent a year, and a rate of 15–16 percent would not be out of the question.

The broad factors discussed above seem to imply that there are good prospects for continued rapid growth of the manufacturing sector in Malaysia, but any such assumption should be qualified by consideration of some recent trends in investment. In particular, there is evidence of a significant deterioration in the rate of investment in the manufacturing sector since 1974. Investment in manufacturing is not measured directly in Malaysia, but investment approvals by the FIDA provide a good indication of investment activity in manufacturing. The level of approvals in 1977 was only half as high as the peak level of 1974 and 40 percent lower than the 1971 level (table 7.3). The investment

30. World Bank, *World Development Report, 1978* (Washington, D.C., 1978), p. 29.

Table 7.3. *Investment Applications to and Investment Approvals by the Federal Industrial Development Authority, 1971–77*

		Approvals			
Year	Number of applications	Number	Capital investment (millions of Malaysian dollars)		Potential employment (thousands of persons)
			Current prices	Constant 1970 prices[a]	
1971	285	305	938	906	48.7
1972	423	355	621	577	56.4
1973	651	473	1,216	1,031	81.5
1974	628	525	1,590	1,166	71.4
1975	471	461	1,436	1,008	36.2
1976	394	425	1,220	816	32.3
1977	429	400	883	552	29.6

Sources: FIDA Annual Report, various years; World Bank estimates.
a. Deflated by investment price index (1970 = 100) of the Department of Statistics.

target of FIDA for the manufacturing sector during the period of the third plan was about M$2 billion a year, but during the early 1970s approvals were averaging less than half that amount. Further evidence of the decline of private investment in manufacturing can be seen in the data on imports of machinery and equipment for manufacturing. It has been estimated that such imports might have declined as much as 37 percent in 1975 and 25 percent in 1976.[31] Although the low level of approvals by FIDA in 1976 and the continuing low levels in 1977 were not encouraging, an upturn was reported in imports of capital goods for the last quarter of 1976 and the first few months of 1977. This might indicate that, although investment approvals still were low, projects that had been approved earlier but had been postponed were beginning to be put into effect.

There are a number of factors that may have contributed to this downturn in investment in manufacturing, but it is difficult to determine their relative importance with any certainty. First, the world re-

31. These estimates were derived by aggregating those imports of capital goods intended exclusively for the manufacturing sector and those of which a significant part was to go to manufacturing. In other words, the estimates were derived by excluding from imports groups 715–719 of the standard international trade classification (SITC)—that is, noncapital goods and capital goods used predominantly elsewhere than in the manufacturing sector.

cession in 1974–75, in addition to being largely responsible for the downturn in the growth of manufacturing output, doubtless had some negative effect on investment activity as well. Second, 1974 was a peak year for private investment in Malaysia. There would probably have been some cyclical decline in the rate of private investment in 1975 in any event. Third, considerable uncertainty has been voiced in the private sector regarding the Industrial Coordination Act, which parliament passed in 1975. Government acknowledged the uneasiness in the business community and amended the act in 1977; a significant change was the establishment of an appeals procedure. Finally, there is the possibility that the manufacturing industry in Malaysia may have lost some of its competitive position, although the evidence for such a view is far from clear.

Although there still was considerable uncertainty about the extent and the causes of the decline in the rate of investment in manufacturing, industrial output increased significantly, although at a declining rate, during 1976 and 1977—almost 19 percent in 1976 and 10.5 percent in 1977.[32] This continued rise in output, despite the evidence of a decline in investment, can be explained by the usual lags in investment and by the substantial increase in capacity created during the investment peak of 1974. On the basis of the estimated decline in the rate of investment in 1975 and 1976, this capacity should have been nearly exhausted by the end of 1977, meaning that continued rapid growth of manufacturing output would require a substantial recovery in investment in manufacturing. Such a view seems to be consistent with the declining trend in the growth of output noted above. In view of the uncertainty about whether cyclical factors or defects in the structure of industry caused the recent decline in manufacturing investment and of the importance of the manufacturing sector in providing employment opportunities for the rapidly growing labor force, a thorough analysis of manufacturing investment deserves to be given a high priority.

---

32. The 1976 estimate is based on the index of industrial production for Peninsular Malaysia; the 1977 estimate is based on actual figures for eleven months.

EIGHT

Alice Galenson

𝄢𝄢

Agriculture and Rural Poverty

THE AGRICULTURE, FORESTRY, AND FISHING SECTOR of Malaysia employs
nearly half the Malaysian labor force and contributes nearly a third of
total value added. During the 1970–75 period output grew at an average
annual rate of 4.2 percent.[1] Rubber remains the most important crop,
contributing more than 30 percent of agricultural value added, but its
relative importance diminished between 1970 and 1975, when palm oil
more than doubled its share in value added and became the second most
important crop (table 8.1). The shares in value added of rice, coconuts,
and other crops and livestock respectively declined to 9.6 percent, 2.1
percent, and 14.1 percent.[2] Forestry, with 16.5 percent of the value
added by the sector, diminished somewhat in importance; fishing maintained its 8.5 percent share. Thus, while most sectoral components
grew in absolute terms between 1970 and 1975, only palm oil grew in
relation to the sector as a whole.

The structure of the agriculture, forestry, and fishing sector is very
different in each of the two major geographical divisions of the country.
The structure in Peninsular Malaysia, which contributes four-fifths of
the value added by the sector and nearly 90 percent of agricultural
value added, is similar to that of Malaysia as a whole, but with rubber—40 percent—and palm oil—21 percent—having larger proportions
and forestry—7 percent—a much smaller proportion of the sector. In
Sabah and Sarawak, on the other hand, forestry contributes half the
value added by the sector. Agriculture contributes only 39 percent, and
fishing supplies the remaining 11 percent.

Malaysia covers an area of 127,330 square miles, of which 60 percent
is in Sabah and Sarawak. Peninsular Malaysia, with 40 percent of the

1. This growth rate is an understatement of the trend growth during the 1970s because
1975 was an abnormally low year. The growth rate for 1970–76, by a least squares calculation, was 5.5 percent.

2. Other crops are cocoa, pineapple, tobacco, coffee, tea, and a number of fruits,
vegetables, and spices.

Table 8.1. *Value Added in Agriculture, Peninsular Malaysia, Sabah and Sarawak, and All Malaysia, 1970 and 1975*
(1970 producers' prices)

| Crop, industry, or sector | 1970 | | | | | |
| | Peninsular Malaysia | | Sabah and Sarawak | | All Malaysia | |
	Millions of Malaysian dollars	Percentage of total	Millions of Malaysian dollars	Percentage of total	Millions of Malaysian dollars	Percentage of total
Rubber planting and processing	1,283	32.8	20	0.5	1,303	33.3
Palm oil	269	6.9	23	0.6	292	7.5
Coconuts	103	2.6	21	0.5	124	3.1
Rice	333	8.5	53	1.4	386	9.9
Other crops and livestock	526	13.4	214	5.5	740	18.9
Total agriculture	2,514	64.2	331	8.5	2,845	72.7
Forestry	266	6.8	454	11.6	720	18.4
Fishing	271	6.9	79	2.0	350	8.9
Agriculture, forestry, and fishing	3,051	77.9	864	22.1	3,915	100.0

Source: World Bank estimates based on Department of Statistics, "Preliminary National Accounts, Peninsular Malaysia 1970–75 and Malaysia 1971–75" (Kuala Lumpur, September 1977; processed) and Graham Pyatt and Jeffrey I. Round, "The Distribution of

land and 84 percent of the population, contains the bulk of Malaysia's cultivated land. Of the 9.6 million acres of land under permanent cultivation in 1975, 7.6 million acres were in Peninsular Malaysia and 2 million in Sabah and Sarawak (table 8.2). During 1965–75 the cultivated area of Malaysia grew at the rate of 1.8 percent a year. The acreage cultivated in Sabah and Sarawak grew at a more rapid rate during the same period, and the share of those states in the total increased from 18 percent to 21 percent.

Rubber, oil palm, rice, and coconuts are the principal crops of Malaysia, together covering more than 90 percent of the cultivated area (table 8.3).[3] Although government has given high priority to diversifi-

3. In table 8.3 the acreages devoted to the most important crops, not the actual acreages cultivated, are presented. To the extent that double-cropping is practiced on land

1975						
Peninsular Malaysia		Sabah and Sarawak		All Malaysia		
Millions of Malaysian dollars	Percentage of total	Millions of Malaysian dollars	Percentage of total	Millions of Malaysian dollars	Percentage of total	Crop, industry, or sector
1,496	31.1	21	0.4	1,517	31.6	Rubber planting and processing
780	16.2	67	1.4	847	17.6	Palm oil
85	1.8	17	0.4	102	2.1	Coconuts
400	8.3	60	1.2	460	9.6	Rice
438	9.1	238	5.0	676	14.1	Other crops and livestock
3,199	66.6	403	8.4	3,602	75.0	Total agriculture
278	5.8	514	10.7	792	16.5	Forestry
298	6.2	112	2.3	410	8.5	Fishing
3,775	78.6	1,029	21.4	4,804	100.0	Agriculture, forestry, and fishing

Income and Social Accounts: A Study of Malaysia in 1970" (Washington, D.C.: World Bank, 1978; processed).

cation—to cocoa, coffee, and tobacco, for example—the predominance of the four principal crops will persist for some time. The relative importance of each of the four has shifted considerably through the years, however. Although rubber still is by far the most widespread crop, its share of the area planted has steadily declined, from 71 percent in 1960 to 57 percent in 1975; the share of oil palm increased from 2 percent to 19 percent during the same period. These shifts reflect the more favorable market position of palm oil in recent years. Of the four crops, only oil palm has significantly increased in acreage since 1965. Rubber is the dominant crop both in Peninsular Malaysia and in Sabah and Sarawak;

planted in rice, the cultivated acreage is greater than that shown in table 8.3. The acreage double-cropped in Peninsular Malaysia is given in table 8.6.

Table 8.2. *Acreage under Cultivation, Peninsular Malaysia, Sabah, and Sarawak, 1965, 1970, and 1975*
(thousands of acres)

Region or state	1965	1970	1975	Percentage annual increase, 1965–75
Peninsular Malaysia	6,500	7,050	7,600	1.3
Sabah	500	650	900	6.0
Sarawak	900	1,050	1,100[a]	2.0
All Malaysia	7,900	8,750	9,600	1.8

Sources: Government of Malaysia, *Third Malaysia Plan, 1976–1980*, p. 209; Economic Planning Unit, unpublished tables, August 1975.

a. In addition, Sarawak has about 5.6 million acres under shifting cultivation, largely devoted to hill rice of low productivity. The annual incomes in 1970 of those who cultivated this acreage ranged from M$160 to M$280.

rice is next in importance in Sabah and Sarawak; oil palm has overtaken all crops except rubber in Peninsular Malaysia.

During the 1960–75 period the production of rubber grew 4.4 percent a year on the average, faster at the beginning and more slowly toward the end of the period; palm oil and palm kernel oil grew 18.7 percent a year, their growth accelerating throughout the period (table 8.4). The value of the output of rubber fell from 24 percent of GNP—M$1.6 billion—in 1961 to 15 percent—M$2.9 billion—in 1974; that of palm oil increased from a negligible amount to 6 percent of GNP—M$1.3 billion—in 1974. Since 1975 the production of rubber has picked up, and the production of palm oil has continued to grow rapidly. Rice production grew nearly 6 percent a year between 1960 and 1970 but only 3.4 percent a year between 1970 and 1975 and, as a result of two successive droughts, did not grow at all in the next few years. The production of coconut oil has shown no steady growth.

After the cultivation of crops forestry is the principal use made of land in Malaysia. Peninsular Malaysia has 20.5 million acres of forest, almost two-thirds of its total area; Sabah and Sarawak together have 38.7 million acres, almost four-fifths of their area. Production of sawlogs grew rapidly during the 1960s but only slightly in the following decade. The production of sawn timber grew more slowly throughout the period but began to grow about 8 percent a year after 1965, reflecting in part a ban on the export of certain types of logs.

Table 8.3. *Acreage Planted in the Principal Crops, Peninsular Malaysia, Sabah, and Sarawak, Selected Years, 1960–75*

Crop and region or state	Thousands of acres				Annual rate of growth, 1960–75 (percent)
	1960	1965	1970	1975	
Rubber	4,420	4,994	5,061	4,936	0.7
Peninsular Malaysia	3,889	4,328	4,331	4,188	0.5
Sabah and Sarawak	531	666	730	748	2.3
Rice[a]	1,180	1,339	1,410	1,345	0.9
Peninsular Malaysia	929	950	992	944	0.1
Sabah and Sarawak	251	389	418	401	3.2
Oil Palm	136	264	786	1,616	17.9
Peninsular Malaysia	135	240	691	1,436	17.1
Sabah and Sarawak	1	24	95	180	41.4
Coconut	599	684	764	797	1.9
Peninsular Malaysia	520	507	528	567	0.6
Sabah and Sarawak	79	177	236	230	7.4
Total, four crops	6,335	7,281	8,021	8,694	2.1
Percentage of cultivated area	n.a.	92.2	91.7	91.2	—

n.a. Not available.
— Not applicable.
Source: Data supplied by the Economic Planning Unit.
a. A substantial portion of the land on which rice is grown is double-cropped. The acreage cultivated in rice, therefore, is substantially greater than the area actually devoted to that crop. Data on the acreage double-cropped in Peninsular Malaysia are presented in table 8.6.

The fishing sector supplied 8 percent of agricultural output and 3 percent of GDP during 1971–75, the period of the second plan. In Peninsular Malaysia, where 80 percent of the Malaysian output of fish is caught, the catch doubled between 1961 and 1972, then jumped 19 percent in 1973, declining thereafter. The fishing industry in Sarawak grew rapidly in the 1970s; the catch in Sabah remained level from 1966 onward. The main reasons for the large increases in the catch in Penin-

Table 8.4. *Production of the Principal Agricultural Commodities,*
Selected Years, 1960–75

Commodity	Thousands of metric tons				Annual rate of growth, 1960–75 (percent)
	1960	1965	1970	1975	
Rubber	770	917	1,269	1,477	4.4
Palm oil and kernel	116	185	522	1,514	18.7
Rice	645[a]	813	1,080	1,288	5.0[b]
Coconut oil	n.a.	70	96	79	n.a.
Sawlogs	n.a.	n.a.	12,701	13,725	n.a.
Sawn timber	983	1,230	1,995	2,734	7.1

n.a. Not available.
Sources: Ministry of Finance, *Economic Report*, various years.
a. 1961.
b. 1961–75.

sular Malaysia and Sarawak were the introduction of trawling and the
heavy investment in large motorized vessels, which can fish farther offshore. This modernization began in the mid 1960s in Peninsular Malaysia and in 1973 in Sabah and Sarawak. In Sabah, however, the increase in the catch made by trawlers may have reduced the catches of
smaller boats.

The farm sector is more market-oriented in Malaysia than in many
developing countries. Exports of agricultural commodities, including
wood products, amounted to M$6.9 billion in 1976, or about a quarter
of GNP and half of all exports. Exports of rubber and palm oil alone
contributed 16 percent of GNP and 33 percent of total exports. From
1960 to 1976 the volume of rubber exports grew to 1,620,000 tons, an
increase of 90 percent; that of palm oil grew to 1,329,000 tons, an increase of more than 1,200 percent. Malaysia supplied 46 percent of all
the natural rubber produced in the world in 1976 and 42 percent of all
the palm oil produced in 1975. Timber is also a significant export commodity. In 1976 sawlogs and sawn timber together accounted for about
9 percent of GNP and 18 percent of exports, of which nearly three-
quarters came from Sabah and Sarawak. During 1966–76 exports of
sawn timber significantly increased in relation to those of sawlogs; the
latter constituted 82 percent of Malaysian exports of the two products
in 1966 but only 63 percent in 1976. The change reflects both the
growth of the sawmill industry and bans on the export of certain popu-

lar species of logs. Malaysia is responsible for about 14 percent of the world market of tropical hardwoods.

Malaysian rice is consumed locally, and additional rice must be imported to meet domestic demand. Government has been active in increasing production in several areas, notably by providing irrigation for double-cropping, with the dual goals of eradicating poverty and promoting self-sufficiency in rice. Because of the comparatively high cost of production in Malaysia, the original target was 90 percent self-sufficiency. But the world food crisis of 1973–75 prompted government to adopt complete self-sufficiency as a goal. In 1970 the country imported 33 percent of its domestic requirement. By 1975 this figure was reduced to about 13 percent, but poor crops in 1977 temporarily increased the need for imports to 18 percent of domestic consumption.

Sector Subdivisions

The agricultural sector of Malaysia comprises three types of landholding: smallholdings, estates, and development schemes (table 8.5). The independent smallholder sector, which encompasses about 60 percent of the agricultural land in Peninsular Malaysia and a somewhat smaller percentage in Sabah and Sarawak, is most important. The largest groups of smallholders are those in rubber, rice, and coconuts. About 30 percent of the total acreage is in estates, which have increasingly been planted in oil palm, though rubber still is important. Because oil palm requires considerably less labor per acre than rubber, employment on estates has fallen as land formerly planted in rubber has been replanted in oil palm. Estates now account for less than a third of total employment in these two crops in Peninsular Malaysia. Land development schemes, in which large numbers of individual settlers work under a common management, constitute about 10 percent of the agricultural acreage of Peninsular Malaysia and produce mostly rubber and palm oil.

About 1.8 million acres have been developed through land development schemes since 1960. The Federal Land Development Authority (FELDA), established in 1956, which has been responsible for more than 50 percent of land developed for smallholders in Peninsular Malaysia, is the most important land development agency. During its first twenty years, FELDA developed 813,000 acres, with a peak development of more than 100,000 acres in 1973. Rubber predominated on FELDA schemes in the early years, but after 1965 oil palm became the most

Table 8.5. *Acreage Planted in the Principal Crops, by Type of Holding, Peninsular Malaysia, Selected Years, 1960–75*

Crop and type of holding	1960		1965	
	Thou-sands of acres	Per-centage of total	Thou-sands of acres	Per-centage of total
Rubber	3,889	66	4,328	66
Estates	1,934	33	1,859	28
Smallholdings	1,955	33	2,469	38
FELDA and state land development schemes	n.a.	n.a.	n.a.	n.a.
Rice (smallholdings)	929	16	950	15
Oil Palm	135	2	240	4
Estates	135	2	208	3
FELDA and other land development schemes	n.a.	n.a.	32	1
Coconut	520	8	507	8
Estates	80	1	68	1
Smallholdings	440	7	438	7
Miscellaneous	452	8	479	7
Total	5,925	100	6,504	100

n.a. Not available.

Sources: Economic Planning Unit and Department of Statistics, unpublished tables, August 1975; *Third Malaysia Plan, 1976–1980*, pp. 293–95; Ministry of Finance, *Economic*

important crop; during the period of the second plan 288,000 acres were developed for oil palm and only 112,000 for rubber. By the end of 1975 FELDA had settled about 33,000 families. During the second plan period FELDA settlements absorbed the equivalent of about a fifth of the 62,000 increase in agricultural households. Other land development agencies include the Federal Land Consolidation and Rehabilitation Authority (FELCRA), the Rubber Industry Smallholders Development Authority (RISDA), and a number of state and private agencies.

Smallholders in rice, one of the poorest groups in the country, made up 16 percent of all agricultural households in Peninsular Malaysia in 1975. Eight percent of all households in Peninsular Malaysia depend upon rice farming as their primary source of income, but rice accounts

1970		1975		
Thou-sands of acres	Per-centage of total	Thou-sands of acres	Per-centage of total	Crop and type of holding
4,331	61	4,188	55	Rubber
1,598	23	1,392	18	Estates
2,290	32	2,796	37	Smallholdings
		n.a.	n.a.	FELDA and state land
443	6			development schemes
992	14	944	13	Rice (smallholdings)
691	10	1,436	19	Oil Palm
478	7	819	11	Estates
				FELDA and other land
213	3	617	8	development schemes
527	7	567	8	Coconut
55	1	44	1	Estates
472	6	523	7	Smallholdings
515	7	405[a]	5	Miscellaneous
7,056	100	7,540	100	Total

Report, 1977–78; data supplied by the Oil Palm Growers' Council.
    a. Residual.

for only 2 percent of GDP. The most important government activity in rice farming has been the provision of irrigation and drainage facilities for both main and off-season crops. The proportion of wet-rice fields that are double-cropped rose from 2 percent in 1960 to 57 percent in 1975. This rise contributed to an increase in production of the off-season crop from 23,000 tons to about 670,000 tons, or from 2 percent to 40 percent of annual rice production (table 8.6). In addition, improved inputs, along with extension and credit services that encourage and facilitate the use of these inputs, contributed to an average annual increase in yields of 2.2 percent between 1955 and 1970 and more than 3 percent between 1970 and 1975.

The Muda Irrigation Project in northwestern Peninsular Malaysia illustrates the possible effect of irrigation and other improvements on

Table 8.6. *Acreage Planted, Production, and Yields of Rice, Peninsular Malaysia, Selected Years and Periods, 1955–75*

Year or period	Acreage planted (thousands)				Production (thousands of long tons)	
	Wet rice				Wet rice	
	Main season	Off season	Dry rice	Total	Main season	Off season
1955	833	6	47	886	658	5
1960	864	21	61	946	868	23
1965	897	90	53	1,040	915	100
1970	938	326	54	1,318	1,002	377
1975	920	527	24	1,471	1,008	668
	Annual rate of growth (percent)					
1955–65	0.8	31.1	1.2	1.6	3.4	34.9
1965–70	0.9	29.4	0.4	4.9	1.9	30.5
1970–75	−0.3	10.1	−23.8	2.9	0.1	12.1
1955–75	0.5	25.1	−3.8	2.7	2.2	27.7

Sources: S. Selvadurai, "Agriculture in Peninsular Malaysia," (Kuala Lumpur: Ministry of Agriculture, April 1977; processed), p. 78; data supplied by Government of Malaysia.

production and incomes.[4] Water was first released into the project area in 1970, and the full area was served by 1975. The switch from single-cropping to double-cropping was accompanied by the rapid adoption of improved varieties of rice and large increases in yields. Between 1969 and 1974 production doubled in the Muda area, where about 40 percent of the rice grown in Peninsular Malaysia was produced by the last year. Net farm income per family also doubled in the project area during the 1969–73 period. Only part of this gain was the result of a 23 percent increase in price; the rest was the result of a 35 percent average increase in yields and, more important, the doubling of crop intensity.[5]

Smallholders in rubber constituted 21 percent of the households in Peninsular Malaysia in 1975. Between 1960 and 1975 the output of smallholders grew at an average annual rate three times that of estates.

4. For a more complete discussion of this project, see Clive Bell and Peter Hazell, "Measuring the Indirect Effects of an Agricultural Project in its Surrounding Region," *American Journal of Agricultural Economics*, forthcoming (February 1980).

5. A doubling of crop intensity alone does not double incomes, because it usually is accompanied by a fall in other income.

Production (thousands of long tons)		Yield (long tons an acre)				Year or period
		Wet rice				
Dry rice	Total	Main season	Off season	Dry rice	Total	
18	681	0.79	0.78	0.38	0.77	1955
33	924	1.00	1.10	0.54	0.97	1960
26	1,041	1.02	1.12	0.49	1.00	1965
28	1,407	1.07	1.16	0.51	1.07	1970
13	1,689	1.10	1.28	0.55	1.15	1975
		Annual rate of growth (percent)				
4.5	4.4	2.6	3.6	3.2	2.7	1955–65
0.0	6.2	1.0	0.9	0.0	1.4	1965–70
−14.2	3.7	0.6	1.8	0.0	3.1	1970–75
−1.6	4.7	1.7	2.5	1.8	2.4	1955–75

In 1973 smallholders surpassed estates in total production because of the shift of estates from rubber to oil palm and the relative improvement of the yields of smallholders, which grew at an average annual rate of 5.6 percent during 1960–75, while the rate of growth on estates was only 2.9 percent (table 8.7).[6] The yields of smallholders now are equal to more than 85 percent of those of estates. This relative improvement of the yields from smallholdings, which include new land settlements, is largely the result of new planting and replanting. Yields were almost constant between 1955 and 1962, when they began to rise rapidly as new trees reached maturity and to close the gap between the yields of smallholdings and those of estates, on which replanting programs had been initiated earlier. Between 1965 and 1974, however, replanting by smallholders slowed. In 1965 about 50 percent of the acreage of registered smallholders had been replanted; in 1976 the percentage had risen only to 67. More than 90 percent of the acreage of estates had been replanted by 1976. Because of declining rubber prices, the share of the acreage of smallholders replanted in crops other than rubber increased from less than 5 percent in 1963 to 37 percent in 1975.

6. The fifteen-year average for estates masks an actual decline in yields during the last five years of the period (see table 8.7).

Table 8.7. *Acreage Cultivated, Production, and Yields of Rubber on Smallholdings and Estates, Peninsular Malaysia, Selected Years and Periods, 1960–75*

Year or period	Mature acreage (thousands)			Production (thousands)		
	Total	Estates	Small-holdings	Total	Estates	Small-holdings
1960	2,968	1,405	1,563	696	420	276
1970	3,300	1,346	1,954	1,215	621	594
1975	3,363	1,308	2,055	1,417	599	818
	Annual rate of growth (percent)					
1960–70	1.1	−0.4	2.3	5.7	4.0	8.0
1970–75	0.4	−0.6	1.0	3.1	−0.7	6.6
1960–75	0.8	−0.4	1.8	4.9	2.4	7.5

— Not applicable.
Sources: Data supplied by the Economic Planning Unit and the Department of Statistics.

Smallholders in rice and rubber are the largest agricultural groups in Malaysia. They also are the least productive (table 8.8). Smallholders in rice and rubber respectively generated value added of only M$1,125 and M$1,194 apiece in 1970; the average for all smallholders in the principal crops was M$1,801. The low productivity of rice farming in relation to the productivity of other groups is largely a function of the small sizes of the holdings, which average 3.4 acres. The productivity of rice land actually exceeds that of smallholdings in both rubber and coconut. The average holdings of smallholders in rubber are somewhat larger than those of rice farmers, but the productivity of their land and their labor is low. The much higher productivity of rubber estates, in both land and labor, shows the extent to which the poor performance of smallholders could be improved by better planting patterns and tapping practices. Coconut land is unproductive, but large average holdings make possible a relatively high output per worker. Finally, holdings in oil palm show the highest productivity of labor and the largest average size. All holdings in oil palm are private or state-owned estates.

It must be recognized that the figures in table 8.8 reflect relative prices in 1970. Changes in the prices of agricultural commodities significantly influenced the incomes of producers during the period of the second plan (table 8.9). Food prices rose more rapidly than the consumer price index as a whole—59 percent rather than 42 percent—and

Yield (tons a mature acre)			Yields of small-holders as percentage of yields of estates	Year or period
Total	Estates	Small-holdings		
0.235	0.299	0.177	59	1960
0.368	0.461	0.304	66	1970
0.421	0.458	0.398	87	1975
Annual rate of growth (percent)				
4.6	4.4	5.6	—	1960–70
2.7	−0.1	5.5	—	1970–75
4.0	2.9	5.6	—	1960–75

because food is by far the largest single item in the budgets of the poor, the change in food prices is of more significance in this analysis. Cultivators of rice and growers of oil palm benefited from price changes during the five years in question. Prices received by these two groups rose more than the prices they paid for food by 10 percent and 8 percent, respectively. The prices of rubber and coconuts, on the other hand, fell substantially in relation to food prices, counteracting government measures to reduce poverty.

Reduction of Rural Poverty under the Second Plan

Under the New Economic Policy, introduced at the beginning of the second plan period, government launched a drive to reduce and eventually eradicate poverty and to accelerate the restructuring of Malaysian society. In 1975 about 87 percent of the poor households of Malaysia were rural; nearly 70 percent of all the poor households were employed in the agricultural sector. Policies for the eradication of poverty have therefore been slanted largely toward agricultural development. Much of the progress made during the period of the second plan was the result of existing government programs to help the rural poor, including the extensive irrigation schemes for rice farmers, the large new land development programs for landless laborers, and a substantial support program for replanting to replace old and low-yielding rubber trees with high-yielding varieties.

Table 8.8. *Productivity of Land and Smallholder Labor Producing the Principal Crops, Peninsular Malaysia, 1970*

Crop and type of holding	Value added (millions of Malaysian dollars)	Acreage (thousands)	Employment (thousands)	Acres per person
Smallholdings in rubber[a]	628	2,733	526	5.2
Rubber estates	655	1,598	197	8.1
Holdings in oil palm[b]	269	691	44	15.7
Holdings in coconuts[c]	103	528	41	12.9
Rice farms	333	992	296	3.4
Total or average	1,988	6,542	1,104	5.9

Sources: Table 8.1, table 8.5, and World Bank estimates.
a. Includes FELDA, which accounts for 16 percent of total acreage.

The second objective of the New Economic Policy—restructuring the ethnic share of incomes and employment—is fundamentally tied to rural poverty. Because a large portion of rural, low-income households are Malay, a reduction in rural poverty would narrow ethnic income imbalances. The concentration of government programs on Malays is particularly evident in rice farming and land development. The estimated 4.4 percent annual rate of real growth of agriculture, forestry, and fishing in Peninsular Malaysia between 1970 and 1975 was accompanied by significant gains in the eradication of rural poverty (table 8.10). This strong performance of the agricultural sector during the period of the second plan generally led to higher incomes, moving a large number of Malay households, as well as non-Malay households, above the poverty line. Poverty among agricultural households fell from 68 percent to 63 percent during the period.

Smallholders in Rubber

Smallholders who plant rubber constitute the largest identifiable group of farmers in Peninsular Malaysia. In 1975 the approximately 400,000 households in this group, of which 234,000 were considered to be in poverty, included 28 percent of the total number of poor. Almost all the smallholders who had low-yielding rubber trees and 41 percent of those who had high-yielding rubber trees earned less than M$500 per

Value added per acre		Value added per worker		
Malaysian dollars	Percentage of average	Malaysian dollars	Percentage of average	Crop and type of holding
230	76	1,194	66	Smallholdings in rubber[a]
410	135	3,325	185	Rubber estates
389	128	6,114	339	Holdings in oil palm[b]
195	64	2,512	139	Holdings in coconuts[c]
336	111	1,125	62	Rice farms
304	100	1,801	100	Total or average

b. Includes FELDA and estates.
c. Largely smallholdings.

capita in 1975 (table 8.11).[7] Yields were a significant determinant of income. Smallholdings planted in low-yielding trees were concentrated in the lowest part of the income range: more than three-quarters of the households working such holdings earned less than M$350 per capita a year; only 9 percent of the households working holdings planted in high-yielding trees were at this income level.

The two main causes of low incomes among rubber smallholders—small size of holdings and low yields—tended to reinforce one another. Low yields were concentrated in small holdings to a far greater extent than high yields. Twenty-eight percent of the low-yield holdings had fewer than 3 acres; only 13 percent of the high-yield holdings were that small. At the higher end of the range, more than 60 percent of the high-yield holdings had more than 5 acres; less than 30 percent of the low-yield holdings were that large. The numbers imply that the smallest holdings in rubber had not yet been adequately reached by programs, such as replanting, that are designed to increase productivity. Pro-

7. The number of smallholdings in rubber does not correspond directly to the number of households engaged in growing rubber: some households own more than one holding; some holdings may employ more than one household. Smallholders, moreover, receive part of their incomes from sources other than growing rubber. To the extent that outside income is derived from crops included in government programs, the incomes of these smallholders are affected both by these programs and by trends in the prices received for those crops.

Table 8.9. *Changes in the Prices of Principal Agricultural Commodities, 1970–75*

Commodity	Price index for products, 1975 (1970 = 1.00) (1)	Price index for food, 1975 (1970 = 1.00) (2)	Change in the terms of trade, 1970–75 (1) ÷ (2)
Rubber	1.10	1.59	0.69
Rice	1.75	1.59	1.10
Coconut oil	1.39	1.59	0.87
Palm oil	1.72	1.59	1.08

Sources: *Third Malaysia Plan*, 1976–1980, p. 127; Ministry of Finance, *Economic Report, 1977–78*, pp. xlvi; Bank Negara, *Quarterly Economic Bulletin*, vol. 9, no. 4 (December 1976), p. 78.

ducers with very small holdings often are reluctant to forgo production during the years required for trees to mature. Replanting small, scattered holdings, moreover, is less efficient than replanting larger blocks of land. Nevertheless a concerted effort is under way to help the poorest smallholders, through replanting, through consolidation of hold-

Table 8.10. *Rural Poverty in Peninsular Malaysia, by Occupational Group, 1970 and 1975*

Occupational group	1970			1975		
	Total households (thousands)	Households in poverty (thousands)	Incidence of poverty (percent)	Total households (thousands)	Households in poverty (thousands)	Incidence of poverty (percent)
Smallholders in rubber	350	226	65	396	234	59
Cultivators of rice	140	123	88	148	114	77
Smallholders in coconuts	32	17	53	34	17	50
Workers on estates	148	59	40	127	60	47
Smallholders in oil palm	7	2	29	10	1	10
Other agricultural workers	138	126	92	158	124	78
Fishermen	38	28	73	42	26	62
Total	853	581	68	915	576	63

Source: *Third Malaysia Plan*, 1976–1980, p. 163.

Table 8.11. *Distribution of Income among Smallholdings in Rubber, Peninsular Malaysia, 1975*

Annual per capita income[a] (Malaysian dollars)	Thousands of smallholdings[b]			Percentage composition
	High yield[c]	Low yield[d]	Total	
Up to 300	12	52	64	16
301–350	13	50	63	16
351–400	16	17	33	8
401–450	37	9	46	11
451–500	33	3	36	9
501–550	25	1	26	7
551–600	22	...	22	6
601–650	20	...	20	5
651–700	20	...	20	5
701 and up	70	...	70	17
Total	268	132	400	100

... Zero or negligible.
Source: World Bank estimates based on background papers of the Economic Planning Unit for the third plan.
a. Includes income from sources other than rubber.
b. Rough estimates.
c. The average is 900 pounds an acre.
d. The average is 450 pounds an acre.

ings, and through relocation by participation in land development schemes.

Despite a 30 percent deterioration of rubber prices in relation to food prices, the Economic Planning Unit of Malaysia estimated that the incidence of poverty among households on holdings planted in rubber dropped from 65 percent in 1970 to 59 percent in 1975 (see table 8.10). Malaysian rubber prices rose 46 percent in 1976, while the increase in the consumer price index was only 2.6 percent, which meant a substantial further reduction in poverty.

The main reason for the decline of poverty among smallholders in rubber—apart from the settlement of approximately 2,750 families of these smallholders on newly developed land—was the increased use of high-yielding trees in subsidized replanting programs and in new planting on settlement and block-planting schemes. The accompanying extension work to teach better care of trees and better tapping practices was also important. Because trees reach maturity in seven to eight years, the eradication of poverty achieved during the period of the second plan was largely the result of replanting and new planting in earlier years. Further benefits are yet to be realized. More than 400,000 acres were replanted in high-yielding trees under the second plan; roughly 500,000 acres had been so replanted under Malaysia's first plan.

Rice Farmers

Accounting for nearly 150,000 households in 1975, rice farmers constitute the second largest agricultural group in Peninsular Malaysia.[8] About 77 percent of these households were considered to be in poverty.[9] The distribution of the income of rice farmers in 1975, analyzed according to whether they grew one crop a year or two and whether they owned or rented their land, indicates some of the reasons for their poverty (table 8.12). Of the farmers who double-cropped their land, 54 percent earned less than M$500 per capita in 1975, whereas 87 percent of those who planted only a single crop earned less than that amount. Owners fared better than tenants: 61 percent of those who owned their land, but 72 percent of those who were tenants, earned less than M$500; 20 percent of those who owned their land, but only 10 percent of those who were tenants, earned more than M$750.

Another important cause of poverty among rice farmers is low productivity per acre planted. Yields obtained on well-managed, closely supervised farms run some 23 percent higher than the national average because of better management and the use of higher yielding seeds and more fertilizers and pesticides. These inputs are available to many small farmers but, given proper irrigation and drainage facilities, whether these farmers adopt them often depends upon the availability of credit and the quality and intensity of extension work. Because only a little more than half of all rice farmers are roughly classified as having high productivity, considerable scope exists for reducing poverty by ensuring, through credit schemes and extension work, that farmers use the best inputs available.

Between 1970 and 1975 the number of rice growers above the poverty line increased from 17,000 to 34,000, and the incidence of poverty

8. For the purposes of the poverty analysis rice farmers are defined as those farmers that plant more than 75 percent of their cultivated acreage in rice. Of 296,000 households in 1970 that grew some rice, only 140,000 specialized in rice farming. The rest were included in other categories of rural households. To the extent that specialists in rice farming also grow other crops, they are helped by the programs discussed in the rest of this section.

9. As noted in chapter two, it is possible that the incidence of poverty among smallholders in rice may be exaggerated, because their own consumption of rice may have been valued at farm-gate prices rather than retail prices.

Table 8.12. *Distribution of Income among Rice Farmers, Peninsular Malaysia, 1975*

| Annual per capita income[b] (Malaysian dollars) | Thousands of farmers[a] | | | | Total | |
| | Owners | | Tenants | | | |
	Double-cropping	Single-cropping	Double-cropping	Single-cropping	Thousands	Percent
Up to 250	7.6	8.4	5.1	3.9	25.0	18
251–300	5.4	7.5	3.2	2.5	18.7	14
301–350	5.8	4.0	3.1	1.4	14.3	11
351–400	5.6	3.1	2.7	0.9	12.3	9
401–450	4.9	2.0	2.4	0.6	10.0	7
451–500	4.4	1.4	2.0	0.5	8.3	6
501–550	3.9	1.0	1.8	0.4	7.0	5
551–600	3.4	0.8	1.5	0.2	5.9	4
601–650	3.3	0.7	1.3	0.2	5.4	4
651–700	2.8	0.4	1.2	0.1	4.5	3
701–750	2.1	0.3	0.5	0.1	3.0	2
751 and up	18.1	1.0	4.0	0.1	23.2	17
Total	67.3	30.6	28.8	10.9	137.6[c]	100

Source: Same as for table 8.11.
a. Rough estimates.
b. Includes income from sources other than rice.
c. This figure differs from that shown in table 8.10 because it is based upon a different set of estimates.

declined from 88 percent to 77 percent. These gains were the result of a sharp, 75 percent increase in the price of rice and a modest, 20 percent increase in production. After allowing for the effects of higher food prices, cultivators of rice gained 10 percent in income as a net result of the relevant price trends. In the future, however, natural price trends cannot be relied upon to improve the incomes of rice farmers.

The 20 percent increase in production was largely the result of the irrigation program. The area of land irrigated increased about 17 percent, and, more important, the percentage of the irrigated area that was double-cropped increased from 46 to 79. Thus it was possible to increase the total area harvested from the main crops and the off-season irrigated crops 43 percent. Because some of the land newly irrigated had in the past been producing rainfed rice, the net increase in production was less than that implied by the increase in irrigated acreage. Nevertheless the potential effects on production of irrigation and improvements in yields were greater than is indicated by the increase of 20 percent for the five years. Production in 1974 was already 27 percent higher than that in 1970, but a drop of more than 5 percent in 1975, attributable to poor weather, led to the lower performance over all.

The high percentage of rice farmers still in poverty, even with the favorable prices of 1975, is explained by the large number of very small holdings, continuing lack of access to the means of irrigation for double-cropping, unfavorable financing agreements, and low productivity of the soil. In 1975 the average rice farmer needed about 5 acres of arable land to earn an income higher than the poverty level, but the size of the average rice farm was only 3.4 acres. As is true for smallholders in rubber, low yields appear to go along with small holdings. For example, 38 percent of the low-yield holdings and 46 percent of the medium-yield holdings had fewer than two acres, while only 27 percent of the high-yield holdings were that small. Similarly, 27 percent of high-yield holdings had 5 acres or more, whereas only 17 percent of the medium-yield holdings and 8 percent of the low-yield holdings were that large.[10] Government programs to increase yields will increase the incomes of all farmers, including those with the smallest holdings, but many of those most in need will remain in poverty unless they can increase their outside income or obtain larger holdings through resettlement or consolidation of land.

Smallholders in Coconuts

Like rubber, coconuts are grown on both estates and smallholdings, though the acreage given to coconuts on smallholdings is more than eight times that on estates. The number of smallholders who grow coconuts is estimated to be about 80,000, but only about 34,000 households depend on this crop for more than half their incomes. The number of households specializing in coconut farming grew by 2,000 during the period of the second plan, but the number below the poverty line remained the same, which means that the incidence of poverty declined from 53 percent to 50 percent. An important cause of poverty is the inadequate size of holdings. Coconuts are a low-yield crop, and more than 7 acres are needed to keep a family out of poverty, but the average holding in Peninsular Malaysia is only 6.5 acres. Furthermore all the important coconut areas have required sizable investments in drainage facilities.

During the period of the second plan, production on smallholdings in

10. Background papers of the Economic Planning Unit for the third plan.

coconuts increased only 10 percent, and increases in the price of coconuts were more than offset by the rise in food prices. The fall in the
incidence of poverty was in part the result of rehabilitating 42,000
acres—9 percent of the total—and replanting 8,000 acres under the
subsidy program administered by the Ministry of Agriculture. Rehabilitation—which includes the removal of uneconomic trees, clearing,
weeding, fertilizing, improving drainage, and planting such intercrops
as cocoa and coffee—increases yields about 25 percent. Replanting increases yields 50 percent. At these rates the rehabilitation and replanting accomplished would have been responsible for only about a third of
the increase in production. The increase in the price of coconuts, despite its having been offset by the increase in consumer prices, may well
have stimulated better care of trees and more attention to harvesting
and marketing. Ample scope still exists for improvements in yields;
average yields on estates are about 50 percent higher than those on
smallholdings, mainly as a result of better management.

Workers on Estates

The number of households working in estates declined from 148,000
in 1970 to 127,000 in 1975, and the incidence of poverty among them
increased from 40 to 47 percent. The labor requirements of estates fell
steadily during 1970–75 for several reasons, including mechanization
and a shift from rubber to oil palm, which requires less labor per acre.
In addition, the use of contract labor, which is excluded from the category of estate workers that have been the subject of poverty estimates,
has increased. The problem of low income among estate workers arises
from underemployment, originating in the surplus of labor, rather than
from low daily wages, and the situation is likely to deteriorate as the
downward trend in labor requirements continues.

Smallholders in Oil Palm

This group is relatively small and is rich in comparison with the
other groups of agricultural households that have been identified (see
table 8.10). The explanation for these facts is that oil palm is basically
an estate crop and is relatively new in Malaysia. Traditional smallholdings do not exist; the smallholder classification refers to farmers on
lands settled by FELDA or other land development schemes. Because
these holdings generally are better supervised and more productive
than traditional smallholdings, and because they are large in relation to

traditional holdings, poverty among so-called smallholders in oil palm is uncommon.

Fishermen

In Peninsular Malaysia two-thirds of the 76,000 fishermen, constituting half the fishing households, are found on the west coast. The catch on the west coast rose almost 10 percent a year between 1965 and 1973, by which time it amounted to 19 tons a boat or 5.6 tons a fisherman, and accounted for 76 percent of the total catch. The catch on the east coast increased 6.4 percent a year between 1966 and 1973, when productivity reached only 12.2 tons a boat and 3.3 tons a fisherman. The share of the west coast, however, has declined in recent years because of overfishing and subsequent depletion of resources in the Straits of Malacca. Between 1970 and 1973 the volume of fish landed grew 18 percent on the west coast and 38 percent on the east coast. The offshore resources of the east coast are not yet fully used, so there is scope for continued increases in yields.

A price increase plus the increase in total catch suggest a better rate of progress in the eradication of poverty than is revealed by the estimated overall decline in the incidence of poverty from 73 percent to 62 percent. The explanation is that gains were not well distributed. Fishermen limited to inshore fishing by traditional methods benefited only marginally; they may even have been hurt by the growing importance of capital-intensive fishing equipment. The catch from small boats held steady on the east coast, but fell by half on the west coast.

Several government programs have been established to fight poverty in the fishing sector. Majuikan, the Fisheries Development Board established at the end of 1971, operates a trawler fleet and an array of marketing and processing facilities. The trawlers are capital-intensive, and their manpower requirement by the end of 1975 was fewer than 1,200 men. A subsidy scheme was created in 1972 to provide capital for fishermen to improve their equipment, but disbursements of funds have been slow. In addition, the grants are large and help only a few fishermen. Training programs in the Fisheries Training Institute have been initiated, but they have difficulty attracting trainees with seagoing experience and placing them once trained. Thus government programs have left the majority of traditional fishermen untouched; in any case the shortage of trained, experienced staff has meant that the programs have had little effect on fishing in Malaysia. Growth that has come about and changes that have been made in the past have been in direct response to market opportunities, and modernization has been financed almost wholly from within the industry.

Other Categories of Rural Households

In 1970 there were 130,000 households in the new villages and 125,000 households of agricultural laborers.[11] These groups overlap with some of the groups already considered to an extent that is unknown. Residents of the new villages may be growers of rice or rubber, and laborers may cultivate small plots of less than two acres, making them smallholders despite the fact that most of their income is from employment elsewhere. Those households not included elsewhere make up a residual category of agricultural families, of whom 78 percent were in poverty in 1975.

It is estimated that nearly half the agricultural laborers of Malaysia work with fair regularity on holdings of 10 to 100 acres planted in rubber. The next largest type of employment probably is in rice growing, which is more seasonal and generally provides lower annual earnings. These laborers suffer from the same conditions that cause high rates of poverty among smallholders who grow rice or rubber. Regulation by the Ministry of Labor of the terms of employment of estate workers and of agreements between unions and management do not apply to these laborers.

The 1970 census estimated the population of 446 new villages to be 920,000; 90 percent were Chinese. About half have no land, and most of the rest either have no legal titles or have only temporary ownership licenses. Unemployment and underemployment of residents of new villages are considerable, especially among the younger job seekers, and little land suitable for agriculture is available for expansion in the surrounding areas. The growing of rice and rubber are the most important uses of land in the less accessible new villages. Residents of new villages in more accessible areas engage in market gardening and the raising of livestock and poultry to make intensive use of their limited acreage. Because opportunities for increasing income from agriculture are so limited, the principal alternatives are nonagricultural employment or resettlement by means of new land development schemes. So far, the

---

11. During the early 1950s inhabitants of remote rural areas were resettled in new villages, where they could be better isolated from insurgents.

former alternative has been more important, because few residents of new villages have been accepted for land development schemes.

Agricultural Services

Malaysia has numerous institutions that provide agricultural support services, which include training, extension, credit, subsidies, and research. Extension services are provided for specific crops—for rubber, for example, by RISDA—and by the departments of agriculture of the various states. Several universities and institutes provide training for extension workers, and during the period of the second plan about M$58 million was spent on agricultural education and training, representing 3 percent of all agricultural development expenditure. Most credit is provided by Bank Pertanian Malaysia, which approved loans worth M$159 million during the period of the second plan. More than 40 percent of the total was for rice growing, with 24 percent for industries based on agriculture, 15 percent for the development of estates, and 10 percent for the growing and marketing of tobacco. The Farmers' Organization Authority and RISDA also provided credit for agricultural inputs, processing, and marketing. Subsidies in the form of planting material, fertilizer, and pesticides are given to smallholders to help them in replanting rubber, coconuts, and other permanent crops. In addition, fishermen benefit from capital subsidies for the purchase and modernization of equipment. Agricultural research is undertaken by the Malaysian Agricultural Research and Development Institute (MARDI) and a number of more specialized agencies. During the period of the second plan that institute released four new varieties of rice and continued its work in developing new strains of oil palm and field crops.

It is difficult to measure precisely the effects of agricultural support services. But the farming practices taught by extension workers and promoted through credit, subsidies, and research undoubtedly are important in raising production and incomes among agricultural households. Even the poorest farmers can benefit from the improvements available if they are given the means and the knowledge to use them. Although the ultimate goal is to lift everyone out of poverty, that goal is not attainable in the short run. It is desirable in the meantime to raise the standard of living of all farmers through whatever means available.

Land Development

As discussed earlier, an important aim of the agricultural program of Malaysia is to accelerate improvement in the use of existing agricultural land. The improvement of yields through irrigation, replanting, and better inputs and farming practices will contribute significantly to attainment of the goal of higher rural incomes. Nevertheless a large number of persons in rural areas either are landless and unable to earn adequate incomes as laborers or they own or operate too little land to realize incomes that will lift them above the poverty line. In all the sectors discussed above, the recurrent theme has been that underemployment and the small size of holdings are important causes of poverty. Until more jobs become available in the other sectors of the economy, most of the very poor agricultural workers must depend on finding additional land to work. The land development program is an attempt to fill this need.

A little more than 1,000,000 acres were developed under the second plan, of which about 800,000 acres were in Peninsular Malaysia. Because of the long gestation period of rubber and oil palm, the two predominant crops on newly developed land, relatively little of the increase in production from land newly developed during 1971–75 was realized during that period. Nevertheless the potential production of this land was equal to about 45 percent of the actual increase in the production of rubber for the period and 100 percent of the increase in palm oil. Land newly developed also accounted for about 10 percent of the increase in the production of rice in Malaysia.

More than 400,000 acres were developed by FELDA, but lags between the beginning of clearing operations and the taking in of settlers limited the intake of settlers to about 14,000 households. Data on the number of households that received indirect benefits from the other parts of the land development program—from employment on a newly developed holding, for example, or from consolidation of land vacated by settlers—are not available, but an optimistic estimate of 25,000 gives a total of 39,000, or more than half the 67,000 agricultural families lifted above the poverty line during the same period. When settlement catches up with land developed under the second plan, further gains in the effort to eradicate poverty will be substantial.

Programs of the Third Plan and Their Effect on Rural Poverty

In the third plan it was projected that agricultural production would grow 6 percent a year during 1976–80; the rate was 4.2 percent a year during the preceding five years (table 8.13).[12] A rapid increase in the

12. See note 1.

Table 8.13. *Growth of Agricultural Output, 1970–75, and Targets for 1976–80*
(percent)

Product	Average annual rate of growth	
	1970–75	*1976–80*
Rubber	3.1	6.0
Palm oil and kernels	24.0	16.0
Rice	3.6	3.6
Coconuts and copra	−3.5	1.5
Pineapple	n.a.	2.5
Pepper	n.a.	7.1
Tea	n.a.	−4.0
Livestock	4.6	5.6
Miscellaneous crops	n.a.	7.5
Fish	3.2	3.8
Sawlogs	2.1	6.7
Total agriculture	4.2[a]	6.0

n.a. Not available.
Sources: Table 8.1 and *Third Malaysia Plan, 1976–1980*, pp. 113, 186.
a. The output of other crops and livestock declined 1.8 percent a year.

production of crops was projected, mainly because of an expected doubling in the production of palm oil and palm kernel. The production of rubber was expected to grow at a rate twice that of the preceding five years. During the first two years of the third plan, the production of rubber grew at an average rate of 8.5 percent a year. The production of rice, projected to grow 3.6 percent a year, did not grow at all during 1976 or 1977 because of poor weather, so the goal may not be attainable. It was projected that growth in the fishing sector would drop sharply, while that in forestry would pick up. Much of this growth, particularly in tree crops, is to be the result of programs undertaken before the third plan was put into effect.

During the period of the second plan, government estimates show that the incidence of poverty among agricultural households fell from 68 percent to 63 percent (see table 8.10), but the incidence of poverty among nonagricultural rural households was virtually unchanged at 35 percent.[13] These figures reflect the concentration of antipoverty pro-

13. The figures on the incidence of poverty probably are an understatement of the average gains made during the period of the second plan, because rubber prices fell 25 percent in 1975 and smallholders who plant rubber are the largest group in poverty.

Table 8.14. *Rural Poverty in Peninsular Malaysia, 1975,
and Projections for 1980*

	1975			1980		
Sector and occupational group	Total households (thousands)	Households in poverty (thousands)	Incidence of poverty (percent)	Total households (thousands)	Households in poverty (thousands)	Incidence of poverty (percent)
Total agriculture	915	576	63	958	472	49
Smallholders in rubber	396	234	59	423	169	40
Rice farmers	148	114	77	150	110	73
Smallholders in coconuts	34	17	50	34	16	47
Smallholders in oil palm	10	1	10	25	2	8
Other agriculturalists[a]	285	184	65	283	153	54
Fishermen	42	26	62	43	22	52
Other rural industries	433	154	35	543	175	32
Total	1,348	730	54	1,501	647	43

Source: *Third Malaysia Plan, 1976–1980*, p. 73.
a. Includes agricultural households in urban areas, agricultural laborers, workers on estates, and farmers who plant more than one crop.

grams on agriculturalists, an emphasis continued under the third plan. Thus the forecast of the plan was that by 1980 poverty among agricultural households would decline further to 49 percent (table 8.14). On the other hand, despite a small decline in the incidence of poverty among nonagricultural rural households, the number in poverty would rise more than 20,000. According to the plan, of the 150,000 new rural households in Peninsular Malaysia during the 1976–80 period, 42,000 were to be employed in agriculture and the rest in nonagricultural activities.[14] The provision of employment for the second group should be given a high priority in Malaysia. Because 70 percent of poor families rely primarily on agriculture for their incomes, however, and because government accords high priority to the eradication of poverty, it is fitting that more than a quarter of all development expenditure under the third plan was earmarked for this sector—more than to any other.

The most important change in emphasis from the second plan to the third is in the distribution of investment resources between programs

14. The estimate of 42,000 additional agricultural households is based on an assumption of growth in agricultural employment that is quite low—only 1.3 percent—while growth in agricultural output is projected at 6 percent a year.

for assisting traditional smallholders and those for developing new agricultural land. The acreage of land newly developed was to be continued at about the same level as that achieved during the period of the second plan, whereas programs for assisting traditional smallholders, excluding drainage and irrigation, were to be doubled (tables 8.15 and 8.16). It should be emphasized that doubling the acreage covered by

Table 8.15. *Land Development, 1971–75, and Targets for 1976–80*
(thousands of acres)

State or region, and type of venture	1971–75	1976–80
Peninsular Malaysia	805	700
FELDA	412	350[a]
Current model component	412	300
New model component	...	50
FELCRA	58	50
Youth component	19	25
Fringe alienation component	39	25
RISDA (block planting)	57	100
Other schemes	278	200
State schemes	151	100
Private ventures	116	100
Joint ventures[b]	11	...
Sabah	74	150
State schemes	74	70
Private ventures	...	30
Joint ventures	...	50
Sarawak	131	150
State schemes	131	70
Private and joint ventures combined	...	80
Total	1,010	1,000

... Zero or negligible.
Source: Economic Planning Unit, "Land Development Strategy" (Kuala Lumpur, August 1975; processed).
a. The target of FELDA was subsequently increased to 500,000 acres.
b. Projects jointly undertaken by the public and private sectors.

programs for assisting traditional smallholders does not necessarily imply doubling the output resulting from such programs. The effectiveness of the programs varies considerably, depending, for example, on whether sufficient extension aid is included with subsidized

Table 8.16. *Development of Existing Agricultural Land,*
Excluding Irrigation and Drainage Programs,
1971–75, and Targets for 1976–80
(thousands of acres)

State or region, development scheme, and type of venture	1971–75	1976–80
Peninsular Malaysia	698	1,265
Crop subsidy and diversification	202	631
Replanting and new planting by RISDA	432	500
Rehabilitation and replanting of coconuts	50	100
Rehabilitation	42	80
Replanting	8	20
Replanting of pineapples	5	26
Rehabilitation by FELCRA	9	8
Sabah	30	60
Crop diversification	14	15
Rehabilitation and replanting of coconuts	...	10
Rehabilitation	...	6
Replanting	...	4
Rehabilitation and new planting by Sabah Rubber Fund Board	16	35
Rubber	8	35
Other crops	8	...
Sarawak	133	343
Crop diversification	59	177
Replanting and new planting of rubber	15[a]	62
Replanting	15	56
New planting	...	6
Pepper acreage	20	44
Mature plants	14	25
New planting	6	19
Rice planting	39	60
Total	861	1,668

... Zero or negligible.
Source: Economic Planning Unit, "Land Development Strategy."
a. The scheme was discontinued in 1972.

inputs. There has been little evaluation of the various support programs used to help increase production on existing farms. The effectiveness of these programs is being studied, but measurement of programs by acreage can give some indication of their size, particularly as they are compared with the results of earlier programs. Expenditure on land development under the third plan was to be 50 percent higher in real terms than that under the second plan; expenditure on all other agriculture will be 108 percent higher, largely as a result of sizable increases in the rubber-replanting and crop-diversification programs.[15] Land development accounts for only 42 percent of agricultural expenditure under the third plan; the comparable figure under the second plan is 54 percent. The share of programs for assisting traditional smallholders is to increase from 30 percent to 38 percent of the total (table 8.17). This change in emphasis is the result of the conviction that land development, although a necessary and dramatic way of reducing rural poverty, can affect only a small number of persons in relation to the number affected by the other programs of agricultural development.

Rubber

Although the expenditure on the replanting of rubber was to more than quadruple in nominal terms under the third plan, the area covered would be 540,000 acres, or only 29 percent more than that covered under the second plan (see tables 8.16 and 8.17). The high expenditure is partly the result of increases in the size of the grants given to smallholders to cover the costs of replanting. The third plan reflects the expectation that the production of rubber would increase at a rate of 6 percent a year and that the incidence of poverty among smallholders who plant rubber would fall to 40 percent by 1980.[16] According to the plan, the area still planted in old, low-yielding trees in 1980 would be more than 300,000 acres, and if constraints on the capacity to implement the program were overcome, the rubber-replanting program could be greatly expanded. The smallholders remaining in poverty

15. The third plan embodies a broad definition of programs for assisting traditional smallholders. Such programs are understood to apply to all agriculture except that on newly developed land and thus include forestry, veterinary services, fishing, agricultural research, credit, and marketing advice, all of which are excluded from the definition used in the rest of this chapter.

16. Projections by the World Bank of rubber prices in 1980 are 35 percent higher than those on which the poverty estimates in the third plan are based. These higher prices would reduce the projected incidence of poverty in 1980 by about a third.

Table 8.17. *Public Development Expenditure for Agricultural Programs, 1971–75, and Projections for 1976–80*
(millions of Malaysian dollars)

Program and crop or activity	Expenditure under the second plan, 1971–75		Projected expenditure under the third plan, 1976–80	
	Malaysian dollars	Percentage of total	Malaysian dollars	Percentage of total
Assisting traditional smallholders	641	30.1	1,793	37.9
Pineapple replanting	4	...	22	0.5
Coconut replanting	27	1.3	62	1.3
Rubber replanting	158	7.4	675	14.3
Drainage and irrigation	271	12.7	621	13.1
Crop diversification, extension, and services	181	8.5	413	8.7
Land development	1,139	53.5	2,010	42.4
Development by FELDA	645	30.3	985	20.8
Development by FELCRA	49	2.3	86	1.8
Other development	445	20.9	939	19.8
Other programs	349	16.4	933	19.7
Forestry	31	1.5	55	1.2
Veterinary medicine	70	3.3	179	3.8
Fisheries	32	1.5	276	5.8
Agricultural research	29	1.4	61	1.3
Credit and marketing	132	6.2	295	6.2
Other activities	55	2.6	67	1.4
Total	2,129	100.0	4,736	100.0

... Zero or negligible.
Source: *Third Malaysia Plan, 1976–1980.*

would be those whose holdings were smaller than three acres, for whom the only long-term solution would be land consolidation or resettlement. Even these hard-core poor would benefit from an expanded program, because their incomes, though still below the poverty line, would rise with replanting. RISDA is unlikely, however, to have the capacity to carry out this expanded program during the period of the third plan.

As the number of outstanding acres to be replanted diminishes, RISDA will be faced with increasing constraints upon replanting. The experience of RISDA during the period of the second plan indicates that replanting in blocks is effective and economical, but some smallholders in a given area often refuse to replant, thereby making block replanting impossible. In addition, ambiguous land titles or lack of interest on the part of absentee landlords sometimes prevents replanting. Because of these and other problems, less than half the anticipated 100,000 acres were replanted in 1976, and there were shortfalls again in 1977, when only about 45,000 acres were replanted. Measures are needed to deal with these constraints, such as bringing more pressure to bear on the individual smallholder, whose decision not to replant is detrimental to the interests of a larger surrounding group, or providing him with incentives to replant. One step considered was an increase in the replanting grant, making it sufficient to cover the full costs and loss of income associated with replanting.[17] The effectiveness of RISDA can also be improved by strengthening supporting technical services. Because the field staff of RISDA is spread very thin, the agency has not been able to provide adequate extension services. An increase in the density of planting, the use of more mature planting material, which can reduce the period of immaturity from seven years to five or four, and the promotion of better tapping practices would all contribute to the improvement of the income of smallholders and provide them with a greater incentive to participate in the program.

Another measure that government might take in the effort to reduce poverty is a reduction of taxes on rubber. In 1976 export duties on rubber amounted to M$500 million, the equivalent of 16 percent of the value of rubber exported, or about M$0.14 a pound. Assuming that the tax was borne entirely by the producer, export duties paid by a family with three acres of rubber trees amounted to roughly M$350 for the year. The replanting cess of 4.5 cents a pound places an additional burden of about M$110 a year on the smallholders. Of course, a general reduction of rubber taxes would affect all producers of rubber, not just those in poverty. Smallholders produce just less than 60 percent of all the rubber in Peninsular Malaysia, and probably somewhat more than half that is produced on holdings of less than 10 acres. Thus only about a third of the tax reduction would accrue to poor rubber farmers. The measure would be more attractive as a means of reducing poverty if a way could be found to direct it exclusively to the small producers.[18]

17. In 1978 the grant for replanting rubber was substantially increased, and a two-year program of income-maintenance subsidies was approved.

18. The budget for 1980 included a reduction in the rubber tax. But because of the

Rice

The most important single determinant of poverty among rice farmers is lack of access to irrigation facilities for double-cropping. Most of the large blocks of land suited for large-scale drainage and irrigation have already been included in such programs, and further expansion of drainage and irrigation facilities must take place on a smaller scale than in the past. It appears, however, that the scope for small-scale irrigation projects is broad. The acreage covered would, of course, be less than was covered in the past by large-scale projects. Projected in the third plan was the provision of new or improved irrigation facilities to about 240,000 acres of rice, about a fourth less than the 324,000 acres irrigated under the second plan. Acreage that can be double-cropped was to increase 16 percent, whereas the increase during the second plan period was 50 percent. Government estimated that poverty among rice farmers would decline from 77 percent to 73 percent. In addition, 359,000 acres were to be provided with new or improved drainage facilities for crops other than rice; 247,000 acres were so provided under the second plan.

In Peninsular Malaysia, where the emphasis now is on improving existing facilities, the total acreage cultivated in rice, including both main and off-season crops, was expected to rise only about 5 percent during the third plan period; the increase during the second plan period was 12 percent. The proposed increase in irrigated and double-cropped acreage was expected to account for about a fourth of the projected 19 percent increase in the production of rice in Peninsular Malaysia between 1976 and 1980. The rest must be achieved by raising yields. Inasmuch as all rice farmers, including those who will remain in poverty, stand to gain from increased yields, programs for reducing poverty should include both improved extension services and rural credit programs to encourage better farming practices and continued research into high-yielding varieties of rice.

MARDI, which is responsible for all agricultural research except that having to do with rubber and fisheries, plans to expand its program and to deal more thoroughly with rice as well as with other field crops, pineapples, cocoa, coconuts, livestock, use of products, engineering, and water management. While the emphasis of research by MARDI is on the selection and breeding of high-yielding, short-maturing, disease-

---

recent increases in the price of rubber and the progressiveness of the tax in relation to price, the burden of the tax on poor rubber smallholders still is substantial.

resistant varieties suitable for double-cropping, the reluctance of farmers to experiment with new varieties and methods can be expected. Despite the introduction of ten new varieties between 1964 and 1975, the one most widely used in 1975 still was Mahsuri, which was developed in 1965 and improved in 1969. In a recent survey of rice farmers it was found that only about half the farmers used high-yielding varieties, even though high-yield seeds were being sold at a research station located in the middle of the survey area.[19] Stronger extension services might improve this situation, as evidenced by the Muda Irrigation Project, for which the extension network is supplied through the Muda Agricultural Development Authority. About seventy varieties of rice were formerly planted in the Muda project area, but by 1973 about 75 percent of the area was planted in three improved varieties developed by MARDI—Jaya, improved Mahsuri, and Bahagia.

Similar contrasts are found in the use of fertilizer. In the Seberang Perak Survey only about half the farmers were found buying fertilizer, despite government subsidies; of those who bought it, most did not use the recommended amounts. In the Muda area the figures are strikingly different. Fertilizer was used on 97 percent of the rice fields in 1973, and fertilizing practices had improved. The average use of nitrogen was 83 percent of the minimum application recommended. In the same year 48 percent of the Muda farmers used pesticides, and the use of pesticides as a preventive measure rather than a corrective measure had increased. The yields for the Muda area exceeded the national average by 30 percent for main crops and 20 percent for off-season crops. Some of the difference may be attributable to better soils and better water supply, but a significant part must be credited to better organized and more intensive support services. Efforts should therefore be made to improve services in other specialized areas where rice is grown.

Coconuts

Incomes from coconut farming and levels of production have suffered from poor land, poor maintenance, poor processing, and smallness of holdings. As a remedy for these conditions government proposed the replanting of 20,000 acres of smallholdings in coconuts in Peninsular Malaysia and the rehabilitation of 80,000 acres during the

19. S. Selvadurai, "Padi Survey: Seberang Perak (Stage 1)" (Kuala Lumpur: Ministry of Agriculture, 1975; processed).

third plan period (see table 8.16). In Sabah 4,000 acres were to be re-planted and 10,000 acres rehabilitated. Poverty among smallholders who grow coconuts was projected to decline slightly, from 50 percent to 47 percent. To achieve this result, subsidies for replanting were increased to M$900 an acre and those for rehabilitation to M$600. The projected 8 percent increase in production was to be the result of a combination of a higher proportion of acreage planted in trees of higher-yielding age—sixteen to sixty years—and an increase in yields for each age group as a result of rehabilitation.

The redress of poverty, however, must depend more on the growth of intercropping than on the yields of coconuts. Intercropping with coffee or cocoa can increase the incomes of coconut growers as much as 300 percent. The third plan called for the acreage of coconuts inter-cropped with cocoa to be increased from 15 percent in 1975 to 30 per-cent in 1980 in Selangor and Perak and from 10 percent to 15 percent in Johore. In the past, farmers did not generally find replanting so attrac-tive as the benefits available from rehabilitation and intercropping. Re-planting should become more attractive as dwarf varieties become more widely available; these new varieties have yields two to three times those of tall varieties, and as far as is known they can also be inter-cropped. Replanting with new varieties and intercropping with unfa-miliar crops may require considerable extension support, which could also help increase the yields of existing coconut stands.

Other Crops and Livestock

The many other crops of Malaysia, which together use only 6 to 7 percent of the total cultivated land, have a collective importance much greater than the acreage given to them might indicate. Fruits and vege-tables are an important part of the domestic food supply; grain crops and tubers can be substituted for imported livestock feed; canned pine-apple is a significant export item; sugar is significant for import sub-stitution. Some of these crops are grown on very small holdings, where they serve to intensify production and raise incomes. Because provid-ing research, extension, and other services for so many crops is ex-pensive, the efforts of government have been primarily devoted to the principal crops, for which the benefits are larger in relation to the costs. Nevertheless subsidies are being provided to encourage the diversifica-tion of crops that would increase and stabilize incomes on small farms.

One crop to which government has given priority under its crop-diversification program is cocoa, because of its suitability for inter-cropping with coconuts. As a result of encouragement by government, there has been a rapid expansion of the cultivation of cocoa in Penin-sular Malaysia. The area planted in cocoa increased from 8,300 acres in 1970 to about 55,000 acres in 1977, while production increased from about 1,100 long tons to 14,200. Besides intercropping with cocoa, there also is interest in growing it as a monocrop, and trial plantings have been made. Malaysia is only a minor producer of cocoa, contrib-uting less than 1 percent of the total world output. Although there is no official forecast of future production of cocoa, 800,000 acres are now planted in coconuts, and there appears to be substantial potential for growth.

The production of livestock was expected under the third plan to grow 5.6 percent a year; under the second plan the rate was 4.6 per-cent. About 95 percent of the domestic supply of dairy products, 75 percent of the supply of mutton, and 15 percent of the supply of beef are imported, and the trend in imports of these products has been up-ward. The production of poultry and pigs, among the more modern, commercialized enterprises, constitutes about 90 percent of the value of all livestock produced, but these enterprises depend on imports for 80 to 85 percent of their feed supply. These facts have led to a good deal of interest in import substitution for feed and for beef and dairy products. The National Livestock Development Authority, which established seven beef and dairy farms under the second plan, was to establish five more under the third plan and expand and reorganize slaughtering fa-cilities. The economic justification for import substitution in beef and dairy products through the operation of large-scale farms is question-able, however, because substantial increases in production may involve high costs and sizable subsidies.

Agricultural Services

In addition to the expenditures for specific crops discussed above, the third plan included expenditures for extension services, subsidies, cred-it, and research. Facilities for training, extension, and research were to be improved and enlarged; the availability of credit was to be ex-panded; subsidies for agricultural inputs were to be continued and new ones provided for the mechanization of farms and for transport services; better infrastructure for processing and marketing crops was to be pro-vided; and measures to improve coordination among the numerous agencies involved in agricultural development were to be taken. A national extension project was established to undertake an evaluation of various support programs, and it was expected that the findings would be used to improve the scope and effectiveness of support services. This improvement is vital, both to ensure that other programs aimed at existing agriculture have the maximum effect possible and to support the farmers who are not affected by those other programs.

Estates

During the period of the third plan the number of households of estate workers was expected to decline 12 percent, while the incidence of poverty was projected to fall from 47 percent to 38 percent. The expected emigration of 15,000 households out of estates during the plan period should have contributed to a reduction in poverty, but the distribution of employment opportunities among the remaining households will have been instrumental in determining their levels of income. During the same period it was expected that more of the acreage of estates would be converted to oil palm, thus decreasing the demand for labor. The programs to aid estate workers were to rely on nonfinancial means. Government intended to be strict in ensuring that employers provide basic amenities to their staffs. For households remaining in the rubber estates, it was projected that price-linked wage increases and the smaller labor force would bring about improvement in their household incomes.

New Villages

The conditions that lead residents of new villages into poverty are readily identifiable and have shown little improvement through the years. Very few own land; fewer than half have access to any land at all; most suffer insecurity of tenure. In addition, residents of new villages have little access to new land developments, and there is reason to believe that many of them would prefer nonagricultural employment. Few funds were allocated to new villages in the third plan; it was asserted that improvements in income among their residents could be expected through trickle-down effects of growth in the nonagricultural sectors in which they work. The plan did, however, contain a proposal for multiracial development and modernization of new villages, for the education of village youths, and for the use of unencumbered land to increase the land holdings of the villages.

Fishing

The plan provided for five new fishing harbors, several jetties, shore facilities, and additional boats. The incidence of poverty among fishing households was projected to fall from 62 percent to 52 percent. Nevertheless offshore fishing was expected to account for most of the 20 percent growth in the catch of fish, and this growth affects only relatively small numbers of the poor fishermen engaged in inshore fishing in small boats. Efforts to help poor fishermen by subsidizing the purchase of gear and conducting training programs also benefit relatively few of those in need. There remains an excess of fishermen for whom land settlement or employment outside the sector is needed. Attempts to relocate fishermen by means of land development schemes have already had some success, and continued efforts in this direction are essential. One other promising source of employment for fishermen is the large-scale development of fish farming in the brackish water of the country's extensive mangrove swamps.

Land Development Programs

The number of people needing agricultural employment in Malaysia was expected to increase during the plan period because of the entry of an estimated 125,000 new laborers, unable to find other employment, into the agricultural sector.[20] The land development program originally proposed for the third plan was similar to that contained in the second plan, with a continuation of all the existing programs (see table 8.15). Against the background of performance under the second plan and in the light of the importance of land development for relieving population pressure on existing land, the land development targets of the third plan appeared conservative. Furthermore the availability of land is not a problem. In 1975 somewhat less than 8 million acres of land were under cultivation in Peninsular Malaysia. The country can expand this area by as much as 4 million acres by developing additional land that is fully suited to cultivation. This provides ample scope for accelerating the land development program. In the longer term, before the end of

20. This number is an estimate made for the plan on the basis of a very low rate of growth in employment—1.3 percent a year—in relation to rates at which employment has grown in the past. The number of workers seeking employment in agriculture was expected to be greater as a result of the failure of other sectors to absorb them at the rate projected.

the period of the perspective plan for 1970–90, the industrial sector should be able to provide a much greater proportion of income and employment, thereby reducing the relative size of the agricultural population and the need for the development of new land. In recognition of these facts, some land development targets, notably those of FELDA, were increased early in the period of the third plan.[21]

The fringe alienation schemes of FELCRA are, in principle, well designed to relieve land shortages by augmenting existing smallholdings. Under these schemes development is restricted to areas on the fringes of existing villages where no new settlements are required. Unfortunately FELCRA, like the other agencies, can respond only to state requests for developing specific land areas and must compete for land with other agencies. Much more land could be developed if the states would make it available: The agency had indicated that it had the capacity to alienate twice as much land as the amount specified in the third plan, or as many as 20,000 acres a year. FELCRA was also to rehabilitate 7,500 acres of unsuccessful state land schemes. State agencies for land development were expected to develop only 100,000 acres in Peninsular Malaysia and 140,000 acres in Sabah and Sarawak under the third plan; they developed 350,000 acres between 1970 and 1975.

Further opportunities for expanding land development appear to exist in the private sector and in joint ventures in which the resources and expertise of the private and public sectors are combined. The third plan called for the development by the private sector of only 100,000 acres in Peninsular Malaysia and none by joint ventures. Development by the private sector was much more important in the past, when foreign-owned estates pioneered in the introduction of tree crops. Under the second plan 130,000 acres were developed in Peninsular Malaysia as a result of private and joint ventures.

The third plan also called for the development of 100,000 acres through the block new-planting program of RISDA. In view of the potential for increasing yields on replanted acreage through improved supervision and of the shortage of extension staff for this purpose, the capacity of RISDA must be considerably increased if expenditures on new planting are to be justified. Replanting 500,000 acres of rubber during the third plan period will still leave about 300,000 acres of trees

21. The land development target of FELDA under the third plan then became 500,000 acres, implying a rate of development of more than 100,000 acres a year during the last three years of the plan. This rate probably represents the limit of what can be expected of FELDA in the short term.

with a tapping age of more than twenty-five years, many of which are low-yielding varieties. The first priority of RISDA should therefore be to strengthen its replanting program.

The land schemes of FELDA are efficiently run. Experienced contractors clear the jungle; level land; build houses, roads, and water-supply systems; plant rubber or oil palm, depending on climate, soil, topography, and location; and, in general, set up a rural area ready for occupancy by settlers according to the classic turnkey enterprise. Production and incomes are high. The potential effectiveness of FELDA, however, is far from having been realized. Between 1956 and 1975 FELDA initiated development of 720,000 acres, but settled only about 33,000 families. During the third plan period, under the authority's latest guidelines, the pace of settlement was to have increased. By the end of the period FELDA should have been able to settle 25,000 families on land for which development began during the second plan period and another 11,000 on land cleared at the beginning of the third plan period. Thus, between 1976 and 1980, FELDA alone should have been able to settle 36,000 families—more than all the families settled during the two preceding decades and a third of the total by which the number of agricultural families in poverty was expected to be reduced.

The total number of families expected to be settled by all agencies during the third plan period is 60,000; about 39,000 were settled during the second plan period. Because of the lag between land development and settlement, many of these 60,000 families will have been settled on land included in programs of the second plan but not settled by the end of the period. Increases in the projected accomplishments of FELDA and the increases recommended for other agencies were not to affect settlement during the remainder of the third plan period, but they would contribute to increases in the number of settlers received in subsequent years. It is possible that settlement will have been accelerated by changes that have been made in the method of land development and from the recent reduction in the acreage allotted to each family.

Beginning in 1971 the rate of settlement of families fell increasingly below the potential rate. The lag between the initiation of development and the actual settlement has increased from three years to as many as five. Part of the reason for this lag is inherent in the method of land preparation, according to which settlers are not allowed on the land until an entire development is launched. Although settlers participated in the clearing and planting stages of development during the early years of the activity of FELDA, the mid-1950s, they were inadequately trained and supervised. As a result, yields were poor. By the mid-1960s emphasis had shifted to productive efficiency, with the implicit goal of matching the performance of the private estate sector. This led to the extensive use of contractors in the development and maintenance phases. An increase in participation by settlers in the early stages of development projects would lead to an initial upward jump in the number of settlers taken in. The third plan includes pilot projects to test the benefits from greater self-help in the development and maintenance of land settlements.

The acreage allotted to each settler family is another important determinant of the rate at which settlers are taken in on a scheme. Until 1977 this allotment was set at twelve acres for the planting of rubber and fourteen acres for oil palm. Holdings of this size generate incomes that are high in relation to those earned in urban or rural areas by persons with similar qualifications. In the mid-1970s the average monthly net income of settler families who grew oil palm was M$800–900 and M$300–400 for those who grew rubber. Of settlers growing oil palm 10 to 15 percent owned cars, 80 percent owned motorcycles, and 50 percent owned television sets. Because of such disparities, allocation of land in FELDA schemes was reduced to ten acres a family; smaller allocations provide a more equitable distribution of land and income, increase the number of settlers, and reduce the per capita costs of the program.

Priorities for Agricultural Development

An increase in the expenditure on agriculture, made possible by the unexpected increase in resources available to government for the third plan, would bring about a more rapid reduction in poverty than was planned. Large irrigation and land development schemes present the fewest problems in execution and offer the most dramatic results. Large-scale irrigation schemes may reach their practical limit in the program outlined in the third plan, but land development could be significantly increased. Several land development agencies are operating at full capacity, but some of them could increase their capacities so that they will be ready to fulfill larger functions, perhaps during the next plan period. Although the land available for development ultimately is limited, there is no reason to delay its use. As the economy of Malaysia grows, the industrial sector will absorb an increasing share of the population, and the need for new land will diminish. Meanwhile any increase above the planned level of settlement will speed the reduction of poverty, both by providing incomes above the poverty level for all settlers and by easing the pressure of population on the land that they vacate to enter a new settlement.

Although land development will remain an important means of increasing rural incomes, expansion of the programs for assisting traditional smallholders is also essential if the incomes of the large number of poor who will not be resettled are to be increased. Programs that are specifically aimed at increasing the productivity and incomes of small farmers and that could be improved or expanded include small-scale irrigation, subsidies to encourage replanting and the use of improved inputs, research for the development of better seeds and planting material, and the provision of credit and extension services to spread improved farming practices. If such institutions as the Ministry of Agriculture, RISDA, and the state planning units are to increase their effectiveness, they will need to have larger technical staffs and better implementation and coordination of policies. The state and rural development project, sponsored jointly by the World Bank and the United Nations Development Program, is one step in this direction. Through this project experts have been placed in various agencies charged with training Malaysian counterparts to assume planning functions and develop new projects. In conjunction with such efforts, technical training was stressed in the third plan as a prerequisite to the effective planning and implementation of agricultural programs. The emphasis was well placed. In the long run the programs for assisting traditional smallholders will become the most important for eradicating poverty.

NINE

Malaysian Exports of Merchandise

CYCLICAL FLUCTUATIONS ASIDE, Malaysian exports of merchandise during 1965–75 were equal to about 40 percent of GNP. During the period
of Malaysia's third plan, 1976–80, this percentage was expected to increase. Thus the outlook for exports of merchandise continues to be of
primary importance to the economic development of Malaysia.[1]

Agricultural products have traditionally been predominant among
the merchandise exports of Malaysia. They made up nearly 60 percent
of the total during 1965–75. Rubber initially was the principal export, but during that decade oil palm and forestry products began to
constitute greatly increased shares of agricultural exports, at the expense of rubber (table 9.1). Within the agricultural group, substantial
diversification has thus taken place. During the early 1970s, the share
of rubber in total agricultural exports fell below half, and a further
gradual decline was projected for the following decade.

During most of the 1965–75 period, the shares in exports of other
products—principally tin and manufactures—remained almost constant. The closing years of the second plan nevertheless brought important changes. The value of petroleum exports sharply increased; there
also was an increase—although less spectacular—in the share of manu-

---

1. The World Bank has made projections of merchandise exports for the period of the
third plan and for 1990. The way in which forecasts of the principal exports were arrived
at is described in some detail in this chapter. In a number of instances—especially tree
crops—there are substantial gestation lags, and it is possible to project capacities for
production and exports with a fair degree of accuracy. In other instances—oil and gas, for
example—there is greater uncertainty with respect to the later years. The standard method of the World Bank was followed in making the price forecasts: The price of a commodity was first projected in constant terms under the assumption of no international
inflation. This projection was then inflated by an estimated international inflation factor.
The average annual rates of international inflation assumed for the projections used in
this report are 7.4 percent from 1976 to 1980 and 7 percent during the 1980s. World
Bank, "Price Prospects for Major Primary Commodities," report no. 814/77 (a restricted-
circulation document) (Washington, D.C., June 1977; processed).

Table 9.1. *Composition of Malaysian Exports, by Commodity or Group of Commodities, 1960–76, and Projections for 1980, 1985, and 1990*
(percent)

Commodity or group of commodities	Average, 1960–64	Average, 1965–69	Average, 1970–74	1975	1976	1980	1985	1990	Commodity or group of commodities
Rubber	47	37	30	22	23	22	19	17	Rubber
Oil palm products	2	3	8	14	9	11	12	12	Oil palm products
Sawlogs	5	11	12	7	11	10	8	6	Sawlogs
Sawn timber	2	3	5	5	6	7	6	5	Sawn timber
Tin	18	20	17	13	11	8	7	6	Tin
Petroleum and petroleum products[a]	3	3	5	9	13	14	17	17	Petroleum and petroleum products[a]
Subtotal, principal commodities	77	77	77	70	74	73	69	63	Subtotal, principal commodities
Manufactures	4	6	10	18	15	17	21	27	Manufactures
All other merchandise	19	17	13	12	11	10	10	10	All other merchandise
Total merchandise	100	100	100	100	100	100	100	100	Total merchandise

Note: Projections are trend values rather than projections for individual years.
Sources: For 1960–76, Bank Negara, *Quarterly Economic Bulletin*, various issues; for projections, World Bank estimates.
a. Includes re-exports of crude petroleum imported from Brunei and exports of liquefied natural gas.

254

Table 9.2. *The Direction of Malaysian Exports, 1961–74*
(percent)

Country or region	1961–64	1965–69	1970–74
United States	11.7	14.4	12.9
Western Europe	24.1	18.0	21.9
Japan	17.3	18.3	17.7
Australia and New Zealand	3.0	2.8	2.4
Canada	...	2.0	1.9
Total, OECD countries	56.1	55.5	56.8
Singapore	21.5	22.6	22.4
Other Asian markets	4.2	4.4	8.5
Total, Asia, excluding Japan	25.7	28.0	30.9
Rest of the world	18.2	16.5	12.3

... Zero or negligible.
Sources: Bank Negara, *Quarterly Economic Bulletin*, various issues.

factured exports. At the same time the contribution of tin and agricultural exports together declined to about 50 percent of total exports of merchandise.[2] Projections for 1975–85 show a stabilization of the shares of agriculture and petroleum and a decline of the share of tin, compensated for by a further increase in the share of manufactured exports.

More than half the exports of Malaysia move into OECD markets (table 9.2). Within the OECD, Western Europe remains the principal trading partner of Malaysia; its next largest markets are in Japan and the United States.[3] Thus the economic situation in OECD countries and the economic policies of those countries strongly affect the demand for Malaysian exports. Because exports of these commodities constitute a large portion of the domestic Malaysian product, changes in the demand of OECD countries for imports affect all sectors of the Malaysian economy. Heavy dependence on industrial countries as trading partners makes Malaysia sensitive to changes in the economic climate in those coun-

2. Because of the severe international recession, 1975 was an atypical year with respect to shares of the export market.
3. Part of what is exported by Malaysia to Singapore is re-exported to OECD countries. The dependence of Malaysia on OECD markets is thus understated in the figures in table 9.2.

tries. The Malaysian government therefore intensified efforts to diversi-fy its trading partners and its products. The principal thrust of its trade diversification policy was toward strengthening trade relationships with countries in Southeast Asia. Because many countries in Southeast Asia have similar resources and exports, however, they are in many ways competitive. This means that Malaysia will for some time contin-ue to be highly dependent on OECD markets for its exports.

The markets for the principal export commodities of Malaysia are highly volatile. Between 1960 and 1974 the prices of exports other than palm oil fluctuated more than the volumes (table 9.3).[4] The Malaysian government has shown considerable interest in trying to stabilize mar-ket prices through international commodity agreements. To stabilize export earnings would require some form of control over supplies. Ma-laysia supplies substantial shares of the markets for tin, natural rubber, and palm oil. By means of controls over supplies and exports of these commodities, Malaysia could influence their market prices. To strengthen this influence Malaysia sought the cooperation of other im-portant producing countries and, later, even the cooperation of con-suming countries.

The Fifth International Tin Agreement, reached in 1976, was for a time the only commodity agreement in effect for stabilizing prices by means of buffer stocks. Negotiations for a similar agreement with re-spect to natural rubber were begun in late 1978, and the International Natural Rubber Agreement for Price Stabilization was concluded in mid-1979. Chances are remote that commodity agreements will be con-cluded concerning the other principal agricultural exports of Malay-sia—forest products and palm oil. The Sabah Timber Association is a member of the Southeast Asian Lumber Producers Association (SEALPA), which was established for the purpose of stabilizing supplies of hardwood. As a private organization, SEALPA is without government support, and it seems unlikely that its policies will lead to an inter-national commodity agreement. Although Malaysia is the largest ex-porter of palm oil in the world, it would be extremely difficult to stabi-lize palm oil prices without stabilizing the prices of all other fats and oils at the same time.

Despite the fact that Malaysia can protect itself against commodity-specific price risks as it attains increasing product diversification, diver-

---

4. The reason may be the choice of linear trend. The growth in actual exports of palm oil more closely resembles a logarithmic pattern. The same is probably true with respect to petroleum.

Table 9.3. *The Instability of the Principal Malaysian Export Commodities, 1960-74*

Commodity	Export earnings		Volume of exports		Export prices	
	Standard deviation[a] (millions of Malaysian dollars)	Standard deviation as percentage of mean	Standard deviation[a] (thousands of metric tons)	Standard deviation as percentage of mean	Standard deviation[a] (Malaysian dollars)	Standard deviation as percentage of mean
Rubber	438.6	25.9	79.6	6.9	30.4	20.3
Palm oil	179.1	76.3	109.7	32.4	178.8	27.9
Tin	134.5	16.1	6,045.1	7.3	1,790.8	17.8
Sawn timber	72.2	40.6	192.6	17.5	29.7	20.3
Sawlogs	89.0	19.0	706.1	10.9	9.5	14.1
Petroleum	112.5	57.3	1,319.8	41.2	40.4	64.9
Total exports	1,184.4	25.4	—	—	—	—

— Not applicable.
Source: Data supplied by Bank Negara.
a. Deviations from linear trends.

sification affords only limited protection against widespread economic recession in the industrial countries. Still, a judicious use of export taxes and subsidies can help to insulate the domestic economy to some extent from the fluctuations of international business cycles, if Malaysia will accept cyclical fluctuations in its international reserves and external borrowing.

Export performance of principal items during the 1960-76 period and export projections for 1980-90 are summarized in table 9.4, which shows the shifts in the absolute and the relative importance of the principal exports. Also shown is a projected increase of 157 percent in the nominal value of Malaysian exports of merchandise during the period of the third plan and a further increase of 240 percent between 1980 and 1990. International inflation between 1975 and 1990 is projected to be 180 percent; thus substantial increases in the volume of exports and improvements in relative prices are foreseen.

How the volume of exports increases and how changes in the terms of trade affect the purchasing power of exports—defined as export value deflated by import price—are shown for the principal items in table 9.5. The aggregate import capacity—that is, the import-purchasing power of exports—will more than triple between 1975 and 1990. In both absolute and relative terms the greatest contributions to the increase in import capacity will come from manufactures and petroleum.

Table 9.4. *Quantities, Prices, and Earnings of the Principal Export Commodities, 1960, 1970, 1975, and Projections for 1980, 1985, and 1990*

Commodity or group of commodities	1960	1970	1975
Quantity	*Thousands of metric tons*		
Rubber	852	1,345	1,460
Palm oil	98	402	1,163
	Thousands of cubic meters		
Sawlogs	2,088	8,914	8,473
Sawn timber	582	1,415	1,890
	Thousands of metric tons		
Tin	78	93	78
Petroleum and petroleum products	1,515	4,778	3,763
	Billions of cubic feet		
Natural gas	...	...	...
Unit value	*Cents a kilogram*		
Rubber	235	128	139
	Malaysian dollars a metric ton		
Palm oil	581	658	1,133
	Malaysian dollars a cubic meter		
Sawlogs	57	72	79
Sawn timber	129	147	234
	Malaysian dollars a metric ton		
Tin	6,513	10,939	15,475
Petroleum and petroleum products	58	42	227
	Malaysian dollars a thousand cubic feet		
Natural gas	...	...	...
Value	*Millions of Malaysian dollars*		
Rubber	2,001	1,724	2,026
Palm oil	61	264	1,318
Sawlogs	119	664	670
Sawn timber	75	208	442
Tin	508	1,013	1,206
Petroleum and petroleum products	147	202	853
Natural gas	...	...	...
Subtotal, principal products	2,922	4,055	6,515
Manufactures	110	344	1,600
All other	613	774	1,118
Total	3,633	5,162	9,231

... Zero or negligible

Sources: Bank Negara, *Quarterly Economic Bulletin*, various issues; World Bank projections.

1980	1985	1990	Commodity or group of commodities
Thousands of metric tons			*Quantity*
1,950	2,325	2,600	Rubber
2,300	3,500	4,600	Palm oil
Thousands of cubic meters			
12,172	11,350	10,580	Sawlogs
3,055	3,055	3,055	Sawn timber
Thousands of metric tons			
80	76	78	Tin
10,329	13,183	16,825	Petroleum and petroleum products
Billions of cubic feet			
...	275	275	Natural gas
Cents a kilogram			*Unit value*
264	354	493	Rubber
Malaysian dollars a metric ton			
1,060	1,464	1,918	Palm oil
Malaysian dollars a cubic meter			
194	290	448	Sawlogs
535	810	1,265	Sawn timber
Malaysian dollars a metric ton			
25,301	36,737	53,428	Tin
340	466	657	Petroleum and petroleum products
Malaysian dollars a thousand cubic feet			
...	4.38	5.87	Natural gas
Millions of Malaysian dollars			*Value*
5,148	8,231	12,818	Rubber
2,438	5,125	8,825	Palm oil
2,365	3,290	4,735	Sawlogs
1,635	2,477	3,866	Sawn timber
2,024	2,792	4,167	Tin
3,510	6,147	11,051	Petroleum and petroleum products
...	1,205	1,615	Natural gas
17,120	29,267	47,077	Subtotal, principal products
4,276	10,569	26,139	Manufactures
2,348	4,326	7,624	All other
23,744	44,162	80,840	Total

Table 9.5. *Indexes of Merchandise Exports, Terms of Trade, and Import Capacity, 1970, 1975, 1976, and Projections for 1980, 1985, and 1990* (1970 = 100)

Commodity or group of commodities	1970	1975	1976	1980	1985	1990
Export quantities						
Rubber	100	109	120	145	173	193
Oil palm products	100	289	335	576	870	1,144
Sawlogs	100	95	137	137	127	119
Sawn timber	100	134	216	216	216	216
Tin	100	84	88	86	82	84
Petroleum and products	100	79	150	216	276	352
Manufactures	100	344	350	613	1,081	1,905
Other	100	104	88	144	191	252
Total	100	126	148	190	253	337
Terms of trade[a]						
Rubber	100	67	89	90	86	85
Palm oil	100	103	78	68	67	63
Sawlogs	100	68	98	117	125	137
Sawn timber	100	98	115	158	171	190
Tin	100	87	99	100	104	108
Petroleum and products	100	333	339	351	343	345
Manufactures	100	86	91	91	91	91
Other	100	86	91	91	91	91
Total	100	87	102	105	104	102
Import capacity[b]						
Rubber	100	62	89	110	132	139
Palm oil	100	308	268	402	630	738
Sawlogs	100	64	133	159	166	162
Sawn timber	100	131	248	341	387	410
Tin	100	73	87	87	89	91
Petroleum and products	100	260	502	754	988	1,207
Manufactures	100	295	353	557	980	1,728
Other	100	89	108	131	181	217
Total	100	110	151	199	264	344
Import price index	100	162	172	230	323	453

Source: World Bank estimates and projections.
a. Export price index divided by import price index.
b. Export value index divided by import price index.

Those contributions are a clear indication of the great structural changes expected in the economy.

Tin, rubber, petroleum, palm oil, and forest products traditionally provide 75 to 80 percent of what Malaysia earns in foreign exchange through exports of merchandise. The market prospects of these commodities will be discussed in the following paragraphs. Projected unit values of exports reflect the most recent projections by the World Bank of growth in GNP among OECD countries, of inflation, and of the prices of these commodities in international markets. Export volumes were projected by members of the World Bank staff, mainly on the basis of information provided by the Malaysian government.

Rubber

The production of rubber dominates Malaysian agriculture. Half the agricultural land of Malaysia is planted in rubber, and a fourth of the labor force finds employment in the rubber industry. In 1977 Malaysia produced 1.6 million metric tons of rubber, or 46 percent of all the natural rubber produced in the world. Because the gestation period of rubber trees is six to seven years, the potential rubber output of Malaysia until the early 1980s is determined by the stock of trees in 1976. The actual output will be determined principally by the weather, prices, application of yield stimulants, and government policies.[5] Replanting and new planting will affect the output only after 1985.

The response of producers to rubber prices is a significant factor in any projection of Malaysian rubber production. In the short term, rubber prices affect the intensity of tapping. A decline in prices would lead to an increase in the acreage of mature rubber left untapped—because the cost of tapping by marginal producers would exceed the revenue from latex sales. The short-term price effect of price changes depends

5. Declining prices and the reluctance of the estate sector to invest in rubber strengthens the importance of such yield stimulants as ethrel. Tapping trees only every four to six days, instead of the normal frequency of every two days, would bring about considerable saving in the costs of tapping, which constitute about 50 percent of total estate costs. Ethrel makes this possible, besides increasing yields about 50 percent. Its effectiveness on old trees provides estates with an alternative to the high costs of replanting. The effect of ethrel and similar stimulants on total production will depend on the extent to which they are adopted by growers and the frequency and methods of their use. Even if it is assumed that ethrel will be applied during the next five years only to trees more than fifteen years old, the level of annual production from estates will be increased 60,000 tons.

largely on alternative employment opportunities and reflects the opportunity cost of estate labor. The intensity of tapping in Sabah and Sarawak, where there are shortages of labor, is closely tied to international market prices. In Peninsular Malaysia, where alternative employment opportunities are few, short-term price effects are less significant. In the long term, rubber prices have a great deal to do with the expansion of rubber production.

According to estimates of elasticities of supply for rubber estates and for smallholdings, the supply response of smallholders to price—0.29—was higher than that of estates—0.028.[6] The average supply elasticity of Malaysian rubber producers was estimated to be 0.15. In addition, it was found that the supply elasticity of smallholders was greater at lower prices; the converse was true of estates. The estimates are confirmed by a World Bank study which shows that the average elasticity of supply of Malaysian rubber is about 0.25.[7] The supply response for rubber is likely to increase in the future as mixed agriculture, such as livestock and intercropping, provides additional income to smallholders who plant rubber and as the use of chemical stimulants is expanded.

Market Outlook for Natural Rubber

The pressing need for rubber during the Second World War, at a time when Western Europe and the United States were cut off from their traditional sources of natural rubber, provided the incentive for the large-scale development of synthetic rubber. Except for a brief period, the synthetic rubber industry continued to expand during the three decades following the war. By 1975 the supplies of synthetic rubber satisfied two-thirds of the demand for elastomers; natural rubber satisfied the remaining third. The structure of the world rubber economy changed significantly as natural rubber yielded its near monopoly position to synthetic rubber.[8]

6. C. S. Chow, "Some Aspects of Price Elasticities of Rubber Production in Malaysia" (paper read at the International Rubber Conference, Kuala Lumpur, October 1975; processed).

7. The World Bank estimate was made econometrically. Enzo R. Grilli, Ray M. Helterline, and Peter K. Pollak, "The Econometric Analysis of the World Rubber Economy," draft, World Bank Staff Commodity Paper, no. 3 (Washington, D.C., January 1979; processed).

8. Enzo R. Grilli, Barbara Bennett Agostini, and Maria 't Hooft Welvaars, The World Rubber Economy: Structure, Changes, and Prospects. World Bank Staff Occasional Papers, no. 30 (Baltimore: The Johns Hopkins University Press for the World Bank, 1980).

Synthetic rubber has long enjoyed a competitive edge over natural rubber because of its ready availability and its lower price. In the post-war period, producers of synthetic rubber expanded their production to meet the rapidly growing needs of the market. At the same time, technological innovations and economies of scale reduced production costs. The availability of chemical monomers at declining prices led to a sharp drop in the prices of synthetic rubber during the 1960s. The prices of natural rubber, although fluctuating widely, followed the declining trend.[9] Natural rubber competes closely with three synthetic products: styrene-butadiene rubber, polybutadiene rubber, and polyisoprene rubber. From a technical point of view polyisoprene is the closest substitute for natural rubber. Its price generally exceeds that of natural rubber, mainly because of higher production costs, and its share in the market for elastomers is smaller than that of natural rubber. Styrene-butadiene rubber and polybutadiene rubber, the other two principal substitutes for natural rubber, together account for about 75 percent of total production of synthetic rubber.

Natural rubber, styrene-butadiene rubber, and polyisoprene rubber compete in all those products in which general-purpose rubber with standard characteristics is needed. Natural rubber is preferred in the manufacture of products that require high strength and low generation of heat, such as airplane tires, giant truck tires, and technical products that need high resistance to fatigue. The potential share of isoprenic rubber (natural and polyisoprene rubber) in the market for all elastomers has been estimated to be 43 percent; its actual share of the market in 1970 was only 35 percent.[10] Other investigators confirm that outside the centrally planned economies the potential market share of natural rubber in 1975 could have been about 42 percent, whereas its actual share was only 34.5 percent.[11]

WORLD DEMAND FOR RUBBER. The demand for all elastomers, although quite insensitive to price changes, responds quickly to changes

9. The reason that the prices of synthetic rubber are more stable than those of natural rubber lies in their different elasticities of supply. In the short run the supply of natural rubber is less price elastic than is the supply of synthetic rubber. Producers of synthetic rubber can adjust more quickly to changing market conditions—by expanding capacity and making more intensive use of existing capacity—than can producers of natural rubber, who find it more difficult, in general, to shift resources into and out of rubber production.

10. P. W. Allen, P. O. Thomas, and B. C. Sekhar, "The Techno-Economic Potential of NR in Major End-Uses" (Kuala Lumpur: Malaysia Rubber Research and Development Board, 1973; processed).

11. Grilli, Agostini, and Welvaars, The World Rubber Economy.

in aggregate economic activity.[12] The world consumption of all rubbers is projected to grow at an average rate of 5.4 percent from the average consumption in 1974–76 until 1990 (table 9.6).[13] This is a slower rate than that of the 1960s and early 1970s. The projected demand reflects the expected pattern of economic growth in industrial countries and the negative effect of changes in the structure of demand for elastomers caused by the oil crisis.[14]

Because world production of natural rubber—taking into account present acreage, plans for expansion, and production technology—is projected to grow only 4 percent a year between 1976 and 1990, the share of natural rubber in the market for all elastomers is projected to decline from 32.3 percent in 1975 to 26.1 percent in 1990. In view of this potential shortfall the Malaysian government in 1975 reaffirmed its policy of expanding production and maintaining Malaysia's share of the market. Table 9.6 illustrates the widening gap between projected output of natural rubber and its potential market, on the basis of a constant but probably conservative estimate of the share of the market held by natural rubber.

WORLD SUPPLY OF RUBBER. In 1975 world production capacity of synthetic rubbers reached 9.5 million tons, nearly 50 percent greater than the depressed demand. It is estimated that by 1980 the synthetic rubber industry will have expanded its capacity to 12 million tons. Although this will be sufficient to cover the greatly expanded demand—including the share not satisfied by natural rubber—it will require greater-than-normal use of capacity and therefore somewhat higher prices than would prevail if only the more efficient plants were in use.

Most of the projected shortfall in the output of natural rubber during the 1980s is attributable to the expected sharp decline in the growth of Malaysian production (table 9.7). Yet Malaysia, more than any other producer of natural rubber, has the capacity to fill this gap. In the mid-1970s it seems likely that of the other two important rubber-producing

12. The staff of the World Bank estimates the following elasticities for all elastomers with respect to real income or aggregate economic activity: 1.3–1.4 in OECD countries, 1.6–2.0 in industrial countries, and 1.4–1.6 in countries having centrally planned economies.

13. The demand for all elastomers is projected to grow 4.3 percent a year in industrial countries, 7.9 percent in developing countries, and 6.5 percent in countries having centrally planned economies between 1976 and 1990.

14. Industrial countries are responsible for about 70 percent of the world demand for elastomers.

Table 9.6. *World Consumption of Natural and Synthetic Rubber,*
Selected Periods, 1955–76, and Projections for 1980, 1985, and 1990
(thousands of metric tons)

Item	Average, 1955–57	Average, 1966–68	Average, 1974–76	1980	1985	1990
Consumption of natural and synthetic rubber	3,518	7,044	10,930	14,500	19,000	14,000
Consumption of natural rubber at current production trends	1,935	2,533	3,427	4,350	5,245	6,135
Potential market[a]	—	—	—	4,710	6,175	7,800
Potential shortfall	—	—	—	360	930	1,665

— Not applicable.
Source: World Bank, Economic Analysis and Projections Department.
a. Assuming that 32.5 percent of the market for all kinds of rubber goes to natural rubber.

countries, Indonesia and Thailand, only Thailand will increase its total production of rubber substantially. The efforts of Indonesia in the mid-1970s to increase its output of rubber materialized more slowly than was expected. Thailand produces about 10 percent of the total output of natural rubber, mostly on smallholdings. Even with a projected growth rate of 7 to 8 percent, Thailand will be responsible for only 18 percent of the production of rubber projected for 1990. Present world acreage, plans for expansion, and production technology seem to indicate that production of natural rubber will expand at a considerably lower rate than in the 1970s—most likely less than 4 percent a year. In order to increase its share of the market to 33–35 percent—feasible in view of the technical and economic potential of natural rubber—producers would have to expand their output at a rate greater than 6 percent a year between 1980 and 1990. Rubber plantings would have to be expanded beyond the goals set forth in existing plans, and Malaysia would have to increase its production of rubber by an additional 4 to 5 percent a year.

PRICE OUTLOOK FOR NATURAL RUBBER. The prices of synthetic rubber determine the range within which the prices of natural rubber move in the long run. The prices of polyisoprene rubber determine the upper limit, those of styrene-butadiene rubber the lower limit. Supplying less than 35 percent of the market for all elastomers, producers of natural

Table 9.7. *World Production of Natural Rubber, 1970, 1976, and Projections for 1980, 1985, and 1990*

Commodity	Thousands of metric tons					Average annual growth (percent)	
	1970	1976	1980	1985	1990	1976–80	1980–90
Malaysia	1,269	1,640	2,000	2,400	2,700	5.1	3.1
Indonesia	815	850	920	1,010	1,100	2.0	1.8
Thailand	287	392	540	785	1,140	8.2	7.8
Sri Lanka	159	152	180	185	195	4.3	0.8
India	90	148	190	200	220	6.4	1.4
Others	324	358	520	465	780	9.8	4.2
Total	3,102	3,540	4,350	5,245	6,135	5.3	3.5

Source: World Bank, Economic Analysis and Projections Department.

rubber will remain price takers. The prices of natural rubber have been projected on the basis of expected future trends in the production costs of styrene-butadiene rubber.[15] The costs of production of styrene-butadiene rubber projected here reflect World Bank estimates of the prices of crude oil and other elements of the process of production of styrene-butadiene rubber. It was assumed that the price of crude oil would remain at US$11.50 a barrel, in 1975 dollars, from 1980 to 1990.[16] On the basis of these assumptions and the supply of and demand for natural rubber, the projected price of rubber is M$2.64 in 1980 and M$3.61 in 1985.

These projected prices would make it possible for profits to exceed 1976 minimum levels by a wide margin. Estimates made in 1977 show production costs in Malaysia in the range of M$1.30 and M$1.40 a kilogram.[17] In view of a difference of 20–25 Malaysian cents a kilogram

15. Styrene-butadiene rubber is by far the most important type of synthetic rubber, constituting about 60 percent of total production of synthetic rubber. Between 1966 and 1975 the price of natural rubber moved between the price of styrene-butadiene rubber, the lowest-priced of all rubbers, and the price of polyisoprene rubber, the highest-priced synthetic rubber, both of which compete directly with natural rubber.

16. An increase in the real price of crude oil would raise the price of feedstocks for synthetic rubber and thereby strengthen the competitive position of natural rubbers. The price sensitivity between crude oil and styrene-butadiene rubber is estimated to be about 0.4. An increase of 10 percent in the real price of crude oil would thus raise the cost of production of styrene-butadiene rubber about 4 percent.

17. Grilli, Agostini, and Welvaars, *The World Rubber Economy.*

between the price FOB Malaysian ports and the price CIF New York, the production of rubber appears to be profitable at the 1976 price of more than M$2 a kilogram. Inflation of the costs of production and investment would squeeze profit margins and might reduce the incentive to expand the production of rubber. To lessen the effect of a decline in the price of natural rubber, the Malaysian government in 1975 established a plan for accumulating buffer stocks of natural rubber and put into effect a program to control the domestic supply.

Development of Buffer Stocks of Rubber

The sharp decline in the price of natural rubber during the late 1960s led to efforts by producers to coordinate the marketing of natural rubber. In October 1970 the Association of Natural Rubber Producing Countries (ANRPC) was formed to set up a coordinated marketing system. As a further step toward an international commodity agreement for natural rubber, the Malaysian government proposed to coordinate the production of natural rubber in member countries of the ANRPC. The primary objective of this proposal was to assure consumers an adequate and stable supply of natural rubber.[18] But the ultimate goal was to stabilize rubber prices at a level high enough to ensure a profit to rubber producers.

The decline in the price of natural rubber in 1975 sparked a new round of discussions for an international agreement on natural rubber in which most of the ideas that had emerged in earlier meetings of the ANRPC would be integrated. In June 1976 the Secretariat of the ANRPC submitted to its member governments the draft of the International Rubber Price Stabilization Scheme. This document was signed during November 1976 by representatives of the governments of Indonesia, Malaysia, Singapore, Sri Lanka, and Thailand. It proposed two mechanisms, both having the purpose of stabilizing prices: first, an international buffer stock; second, a supply-rationalization scheme. The buffer-stock operation was modeled after the buffer stock of tin, but its size—only 100,000 tons for the first two years of operation—is clearly too small to ensure any substantial degree of price stabilization. The supply-rationalization scheme follows the concept of the Malaysian crash program for rubber. To prevent a further decline in the prices of natural rubber, Malaysia put a crash program into effect in December

---

18. Fluctuations in the supply of natural rubber were recognized as the principal cause of the decline in the share of the market held by natural rubber.

1974. With the aim of reducing the flow of natural rubber into export markets, this program contained two sets of measures: those intended for keeping the rubber in the trees, and those directing the excess flow of rubber into government stocks. The success of the government program to arrest the decline of rubber prices contributed to the enthusiasm for bringing about an agreement among the members of the ANRPC.[19]

The ANRPC plan, which requires that countries reduce their exports when demand is weak and expand production when demand exceeds supply, has yet to become effective. Negotiations for an international agreement concerning natural rubber have shifted to the United Nations Conference on Trade and Development (UNCTAD), within the framework of the Integrated Program for Commodities. In March 1978 producers and consumers of natural rubber agreed to begin negotiation of an international rubber agreement in which both sides would participate directly. A buffer stock—much larger than the one envisaged in the International Rubber Price Stabilization Scheme—supplemented when necessary by supply-rationalization measures, was to be the main regulatory instrument. The prospects for an international agreement on natural rubber remain good.

Conclusions

The average volume of rubber exported by Malaysia is projected to increase about 3.9 percent a year between 1975 and 1990. Combined with a 27 percent increase in the relative price of rubber, the import capacity for which exports of rubber are responsible would increase 125 percent by 1990. It was projected that exports of rubber would grow at an average annual rate of 6 percent between 1975 and 1980; this growth will slow to 3.6 percent a year between 1980 and 1985, mainly because of a decline in the rate of output. Barring any large new investments in rubber during the next few years, the growth of rubber exports from Malaysia will be even slower—about 2.2 percent—between 1985 and

---

19. To achieve the objectives of the crash program, the Malaysian government imposed the following rules:
- tapping holidays—that is, a ban on tapping on certain days;
- a ban on the use of yield stimulants;
- the imposition of lower frequency of tapping in the estate sector;
- the adoption of an accelerated replanting program;
- the holding of stocks of rubber by the packer-remiller-exporter-dealer sector;
- direct purchase of rubber from smallholders by the government.

1990. During the entire 1975–90 period the value of rubber exports in nominal terms is expected to increase more than sixfold. Despite this substantial increase, the share of rubber in total exports will decline from 30 percent during 1970–74 to 16 percent by 1990 as a result of gains in other export commodities.

Palm Oil

Malaysia is the leading producer and exporter of palm oil in the world. Although the oil palm was introduced in Malaysia around the turn of the century, the Malaysian palm oil industry did not expand significantly until the early 1960s. Three factors were responsible for the rapid expansion of oil palm plantings in Malaysia. Soil and climate provided an ideal environment for the cultivation of oil palm; land development schemes and estates provided the level of management necessary to achieve maximum yields; and the decline in the price of rubber during the 1960s provided the economic incentive for investment in oil palm.[20]

The output of palm oil and palm kernel products during the period of the third plan, the potential for which is determined by the age and number of oil palms existing at the beginning of the period, could increase at an annual rate of 16.5 percent.[21] This would have raised Malaysian production of palm oil to 2.5 million tons by 1980 and that of palm-kernel oil to 250,000 metric tons (table 9.8). It is projected that by 1985 production will surpass 3.7 million tons and by 1990 will reach 4.8 million tons. For these projections it was assumed that acreage under oil palm would be replanted in oil palm but that newly developed land, to whatever extent is feasible, would be planted in other crops.

20. The principal institution responsible for land development in Peninsular Malaysia is the Federal Land Development Authority (FELDA). Before 1956, when FELDA came into existence, the development of the oil-palm sector was entirely in the hands of the large privately owned estates, on which land formerly planted in rubber was replanted in oil palm. From its establishment until 1974 FELDA opened a total of 251,000 hectares in 149 settlement schemes to the cultivation of oil palm. In addition, the Federal Land Consolidation and Rehabilitation Authority (FELCRA), another government agency concerned with development of land for oil palm and rubber, opened 4,500 hectares to the cultivation of oil palm during the first three years of the second plan.

21. Oil palm planted during 1976 and 1977 would have affected potential output during the final years of the third plan, 1979–80, only marginally. Actual output depends on other factors, such as rainfall and the quantity of fertilizer applied, as well.

Table 9.8. *Supply and Disposition of Palm Oil, 1960–76, and Projections for 1980, 1985, and 1990*

	Supply				Disposition (thousands of metric tons)	
	Area planted in oil palm (thousands of acres)			Total production (thousands of metric tons)		
Year	Peninsular Malaysia	Sabah and Sarawak	Total		Domestic consumption	Exports
1960	135.0	...	135.0	91.7	n.a.	97.7
1961	141.2	...	141.2	94.8	n.a.	95.0
1962	153.4	...	153.4	108.2	n.a.	107.4
1963	185.3	6.5	191.8	125.6	n.a.	116.9
1964	205.6	17.5	223.1	122.0	n.a.	126.1
1965	239.8	24.3	264.1	148.6	n.a.	143.2
1966	303.7	47.8	351.5	186.3	n.a.	184.7
1967	402.0	54.3	456.3	216.8	n.a.	189.0
1968	497.5	70.4	567.9	264.9	n.a.	286.0
1969	598.2	85.0	683.2	326.1	n.a.	356.8
1970	692.5	91.0	783.5	402.4	n.a.	402.0
1971	772.5	100.7	873.2	550.8	n.a.	573.4
1972	887.0	114.0	1,001.0	657.0	n.a.	697.1
1973	960.0	153.0	1,113.0	739.3	n.a.	797.9
1974	1,180.0	160.0	1,340.0	942.3	n.a.	901.2
1975	n.a.	n.a.	1,616.0	1,257.0	94	1,163.0
1976	n.a.	n.a.	1,719.0	1,389.0	54	1,335.0
1980	n.a.	n.a.	2,200.0	2,500.0	200	2,300.0[a]
1985	n.a.	n.a.	2,700.0	3,750.0	250	3,500.0[a]
1990	n.a.	n.a.	3,100.0	4,870.0	270	4,600.0[a]

... Zero or negligible.
n.a. Not available.
Sources: Supply: for 1960–76, Oil Palm Growers Council; for 1978–90, World Bank projections. Disposition: for 1960–76, Department of Statistics; for 1978–90, World Bank projections.
    a. Includes the crude-oil equivalent of exports of refined palm oil.

This assumption is based on the market prospects for palm oil. It does not imply that oil palm should be excluded from the list of potential crops for newly developed land, on which it has a comparative advantage over other crops. Replanting in oil palm would help to ensure, moreover, that existing plants for the extraction of palm oil could be operated efficiently.

Market Outlook for Palm Oil

Between 1955 and 1975 the world production of fats and oils increased at an average rate of 2.5 percent a year. Between 90 and 95 percent of the total output of fats and oils falls into the category of edible soap oils. These fats and oils are used both for edible products, such as margarine and shortening, and for industrial products, such as soaps and detergents. Table 9.9 shows the shares of the export market held by major fats and oils. It illustrates two important aspects of the market for fats and oils: First, no fat or oil dominates the market; second, palm oil will be expanding its share of the market rapidly.

Technically most fats and oils are interchangeable. Nevertheless the costs of refining and the requirements of specific products limit the range within which individual fats and oils can be substituted. Each oil or fat has its distinct chemical composition, and the importance attached to a specific component varies with the products in which they are used. Palm oil is used mainly in the manufacture of margarine, shortening, and soaps. Refining and fractionation bring palm oil into close competition with lard, soybean oil, rapeseed oil, and other low-priced fats and oils.

The demand for fats and oils largely depends on per capita income. The income elasticity of demand is high at low income levels and is almost zero at the present levels of per capita income in the industrial countries. Annual per capita consumption of fats and oils in most industrial countries has reached about 25–30 kilograms; in many developing countries it is less than 5 kilograms. Thus the developing countries represent a large potential market for fats and oils. Whether those countries will be able to turn this potential demand into an effective demand remains uncertain. Considering that consumption of fats and oils in many industrial countries will expand only slowly in the future, a large portion of world supplies of fats and oils will have to be marketed in developing countries—possibly at prices significantly lower than historical prices. Considering the low costs of production of palm oil, a decline in prices could reduce the share of the market taken up by high-priced oils.

WORLD PRODUCTION OF PALM OIL. A steep increase in world production of palm oil is projected for the 1975–90 period. Malaysia will continue to be the leading producer and exporter, followed by Indonesia and the Ivory Coast (table 9.10). The share of palm oil in total world exports will almost be equal to that of soybean oil by 1990. With a growing but still limited share of the market, the Malaysian palm oil

Table 9.9. *Projections of World Exports of Selected Fats and Oils, Selected Years, 1975–90*

	1975		1980	
Fat or oil	Thousands of metric tons	Percent- age share	Thousands of metric tons	Percent- age share
Soybean oil	3,500	27.1	5,000	28.9
Palm oil	1,774	13.6	3,000	17.4
Coconut oil	1,532	11.8	1,700	9.9
Tallow	1,437	11.0	1,750	10.1
Peanut oil	742	5.7	980	5.7
Sunflowerseed oil	729	5.6	900	5.2
Butter	728	5.6	800	4.6
Rapeseed oil	611	4.7	1,000	5.8
Fish oil	580	4.5	580	3.4
Lard	516	3.9	530	3.2
Cottonseed oil	404	3.1	420	2.4
Palm kernel oil	369	2.8	450	2.6
Olive oil	73	0.6	140	0.8
Total	13,025	100.0	17,250	100.0

Source: World Bank estimates and projections.

industry has had little influence on international market prices of fats and oils. Its influence will grow, however, with the substantial increase in the output of palm oil expected during the period of the third plan. By 1990 Malaysia will be second only to the United States as an exporter of fats and oils.

PRICE PROJECTIONS. A decline, in real terms, was projected in the general price trend of all fats and oils between 1975 and 1980. The principal assumptions underlying this projection are a weakening of the market for fats and oils caused by the rapid expansion in the acreage planted in oil-bearing tree crops in recent years and the growing demand for oilseed meals and a declining potential market for fats and oils in industrial countries, where consumption approaches the saturation level. An increase in the demand for fats and oils in these countries is likely to come only from the development of new products. The price trend of fats and oils between 1980 and 1985 will depend largely on the capacity of developing countries to absorb the projected increase in the

1985		1990		
Thousands of metric tons	Percent- age share	Thousands of metric tons	Percent- age share	Fat or oil
6,100	28.5	7,400	28.7	Soybean oil
5,100	23.8	7,200	27.9	Palm oil
1,800	8.4	1,950	7.6	Coconut oil
1,900	8.9	2,000	7.8	Tallow
1,050	4.9	1,200	4.6	Peanut oil
1,100	5.1	1,200	4.6	Sunflowerseed oil
950	4.4	1,100	4.3	Butter
1,100	5.1	1,200	4.7	Rapeseed oil
640	3.1	700	2.7	Fish oil
560	2.7	570	2.2	Lard
450	2.1	500	1.9	Cottonseed oil
500	2.3	600	2.3	Palm kernel oil
150	0.7	180	0.7	Olive oil
21,400	100.0	25,800	100.0	Total

production of fats and oils. A slight rise during this period is projected in the general trend of prices of fats and oils. This projection rests on the assumption that producers will reduce plantings in response to declining prices during the first half of the decade and that developing countries will absorb an increasing share of the total output of fats and oils. Between 1985 and 1990 the general price level of fats and oils is projected to decline slightly as increasing supplies of oils from tree crops, mainly palm oil and coconut oil, flow into international markets.

Conclusions

A decline of about a third in the relative price of palm oil between 1975 and 1980 was projected; a more moderate decline of about 6 percent is projected for the 1980s. For the period of the third plan this decline in the real price substantially offsets the expected growth of 100 percent in the volume of exports of palm oil to such an extent that an increase in import capacity of only 30 percent would be attained. In nominal terms the increase in exports of palm oil would be about 85

Table 9.10. *Projections of the Production of Palm Oil by the Principal Producing Countries, Selected Years, 1975–90*

Country	1975		1980	
	Thousands of metric tons	*Percent- age share*	*Thousands of metric tons*	*Percent- age share*
Malaysia	1,257	42.4	2,500	56.8
Indonesia	380	12.8	520	11.8
Ivory Coast	150	5.1	260	5.9
Zaire	168	5.7	90	2.0
Nigeria	480	16.2	350	8.0
Cameroon	60	2.0	80	1.8
Ghana	65	2.2	90	2.0
Sierra Leone	55	1.9	70	1.6
Others	348	11.7	440	10.0
World total	2,963	100.0	4,400	100.0

Source: World Bank estimates and projections.

percent. Although the decline in the relative price of palm oil would be much smaller during the 1980s, the growth in volume would also be significantly smaller—7.2 percent a year instead of the growth of almost 15 percent expected to take place between 1975 and 1980. As a result, the growth of import capacity made possible by exports of palm oil would increase slightly, from 5.5 percent a year between 1975 and 1980 to about 6.3 percent a year between 1980 and 1990, and exports of palm oil throughout the entire fifteen-year period would perform better than total exports. The share of palm oil products in total exports would increase from 8 percent between 1970 and 1974 to about 11 percent by 1990.

Forest Products

As the most important sources of tropical hardwood in the world, Malaysia, Indonesia, and the Philippines are responsible for 60 percent of world production and almost 80 percent of world exports (table 9.11). The tropical belt of this region contains about 750 million acres of forest land. About 97 percent of the forest reserves are tropical hardwood, representing 11 percent of the world's total hardwood resources.

1985		1990		
Thousands of metric tons	Percent- age share	Thousands of metric tons	Percent- age share	Country
3,750	61.5	4,870	61.7	Malaysia
900	14.8	1,100	13.9	Indonesia
330	5.4	510	6.5	Ivory Coast
90	1.5	110	1.4	Zaire
355	5.8	470	5.9	Nigeria
100	1.6	130	1.7	Cameroon
100	1.6	120	1.5	Ghana
				Sierra
80	1.3	90	1.1	Leone
395	6.5	500	6.3	Others
6,000	100.0	8,000	100.0	World total

Demand for Hardwood

Since the Second World War the use of tropical hardwoods in the housing and furniture industries has increased at about the same rate as per capita incomes in industrial countries.[22] About 60 percent of the output is marketed in the form of logs. Pulpwood and industrial wood products industries each take about a fourth of the remaining output.

Tropical hardwood has faced increasing competition from softwood and from materials other than wood. In the early 1940s plywood began to replace sawn wood. Then, in the 1960s, particle board was increasingly substituted for plywood. In addition, such materials as plastics, aluminum, cement, and steel replaced hardwood in many products— aluminum window frames, concrete buildings, plastic and vinyl flooring, and so on. Because the cost of plastics, aluminum, and steel began to rise following the increase in petroleum prices in the early 1970s, it is expected that the substitution of these materials for wood will proceed more slowly between the late 1970s and 1990.

22. Tropical hardwood logs are processed into sawn wood, plywood, veneers, and sometimes railroad ties. These products are then used for construction, furniture, ships and boats, containers, packaging, and so on. Construction and furniture account for roughly 80–95 percent of the consumption of tropical hardwood.

Table 9.11. *World Exports of Hardwood, 1965, 1970, and Projections for 1980, 1985, and 1990*
(millions of cubic meters)

Country or region	1965	1970	1980	1985	1990
Indonesia	0.2	7.9	25.0	25.0	27.0
Malaysia	5.5	10.3	15.2	14.4	13.6
Philippines	10.0	14.0	11.0	9.0	10.0
Other tropical countries	8.0	12.5	26.2	45.9	58.7
Subtotal	23.7	44.7	77.4	94.3	109.3
Temperate zones	5.9	7.5	10.0	8.0	6.0
World total	29.6	52.2	87.4	102.3	115.3

Note: Exports of hardwood include logs, sawn wood and sleepers, veneer, and plywood.

Sources: Food and Agriculture Organization, *Yearbook of Forest Products*, annual volumes, 1962–73; World Bank projections.

Supply of Hardwood

Annual world production of wood in the late 1970s is estimated to be 2.5 billion cubic meters, of which more than half is industrial wood; the remainder is used for fuel. Industrial wood includes logs—sawlogs, veneer logs, and logs for railroad sleepers—pulpwood, and such lesser items as poles, posts, pilings, and pitprops for the roofs of underground mines. Although developing countries contribute only a small share— 13.2 percent in 1972—to the total supply of industrial wood, about three-fourths of their production consists of tropical hardwoods. Industrial countries and those having centrally planned economies mainly produce softwoods.

Malaysia, Indonesia, and the Philippines dominate the world trade in tropical hardwoods for several reasons: first, the timber resources of these three countries are in easily accessible locations; second, the large number of tropical hardwoods is distributed with fair uniformity in these countries; third, their forests are richer than those of other hardwood-exporting countries, in output per acre of commercially acceptable species. Average logging costs are therefore lower than those in Africa and Latin America.

About three-fourths of the exports from the region enter the market in the form of logs; the rest is divided among sawn wood, plywood, and veneer. Only the Philippines and Peninsular Malaysia have succeeded in significantly increasing their exports of processed tropical hardwood. Japan, Korea, Taiwan, and Singapore receive most of the logs exported by these countries and re-export them in some processed form, principally as plywood. The main reason for this pattern of activity is the difference in the efficiency of the timber-processing industries among these countries. Malaysia, for example, has more than 700 sawmills, most of which are poorly equipped backyard operations employing fewer than fifty workers. The rate of timber recovery is less than 55 percent, which leaves substantial room for improvement.

In 1975 the Malaysian government adopted a national forest policy to conserve forest resources, to realize sustained yields from the productive forest, and to curb the export of logs in favor of increased exports of wood products. To accomplish all this would require substantial investments in the Malaysian timber-processing industry.

In an effort to stabilize the prices of tropical hardwoods, Malaysia, Indonesia, and the Philippines established SEALPA in 1974. The primary objective of SEALPA has been to improve prices by concerted efforts to restrict exports of logs. In 1975 total exports of sawn logs were limited to 20.5 million cubic meters. The export shares agreed upon for Malaysia, Indonesia, and the Philippines were 29, 49, and 23 percent. Despite this restriction upon exports of hardwoods, prices continued to decline until the middle of 1975, mainly because the principal importing countries were reducing their large inventories. It remains to be seen whether the efforts of SEALPA will be more successful in the future. Malaysia is also participating in preparatory meetings sponsored by UNCTAD, the objective of which is to codify an agreement between producers and consumers of tropical hardwoods in an effort to rationalize supply and demand and to stabilize prices.

Price Outlook

About fifty years are required for tropical hardwood trees in Southeast Asia to grow large enough to produce veneer logs; only 25 to 35 years are required for softwood trees. Thus many preferred species of temperate and tropical hardwoods can be regarded as virtually nonrenewable resources. Although additional supplies could become available from traditional exporting countries under the pressure of sustained demand, the potential supply is limited. The bulk of additional supplies will have to come from new regions, such as some areas of Central Africa. The cost of marketing tropical hardwoods from these regions is likely to exceed the costs incurred by traditional suppliers.

Sizable investments and price incentives will be required to open up these untapped forests. The cost of production in these new regions is estimated to be 1.5 to 2 times as high as the cost in the traditional export countries. On the basis of these estimates, it was projected that the prices of tropical hardwoods, in real terms, would increase at a rate of about 11 percent a year between 1975 and 1980. After 1980 the increase in real prices is expected to slow to 2 percent a year.

This relatively favorable price outlook offsets to a considerable extent the projections of constrained volume for exports of wood from Malaysia. The forecast of high prices in particular would cause the import capacity for which exports of wood are responsible to increase about 20 percent a year between 1975 and 1980; that produced by total exports would be only 12 percent. The forecast of more moderate prices after 1980, together with the anticipated decline in the overall volume of exports of sawlogs, would reverse this trend: The value of wood exports is expected to expand about 2 percent a year between 1980 and 1990, whereas the expansion of total exports should increase only about 5 percent a year. As a result of these trends the share of wood exports in total exports should have increased from 12 percent in 1975 to almost 17 percent in 1980, and should then decline to 11 percent by 1990.

Tin

Malaysia is responsible for about 40 percent of world production of tin. Like other important tin-producing countries, Malaysia has passed the peak of the capacity of existing mines. The bulk of Malaysian tin comes from alluvial deposits. Although the quality of ore in the more important fields declined steadily during the 1970s, the easy accessibility of tin mines combined with high prices of tin made it again economically possible to mine low-grade ores and remine accumulated tailings. Actually Malaysia has reworked many of its tin fields two or three times since the Second World War. Declining output and rising operating costs forced the mining industry to improve its efficiency. Most mines have increased the capacity and efficiency of their equipment. They have attached more powerful motors to larger and more efficient pumps, have increased the capacity of their dredges, and have improved techniques of recovery.[23] This has made it possible to mine fields formerly considered unprofitable.

23. Malaysian mining companies use only land-based dredges. Conventional land-based bucket dredges can operate to a depth of about 110 feet. Below this depth the

In addition to improving mining operations, Malaysia will have to intensify the search for new deposits. It is estimated that nearly 2,000 square miles in Peninsular Malaysia have potential reserves of tin. Only a third of this area has been leased for mining. Exploration for deposits of tin and other minerals warranted more attention during the period of the third plan. Because mining tin from established fields will remain profitable at 1978 prices, the private sector lacks the incentive to explore less accessible areas. Although improvements in the network of roads along the east coast of Malaysia, such as completion of the east-west highway through North Perak and Kelantan, will stimulate prospecting for tin in these areas, government will have to bear the main burden of mineral exploration on land situated in undeveloped areas and offshore.[24] Whether exploration continues and new reserves are developed during the early 1980s will depend largely on the relations among tin prices, mining costs, and taxes. Declining tin prices and increasing mining costs would cause investments in tin mining to decline, particularly in such risky ventures as offshore dredging.

Of all the tin produced in the world, 75 percent is consumed by the industrial countries. Of that, 47 percent is tinplate and 23 percent is solder. The preponderance of tinplate among tin products has been the principal reason for the slow growth of the demand for tin in the past. The demand for tinplate has been reduced by increasing use of tin-free steel and aluminum in the manufacture of containers for beer and soft drinks and by such technological advances as the introduction of the electrolytic tinplate process. In the electronics industry soldered connections have largely been replaced by miniature circuits and integrated circuits. In the automobile industry new designs and new welding practices have made it possible to substitute aluminum and plastic increasingly for solder.

Demand for Tin

Between 1955 and 1974 demand for primary tin grew 1.7 percent a year. The growth of demand during this period was higher in devel-

---

productivity drops rapidly. It is believed that dredging will increase as Malaysia finds ways to overcome the lack of capital for larger and more efficient dredges and the lack of technical expertise in mining by dredging.

24. Large alluvial areas of Malaysia have not yet been fully explored, and little systematic work has been done on primary deposits. Prospecting licenses were issued in 1973 for offshore areas near Penang, Perak, and Selangor. The analysis of some 400 samples of marine sediments from off the east coast and from the Singapore Straits points to the existence of rich deposits.

oping countries and those having centrally planned economies, but only 1.3 percent a year in industrial countries. The amount of tin consumed will continue to depend to a large extent on the demand for tinplate. In industrial countries the container industry will continue to grow steadily, but technological substitution in this industry is expected to allow only a modest growth in the use of tin. It is less likely, however, that substitution will take place as rapidly in developing countries and those having centrally planned economies as in industrial countries. Changes in the demand for tin for use in bronze, brass, solder, and other alloys are expected to be uniform throughout the world, but a more rapid increase in domestic demand is possible in developing countries. The greatest potential for growth in the use of tin is in chemicals. Although the forecasts of the tin industry of the use of tin in chemicals are optimistic, such uses constitute only a small proportion of the total consumption of tin, and the effect on total demand for tin will thus not be particularly strong for some time.

World demand for tin is projected to increase 1.5 percent a year from its average for 1972–74 to that in 1990. The sharp increase in tin prices from 1973 onward hurt the consumption of tin in industrial countries, and a full recovery is not expected until the early 1980s.

World Production of Tin

World production of tin, in concentrates, is projected to grow about 1.5 percent a year between 1975 and 1990, mainly in response to the relatively high prices of the early 1970s (table 9.12). A stagnation in world production of tin ore is projected for the mid-1980s in response to the decline in real prices projected for the early 1980s. The assumption underlying these projections is that overall production of tin ore will follow historical patterns in response to price changes.

In the past, production of primary tin has grown faster than consumption. Most of the excess supply in the 1950s was stockpiled by the United States. The creation of buffer stocks and the imposition of export quotas by the International Tin Council in 1956 alleviated the periodic problem of excess supplies, while releases from the U.S. government stockpile mitigated the problems of shortages in boom periods of demand. Thus both the U.S. stockpile and the International Tin Council contributed to the maintenance of stable tin markets.

Effects of Tin Agreements

Tin is one of the few commodities—and the only metal—for which the market is regulated by a commodity agreement. The forces that impelled the making of the tin agreements were overproduction, fear of widespread unemployment in the tin industry, uncertainties associated with the dispersal of strategic stocks, and the belief that commodity agreements aimed at price stabilization in the short term and development of markets for the long term could significantly assist tin-producing countries. The main purpose of these agreements continues to be the stabilization of international tin prices. It is the task of the International Tin Council to keep the price of tin within a range determined by the council, using the price of tin in Penang as a reference. For this purpose, the council operates a buffer stock and controls the volume of exports through the imposition of quotas whenever they are needed.

The management of buffer stocks is now tied to the movement of tin prices at Penang. The manager of the buffer stocks is obliged to sell when the Penang price reaches the ceiling price. In the top sector of the price range, the manager may sell at the prevailing price if doing so can be expected to reduce the upward pressure on prices.[25] In the lower sector, he may buy tin at the prevailing price if doing so can be expected to reduce the downward pressure on prices. If prices drop to the lower limit, the manager must buy tin until his funds are exhausted.

Price Outlook

In the late 1970s the real price of tin was expected to decline from its 1977 peak. The supply deficit was expected to be eradicated by 1980 with the response of production to the recent price increase, and the London tin price in constant 1977 dollars was expected to decline to about US$4.40 a pound. During the 1980s prices will move upward, reflecting the rising real cost of mining tin.

Largely as a result of depleted reserves, the volume of Malaysian tin production is projected to increase slowly from 64,000 metric tons to 74,000 between 1975 and 1990. About 20 percent of Malaysian exports of tin are re-exports after smelting. Under the assumption that the smelting capacity of neighboring countries from which tin is exported to Malaysia for smelting increases, re-exports can be expected to decline. Under the assumption that this trend will approximately offset the increase in domestic production, no increase in the volume of exports of tin is projected for the long term. The increase of about 25

25. The width of the range was determined by the objective of limiting price fluctuations to 10–15 percent above or below the midpoint of the range. Within the range the decisions open to the manager of the buffer stocks were designed to retard changes as the prices approached the limit of the range.

Table 9.12. *Production of Tin in Concentrates by the Principal Producing Countries, 1970, 1975, and Projections for 1980, 1985, and 1990*

	1970		1975		1980	
Country	Thousands of metric tons	Percent- age share	Thousands of metric tons	Percent- age share	Thousands of metric tons	Percent- age share
Malaysia[a]	74	39.9	64	36.2	67	33.0
Bolivia	30	16.3	28	15.8	34	16.7
Thailand	22	11.8	16	9.0	26	12.8
Indonesia	19	10.3	25	14.1	28	13.8
Australia	9	4.8	9	5.2	12	5.9
Nigeria	8	4.3	5	2.8	4	2.0
Zaire	6	3.5	5	2.8	4	2.0
Brazil	4	1.9	5	2.8	8	3.9
Others[b]	13	7.1	20	11.3	20	9.9
World total[c]	185	100.0	178	100.0	203	100.0

Note: Figures may not reconcile because of rounding.
Source: World Bank estimates and projections.
   a. Malaysian exports of tin have exceeded domestic production because tin in concentrates is imported from neighboring countries and processed into tin in Malaysia.

percent in import capacity between 1975 and 1990 for which tin is responsible will thus be entirely the result of the increase in the relative price of tin. This increase would not, however, be enough to offset the decline projected in the share of tin in exports from 13 percent in 1975 to 5 percent in 1990.

The Effects of Disposals from the U.S. Government Stockpile

The United States had a stockpile of about 200,000 tons of tin for strategic purposes in 1976. Since 1956 the U.S. government has been reducing the size of this stockpile. Although the U.S. authorities have declared that they would dispose of their stocks in a way that would minimize the effect on international tin prices, producers are concerned about the availability of additional tin, especially in times of surplus, and the constant threat of the disposal of large stocks of tin. Considering that an annual increase in demand of only 1 or 2 percent is projected, it is likely that a massive release of U.S. tin stocks would depress tin prices and thus reduce the export earnings of tin-exporting countries. The International Tin Council has an understanding with the U.S. government on disposals of tin from its stockpile; the parties

1985		1990		
Thousands of metric tons	*Percentage share*	*Thousands of metric tons*	*Percentage share*	*Country*
72	33.5	74	32.7	Malaysia[a]
35	16.3	37	16.4	Bolivia
27	12.6	28	12.4	Thailand
31	14.4	34	15.0	Indonesia
13	6.0	14	6.2	Australia
5	2.3	6	2.7	Nigeria
5	2.3	6	2.7	Zaire
9	4.2	10	4.4	Brazil
18	8.4	17	7.5	Others[b]
215	100.0	226	100.0	World total[c]

b. Countries of Western Europe, Japan, and so on.
c. Excludes countries having centrally planned economies, which, as a group, are marginal net exporters; between 1971 and 1973 the total net exports of tin by this group amounted to 1,000 tons a year.

to the International Tin Agreement will be under severe pressure to consider measures for maintaining the projected price trend.

Petroleum and Natural Gas

Petroleum emerged in the early 1970s as one of the principal export commodities of Malaysia. Reserves of crude oil, estimated to be a billion barrels, and natural gas, estimated to be 22,500 billion cubic feet, may make Malaysia the second largest producer of petroleum in Southeast Asia.

Until 1974 the oil companies operated under concession agreements. In July 1974 the Malaysian government canceled these agreements and passed the Petroleum Development Act, thereby tightening its control over the petroleum industry. Ownership of the crude-oil reserves of Malaysia—and thus of the right to explore and exploit these reserves— was transferred to Petroliam Nasional Berhad (PETRONAS), a corporation under the direction of the Prime Minister. The final authority over all petroleum-related issues rests with the Prime Minister, who is advised by a national advisory council. He exercises this authority by means of regulations. Under the petroleum regulations issued in 1974, oil companies and manufacturers and suppliers of drilling equipment had to apply to PETRONAS if they wanted to continue their operations or start new ventures. Oil companies that had been issued exploration licenses or had concluded petroleum agreements under the Petroleum Mining Act of 1966 were required to submit all data, information, and records concerning their surveys, research, exploration, and production to PETRONAS.

The uncertainty about the outcome of government negotiations with oil companies operating in Malaysia slowed production during 1975. Esso, one of the largest refining and marketing companies in Malaysia, suspended all exploration. The development of its Tembungo field was suspended, and its production remained at 4,000 barrels a day, the same as that of the preceding year. Similarly the development of other oil fields, such as Pulai and Conoco's Sotong field, was temporarily halted. The agreement made by PETRONAS with Shell and Esso allows the two companies to deduct as much as 20 percent of production for the costs of exploration, development, and production and 10 percent for royalties. The remaining 70 percent is to be divided between PETRONAS and Shell and Esso, with PETRONAS taking 70 percent and the foreign oil companies together taking 30 percent. In addition, the oil companies are to pay income taxes. The production-sharing agreement is to last twenty years, with the option of a four-year extension. The contract for gas is for twenty years, with the option of a fourteen-year extension.

Until October 1974 all the crude oil produced in Malaysia came from Sarawak Shell's West Lutong, Baram, and Baronia fields and, more recently, from the Bakau field. The average production of Sarawak Shell in 1974 was 80,000 barrels a day, 50,000 barrels of which came from Baram and 30,000 from West Lutong. In October 1974 Esso started to pump oil from two wells in its Tembungo field in Sabah at the rate of 5,000 barrels a day. Although the drilling equipment installed at the Tembungo field could serve as many as eighteen wells, production remained within the range of 4,000 to 5,000 barrels a day. Total production amounted to about 80,000 barrels a day in 1974 and 100,000 barrels a day in 1975. By 1977 the effective rate of production of crude oil in Malaysia had increased to more than 200,000 barrels a day. More than 82 percent of this came from the four offshore fields of Sarawak—Bakau, Baram, Baronia, and West Lutong—operated by a subsidiary of Royal Dutch Shell. The remaining 18 percent of produc-

tion came from the offshore Sabah fields—Tembungo and Samarang—
the former operated by Esso and the latter by Shell.

PETRONAS has divided international oil companies into four groups.
The first group consists of the original producers, Shell and Esso, with
whom PETRONAS has already signed production-sharing contracts. The
second consists of the Continental Oil Group, which discovered oil off
the east coast of Malaysia in 1974. The third group is made up of companies that have explored offshore Sabah—Aquitaine, Sabah Teiseki,
and the Oceanic Exploration Forest Oil Consortium. All newcomers
are placed in the fourth group. Areas not pre-empted by the first three
groups are to be made available to the fourth group. In addition, new
onshore and offshore acreage is to be offered to interested companies.
The recoverable reserves of Malaysia were estimated by PETRONAS to be
about 1 billion barrels of crude oil and 22.5 billion cubic feet of natural
gas in June 1977. At the 1977 production rate of about 200,000 barrels a
day, Malaysian reserves will not last more than thirteen years.

Any projections of the production of crude oil in Malaysia will be
affected by the rate at which new fields are developed. Among these
fields are Shell's South Furious, Samarang, and Erb West oil fields in
Sabah; the Conoco group's Sutong, Duyong, and Anding fields in the
Peninsula; and Esso's Pulai and Kikok fields. Provisional estimates by
the government indicated an increase in production from 120,000 barrels a day in 1976 to 240,000 by 1978 through 1980. It was possible that
the production of oil would expand more rapidly, but the projection set
forth here is based on the more conservative official estimates.[26]

Malaysia has two refineries, the combined capacity of which is about
100,000 barrels a day. These refineries are located at Port Dickson and
operated by Shell and Esso. The capacity of the Shell refinery was
increased in 1976 from 32,000 to 65,000 barrels a day. Shell expanded
the capacity of its refinery shortly before the decline in the demand for
oil in 1974. Since then refineries have been operating at about 80–86
percent of capacity, which is considerably less than the economic opti-
mum of 92 percent. In 1976 Caltex Petroleum, supported by Japanese
interests, submitted a proposal to construct a refinery with a capacity of
84,000 barrels a day on the west coast. In view of the fact that refineries
in Singapore, the main refining center in the area, operate at 50 percent

26. None of these projections includes re-exports, and the underlying assumption is
that most of the oil consumed domestically is imported and that all high-quality Malaysian oil is exported.

of capacity, it seemed doubtful that Malaysia would increase its refining capacity before 1980. A small increase in refining capacity would be sufficient to meet the domestic needs of Malaysia, which are estimated to be 112,000 barrels a day by 1980.

In summary, even if real oil prices should increase only slightly between 1975 and 1980, an increase in the production of oil to 240,000 barrels a day would bring about more than a doubling of the import capacity of petroleum products during the period of the third plan. In nominal terms there would be a threefold increase in export revenues, from less than M$1 billion, an amount equal to 10 percent of exports, in 1975 to more than M$3 billion, an amount equal to 15 percent of exports, in 1980. There are no official forecasts of production beyond 1980. Nevertheless offshore exploration is continuing—the six oil companies, for example, spent M$133 million on exploration for oil and gas in 1977—and the prospects of additional discoveries are good. It therefore is assumed that production during the 1980s will increase an average of 5 percent a year, which means production of 375,000 barrels a day by 1990.

Natural gas resources may also be of great importance to the Malaysian economy in the future, yet they have remained largely undeveloped. Less than 10 percent of the output of natural gas is now marketed; the rest is flared or reinjected into producing oil fields to maintain the required pressure. The discovery by Shell in the Bintulu field off the west coast of Sarawak is so far the largest gas find. Reserves are estimated to be 6 trillion cubic feet. A plant to produce liquefied natural gas is planned that will liquefy about 750 million cubic feet of gas a day for export to Japan under a twenty-year contract executed in May 1977. Shell, Mitsubishi, and PETRONAS are the parties to this project. Shell, Mitsubishi, Tokyo Gas, Tokyo Electric, and PETRONAS, moreover, have agreed to form a company in Japan to market the liquefied natural gas. PETRONAS owns an interest of 70 percent in the marketing company; Shell and Mitsubishi hold 15 percent each. Construction of the liquefaction plant was to begin in 1978; exports should begin in 1983. The liquefied gas is to be shipped by the Malaysia International Shipping Corporation.

The unit cost of liquefied natural gas includes the wellhead price of gas, the cost of delivery to the liquefaction plant, the cost of liquefaction, and the cost of marine freight to the receiving terminal. The costs exclusive of marine freight can range from US$0.30 to US$1.00 a million British thermal units. Freight costs vary from US$0.15 a million British thermal units for short hauls to considerably more than

US$1.50 for long distances. Prices of natural gas are projected to be US$2.00 a million British thermal units CIF Japanese ports by 1980; freight costs are estimated to be about US$0.45. Thus the projected price of liquefied natural gas FOB Sarawak will be about US$1.55 a million British thermal units. Exports of natural gas from the Bintulu field could begin to add about M$1.2 billion to annual export earnings in the early 1980s.

Manufactured Exports

Malaysia made considerable progress in increasing manufactured exports during the 1970s. Between 1970 and 1975 manufactured exports grew more than 24 percent a year in real terms; their share in exports of merchandise increased from 7 percent in 1970 to 17 percent in 1975. Four industries—wood products, textiles and clothing, rubber products, and electronics components and assembly—were responsible for nearly all the growth in manufactured exports. This performance was significantly better than that of developing countries as a whole, whose exports during the same period increased only about 13 percent a year. A further examination of the data reveals, however, that before 1970 the growth of Malaysian exports was slightly lower than the average (table 9.13) and that the excellent performance of Malaysia in the 1970s was largely attributable to the spurt of growth in 1973–74 following the initiation of exports from the free-trade zones established in 1970.

There is considerable uncertainty about the future of Malaysian exports. A prime determinant, of course, is the growth in demand for manufactured exports from developing countries. World Bank projections, in which no substantial changes in trade barriers are assumed, indicate some slackening in the overall growth of manufactured exports from developing countries during the 1980s from the levels of the early 1970s. Thus it is projected that between 1975 and 1985 manufactured exports of developing countries will increase at a real annual rate of 12 percent, which is the same as the rate of increase between 1960 and 1975 but is significantly lower than the rate of 15 percent at which they increased between 1970 and 1975. Although this projected rate of growth of manufactured exports is highly speculative in the light of the unexpectedly dynamic performance of the 1970s, it is a useful benchmark for projecting the performance of Malaysian exports.

For a number of reasons some slackening in the rapid growth of manufactured exports of Malaysia is to be expected. First, the export base

Table 9.13. *Rates of Growth of Manufactured Exports by Malaysia and by All Developing Countries, 1960–75, and Projections for 1975–85*
(average annual percentage rates)

Exporting country or group of countries	1960–70	1970–75	1960–75	1975–85
Malaysia[a]	10.6	24.5	15.1	12.2
All developing countries[b]	11.0	14.9	12.3	12.2

Sources: Bank Negara, *Quarterly Economic Bulletin*, various issues World Bank estimates.
a. Standard international trade classifications 5–8, excluding 68.
b. Standard international trade classifications 5–9, excluding 68.

was much larger in 1979 than it was in 1970. Between 1970 and 1975, for example, the share of manufactured exports in exports of merchandise more than doubled, increasing from 7 percent to 17 percent. Second, in the late 1970s there was a significant decline in investment in manufacturing activities. Third, the outlook for continued rapid growth in exports of clothing and textiles from developing countries is not good. It is roughly estimated that if the quantitative restrictions on imports of textiles and clothing by industrial countries are enforced with some strictness, the growth of these exports could be significantly less than 10 percent; their annual growth was almost 20 percent between 1970 and 1975. Because a significant part of the growth of Malaysian exports has been in textiles and clothing, some future dampening of the growth of manufactured exports is likely.

On the assumption that domestic conditions do not inhibit a recovery in manufacturing investment, and in view of the past performance of Malaysia in exports, there is no obvious reason to expect the performance of Malaysia to be worse than that of the average of developing countries. If it is assumed that Malaysia does as well as the average in each of the main categories of manufactured exports—clothing, textiles, chemicals, iron and steel, and machinery and equipment—and given the composition of Malaysian exports (see table 2.4 in chapter two), Malaysia should be able to achieve an average growth of manufactured exports of about 12 percent a year. If this rate of growth were to be sustained, the share of manufactured exports in exports of merchandise would increase significantly, from 17 percent in 1975 to almost a third by 1990.

𐂷𐂷𐂷𐂷𐂷𐂷𐂷𐂷𐂷𐂷𐂷𐂷𐂷𐂷𐂷𐂷𐂷𐂷𐂷𐂷𐂷𐂷𐂷𐂷𐂷𐂷𐂷𐂷𐂷𐂷𐂷𐂷𐂷𐂷𐂷𐂷𐂷𐂷𐂷

Estimated Effects of Different Investment Levels on Growth, Incomes, Employment, and Restructuring, 1975–90

THIS APPENDIX PRESENTS A DISCUSSION of the consequences of different investment levels in Malaysia during 1975–90, the last fifteen years of the period of the perspective plan. With the help of a simple model of the economy, it first sets out to project the macroeconomic outcomes of three different growth paths of private investment and public expenditure. It next assesses the consequences for the growth in output, employment, and incomes by principal sector. It then reviews the prospects for attaining the goals of the New Economic Policy with regard to eradicating poverty and restructuring employment under the various alternatives.

Alternative Scenarios for Manufacturing Investment and Public Expenditure

The seven-sector model used to determine the quantitative outcome of alternative scenarios is partly supply-determined and partly demand-determined. The fundamental distinction was to determine the output of certain sectors on the basis of investment and to let other sectors be determined by demand. This dichotomy was used to capture the demand effects of additional expenditure and the capacity effects of changes in investment. In particular this formulation illustrates the limitations of a pure demand-pull strategy—for example, through lower taxes—which would result in large import leaks if capacity were not being simultaneously created. As for any model, this model has numerous simplifications and shortcomings when judged in the light of the complexities of an economy. Nevertheless a number of the principal relations have been accounted for, and the results may provide a useful guide to policy decisions.

The principal characteristics of the model are the following. The supply-determined sectors are principal agricultural exports, mining, manufacturing, and utilities. The demand-determined sectors are other agriculture, construction, and services. Imports are determined as a residual; investment is exogenous. The model is run in constant 1970 prices, and exports are included in terms of their purchasing-power equivalent, with a subsequent conversion to current dollars. The incremental capital-output ratio (ICOR) used in the manufacturing sector is 2.2, with a two-year lag; it was derived from the input-output model presented in an earlier World Bank report.[1] Demand relations are also derived from this model. The tax function is based on historical relations for all taxes except excise and oil taxes, which are derived from the analysis in chapter six. Consumption functions for both public and private consumption are based on historical data.

With regard to principal exogenous inputs into the model, the growth of the agricultural export sector—rubber, palm oil, sawlogs, and sawn timber—is based on the analysis of both public investment in agriculture and world market conditions, as discussed in chapter nine. Additional public investment in this area is assumed to affect output through an ICOR of 4.0 and a four-year lag. The output of the mining sector is also based on an analysis of investment and world market conditions, again as discussed in chapter nine. The output of the utilities sector is based on the implicit relation between public investment and growth in the third plan.

---

1. As noted in chapter three, a fixed ICOR was used to determine the investment-output relations in the manufacturing sector. Although this was largely done for analytical convenience, it is not clear that it seriously misstates the true relation. A number of factors affect the ICOR over time: capital deepening within manufacturing subsectors; shifts in the structure of manufacturing toward more or less capital-intensive subsectors; the growth rate of manufacturing value added; and greater or less capital use. The first factor will always tend to increase the ICOR; the third factor will always tend to have the opposite effect; the second and fourth factors may have either positive or negative effects on the size of the ICOR. Because the net impact of all these factors may be positive or negative, little can be said a priori about the direction of the bias in using a fixed manufacturing ICOR. Because manufacturing investment accounts for between a quarter and a third of total investment, it would take a very large change in the manufacturing ICOR to produce a significant impact on the required overall investment rate. World Bank, "Malaysia: Second Plan Performance and Third Plan Issues," report no. 1177a-MA (a restricted-circulation document), 2 vols. (Washington, D.C.: World Bank, 1976; processed), vol. 2, annex V.

The model operates sequentially in the following way. First, investment is specified. Second, output in the investment-determined sectors is estimated. Based on this estimate and assumptions about world demand, exports are projected. Third, with investment and exports given, the model solves for income, consumption, and output in the demand-determined sectors. Fourth, imports are calculated as the difference between gross demand and domestic supply. Fifth, the balance of payments implications can be derived by converting exports and imports to current prices. In view of Malaysia's highly open economy, it is reasonable to expect that excess demand would quickly be satisfied with additional imports rather than by initiating domestic inflation. Thus, by assuming a fixed exchange rate, domestic inflation is assumed to be the same as international inflation, an assumption which is borne out historically.

Given the decline of manufacturing investment in the mid-1970s, the uncertain outlook for manufacturing investment activity in the future, and the uncertainty about the reaction of the public sector to its improved resource position, various alternative scenarios are examined with different assumptions about public and private resource use (table A.1). Three basic alternatives are examined in detail; various modifications to these basic alternatives are discussed in passing. The basic framework for external resources and those of the public sector is consistent with the forecasts set out in chapters three and six.

Alternative I: Moderate Growth—Low Investment in Manufacturing

This alternative assumes that the factors affecting the climate for private investment in 1975 and 1976 are serious and permanent and that there will be no recovery in the rate of investment in the manufacturing sector. Thus investment in manufacturing, which is estimated to have declined to about 3 percent of GDP in 1976, is projected to stay at that relative level throughout the 1976–90 period. This alternative therefore presents what might be called a pessimistic outlook. Although it is not a forecast of the likely course of events, it illustrates the significance of the manufacturing sector for the overall performance of the economy in the context of continuing expansion in other sectors.

Other investment is assumed to increase more rapidly. Public investment is projected to increase about 9 percent a year, which is in line with the long-term targets of government. Investment in oil and related areas is also projected to grow rapidly during the late 1970s and early

Table A.1. *Investment Projections under Three Scenarios, 1976–90*

Item	Alternative I	Alternative II	Alternative III
	Billions of Malaysian dollars, 1990 *(constant 1970 prices)*		
Fixed investment	20.6	14.1	15.9
Public	5.2	6.2	6.2
Private	5.4	7.9	9.7
Manufacturing	1.2	3.7	5.5
Oil	0.3	0.3	0.3
Other	3.9	3.9	3.9
	Investment in relation to GDP, 1990 (percent)		
Fixed investment	27.4	27.9	26.7
Public	13.3	12.2	10.4
Private	14.0	15.7	16.3
Manufacturing	3.2	7.4	9.3
Oil	0.8	0.6	0.5
Other	10.0	7.7	6.5
	Average annual rate of growth, 1976–90 (percent)		
Fixed investment	7.2	9.4	10.4
Public	9.1	10.5	10.5
Private	5.8	8.7	10.3
Manufacturing	5.2	14.0	16.0
Oil	2.4	2.4	2.4
Other	6.4	6.4	6.4

Source: World Bank estimates.

1980s, reflecting proposed investments, particularly in a liquefied natural gas plant in Sarawak. That plant, at a cost of M$2.4 billion, probably is the largest single project ever undertaken in Malaysia. Once this project is completed (by about 1983) investments in this area are expected to decline somewhat in the second half of the 1980s. Other private investment—in buildings, agriculture, and services—is projected to grow about 6.5 percent a year through 1990.

Over all, the assumptions result in an average growth of gross fixed investment of 7.2 percent a year, but the growth rates of various components would differ substantially. Because the GDP growth rate under this alternative would be lower than that projected by government, the investment rate would, even under this alternative, still rise substantially. Investment in fixed assets, which in 1970 prices was 25 percent of GDP in 1974 and 21 percent in 1976, would recover to 25 percent of GDP in the early 1980s and reach 27 percent by 1990. In this sense, therefore, alternative I is not pessimistic. Most of the increase in the investment rate would nevertheless originate in the public sector.

Alternative II: Rapid Growth—Recovery in Manufacturing and Higher Public Expenditure

This alternative varies in two important respects from alternative I. First, it is assumed that manufacturing investment will have recovered by 1980 to 4.5 percent of GDP, the average level prevailing in the early 1970s. This recovery implies an average growth rate of 17 percent a year in the four years 1977–80, a rate which does not appear to have been realized in 1977. Beyond 1980 it is assumed that manufacturing investment will continue to grow rapidly, at 12.6 percent a year. Second, it is assumed that government substantially accelerates spending both for programs relying heavily on current expenditure and for development expenditure. Specifically, it is assumed that by 1990 public investment will be about 20 percent higher, and public consumption about 30 percent higher, than under alternative I. Still the investment rate under alternative II would by 1990 be only slightly higher, 28 percent, than under alternative I because the GDP would be substantially larger. The structure of investment would nevertheless be markedly different, with manufacturing investment taking a larger share of the total.

Alternative III: Accelerated Growth —Attainment of Perspective Plan Targets for Manufacturing

This alternative is designed to show what is necessary to achieve the long-term target that the perspective plan sets for growth of the manufacturing sector. This target is very ambitious. It is examined to provide some insight into what is required to achieve the government targets. Specifically this alternative is the same as alternative II, except that manufacturing investment is expected to grow even more rapidly. Thus it is assumed that manufacturing investment grows 17 percent a year, the rate required to achieve the government's target for growth of about 13 percent a year in manufacturing output during 1976–90. Under this alternative, fixed investment would increase more than 10 percent a year during 1976–90. The overall investment rate would reach 27 percent of an even larger GDP by 1990.

As this discussion and table A.1 indicate, the overall investment rate under the three alternatives does not significantly vary. It even is somewhat lower under alternative III than alternative II. There is, however, a substantial difference in the level and composition of investment under the three alternatives. In fact, the pattern of investment rates is the result of the substantially different composition of investment. Thus the increasing share of manufacturing investment, with lower ICORs than for other sectors, tends to lead to a lower investment rate in alternatives II and III. This is offset to some extent, however, by the relative increase in public investment in those alternatives. Because public investment is the same under alternatives II and III, the increasing share of manufacturing investment under alternative III is not offset, and the investment rate is somewhat lower as a result.

Macroeconomic and Sectoral Results of Alternative Strategies

The consequences of the three alternatives for overall growth and for individual sectors are summarized in table A.2. In output growth it can be seen that only alternative III matches the government's long-term GDP growth target of more than 8 percent a year. Under the assumptions of alternative I, the GDP growth rate is only 5.5 percent, significantly short of the government's target. Under alternative II, the GDP growth rate is 7.4 percent a year. In income, however, the three alternatives appear relatively more favorable. The commodity price projections by the World Bank indicate a 16 percent improvement in the terms of trade between 1975 and 1990.[2] It was projected in the third plan that there would be a 7 percent decline during 1976–80. If no further decline is assumed, the government's long-term output projection would imply growth in income of 8 percent a year; the World Bank's projections would respectively lead to income growth of 5.9 percent, 7.8 percent, and 9 percent for alternatives I, II, and III. In summary, the growth path under alternative II would fulfill the government's targets for income, but only a growth path close to that of alternative III could fulfill the government's targets for production and employment.

The significance of these different growth rates is more striking when the implied levels of per capita income are examined. In 1976 prices and exchange rates, Malaysia's per capita income in 1976 was about

2. All of that improvement occurred in 1976, when the terms of trade increased from 87.4 to 101.2 (1970 = 100). For 1976–90 the terms of trade are projected to remain relatively constant.

Table A.2. *Alternative Growth Strategies, 1976-90*

Item	Average annual rate of growth (percent)			
	Perspective plan	Alternative I	Alternative II	Alternative III
Gross domestic income	8.0[a]	5.9	7.8	9.0
Gross domestic product	8.2	5.5	7.4	8.6
Agriculture	5.3	4.3	5.3	5.6
Mining	5.0	3.4	3.4	3.4
Manufacturing	12.7	7.7	10.6	13.0
Utilities	9.7	9.7	10.2	10.4
Construction	8.3	7.4	9.6	10.5
Services	8.4	4.9	6.9	8.0

Note: All figures are in constant 1970 prices.
Sources: Third Malaysia Plan 1976-1980; World Bank estimates.
a. The third plan does not project gross domestic income for 1990. The 8 percent estimate assumes that there is no further loss in the terms of trade beyond the 7 percent decline projected by the third plan for 1976-80. If that rate of decline were to continue through to 1990, the growth of gross domestic income would be 7.6 percent a year.

US$910. Under alternative I this level would increase to about US$1,230 in 1976 prices in 1990; under alternative II it would reach US$1,600; under alternative III US$1,875. Thus the range of increase indicated by these alternatives is from 35 percent to more than 100 percent. Apart from the consequences for restructuring, this wide range in possible outcomes highlights the importance of the policy options facing Malaysia.

The sectoral growth rates under the projections of the perspective plan and the three alternative scenarios also differ considerably. Output in agriculture would—under all projections but especially alternative I—expand somewhat more slowly than the average of about 6 percent a year achieved during 1960-75.[3] First, even if the pace of land development were to remain constant over the period, the resulting increased output would become a smaller and smaller proportion of total output. Similarly, the benefits of the rubber-replanting program will begin to decline relatively as the proportion of acreage replanted with high-yielding clones increases. For example, if the targets of the third plan are met, less than 10 percent of the rubber acreage would still require re-

3. There is no consistent series of national income in constant prices extending back to 1960. This estimate of 6 percent is from the agricultural production index of the Food and Agriculture Organization of the United Nations for 1960-75.

planting in 1980. Second, production from forestry is expected to decelerate substantially (see chapter three). Third, most of the more obvious investments to increase rice yields have already been made. It was estimated that irrigation would by 1980 have been extended to most of the rice land best suited to double-cropping and that the further expansion of drainage and irrigation would be limited by lack of water and unsuitable topography (see chapter eight). For the alternatives of higher overall growth, the tendencies toward deceleration are at least partly compensated for by the demand-pull effects of higher income growth on the demand for such high-value products as vegetables, fruits, and livestock. For alternative I, the absence of these additional demand-pull effects explains why the agricultural growth rate is lower than that in the perspective plan, despite the similarity of assumptions for land development and other agricultural development. For alternative II, the demand growth is similar to that in the perspective plan, but land development and other agricultural programs are stepped up. The difference between alternatives II and III is the result of further impulses from the demand side.

The growth rate of 3.4 percent a year for mining is based on three assumptions: oil production will grow about 5 percent a year after reaching the target rate of 240,000 barrels a day in 1980; the production of liquefied natural gas will begin in 1983; these increases in production will be offset by a continuing sluggish growth in tin output (see chapter three). Because the prices are based on those in 1970, which predates the oil price increase, the weight given to the growth of oil production is much less than if 1976 prices were used. Thus, in relation to import capacity—the value of production deflated by the import price index— the growth of mining would be significantly higher, at 7.8 percent a year, during 1975–90.

The manufacturing growth rates, ranging from 7.7 percent to 13 percent, vary substantially. The reason is that the assumptions about investment in that sector are very different.[4] These long-term average

---

4. These estimates are based on those discussed earlier for manufacturing investment. For long-term projections, this procedure is appropriate. In the short term, however, the relation may be disturbed by variations in capacity use. For example, it has been reported that while manufacturers may be unwilling to invest, they are increasing production by using capital more efficiently—for example, by increasing from two to three shifts. To the extent this is occurring, the adverse consequences of low manufacturing investment will be ameliorated for production and employment. But with regard to the outlook for the longer term, this is not likely to be a panacea, because capital use has generally been high in Malaysia. The scope for increasing it further is therefore limited. Moreover, this

rates nevertheless mask a substantial change within the period. Under alternative I the growth decreases over the period such that manufacturing is growing only 6.3 percent a year in the latter half of the 1980s. Under alternative II the pattern is reversed: the growth of output gradually accelerates to 11.2 percent a year during 1985–90. Under alternative III the growth of manufacturing output reaches a peak of 16.3 percent a year during 1985–90. Under alternatives II and III, however, the rate of investment growth, if continued, would put manufacturing on a long-term growth path of about 12.6 percent a year by 1990.[5]

Under alternative I utilities are projected to grow at the same rate as in the perspective plan: 9.7 percent a year. The reasons are that this sector is largely in the public domain and the public investment in utilities is assumed to be the same as in the plan. Although it might appear inconsistent to have utilities growing so much faster than overall output under alternative I, given the low rate of electrification in the country, there is considerable backlog of demand that could be provided for before the increase in demand becomes a constraint on output growth. Under alternatives II and III it is assumed that public investment in utilities is increased to service the rapidly expanding manufacturing sector. Because it is assumed that about a quarter of the increase in public investment is directed toward this sector and that the ICOR is 7.5, the annual growth of utilities output is 10.2 percent under alternative II and 10.4 percent under alternative III.

As noted earlier, the growth of the construction sector is largely dependent on the growth of investment. Because gross investment grows relatively rapidly under all three alternatives—varying from about 7 percent to 10.5 percent a year—the growth of construction also is high, ranging from about 7 percent to 11 percent a year.

It is worth noting that the services sector is projected to grow slightly more slowly than GDP under the three alternatives, but slightly faster under the perspective plan. The change in the structure of demand accounts for almost all of this difference. The demand equation used to determine the output of services in the World Bank projections has an

---

is basically a once-and-for-all effect, which, following the recovery in manufacturing output during 1976 and 1977, may already have been exhausted.

5. The reason for these different patterns is that with a fixed ICOR the output growth gradually approaches the growth of investment. Because output growth initially is higher than the 5 to 6 percent growth in investment under alternative I, it thus declines over the period toward that level. Under alternatives II and III, on the other hand, the growth of investment is more rapid than the initial output growth; output growth thus increases over the period toward the rate of growth of investment.

implicit elasticity of unity, under the assumption of an unchanged structure of demand. But because the weight given to consumption in the demand for services is much greater than that for either exports or investment and because the share of consumption in aggregate demand decreases, the growth rate of the services sector is kept below that of GDP. The reason for the decline in the relative weight of consumption is that the share of taxes in GDP significantly increases over time in relation to the level implicit in the third plan. This increase is the result of the unanticipated increase in oil revenue from income taxes, royalties, and PETRONAS surpluses, as well as of an increase in export duties associated with the relatively favorable commodity price projections of the World Bank. These factors are only partially compensated for by higher public expenditure under alternatives II and III.

Another result that merits explanation is this: although the investment rates under the three alternatives are as high or higher than that in the government forecast, the GDP growth rates under alternatives I and II are lower. The principal reason for this result is the difference in composition of gross investment. The perspective plan does not disaggregate the rate of private investment, but it is implied that the level of investment in the manufacturing sector is high and growing, so as to sustain the high rate of growth in manufacturing value added. To achieve growth in manufacturing of 12.7 percent a year, manufacturing investment must grow at close to 13 percent a year. Because overall private investment is forecast by government to grow only 9 percent a year, the share of manufacturing in investment must be increasing while that of other sectors is decreasing. Because the ICOR is considerably less in manufacturing than in other sectors, the increase in output resulting from this structure of investment is considerably greater than that under a pattern in which the share of manufacturing investment is less, as in alternatives I and II. In the alternative projections by the World Bank, the investment in oil and such related areas as the liquefied natural gas plant, which have very high ICORS and which the perspective plan does not explicitly include, is assumed to be substantial. In addition, the World Bank projections allowed for considerable investment in building construction, which appears to have been less affected by the slowdown in private investment in 1975 and 1976. Furthermore all three alternatives, but especially II and III, have allowed for a continuing rapid increase in public investment because of the favorable resource position of government. Such investment tends, however, to have a longer gestation period and a higher ICOR than the average.

The implications of these projections for resources also are different (table A.3). For external resources the projected surpluses decline as the economic growth rate increases. Under alternative I the surplus in 1990 is more than 9 percent of GDP (in current prices); under alternative III this surplus is 6 percent. If it is assumed that net factor-service payments and transfers continue at their historic average of about −4 percent of GDP, the current account in the balance of payments would show a surplus of 5 percent under alternative I, a balance under alternative II, and a surplus of 2 percent under alternative III. Therefore external resources would be sufficient to finance the high growth alternatives.[6]

For public resources the substantial increase in revenue, largely from taxes and royalties on oil and natural gas, leads to a significant increase in the current surplus, an increase equivalent to about 5 percent of GDP under alternatives II and III. This increase would enable a significant increase in development expenditure and still enable a reduction in the overall deficit. Because of the good external prospects of Malaysia and the proven domestic borrowing capacity of the public sector (see chapter six), financing a deficit of 10 to 12 percent of GDP should be within the capacity of the public sector.

Other Possible Strategies

As is clear from the foregoing discussion, alternatives I and III span a considerable range in private investment activity, particularly manufacturing investment activity. It appears unlikely that government will allow this activity to fall below the level of alternative I or succeed in stimulating it beyond that of alternative III. Other possible strategies should therefore reflect alternative assumptions for the public sector or for a mix of the public and private sectors. For that mix, a decomposition of the differences between alternatives I and II, which reflect changes in the assumptions for both sectors, throws light on the relative influence of each. Such a decomposition reveals that, in moving from alternative I to alternative II, about 30 percent of the increase is the result of an expansion of government spending; the balance, about 70 percent, is the result of higher private investment. Thus, while an ex-

6. Although the current account would be in balance, some borrowing would be required to finance the required increase in foreign exchange reserves. Thus to maintain reserves equal to seven or eight months of imports, net borrowing would have to be equivalent to about 4 percent of GDP in 1990 under alternative II and about 2 percent under alternative III.

Table A.3. *Availability of Resources in Current Prices, 1971-75, 1975, 1976, and Projections for 1990*

Sector and item	Percentage of GDP			1990 Alternative I	
	1971–75	1975	1976	Billions of Malaysian dollars	Percentage of GDP
External resources[a]					
Exports	42.2	45.2	52.2	80.6	54.2
Imports	40.8	42.8	41.0	67.0	45.1
Resource balance	1.4	2.4	11.2	13.6	9.1
Public resources[b]					
Revenue	24.1	26.2	25.6	48.6	32.7
Operating expenditure	23.4	25.2	24.3	33.4	22.5
Current surplus	0.7	1.0	1.3	15.2	10.2
Development expenditure	10.7	12.3	11.8	28.2	18.9
Overall balance	−10.0	−11.3	−10.5	−13.0	−8.7

Sources: Historical figures are World Bank estimates based on data supplied by the Treasury, the Economic Planning Unit, and the Department of Statistics; projections are World Bank estimates.

a. Uses national-accounts concepts, which differ somewhat from balance-of-payments concepts. Exports and imports include nonfactor services.

b. The model uses national-accounts concepts of public consumption and public in-

panded government program can have a significant effect on the growth of income, it has much less potential for increasing income than for fostering a recovery in manufacturing investment. Still, if government succeeds in giving its additional expenditure a specific antipoverty focus, the effect on poverty alleviation may be significant.

Implications for the Targets of the New Economic Policy

As can be seen in table A.4, the various growth alternatives have very different implications for the growth of employment and productivity.[7] In the low-growth forecast of alternative I, the implied growth

7. The employment implications of the three alternative growth paths were derived in the following manner. First, the growth rates of labor force and employment in the

1990				
Alternative II		Alternative III		
Billions of Malaysian dollars	Percentage of GDP	Billions of Malaysian dollars	Percentage of GDP	Sector and item
				External resources[a]
91.9	47.9	104.1	46.1	Exports
82.9	43.2	90.2	40.0	Imports
9.0	4.7	13.9	6.1	Resource balance
				Public resources[b]
59.5	31.0	67.4	29.9	Revenue
49.8	25.9	57.2	25.3	Operating expenditure
9.7	5.1	10.2	4.6	Current surplus
32.2	16.8	32.2	14.4	Development expenditure
−22.5	−11.7	22.0	−9.7	Overall balance

vestment, which are considerably different from the concepts of operating expenditure and development expenditure used for budgeting in the public sector. The estimates for the public sector are therefore based on the projected change in public investment and consumption and then inflated by 38 percent and 44 percent respectively to arrive at the budget concepts of development and operating expenditure. The inflation factors are derived from the actual relations of these variables during 1971–76.

of productivity is substantially below the plan targets in all sectors, especially in agriculture, in which employment grows 3.5 percent a year and productivity grows less than 1 percent a year.[8] In alternative

---

perspective plan were taken as given. Second, the employment elasticities from the plan for all sectors but agriculture were multiplied by the growth rates of output for the various sectors to determine employment for those sectors. Third, given total employment, agricultural employment was determined as a residual. In Malaysia's circumstances, and given the high employment elasticity already assigned to the services sector in the plan, it appears reasonable to let agriculture be a residual, rather than services, for example. Thus a greater or lesser availability of jobs in the industrial and services sectors would for the most part result in less or more labor remaining in agriculture. An alternative might be to allow unemployment to be the residual.

8. As noted above, the figure of 3.5 percent is residually determined. If unemployment were allowed to increase, there would be a corresponding reduction in the required absorption of labor in the agricultural sector. Although it is likely that there would be

Table A.4. *Growth of Employment and Productivity, by Sector, Projections for 1976-90*

Sector	Average annual rate of growth (percent)			
	Perspective plan	Alternative I	Alternative II	Alternative III
	Employment			
Agriculture	1.0	3.5	2.2	1.0
Mining	0.5	0.3	0.3	0.3
Manufacturing	6.8	4.1	5.7	7.0
Utilities	4.3	5.3	5.6	5.8
Construction	4.7	4.1	5.4	5.9
Services	4.6	2.7	3.8	4.4
Total	3.2	3.2	3.2	3.2
	Output per worker			
Agriculture	4.3	0.8	3.0	4.6
Mining	4.5	3.1	3.1	3.1
Manufacturing	5.5	3.4	4.6	5.6
Utilities	5.2	4.2	4.4	4.4
Construction	3.4	3.2	4.0	4.3
Services	4.1	2.1	3.0	3.4
Total	4.8	2.2	4.1	5.2

Sources: Third Malaysia Plan, 1976-1980; World Bank estimates.

II the productivity growth rates are much closer to the plan targets; in alternative III productivity growth exceeds the plan target.

Reducing Poverty

The different effect on poverty reduction of the various growth rates of productivity would obviously be considerable. To measure precisely the extent of this effect is impossible without information on the distributions of poverty incomes and growth benefits. Economic research of this critical issue is just beginning, however, and this entire process still is shrouded in considerable mystery. Analysis of cross-sectional data of sixty countries by Ahluwalia confirms the Kuznets hypothesis that there typically is a deterioration in the distribution of income in the

some spillover into unemployment, the negative impact on poverty reduction would be increased, not lessened. Thus the assumption used in this analysis is, if anything, an understatement of the negative effect of lower growth on poverty.

early stages of development and a reversal of this trend in later stages.[9] His analysis of turning points would seem to indicate that Malaysia has passed the initial phase and that a deterioration in income distribution is not likely. On the other hand, the analysis suggests that the estimated improvement in income distribution with greater levels of development is much less steep than the initial decline. This finding, together with the obvious limitations of using cross-sectional analysis in these circumstances, makes it difficult to quantify the exact relation between growth and the distribution of income in Malaysia over a long period. For this analysis it is assumed that there would be no change from the distribution of income in 1970. On this basis, it is possible to estimate roughly the impact on poverty reduction.

The estimates suggest that under the lower growth of alternative I there would be almost twice as many households in poverty in 1990 as are projected in the perspective plan (table A.5). Under alternative II the incidence of poverty would be reduced to about 19.4 percent; under alternative III to 13.4 percent. Although these estimates are merely illustrative, they indicate that rapid growth is essential to achieving the targets of the New Economic Policy for reducing poverty.

Restructuring Society

On the basis of sectoral employment growth rates discussed above, the estimates for restructuring employment have been re-evaluated.[10] The analysis proceeds by accepting the estimates of labor force and employment growth in the perspective plan and calculating the growth rates of sectoral employment under the various alternatives. Next the growth rates of employment of Malays and non-Malays required to achieve restructuring targets by sector in industry and services are calculated. Employment by race in agriculture is then determined as a residual.

Under alternative I, the low-growth projection, satisfying the employment objectives by race in industry and services implies holding the growth of non-Malay employment in these sectors substantially below the growth of labor force (table A.6). Looked at from a different

9. Montek S. Ahluwalia, "Inequality, Poverty and Development," *Journal of Development Economics*, vol. 3 (1976), 307–42.

10. For purposes of comparison with the perspective plan, the discussion of restructuring employment centers on Peninsular Malaysia.

Table A.5. *Incidence of Poverty in Agriculture and Nonagriculture, Peninsular Malaysia, 1975, and Illustrative Projections for 1990*

Sector or projection and sector	Thousands of households	Thousands of poor households	Percentage incidence of poverty
1975			
Agriculture	915	577	63.0
Nonagriculture	987	258	26.1
Total	1,902	835	43.9
1990			
Perspective plan			
Agriculture	909	242	26.6
Nonagriculture	2,162	272	12.6
Total	3,071	514	16.7
Alternative I			
Agriculture	1,532	801	52.3
Nonagriculture	1,539	183	11.9
Total	3,071	984	32.0
Alternative II			
Agriculture	1,251	424	33.9
Nonagriculture	1,820	171	9.4
Total	3,071	595	19.4
Alternative III			
Agriculture	1,042	250	24.0
Nonagriculture	2,029	160	7.9
Total	3,071	410	13.4

Note: The estimates for alternatives I, II, and III are based on the distribution of rural and urban income in 1970, rebased to 1975 on a split into agricultural and nonagricultural income. The income estimates take into account changes in the terms of trade, and household growth is assumed to be proportional to employment growth in each sector. It is assumed in the calculations that income gains by sector are proportionately distributed to income classes.

Sources: Third Malaysia Plan, 1976–1980; World Bank estimates.

perspective, the targets would mean that almost 75 percent of the new jobs in industry and more than 60 percent of new jobs in services would go to Malays (see table A.7). This outcome would lead to either substantial reverse migration of non-Malays to the agricultural sector (as is implicit in tables A.6 and A.7) or, if the racial objective target in agri-

Table A.6. *Growth of Employment, by Race, Peninsular Malaysia, Projections for 1976–90*

Sector and race	Average annual rate of growth (percent)			
	Perspective plan	Alternative I	Alternative II	Alternative III
Agriculture	1.0	3.7	2.2	1.0
Malay	0.4	2.7	1.4	0.3
Non-Malay	2.1	5.6	3.8	2.1
Industry	4.9	3.3	4.8	5.7
Malay	7.5	5.9	7.3	8.2
Non-Malay	3.1	1.6	2.9	3.8
Services	4.9	2.7	3.7	4.4
Malay	5.8	3.6	4.7	5.3
Non-Malay	4.1	1.9	3.0	3.6
Total	3.4	3.4	3.4	3.4
Malay	3.5	3.5	3.5	3.5
Non-Malay	3.2	3.2	3.2	3.2
Labor force	3.1	3.1	3.1	3.1
Malay	3.3	3.3	3.3	3.3
Non-Malay	2.9	2.9	2.9	2.9

Sources: Third Malaysia Plan, 1976–1980; World Bank estimates.

Table A.7. *Implications for Restructuring Employment, Peninsular Malaysia, 1976–90*
(percent)

Item	Agriculture	Industry	Services	Total
Malay share in 1975	67.3	36.5	42.3	52.6
Malay share in incremental employment, 1976–90				
Perspective plan	23.7	66.2	54.2	55.2
Alternative I	44.1	74.6	60.8	55.2
Alternative II	38.9	67.1	56.6	55.2
Alternative III	20.3	63.7	55.1	55.2
Targeted Malay share in 1990	61.4[a]	51.9	48.4	53.6

Sources: Third Malaysia Plan, 1976–1980; World Bank estimates.
a. Because agriculture is a residual, the Malay share varies as follows under each alternative: alternative I, 57.9 percent; alternative II, 59.2 percent; alternative III, 61.2 percent.

culture were to be achieved, widespread non-Malay unemployment. The first of these outcomes does not seem feasible; the second obviously could not be tolerated within the framework of the New Economic Policy, which emphasizes that gains of one group are not to be at the direct expense of another group, but are to come from a redistribution of growth benefits. The clear implication then is that by providing for employment growth of non-Malays in industry and services, growth that is at least equal to their increase in the labor force, the racial restructuring targets could not be met. Under alternative II these negative results would be considerably ameliorated, but some pressure in the non-Malay labor market would still exist and some migration to agriculture by non-Malays would still be implied. To achieve reasonably the targets for employment by race, it is imperative that the economy grow at least as fast as is implied in the growth projection of alternative II; achieving the accelerated growth of alternative III would fully satisfy the targets.

The implications of the various growth alternatives for achieving the targets for racial restructuring by occupational category are not as straightforward. The reason is that the perspective plan assumes some significant changes in the occupational pattern within sectors over the period. Because the focus of much of the occupational restructuring effort is to increase the Malay share in the two highest-level occupational categories in the secondary sector—professional and technical, and administrative and managerial—an examination of the effect on these two job categories highlights the principal issues involved.

By looking first at the category of professional and technical workers, it can be seen that the perspective plan projects a substantial increase in the relative share of jobs in that category, from 2.5 percent in 1975 to 4.3 percent in 1990 (table A.8). The effect of such an increase is twofold. First, combined with the target of increasing the Malay share in this category from 40 percent to 57 percent, the growth of Malay jobs required in this category is very high—11.4 percent a year over the period. That growth concurrently allows for an increase of 6.5 percent a year in non-Malay jobs in this category. The second effect is to dilute substantially the effect of slower industrial growth on meeting this target. For example, under the low-growth alternative non-Malay employment growth in this category, at 4.9 percent a year, still is substantially above labor force growth. This increase in the relative share of the professional and technical category essentially provides the cushion for slower growth.

A constant or declining share in the occupational structure would

Table A.8. *Restructuring of the Secondary Sector, by Occupation, Peninsular Malaysia, 1976–90*
(percent)

Item	Professional and technical workers		Administrative and managerial workers	
	1975	1990	1975	1990
Projected share of jobs in sector	2.5	4.3	2.3	2.1
Perspective plan target for Malay share	40.0	56.6	21.7	43.2
	1976–90		*1976–90*	
Malay share of additional jobs required to meet target				
Perspective plan	63.0		66.6	
Alternative I	65.6		84.1	
Alternative II	63.2		69.3	
Alternative III	62.1		62.7	
Average annual rate of growth required to meet targets				
Perspective plan				
Malay	11.4		9.4	
Non-Malay	6.5		2.3	
Alternative I				
Malay	9.8		7.7	
Non-Malay	4.9		0.7	
Alternative II				
Malay	11.3		9.1	
Non-Malay	6.4		1.9	
Alternative III				
Malay	12.1		10.1	
Non-Malay	7.3		2.8	

Sources: Third Malaysia Plan, 1976–1980; World Bank estimates.

have much more severe consequences, as is clear from examining the administrative and managerial category. The perspective plan projects a slight decline in the relative share of this category, from 2.3 percent to 2.1 percent. That decline, when combined with the target of substantially increasing the Malay share, seriously constrains the possible growth of non-Malay jobs in this category. Thus, even under the accelerated growth of alternative III, the growth of non-Malay employment is below the growth of labor force; under the moderate growth of alternative I, the growth of non-Malay employment would be restricted to less than 1 percent a year if the target were to be met. Consequently, one conclusion is that restructuring the occupational categories is considerably easier, in allowing for non-Malay growth, if there is a significant increase in the relative size of the occupational category—in the group of professional and technical workers, for example. This is a double-edged sword, however. Such an increase also requires significantly more rapid growth of Malay employment in these occupations. That growth would in turn require an intensified effort to provide Malays with the requisite education and skills.

Calculation of Probabilities of Supply, Demand, and Consumption: Public Utility Services

To CARRY OUT THE ANALYSIS of supply, demand, and consumption, a linear regression model was used, in which the basic building block is the equation:

$$(1) \qquad P^C = (P^S)(P^D).$$

The probability of a household consuming the service, P^C, is the product of its probability of effectively demanding the service, P^D, given that it has access, P^S. The probabilities of access and demand are estimated independently. Because I rely on linear regression, the first estimation equation is:

$$(2) \qquad P^S = s_0 + s_1 X_1 + s_2 X_2 + \cdots + s_k X_k.$$

The independent variables X_1 to X_k are oriented toward explaining access: for example, townsize, regions, subsistence income. For any given household, the value of the dependent variable is zero or unity (if it is on the supply), although the probability will normally be between zero and unity. The effective demand equation is:

$$(3) \qquad P^D = d_0 + d_1 X_1 + d_2 X_2 + \cdots + d_k X_k.$$

Hence the independent variables are those oriented toward explaining demand: for example, household per capita income. Unlike equation (2), equation (3) includes only the partition of households which have access or are "on the supply." Thus it measures the probability of P^D, given that the household in question has access.[1]

---

1. The technique does not constrain the dependent variable within the range of probability, although for household vectors of interest, values greater than zero and less than

Figure B.1. *Partitioning of Sample by Characteristics*

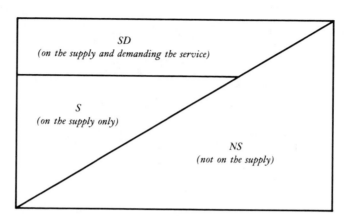

In rigor P^C should be estimated as the product of equations (2) and (3). This implies a formulation involving quadratic and other nonlinear terms. Experimenting with this approach led to no stronger but far more complicated results than independent linear estimation of P^C. Consequently I have opted for the simpler linear approach in the analysis that follows. With P^C as the regressand, the equation for probability of consumption is:

$$(4) \qquad P^C = c_0 + c_1X_1 + c_2X_2 + \cdots + c_kX_k.$$

As indicated, even if the residual term in the regression equation is zero, the fact of a household's access or nonaccess to a service will necessarily differ from its estimated probability of access, P^S, unless the probability itself is zero or unity. This also is true of P^D. For the sample as a whole, however, the shares of households with the characteristics $S=1$ or $D=1$—that is, being on the supply or having effective demand—equal the means for P^S and P^D. Thus I can partition the sample as in figure B.1 (the relative proportions in the rectangle have no significance). Then for the sample as a whole, the means (and probabilities for each household at random) are:

$$(5) \qquad P^S = (S + SD)/(S + SD + NS)$$

---

one are rare. A common solution to this problem—and the one used here—is to define negative values as zero and those exceeding unity as one.

(6) $$P^D = SD/(S + SD)$$

(7) $$P^C = (P^S)(P^D) = SD/(S + SD + NS)$$

I can usefully amplify this discussion with illustrations from the case of electricity. From the perspective of the household, the degree of access is measured by the cost to the household of connection. (This concept is very different from economic cost.) As the range of access is increased, the costs to households increase. Ideally I should define all households whose access costs are below a well-defined cutoff cost to the household as having access. It is impossible, however, to generate data consistent with such a criterion. As a substitute I define the cutoff point in relation to the needed length of line. But this is a rough substitute. Note further that if the economic costs of connecting to the supply network are equal, the connection fee borne by the individual household or village will probably be greater under autogeneration than under supply by the National Electricity Board. Thus the objective situation in terms of connection fees facing households that are to be considered on the supply may substantially differ, even if economic connection costs are identical. But because I define all households within a maximum length of connecting line as being on the supply, the economic connection costs themselves will vary substantially.

The means of the connection costs and their variance are a function of the cutoff point for supply. If the cutoff cost is extremely low—for example, if only urban communities with complete electrification are considered to be on the supply—the mean connection cost will necessarily be very low and P^D will be correspondingly higher. This relation is consistent with economic theory, which predicts that P^D is a negative function of connection costs: that is, households are more likely to purchase low-cost electricity than high-cost electricity. The outcome also conforms to the mathematics of the model. Because P^C is well defined, reducing the range of access—that is, reducing P^S—necessarily increases P^D.

A simple graphic illustration can be useful. In figure B.2 the vertical axis measures probability within a range of zero to one. The horizontal axis measures marginal connection costs per household (lump sum plus present value of any periodic payments). For a given community at a given time, I can then define the P^S schedule as a function of marginal connection costs. I define as being on the supply the maximum proportion of households that can be supplied with electricity, other things being equal, at the given marginal connection cost per household. In moving up and down the P^S schedule, the only thing that changes is the

Figure B.2. *Probabilities of Supply, Demand, and Consumption in Relation to Marginal Connection Costs*

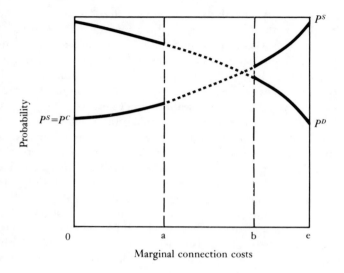

Marginal connection costs

Table B.1. *Percentage of Households Supplied and Demanding Electricity, and Corresponding Mean Probabilities, Peninsular Malaysia, 1974*

Location	On the supply	Service demanded	Off the supply	P^S	P^D	P^C	Total
Urban	41	34	2	95	82	78	44
Rural	39	22	18	70	57	39	56
Total	80	56	20	80	70	56	100

Source: Distributive Effects of Public Spending Survey (see note 2 in chapter five).

definition of being on the supply in relation to the marginal connection cost per household. By the time that cost is defined as e, all households are included as being on the supply and P^S equals 1. Because P^C equals the proportion of households already consuming electricity, their connection costs necessarily are zero. Thus, if the marginal connection cost is zero, $P^S = P^C$. Because $(P^S)(P^D) = P^C$ and P^C is a constant, corresponding to the P^S schedule, there is a "reflected" P^D schedule. At the extremes, if $P^S = P^C$, $P^D = 1$; if $P^D = P^C$, $P^S = 1$.

The rationale for disaggregating P^C into $(P^S)(P^D)$ rests on the belief that in Malaysia as elsewhere, marginal connection costs are discontin-

Table B.2. *Electricity: Estimates of the Linear Probability Function, Peninsular Malaysia, 1974*
(*t* scores in parentheses)

Item	Mean	P^S	P^D	P^C	Monthly bill
		Total sample			
Constant	—	0.58	− 0.03	− 0.14	−20.68
		(8.35)	(0.30)	(1.77)	(9.97)
Log of household per capita income	4.09	0.04	0.14	0.14	4.87
		(2.88)	(9.03)	(9.90)	(13.29)
Number in household	5.83	0.01	0.03	0.03	0.92
		(3.18)	(6.92)	(7.63)	(10.00)
Age of household head	45.88	0.0008	−0.001	−0.0006	0.05
		(1.16)	(1.39)	(0.81)	(2.33)
Subsistence income	17.78	−0.002	−0.002	−0.002	—a
		(5.21)	(4.25)	(6.04)	
Income from owner-occupied house	32.95	−0.00004	0.0003	0.0001	0.01
		(0.27)	(0.21)	(0.68)	(4.12)
Region					
Selangor	0.17	0.03	−0.02	0.002	−0.84
		(1.13)	(0.75)	(0.11)	(0.99)
North	0.29	−0.12	−0.12	−0.13	1.58
		(4.86)	(3.63)	(5.01)	(2.24)
Race					
Chinese	0.31	0.08	0.13	0.16	−0.89
		(3.44)	(4.58)	(6.12)	(1.52)
Indian	0.10	0.13	0.13	0.18	−0.96
		(4.22)	(3.52)	(5.22)	(1.04)
Size of community					
Metropolitan	0.16	0.07	0.07	0.13	3.45
		(2.23)	(2.06)	(3.68)	(4.93)
Large urban	0.15	0.15	0.11	0.17	1.88
		(5.14)	(3.15)	(5.35)	(2.37)
Small urban	0.12	0.12	0.07	0.13	—a
		(4.21)	(1.96)	(4.05)	
Poverty occupation	0.34	−0.17	−0.17	−0.21	1.73
		(7.28)	(5.36)	(7.93)	(1.99)
Mean	0.34	0.80	0.70	0.56	10.18
R^2	—	0.27	0.30	0.42	0.40
Number of households	1,462	1,462	1,170	1,462	737

— Not applicable.
Source: Regression analysis of data from the Distributive Effects of Public Spending Survey.
a. No relation.

uous over much of their hypothetical range in the short run. At marginal costs less than a, connection can be thought of as being to the existing network, including autogeneration. But at marginal costs of b, the choice would be the large public alternative, for which connection charges are far higher because of the length of line, difficult terrain, and so forth. Between a and b, there would be a technological void.[2]

Because of these difficulties I also considered an alternative: only nonusing households that claimed access, were urban, and needed a connecting line less than a mile in length were defined as being on the supply. Rural households claiming access with a connecting line of a mile or less were classified as being in limbo (17 percent of the sample). By using this definition, it was found that the regression results with P^s as the regressand were similar to those for the extended definition. The R^2 increased to 0.46 in the limbo case, compared with 0.27 in the extended case. But the coefficients and signs of the independent variables were very similar. The t scores were higher but largely congruent with those for the extended definition. This outcome was a factor in using the extended definition in the analysis. Table B.1 presents the basic dimensions of the results using the extended definition.

The regression results from using this model are given for electricity in table B.2. The results for pure water and flush systems are in the source cited in note 2. For all three utilities the values of R^2 for the various regressions nearly always are significant, as are the regression parameters for the log of household per capita income, the number in household, and subsistence income. The variables for race, residence, and region, as well as poverty occupation, are all dummies, with rural Malays as the omitted group.

2. For detailed discussion of similar procedures for estimating access in the cases of water and sewage disposal, see Jacob Meerman, *Public Expenditure in Malaysia: Who Benefits and Why?* (New York: Oxford University Press, 1979), ch. 6.

᠎᠎᠎᠎᠎᠎᠎᠎᠎᠎᠎᠎᠎᠎᠎᠎᠎᠎᠎᠎᠎᠎᠎᠎᠎᠎᠎᠎᠎᠎᠎

Social and Economic Statistics

THE GENERAL MACROECONOMIC INFORMATION in this appendix is presented, when feasible, as time series for the 1961–76 period. For instances in which such general information has already been presented in the text—such as for employment, poverty, and saving and investment—the data are not repeated here. The basic official sources for social and economic statistics on Malaysia are the following: *Economic Report*, published annually by the Ministry of Finance; *Annual Report* and *Quarterly Economic Bulletin*, published by the Bank Negara; and *Monthly Statistical Bulletin*, published by the Department of Statistics.

The national accounts of Malaysia are in a period of transition to the new United Nations System of National Accounts. There consequently is no consistent official series of national accounts for the entire 1961–76 period. Because such a series is critical for historical analysis, the World Bank made provisional working estimates to serve as the basis for the analysis in this report. These estimates are reproduced in tables C.4–C.6. The data on expenditure in table C.4 are a synthetic series linking the former series of national accounts for 1961–70 to the new system of national accounts for 1971–76. This link was made in current prices, in which both series are available. To estimate the constant price series for 1961–70, the linked current-price series was adjusted by the national accounts deflators of the United Nations for Malaysia.

Estimating a consistent synthetic series for GDP by industrial origin is more difficult because the estimates under the former system are only in current prices; the estimates under the new system, only in constant prices. Thus the data in table C.5, which covers the 1961–70 period, are reported only in current prices. That series has nevertheless been linked to the new estimates of national accounts and, to ensure consistency with the new format, rebased from factor cost to market prices by allocating indirect taxes among the various sectors. The series for 1971–76 in table C.6 is in constant prices estimated under the new system.

Because of the numerous simplifying assumptions used to estimate these national accounts, not too much significance should be placed on any single number. Instead the data should be considered as indicating broad, long-term trends.

Table C.1. *Important Growth Rates, 1961–70, 1970–76, and 1961–76*

Item	Average annual rate of growth (percent)		
	1961–70	1970–76	1961–76
Population	2.8	2.6	2.7
Gross national product	6.4	7.7	6.7
Consumption	4.7	6.8	5.4
Investment	6.7	9.4	8.7
Exports	6.0	7.9	6.4
Imports	2.9	6.9	4.7
Gross domestic product[a]	6.3	7.8	6.8
Agriculture	5.8	5.5	5.7
Industry	7.6	9.2	8.0
Services	5.5	8.5	6.5
Consumer prices	1.1	7.7	3.0
Money supply[b]	9.9	21.5	13.9

Note: Unless otherwise noted, the growth rates are in real terms. Except for the growth of population, which is based on point-to-point calculations, the growth rates are estimated by the least squares method.

Sources: Computed from other tables in this appendix, with the exception of value added in agriculture for 1961–70, which is based on nominal value added in agriculture in table C.5 and deflated by World Bank estimates of the agricultural price index.

   a. At market prices.

   b. Includes quasi money.

Table C.2. *Population and Vital Statistics, 1961–75*

Year	Population[a] (millions)	Birth rate[b] per thousand	Death rate[b] per thousand	Infant mortality rate per thousand live births[b]
1961	8.4	41.8	9.2	59.7
1962	8.7	40.3	9.3	59.3
1963	8.9	39.4	8.9	56.8
1964	9.2	39.1	8.0	48.4
1965	9.5	36.7	7.9	50.0
1966	9.7	37.3	7.6	48.0
1967	10.0	35.3	7.5	45.1
1968	10.3	35.4	7.6	42.2
1969	10.5	33.3	7.3	43.2
1970	10.8	32.5	7.0	40.8
1971	11.1	33.0	6.9	38.5
1972	11.4	32.0	6.6	37.9
1973	11.7	30.7	6.6	38.5
1974	12.0	30.9	6.3	35.4
1975	12.3	30.3	6.2	33.2

Note: The figures in this table are based on revised population estimates for 1970, estimates which have not been consistently adopted in all official publications. There consequently are small discrepancies between this table and some official publications and between those official publications as well.

Sources: Infant mortality from Department of Statistics, *Monthly Statistical Bulletin, Peninsular Malaysia* (December 1975 and June 1978). Other estimates for 1961–70 are from idem, "Revised Inter-censal Population Estimates, Malaysia" (Kuala Lumpur, 1974; processed). Other estimates for 1971–75 are from idem, "Vital Statistics, Malaysia," as reported in National Family Planning Board, *The Malaysian Family Planning Programme* (Kuala Lumpur, 1978); Department of Statistics, "Annual Statistical Bulletin, Sarawak, 1976" (Kuching, 1977; processed); and idem, "Monthly Statistics, Sabah" (Kota Kinabalu, July 1976; processed).

    a. At midyear.

    b. Peninsular Malaysia only.

Table C.3. *Estimates of Population, by Race and Region, 1975*

Race	Peninsular Malaysia		Sabah		Sarawak		Total	
	Millions of persons	Percentage composition	Millions of persons	Percentage composition	Millions of persons	Percentage composition	Millions of persons	Percentage composition
Malay	5.5	53	...	5	0.2	19	5.8	47
Other indigenous[a]	...	...	0.5	61	0.6	49	1.0	8
Chinese	3.7	36	0.2	20	0.3	31	4.2	34
Indians	1.1	10	—[b]	—[b]	—[b]	—[b]	1.1	9
Others	0.1	1	0.1	14	...	1	0.2	2
Total	10.4	100	0.8	100	1.1	100	12.3	100

... Zero or negligible.
Sources: Government of Malaysia, *Mid-term Review of the Third Malaysia Plan, 1976–1980* (Kuala Lumpur: Government Press, 1978); Department of Statistics, "Annual Statistical Bulletin, Sarawak, 1976" (Kuching, 1977; processed); idem, "Monthly Statistics, Sabah" (Kota Kinabalu, July 1976; processed).
   a. Kadazans, Muruts, Bajaus, Melanaus, Sea Dayaks, Land Dayaks, and other indigenous peoples.
   b. Included under "Others."

Table C.4. *Expenditure on Gross Domestic Product, 1961-76*

Item	1961	1962	1963	1964	1965	1966	1967
	Millions of current Malaysian dollars						
Consumption	5,437	5,725	6,197	6,664	7,096	7,592	7,977
Government	829	892	1,029	1,201	1,341	1,522	1,562
Private	4,608	4,833	5,168	5,463	5,755	6,070	6,415
Gross domestic investment	1,154	1,415	1,465	1,541	1,674	1,777	1,901
Exports	3,403	3,424	3,513	3,609	4,063	4,157	4,000
Imports	3,022	3,242	3,380	3,467	3,658	3,771	3,760
Gross domestic product	6,972	7,322	7,795	8,347	9,175	9,755	10,118
Net factor income							
from abroad	−206	−153	−171	−227	−264	−240	−115
Gross national product	6,766	7,169	7,624	8,120	8,911	9,515	10,003
	Millions of constant 1970 Malaysian dollars						
Consumption	6,072	6,385	6,691	7,123	7,565	7,981	8,092
Government	1,000	1,057	1,171	1,352	1,468	1,634	1,646
Private	5,072	5,328	5,520	5,771	6,097	6,347	6,446
Gross domestic investment	1,171	1,406	1,487	1,517	1,681	1,783	1,908
Exports	3,244	3,400	3,599	3,474	3,762	3,997	4,211
Imports	3,422	3,672	3,706	3,611	3,851	3,888	3,958
Gross domestic product	7,065	7,519	8,071	8,503	9,157	9,873	10,253
Net factor income							
from abroad	−206	−153	−171	−227	−274	−240	−115
Gross national product	6,859	7,366	7,900	8,276	8,883	9,633	10,138

Source: World Bank estimates based on estimates by the Department of Statistics of national accounts for Malaysia for 1961-70 under the former system of national accounts and the new system for 1971-76. For a discussion of method, see the introduction to this appendix.

a. Provisional.

1968	1969	1970	1971	1972 [a]	1973 [a]	1974 [a]	1975 [a]	1976 [a]
			Millions of current Malaysian dollars					
8,216	8,656	9,255	10,081	11,347	13,369	16,303	17,107	18,807
1,599	1,674	1,890	2,170	2,738	2,919	3,516	3,924	4,178
6,617	6,982	7,365	7,911	8,609	10,450	12,787	13,183	14,629
1,981	1,864	2,438	2,688	3,174	4,222	6,512	4,986	5,865
4,407	5,295	5,367	5,242	5,111	7,766	10,981	10,092	14,493
4,050	4,157	4,807	5,056	5,412	6,735	10,938	9,853	11,385
10,554	11,658	12,253	12,955	14,220	18,622	22,858	22,332	27,780
−120	−276	−355	−363	−366	−629	−998	−903	−947
10,434	11,382	11,898	12,592	13,854	17,993	21,860	21,429	26,833
			Millions of constant 1970 Malaysian dollars					
8,294	8,758	9,255	9,809	10,557	11,458	12,648	12,817	13,475
1,650	1,694	1,890	2,078	2,429	2,540	2,919	3,117	3,232
6,644	7,064	7,365	7,731	8,128	8,918	9,729	9,700	10,243
1,990	1,871	2,438	2,583	2,888	3,575	4,702	3,501	3,906
4,879	5,141	5,367	5,480	5,581	6,384	7,359	7,123	8,362
4,091	4,157	4,807	4,856	4,788	5,513	7,482	6,076	6,646
11,072	11,613	12,253	13,016	14,238	15,904	17,227	17,365	19,097
−120	−276	−355	−349	−324	−515	−683	−557	−553
10,952	11,337	11,898	12,667	13,914	15,389	16,544	16,808	18,544

Table C.5. *Gross Domestic Product by Industrial Origin, 1961–70*
(millions of Malaysian dollars in current prices)

Sector or item	1961	1962	1963	1964
Agriculture	2,684	2,675	2,742	2,767
Mining	424	537	575	690
Manufacturing	591	655	731	846
Construction	235	294	332	358
Utilities	88	97	110	127
Transport	343	366	385	416
Trade	1,338	1,399	1,515	1,530
Other services	1,269	1,299	1,405	1,613
GDP at market prices	6,972	7,322	7,795	8,347
Indirect taxes	1,053	1,088	1,144	1,190
GDP at factor cost	5,919	6,234	6,651	7,157

Source: Same as for table C.4.

1965	1966	1967	1968	1969	1970
2,851	3,083	3,133	3,246	3,776	3,915
787	814	702	630	723	768
935	1,030	1,155	1,223	1,490	1,663
378	393	422	426	431	471
144	162	181	199	213	225
456	470	495	532	541	575
1,673	1,746	1,873	1,992	2,042	2,138
1,951	2,057	2,157	2,306	2,442	2,498
9,175	9,755	10,118	10,554	11,658	12,253
1,604	1,679	1,567	1,682	1,768	1,801
7,571	8,076	8,551	8,872	9,890	10,452

Table C.6. *Gross Domestic Product by Industrial Origin, 1971–76*
(millions of Malaysian dollars in constant 1970 prices)

Sector or item	1971	1972[a]	1973[a]	1974[a]	1975[a]	1976[a]
Agriculture	3,852	4,146	4,634	4,954	4,804	5,270
Mining	834	889	852	796	792	948
Manufacturing	1,858	2,047	2,508	2,768	2,850	3,377
Construction	541	571	651	729	654	713
Utilities	238	275	304	337	365	400
Transport	632	720	827	947	1,071	1,153
Trade	1,579	1,695	1,874	2,025	2,019	2,196
Other services[b]	3,482	3,895	4,254	4,671	4,810	5,040
GDP at market prices	13,016	14,238	15,904	17,227	17,365	19,097
Indirect taxes	1,873	2,116	2,481	2,806	2,573	3,058
GDP at factor cost	11,143	12,122	13,423	14,421	14,792	16,039

Source: Department of Statistics provisional estimates under the new system of national accounts.
a. Provisional.
b. Includes import duties.

Table C.7. *Consolidated Financial Position of the Public Sector, 1966–76*
(millions of Malaysian dollars)

Item	1966	1967	1968	1969
Revenue and Expenditure[b]				
Government revenue	1,964	2,187	2,289	2,514
Government current expenditure	1,804	1,991	2,010	2,142
Current surplus	160	196	279	372
Public authorities' current surplus	54	58	67	80
Public sector's surplus[c]	214	254	346	452
Public sector development expenditure	841	821	854	867
Federal and state governments	724	698	728	761
Public authorities[c]	117	123	126	106
Overall deficit	627	567	508	415
Sources of Finance				
Net domestic borrowing[d]	287	349	428	379
Net foreign borrowing	35	135	104	180
Special receipts[e]	93	57	46	29
Asset changes[f]	212	26	−70	−173

Sources: Ministry of Finance, *Economic Report*, 1976–77 and 1977–78.

a. Preliminary.

b. The telecommunications account is, from 1971 onward, included in public authorities and not in the central government accounts.

c. Adjusted for transfers between government and public authorities.

d. Includes borrowing from federal funds.

e. Defense and economic grants; 1976 includes M$265 million from an IMF loan.

f. A minus sign indicates an increase. Because of some accounting discrepancy, asset changes for the consolidated public sector do not equal the sum of the changes from federal and state governments and public authorities.

1970	1971	1972	1973	1974	1975	1976[a]
2,877	2,961	3,482	4,146	5,533	5,849	7,103
2,424	2,737	3,529	3,886	4,850	5,540	6,562
453	224	−47	260	683	309	541
95	141	144	177	147	96	204
548	365	97	437	830	405	745
969	1,427	1,650	1,607	2,342	2,748	3,282
888	1,271	1,498	1,362	1,997	2,285	2,639
81	156	152	245	345	463	643
421	1,062	1,553	1,170	1,512	2,343	2,537
308	676	826	877	826	1,209	1,636
3	345	313	118	295	1,012	539
20	41	68	33	31	9	275
90	0	346	142	360	113	87

Table C.8. *Balance of Payments. Summary Statement, 1961–76*
(millions of Malaysian dollars)

Item	1961	1962	1963	1964	1965	1966	1967
Trade account	511	337	283	272	522	553	475
Exports f.o.b.	3,208	3,232	3,296	3,346	3,753	3,808	3,679
Imports f.o.b.[b]	2,697	2,895	3,013	3,074	3,231	3,255	3,204
Services (net)	−334	−310	−321	−326	−341	−407	−351
Transfers (net)	−193	−194	−181	−74	−58	−106	−142
Current account balance	−16	−167	−219	−128	122	40	−18
Long-term capital (net)	21	322	416	394	324	388	495
Official capital	−159	87	146	229	174	218	365
Commercial loans[c]	...	...	...	...	...	...	...
Corporate investment[d]	180	235	270	165	150	170	130
Private monetary capital and unrecorded transactions (net)	−24	−72	−153	−204	−337	−363	−518
Commercial banks	77	23	59	...	−102	33	8
Other[e]	...	...	...	...	...	...	...
Errors and omissions including short term	−101	−95	−212	−204	−235	−396	−526
Overall balance	−19	83	44	62	109	65	−41
Allocation of special drawing rights	0	0	0	0	0	0	0
Drawing on IMF	0	0	0	0	0	0	0
Net change in central bank reserves[f]	—	−83	−44	−62	−109	−65	41

— Not applicable.
... Zero or negligible.
Source: Bank Negara, *Quarterly Economic Bulletin*, vol. 6, no. 1 (March 1973) and vol. 10, no. 4 (December 1977).
   a. Preliminary.
   b. Includes nonmonetary gold.
   c. Net loans inflows of the Malaysian International Shipping Company and the Malaysian Airlines System.
   d. Includes direct private investment, borrowing by the private sector, and reinvestment of retained earnings by foreign companies operating in Malaysia.
   e. From 1976 onward this item is largely comprised of PETRONAS earnings that are deposited abroad.
   f. A minus sign indicates an increase.

1968	1969	1970	1971	1972	1973	1974[a]	1975[a]	1976[a]
637	1,613	1,067	686	365	1,594	755	941	3,715
4,070	4,921	5,020	4,884	4,736	7,263	9,991	9,042	13,265
3,433	3,308	3,953	4,198	4,371	5,669	9,236	8,101	9,550
−400	−702	−862	−878	−906	−1,197	−1,365	−1,225	−1,835
−143	−180	−180	−137	−157	−151	−140	−125	−145
94	731	25	−329	−698	246	−750	−409	1,735
245	505	325	714	1,169	600	1,109	1,380	933
152	265	35	409	692	120	276	848	440
...	−5	3	−1	157	60	−67	−18	163
93	245	287	306	320	420	900	550	330
−162	−742	−282	−182	−82	−256	93	−800	−614
115	−126	−16	68	−15	259	65	−108	66
...	−27	6	5	9	−5	36	25	−241
−277	−589	−272	−255	−76	−524	23	−717	−439
177	494	68	203	389	576	452	171	2,054
0	0	64	61	60	0	0	0	0
0	0	0	0	0	0	0	0	265
−177	−494	−132	−264	−449	−576	−452	−171	−2,319

Table C.9. *Exports of Selected Commodities, 1960–76*

Commodity group	1961	1962	1963	1964	1965
Rubber					
Volume[a]	874.9	871.0	922.1	928.3	966.0
Value[b]	1,566.9	1,476.9	1,475.7	1,395.8	1,461.8
Unit value[c]	179.1	169.6	160.0	150.4	151.3
Tin					
Volume[d]	75,985.0	83,387.0	86,657.0	72,985.0	75,273.0
Value[b]	533.1	620.3	642.5	728.3	871.8
Unit value[e]	7,281.4	7,438.9	7,144.4	9,978.4	11,608.2
Petroleum, crude and partly refined[f]					
Volume[a]	1,909.8	1,902.0	1,590.3	1,711.1	1,747.4
Value[b]	107.2	106.7	89.1	84.6	86.7
Unit value[e]	56.1	56.1	56.0	49.9	49.6
Sawlogs					
Volume[g]	2,581.6	2,936.5	3,642.6	4,045.4	4,780.7
Value[b]	136.6	163.1	204.9	205.4	263.3
Unit value[h]	52.9	55.5	56.3	50.8	55.1
Sawn timber					
Volume[g]	453.8	481.1	569.8	725.6	753.0
Value[b]	51.3	60.2	65.2	92.4	96.9
Unit value[h]	113.0	104.4	114.5	127.5	128.7
Palm oil					
Volume[a]	94.9	107.4	116.8	126.1	143.2
Value[b]	61.3	65.1	70.0	81.1	107.2
Unit value[e]	645.6	606.6	590.7	643.3	748.8
Manufactured goods[b, i]	146.4	146.3	152.4	170.6	189.3
Other exports[b, j]	615.4	620.9	630.2	620.7	705.5
Total exports f.o.b.[b, j]	3,238.2	3,259.5	3,330.0	3,381.9	3,782.5

Source: Bank Negara, *Quarterly Economic Bulletin*, vol. 10, no. 4 (December 1977)
  a. Thousands of metric tons.
  b. Millions of Malaysian dollars.
  c. Malaysian cents a kilogram.
  d. Metric tons.
  e. Malaysian dollars a metric ton.
  f. Includes re-exports of crude petroleum imported from Brunei.
  g. Thousands of cubic meters.
  h. Malaysian dollars a cubic meter.
  i. SITC groups 5–8, excluding tin.
  j. These export figures are based on trade data and differ from those adjusted for valuation and coverage to a balance-of-payments basis in table C.8.

1966	1967	1968	1969	1970	1971
1,011.1	1,043.3	1,171.6	1,354.9	1,345.4	1,390.4
1,473.9	1,274.7	1,353.2	2,031.1	1,723.7	1,460.3
145.8	122.2	115.5	149.9	128.1	105.0
73,535.0	75,607.0	88,157.0	92,017.0	92,631.0	87,142.0
793.0	755.6	829.6	939.8	1,013.3	905.8
10,784.4	9,993.2	9,410.7	10,212.8	10,939.1	10,394.7
2,240.5	2,670.4	3,859.4	3,993.2	4,778.2	7,926.7
104.2	124.0	173.1	168.2	201.5	389.9
46.5	46.4	44.8	42.1	42.2	49.2
6,432.4	7,090.9	8,240.3	8,768.2	8,913.8	8,772.2
385.1	475.6	549.5	604.3	643.6	642.0
59.9	67.1	66.7	68.9	72.2	73.2
712.8	857.6	1,114.1	1,234.7	1,414.9	1,343.7
82.6	106.9	149.3	172.4	208.1	197.7
115.9	124.7	134.0	139.6	147.0	147.1
184.6	188.9	286.0	356.7	401.9	573.4
120.0	116.0	124.5	153.0	264.3	380.4
649.9	614.0	435.3	428.9	657.5	663.5
188.0	192.0	231.1	287.4	334.1	377.3
699.0	678.9	712.3	698.5	773.8	663.4
3,845.8	3,723.7	4,122.6	5,054.7	5,162.4	5,016.8

(*table continues on the following page*)

Table C.9 (continued)

Commodity group	1972	1973	1974	1975	1976
Rubber					
Volume[a]	1,365.0	1,638.8	1,570.1	1,459.6	1,620.1
Value[b]	1,298.3	2,507.2	2,887.7	2,025.5	3,097.8
Unit value[c]	95.1	153.0	183.9	138.8	191.2
Tin					
Volume[d]	89,609.0	82,537.0	85,111.0	77,940.0	81,532.0
Value[b]	924.0	897.0	1,515.0	1,206.1	1,524.0
Unit value[e]	10,311.2	11,000.0	17,675.4	15,475.1	18,691.5
Petroleum, crude and partly refined[f]					
Volume[a]	4,255.3	3,834.6	3,167.8	3,763.2	7,143.9
Value[b]	222.9	268.7	678.1	852.8	1,746.5
Unit value[e]	52.4	70.1	214.1	226.6	244.5
Sawlogs					
Volume[g]	9,118.5	10,122.4	9,553.1	8,473.2	12,172.1
Value[b]	592.5	987.0	1,032.8	669.5	1,471.9
Unit value[h]	65.0	97.5	108.1	79.0	120.9
Sawn timber					
Volume[g]	1,798.6	2,229.8	1,998.3	1,889.6	3,055.3
Value[b]	287.7	574.4	507.3	441.5	887.3
Unit value[h]	160.0	257.6	253.9	233.7	290.4
Palm oil					
Volume[a]	697.1	797.8	901.2	1,162.8	1,345.7
Value[b]	362.7	466.5	1,085.6	1,317.5	1,220.2
Unit value[e]	520.3	584.7	1,204.5	1,133.0	906.8
Manufactured goods[b, i]	502.7	858.8	1,326.3	1,600.1	2,028.8
Other exports[b, j]	663.4	813.8	1,161.9	1,118.1	1,466.4
Total exports f.o.b.[b, j]	4,854.2	7,373.4	10,194.7	9,231.1	13,442.9

Source: Bank Negara, *Quarterly Economic Bulletin*, vol. 10, no. 4 (December 1977)
a. Thousands of metric tons.
b. Millions of Malaysian dollars.
c. Malaysian cents a kilogram.
d. Metric tons.
e. Malaysian dollars a metric ton.
f. Includes re-exports of crude petroleum imported from Brunei.
g. Thousands of cubic meters.
h. Malaysian dollars a cubic meter.
i. SITC groups 5–8, excluding tin.
j. These export figures are based on trade data and differ from those adjusted for valuation and coverage to a balance-of-payments basis in table C.8.

Table C.10. *Gross Imports, by Commodity Group, 1961–76*
(millions of Malaysian dollars)

Year	Food and live animals	Beverages and tobacco	Crude materials inedible	Mineral fuels	Animal/ vegetable oils and fats	Chemicals	Manu- factured goods[a]	Machinery and transport equipment	Miscel- laneous manu- factured articles	Other imports	Total
1961	665.2	127.4	310.9	358.6	15.7	181.9	473.2	458.0	160.7	64.1	2,815.7
1962	670.1	125.6	361.2	376.0	15.7	173.3	534.8	561.4	171.7	66.5	3,056.3
1963	783.1	130.5	307.3	355.5	14.4	189.9	545.3	613.0	187.4	66.2	3,192.6
1964	835.4	114.3	241.4	364.8	15.3	201.3	544.2	631.3	191.3	66.0	3,205.3
1965	749.6	123.5	237.7	388.5	18.2	233.9	597.6	728.6	206.3	72.2	3,356.1
1966	748.0	90.6	163.7	437.0	15.2	252.0	608.4	799.7	188.9	76.2	3,379.9
1967	762.1	90.2	165.8	446.6	15.2	248.2	592.5	735.8	193.5	75.1	3,325.0
1968	766.2	77.9	284.2	500.7	21.9	239.5	613.5	792.7	188.4	66.6	3,551.6
1969	727.5	87.0	302.6	485.7	19.2	274.7	624.2	840.9	182.8	60.4	3,605.0
1970	787.8	96.7	322.3	518.8	24.0	314.7	773.1	1,231.5	204.2	67.0	4,340.1
1971	734.8	92.1	266.9	572.8	23.1	349.0	780.9	1,363.3	194.9	56.0	4,433.8
1972	812.1	82.2	310.0	370.3	22.9	381.5	852.9	1,607.6	199.6	56.2	4,695.3
1973	1,079.0	103.9	371.3	397.0	28.5	534.0	1,257.9	1,888.7	341.4	68.2	6,069.9
1974	1,585.0	114.9	543.1	1,003.5	44.1	879.0	1,864.6	3,275.8	559.7	90.3	9,960.0
1975	1,401.6	119.3	557.7	1,021.1	26.0	709.2	1,389.3	2,881.8	465.4	67.0	8,638.4
1976	1,442.8	116.8	533.2	1,310.6	21.1	922.8	1,620.1	3,428.6	494.1	76.9	9,967.0

Note: Imports, classified by commodity sections based on the standard international trade classification, have been adjusted to exclude intra-regional trade. They include imports of ships and aircraft, but exclude military imports.
Source: Bank Negara, *Quarterly Economic Bulletin*, vol. 10, no. 4 (December 1977).
a. Refer to manufactured goods classified chiefly by materials.

Table C.11. *Money Supply and Its Determinants, 1961–76*
(millions of Malaysian dollars)

Year-end	Money		Money supply		Broad money supply[b]		Determinants of money supply (changes during period)		
	Total[c]	Currency[c]	Demand deposits	Quasi money[a]	Total	Percentage change	Foreign assets[d]	Credit to private sector	Claims on government (net)[e]
1961	1,197	691	506	560	1,757	6.2	-98	168	40
1962	1,254	716	537	622	1,876	6.8	68	86	-40
1963	1,342	749	593	713	2,055	9.5	-15	142	60
1964	1,417	797	620	804	2,221	8.1	61	144	-67
1965	1,514	846	668	943	2,457	0.6	212	59	8
1966	1,652	909	743	1,084	2,736	1.4	33	148	115
1967	1,525	772	753	1,300	2,825	3.3	-232	135	75
1968	1,697	805	892	1,568	3,265	15.6	62	285	121
1969	1,882	931	952	1,842	3,724	14.1	436	151	-177
1970	2,033	1,000	1,032	2,098	4,131	10.9	84	404	0

							Outstanding	
1971	2,120	1,061	1,060	2,554	4,674	13.1	135	326	120
1972	2,716	1,269	1,446	3,056	5,772	23.5	404	443	287
1973	3,735	1,718	2,017	3,838	7,573	31.2	318	1,571	129
1974	4,055	2,030	2,026	4,674	8,729	15.3	400	692	393
1975	4,349	2,239	2,110	5,653	10,002	14.6	269	799	−354
1976	5,257	2,628	2,629	7,514	12,771	27.7	2,258	1,434	−491
1976							5,818	7,511	822

Source: Bank Negara, Quarterly Economic Bulletin, vol. 10, no. 4 (December 1977).

a. Fixed and savings deposits, deposits against letters of credit, guarantees, open contracts, and rental and safe deposits—all of the private sector. Includes private sector holdings of fixed deposits with the central bank.

b. The sum of money and quasi money.

c. Until year-end 1968 the series includes the estimated amount of Malayan currency issued by the Board of Commissioners of Currency, Malaya and British Borneo. That currency ceased to be legal tender on 16 January 1969.

d. Of the central bank and commercial banks. Includes Malaysia's estimated share of the Currency Board's external assets up to year-end 1968, the IMF gold tranche position, and, since 1970, special drawing rights allocated. For commercial banks, includes bills discounted or purchased and bills receivable that are payable abroad.

e. Federal and state governments only.

Table C.12. *Public Debt, Year-end 1976*
(thousands of U.S. dollars)

Type of credit and creditor	Debt outstanding		
	Disbursed	Undisbursed	Total
Supplier credits			
Australia	1,278	1	1,279
France	528	0	528
India	7,760	0	7,760
Japan	20,193	0	20,193
Korea, Republic of	0	3,579	3,579
United Kingdom	495	0	495
United States	24	0	24
Total	30,278	3,580	33,858
Private bank credits			
Belgium	39	0	39
France	9,489	557,538	567,027
Germany, Federal Republic of	0	5,780	5,780
Japan	86,580	0	86,580
Sweden	24,853	7,953	32,806
Switzerland	20,404	0	20,404
United States	104,517	150,000	254,517
United Kingdom	50,000	0	50,000
Multiple lenders	509,916	18,973	528,889
Total	805,798	740,244	1,546,042
Bonds			
Germany, Federal Republic of	27,090	0	27,090
United Kingdom	16,852	0	16,852
Brunei	19,862	0	19,862
Multiple lenders	20,350	0	20,350
Total	84,154	0	84,154
Loans from international organizations			
Asian Development Bank	90,971	152,862	243,833
World Bank	305,506	375,970	681,476
Total	396,477	528,832	925,309

Type of credit and creditor	Debt outstanding		
	Disbursed	Undisbursed	Total
Loans from governments			
Abu Dhabi	0	8,360	8,360
Austria	662	441	1,103
Canada	6,479	8,829	15,308
Denmark	4,561	52	4,613
France	6,047	11,342	17,389
Germany, Federal Republic of	15,742	34,692	50,434
Japan	168,879	68,285	237,164
Kuwait	0	26,485	26,485
Netherlands	213	601	814
Saudi Arbia	0	75,935	75,935
United Kingdom	48,563	2,344	50,907
United States	64,345	27,509	91,854
Total	315,491	264,875	580,366
Total external public debt	1,632,198	1,537,531	3,169,729

Note: Only debt with an original or extended maturity of more than one year is included in this table. Debt outstanding includes principal in arrears but excludes interest in arrears. The following uncommitted part of frame agreements and standbys is not included in this table: loan from Japan, U.S. $17.3 million.

Source: World Bank, External Debt Division.

Table C.13. *Index of Industrial Production, by Commodity Group, Peninsular Malaysia, 1968-76*
(1968 = 100)

Commodity group	Weight	1969	1970	1971	1972	1973	1974	1975	1976
Mining[a]	31.4	97.6	95.5	85.3	85.0	80.6	75.4	70.7	49.6
Electricity[b]	9.2	105.7	115.3	123.1	138.8	153.5	170.0	185.0	206.0
Manufacturing[c]	59.4	115.6	129.8	137.8	156.1	187.1	215.8	216.0	256.9
Processing agricultural products	7.3	110.9	130.1	144.5	164.8	182.2	210.4	235.5	254.1
Food	9.8	108.7	115.9	111.9	115.4	130.3	128.5	136.2	156.3
Beverages	2.7	124.2	131.0	129.4	135.9	169.7	195.1	184.6	214.0
Tobacco products	4.3	115.0	119.9	123.5	130.6	154.5	167.5	166.9	174.1
Textiles	1.3	111.6	114.6	122.0	156.1	196.8	141.0	213.8	302.5
Wood products	7.1	107.7	125.5	140.4	183.7	203.3	185.9	190.2	265.2
Paper and paper products	0.5	131.7	141.3	155.2	175.0	218.4	214.2	203.8	276.1
Rubber products	3.8	109.1	125.3	131.9	139.8	166.5	161.7	164.1	185.4
Chemicals and chemical products	5.7	111.5	118.9	121.6	144.2	165.6	175.1	154.7	176.3
Products of petroleum and coal	3.0	100.1	99.5	92.0	96.6	99.1	101.5	117.9	150.3
Nonmetallic mineral products	4.5	111.9	118.2	119.3	129.2	147.0	154.6	161.3	189.5
Basic metals	1.5	143.9	139.3	166.5	192.2	225.5	237.5	227.5	242.2
Metal products	2.5	106.7	131.4	141.3	171.7	242.8	267.5	186.0	207.9
Electrical machinery[d]	1.2	128.6	171.5	188.9	192.4	200.6	247.0	287.0	338.4
Transport equipment	1.4	210.2	272.5	281.9	268.3	393.0	531.4	412.1	416.6
Other pioneers[e]	2.7	147.2	193.9	239.4	313.6	474.5	906.0	915.3	1,179.4
All groups	100.0	109.1	117.7	120.0	132.2	150.6	167.6	167.6	193.4

Source: Bank Negara, *Quarterly Economic Bulletin*, vol. 10, no. 4 (December 1977).

a. The series covers production of tin and iron ore, which accounted for 97 percent of the value added in mining in 1968.

b. Electricity generated covered 97 percent of total electricity output in 1968.

c. The index covers 145 manufactured items classified under 55 individual industries and 16 principal groups, which together accounted for 76 percent of total value added in 1968. Six principal groups are excluded from the index: footwear; other wearing apparel and made-up textiles; furniture and fixtures; printing and publishing; leather, fur, and leather products; miscellaneous industries; and machinery except electrical machinery.

d. Includes electrical apparatus, appliances, and supplies.

e. Refers to establishments granted pioneer status but not falling within the industries covered by the survey.

Index

Pollak, Peter K., 262n
Population: density of, 10, 72; ethnic composition of, 10–11, 97; growth of, 4, 43, 72, 90, 97; immigration and, 97. *See also* Chinese; Indians; Malays
Poverty: of agricultural workers, 50–51, 223; definition of, 61; economic growth to reduce, 71, 73; factors causing, 43–44; government efforts to eradicate, 5, 6, 9, 41, 88, 96, 180; household per capita income to measure, 128–29; incidence of, 3, 43, 52, 61, 130–31; lines for, 113, 115–16; population growth and, 4; by racial group, 61, 113–15; rural development to eradicate, 42, 44, 74, 88–89, 223, 235–40; rural versus urban, 116
Power, John H., 187n
Prices: consumer, 35, 36, 163; food, 222–23; stability of, 162
Private sector, 4; investment by, 7, 41–42, 59
Public assistance, for education, 133, 137
Public debt; extent of, 39; financing of, 158–62; service rate for external, 162
Public expenditures: borrowing and, 159; for development, 176–77; growth in, 165, 166; on health, 141–43; and manufacturing investment, 293; on poverty-related programs, 180; projections of, 176–77; under second plan, 155
Public finance, 159–62
Public sector: development program for, 58, 74–75, 91–92, 155; domestic borrowing of, 159, 169, 170, 173, 175–76; economic planning by, 57–59; foreign market loans of, 159, 169–70, 179; increase in resources of, 169–70, 177, 180; investment by, 3, 59; manpower scarcity in, 91; revenue prospects of, 82–83; savings of, 83; services of, 127–28; surplus of, 76. *See also* Education; Medical care; Public utilities
Public trust agencies, 59; capital ownership by, 54–55, 69, 70
Public utilities, 134n; accessibility to, 90, 91, 152; factors influencing demand for, 147–48, 150–51; investment in, 297; model for, 309–14; output of, 290; for poor, 128; spatial distribution of, 145–

47. *See also* Electricity; Sewage disposal; Water supply
Public Works Department, 204
Pyatt, Graham, 99n

Rabenau, Kurt von, 182n, 184n, 186
Race: employment and, 8, 63–65; imbalance relating to, 5, 8, 60, 75; and income distribution, 103–04; and poverty, 61, 113–15; restructuring occupations by, 303–04, 306–08
Religion, 12, 16
Research, agricultural, 243
Reserves, external, 37, 39
Resources allocation: into inefficient industries, 190; projections for, 299–300
Restructuring program: for agriculture, 8, 224, 303; categories for, 199; economic growth for, 86; for education, 55–57; for employment, 53–54; flexibility in implementation of, 86; objectives of, 8–9; for ownership, 54–55; shortcomings in efforts toward, 201. *See also* New Economic Policy
Revenue. *See* Tax revenue
Rice: double cropping of, 49; poverty among growers of, 50–51; price of, 43n; production of, 4, 31, 48–49, 214; self-sufficiency in, 217; smallholders in, 218–19, 222, 228–30; under third plan, 243–44
Riots, 23, 32
RISDA. *See* Rubber Industry Smallholders Development Authority
Road system, 10
Round, Jeffrey I., 99n
Rubber: British introduction of, 13; buffer stocks of, 267–68; export price of, 25; exports of, 3, 25, 30, 253, 268; land development schemes for, 217; prices of, 4, 43, 47, 98, 170, 223, 261, 265–67; production of, 4, 6, 23, 25–26, 30, 47, 79, 89, 214, 261; real earnings from, 39; replanting program for, 249–50, 261, 295; revenue from exports of, 171; share of land area to, 213; smallholdings for, 30, 46–47, 89, 220–22, 224–28, 242; supply elasticity of, 262; synthetic, 262–